Religion and Innovation

Also available from Bloomsbury

Meditation in Judaism, Christianity and Islam, edited by Halvor Eifring

Religion, Material Culture and Archaeology, Julian Droogan

Secularization and Its Discontents, Rob Warner

Religion and Innovation

Antagonists or Partners?

Edited by
Donald A. Yerxa

Bloomsbury Academic
An imprint of Bloomsbury Publishing Plc

B L O O M S B U R Y
LONDON · OXFORD · NEW YORK · NEW DELHI · SYDNEY

Bloomsbury Academic

An imprint of Bloomsbury Publishing Plc

50 Bedford Square	1385 Broadway
London	New York
WC1B 3DP	NY 10018
UK	USA

www.bloomsbury.com

**BLOOMSBURY and the Diana logo are trademarks of
Bloomsbury Publishing Plc**

First published 2016

British Library Cataloguing-in-Publication Data

A catalogue record for this book is available from the British Library.

ISBN: HB: 978-1-4725-9101-2
PB: 978-1-4725-9128-9
ePDF: 978-1-4725-9102-9
ePub: 978-1-4725-9100-5

Library of Congress Cataloging-in-Publication Data

Religion and innovation: antagonists or partners? / edited by Donald A. Yerxa. – 1 [edition].
pages cm
Includes bibliographical references and index.
ISBN 978-1-4725-9101-2 (hb) – ISBN 978-1-4725-9128-9 (pb) – ISBN 978-1-4725-9100-5
(epub) – ISBN 978-1-4725-9102-9 (epdf) 1. Religion and culture. 2. Civilization, Modern.
3. Technology–Religious aspects. I. Yerxa, Donald A., 1950- editor.
BL65.C8R4445 2015
201'.7–dc23
2015017884

Typeset by Deanta Global Publishing Services, Chennai, India
Printed and bound in India

Contents

List of Figures and Tables

Figures

Tables

Acknowledgements

The chapters in this volume are the result of studies sponsored by the Religion and Innovation in Human Affairs (RIHA) grants initiative of The Historical Society, a professional organization, now inactive, that was located in Boston, Massachusetts. I served as director of the RIHA program until its completion in the summer of 2014. Generous funding for RIHA came from the John Templeton Foundation. For their encouragement, support and patience, I am enormously grateful to the Foundation's president and chairman the late Dr Jack Templeton, program associate Heather Micklewright and, especially, vice president of life sciences and genetics Dr Paul K. Wason. Paul's vision, keen insight and gentle prodding made RIHA and this book possible.

RIHA's six distinguished advisory board members (Ian Hodder, William B. Hurlbut, David N. Livingstone, Wilfred M. McClay, Patrick K. O'Brien and William R. Shea) also provided strategic advice and invaluable encouragement, especially at the outset and during an RIHA conference held at Harris Manchester College, Oxford, in July 2013. Throughout the RIHA project, I have especially relied on the experience, perspective and support of Bill Hurlbut, Bill Shea and Bill McClay. I count it a privilege not only to have worked closely with them but also to call them friends. The RIHA board functioned in an advisory capacity, and its members are in no way responsible for either the intellectual direction of RIHA or the contents of this volume.

And to the scholars who contributed to this volume and those whose projects are not represented here, I have enjoyed and benefited from our collaboration enormously. You have added substantially to our understanding of an important 'big question'.

Donald A. Yerxa
February 2015

Introduction

DONALD A. YERXA

Has religion inhibited innovation in human societies? At first blush, the answer might seem obvious. Of course, it has! Religion, it is commonly assumed, resists change and functions as an agent of tradition and social control.[1] Its relationship to innovation is fundamentally antagonistic. But this volume asks a question that runs against the grain of such thinking: Could it be that religion has actually helped to generate innovation? The contributing scholars address this from a variety of chronological, cultural, disciplinary, conceptual and methodological perspectives.

The view that religion is implacably opposed to novelty and innovation has become a staple of recent polemical writing. Unfortunately, it is also far from rare in academic discourse. To be sure, religion has at times resisted innovation, but to argue that religion has consistently done so ignores evidence to the contrary. Over the last few decades, scholarship dealing with the complex interfaces between science and religion has demonstrated how distorted this claim is.[2] The interdisciplinary work in this volume should be viewed in this context. By presenting evidence for a much more complex and compelling reality, it challenges facile assumptions. Based on the work presented here, a persuasive case is made that in some notable contexts, religion and innovation have, indeed, been partners.

In Part 1, we begin our examination of the interaction of religion and innovation with three chapters dealing with pre-Columbian societies. These case studies, all based on archaeological fieldwork, may well provide a New World complement to the 'controlled speculation' about the relation of innovation to prehistoric material and spiritual culture based on findings at Upper Paleolithic era sites in Europe.[3] The pre-Columbian explorations should also be seen in the light of the extensive fieldwork in Turkey at Çatalhöyük, which suggests that 'changes in spiritual life and religious ritual are a prelude to or accompany the social and economic changes that lead to "civilization"'.[4]

Archaeologist John Rick catalogues in Chapter 1 a series of innovations at the iconic Peruvian ceremonial site of Chavín de Huántar during the later Formative period (approximately 1200 to 500 BCE). These include monumental architecture; manipulation of light, sound and, perhaps, other senses; the use of psychoactive drugs; development of cut-stone architecture; hydraulic technologies; and the use of powerful images through iconic art style. Innovation, Rick maintains, was a major factor in the competition, and the resulting success and survival, of some cults over others. When interpreted in the overall central Andean context, the 'range, extension, creativity, and originality' of the 'belief-system-driven innovation' at the Chavín temple complex signal a 'major restructuring' and represent 'an exceptional development along the human trajectory'.

In Chapter 2, Arthur A. Joyce and Sarah B. Barber examine the interplay of religion and politics during the later Formative period of Mesoamerica by comparing two regions in modern-day southern Mexico. Archaeological evidence points to the different roles religion played in political innovation in these regions. In the lower Río Verde Valley, religion was a conservative force, constraining innovations that could have led to political centralization. In contrast, in the Valley of Oaxaca, fieldwork suggests that religion fostered innovations that would eventually give rise to a politically centralized polity. Both regions show that religion was not necessarily a unifying factor in social change as has often been assumed; rather, it could have been a crucible of tension and conflict out of which political innovations emerged.

Drawing from their fieldwork at multiple sites of the sprawling indigenous North American city of Cahokia, Timothy Pauketat and Susan Alt explore in Chapter 3 'the innovative potential of religion conceived not as pre-existing systems of belief but as the very terrain of social relationships'. Religion properly understood in this 'early context' was fundamental to the rise of an important Mississippian urban centre located in and around contemporary St Louis, Missouri, that reached its height in the early twelfth century CE.

The middle chapters of this book, forming Part 2, deal with the complexities of the interaction between religion and innovation witnessed in the West during the early modern and modern eras. The contributing scholars deal with such broad themes as secularization, naturalism, the Reformation, the Enlightenment and 'Christian transnationalism'. In some respects, historians William Bulman and Robert Ingram summarize the collective conclusion of this section when they assert that the notion that religion has existed 'in an inherently antagonistic relationship with modernity, Enlightenment, and secularization is … an illusion'.

Chapter 4 sets the stage for these discussions. In it political scientist Timothy Samuel Shah argues that some of the earliest persecuted Christian communities incubated innovative doctrines of individual and institutional religious freedom, which themselves generated new concepts of political freedom. In the work of some of the earliest Greek and Latin fathers of the church, Shah traces innovative articulations of a principle of universal religious freedom.[5] These Patristic arguments for religious freedom, he argues, amount to the 'First Enlightenment' and 'constitute one of the most radical conceptual innovations in human history'.

In the next two chapters, historian Peter Harrison explores the relationship between religion and innovation as it relates to secular modernity and scientific naturalism and progress. In Chapter 5, he evaluates three models of secularization: (1) Auguste Comte's stages-of-history model in which religion is destined to be replaced by a more advanced form of thought – science; (2) Max Weber's disenchantment model in which religion itself – Protestant Christianity in particular – is the initial driver of secularization; and (3) the 'nostalgic secularization' story narrated by Alasdair MacIntyre, Charles Taylor and Brad Gregory that focuses more on what is lost than what is gained in the transition to modernity. Harrison shows how these models of secularization lead to differing narratives about the relationship between religion and innovation.

In Chapter 6, Harrison takes on the notion that scientific naturalism has been a primary driver of historical progress, with religion playing a basically negative role. He demonstrates that there are surprisingly positive connections between religion and naturalism; indeed, scientific naturalism itself has religious roots. From this it follows that any historical arguments positing 'a simple alliance between science and progress, while attributing to religion an essentially conservative or inhibitory role, may need to be revised'.

In Chapter 7, we get a fascinating glimpse of the complexities to be found in the religion–innovation interface. William Bulman and Robert Ingram demonstrate how the English considered innovation and novelty to be inherently destabilizing after the bloody civil wars of the mid-seventeenth century. Yet the Anglican Enlightenment, the very intellectual project meant to forestall the negative effects of innovation and novelty, inadvertently spurred intellectual and political innovation. So we have an instance of 'the paradoxical, counter-intuitive ways in which religion and innovation can find themselves in a mutually-sustaining relationship'.

With Chapter 8, we move to an examination of two important anniversaries of the Reformation in Germany: its tricentennial in 1817 and the 400th anniversary of Martin Luther's birth in 1883. Thomas Albert Howard argues that these commemorative occasions provided opportunities for celebrants to distance themselves from earlier, largely confessional remembrances of the Reformation and to connect the commemorations to the new, distinctively nineteenth-century ideologies of liberalism and nationalism. So even the retrospective gaze of anniversary commemorations served as a mirror and agent of social change.

In Chapter 9, historians of religion David Hempton and Hugh McLeod draw from a conference they ran at Harvard Divinity School to examine 'whether American Christians have responded to the threat of secularization in more innovative ways than their European counterparts'. On balance, they conclude, American Christians have been more innovative than Christians in Europe. But they question whether this provides a sufficient explanation for the so-called '"God Gap" between a more "religious" United States and a more "secular" western Europe'.

In the concluding chapter of this section, historian of Christianity Dana Robert makes a significant contribution to our understanding of how missionary Protestantism was a major source of social innovation and modern democratic notions at the beginning of the twentieth century. The innovative dynamics are evident in what Robert calls 'Christian transnationalism'. She demonstrates how non-Western Christian intellectuals – namely, Inazô Nitobé (Japan), Silas Modiri Molema (South Africa) and Philip Hitti (Lebanon) – wrote national histories in the early twentieth century that 'envisioned a common global civil society'. These Christian transnationals 'used ethnic nationalism as a tool for democratic internationalism'. Robert's sophisticated argument 'challenges interpretations of modern transnationalism that ignore the essential role of Christianity in its construction'.

––––––––––––––––––––––––

In Part 3, we explore a variety of contemporary topics related to religion, innovation and progress. In this most interdisciplinarily oriented section in the volume, we hear from an intellectual historian, an economist, an architect and a historian of science. Their vantage points and methods vary greatly and suggest a number of fruitful future lines of inquiry.

Chapter 11 is a brilliant examination of an underappreciated dilemma that cuts to the core of the religion–innovation question. Wilfred McClay contends that despite its manifest achievements, modern science 'cannot do anything to relieve the weight of guilt' that burdens people in the contemporary West. In fact, there is an 'ominous linkage' between progress and guilt, and this, McClay warns, could fatally undermine 'the energies of innovation that have made the West what it is'. He suggests that in order to be sustained, human progress may need religion and 'something very like the moral economy of sin and absolution that has hitherto been secured by the religious traditions of the West'.

The next two chapters in the book approach religion and innovation from very different perspectives. In Chapter 12, economist Rebecca Samuel Shah provides a contemporary example of religious innovation. She summarizes an empirical study of Dalit (outcaste) women in Bangalore, India, designed 'to probe the plausibility of the hypothesis that faith-inspired virtues and practices contribute in measurable ways to the economic well-being'. She believes that her longitudinal studies demonstrate how 'certain religious practices and networks may help vulnerable Dalit women harness their spiritual capital in innovative ways'. Going further, she contends that religion 'provides innovative resources that can – if properly tapped – alleviate poverty'.

In Chapter 13, Philip Bess, a professor of architecture, describes an urban design project he has directed at the University of Notre Dame that critically extends Daniel Burnham's 1909 *Plan of Chicago* and imagines a metropolitan Chicago in 2109 informed by classical humanist urbanism and Catholic metaphysics and social teaching. Bess's *After Burnham* project seeks 'to locate the modern metropolis in both nature and sacred order' so that human beings might better flourish. *After Burnham* is conceived as a 'counter-project' intended to critique contemporary architecture, urban design and planning. Were its features ever to be implemented, Bess suggests, they might be innovative but would certainly represent progress.

In the book's final chapter, historian of science J. Benjamin Hurlbut uses the 'transhumanist imagination' as a point of entry for exploring some ways in which technological innovation is seen as an agent of social change and progress. Transhumanism preaches 'a vision of innovation as a gospel of progress' that undertakes 'a mission of world-transformation'. Hurlbut makes the case that secular modernity 'privileges visions of innovation – of possible technological futures – as a site of collective moral imagination and public reasoning'.

And in his 'Afterword', Adam Keiper, editor of the The New Atlantis, maintains that the approaches to religion and innovation found in this volume are a valuable counter to the simplistic and confused understanding of both religion and innovation often found in public and academic discourse. He turns readers' attention to the future, speculating that changes in religion as well as advances in science and technology, including the futuristic possibilities of transhumanism, will likely 'tie religion and innovation to the deepest questions of human meaning and destiny'.

As the contributors demonstrate, probing the relationship between religion and innovation does, indeed, raise important questions of human meaning, flourishing and destiny. It also prompts us to think about the nature of *religion* and *innovation*, concepts that some consider 'imprecise' and somewhat slippery. For example, the diversity of religious traditions and expressions, as Peter Harrison puts it, 'is too great to warrant speaking of *religion* in general as having some kind of unitary historical force'. And, as Harrison and other contributors note, *innovation* has not always had the connotation of 'positive change' it has enjoyed in the modern era.

Definitions matter. But dangers abound in the definitional enterprise. It can lead to endless debate, as decades of discussion about the meaning of *religion* attest. Intellectualized substantivist definitions privilege propositional religious belief at the expense of things such as ritual practice, materiality, the experiential and expressive dimensions of faith, and Geertzian symbolism.[6] The limits of approaching religion in this manner are apparent in how the archaeologists deal with the question of religion in the pre-Columbian context in Part 1. Although there is no consensus on what constituted religion in early societies or, even, if *religion* is an appropriate term to employ, archaeologist Ian Hodder contends there is some agreement that early societies dealt with 'the beyond'. And this focus on 'the beyond' was not part of a separate proto-religious sphere, but was embedded and inextricably 'entangled' within those societies' social and material lives.[7]

Clearly, any working definition of religion must go beyond an emphasis on propositional beliefs. But there is also danger in embracing a more functionalist approach that relates religion to virtually anything humans do that gives their lives order and meaning. This risks making religion such a broad concept that it serves no useful analytical purpose.[8] We also need to take into account that *religion* as a transcultural and transhistorical concept appears to have been the rather recent creation of the modern Western mind intent on separating religion from its larger cultural and political contexts.[9] No wonder, then, that anthropologist Harvey Whitehouse suggests that the effort to pin down a definition of religion could be an intellectual red herring.[10]

Rightly, the contributors to this volume do not subscribe to essentialist notions of religion. That does not mean that there is no such thing as religion; rather, it suggests that not all religions 'exhibit the same essential features'. To state the obvious, religion in pre-Columbian societies is not the same thing as Reformed Protestantism or Vatican II Catholicism. The authors avoid lockstep definition and adopt conceptions of religion – and innovation – that work best in the various contexts of their investigations.[11]

The same goes, more or less, for innovation. As is the case with religion, the term *innovation* can be problematic. Innovation is so ubiquitous, especially in the business world, that it runs the risk of not meaning anything.[12] One recent work of evolutionary anthropology faulted the common-sense definition of innovation as 'something new or different' for failing to account for such things as how we recognize something as an innovation, how it originates, how it is transmitted and how it differs from invention.[13] We could add its failure to address how innovation should be distinguished from incremental improvement. But it seems unnecessary, perhaps even petty, to burden a working definition with interpretative qualifications such as these. Over sixty years ago, social anthropologist H. G. Barnett offered a serviceable definition of innovation: 'Any thought, behavior, or thing that is new because it is qualitatively different from existing forms.'[14] We might modify that slightly to 'change that is perceived at the time of its inception, diffusion, or in retrospect as being new and significant'. Such a working definition, like most, contains 'weasel words', such as *positive*, *perceived* and *significant*.[15] But its openness enhances its practical utility. As with religion, jettisoning the concept of innovation because we lack definitional precision is a mistake.[16]

The chapters of this book stand on their own as valuable contributions to our understanding of the interactions between religion and innovation in a wide variety of contexts – from the innovative role of Christianity in fostering political freedom in Late Antiquity and alleviating poverty among outcaste women in contemporary India to the impact of persistent guilt on innovation to the transhumanist vision of an innovative future. But what can we say by way of summary based on these various explorations ranging over continents and millennia, not to mention academic disciplines?

It should be emphasized that the studies in this volume give no warrant for claiming a uniform causal connection between religion and innovation. There is simply insufficient, and at times contradictory, evidence for advancing a general theory of religion and innovation. Again, context matters enormously. And the complexity of forces operating at the interface of religion and innovation poses a substantial obstacle for any general theory.[17]

That said, these fourteen case studies do permit us to say some important things about the relationship of religion and innovation. One obvious conclusion to be drawn is that innovation need not be captive to the worlds of business and entrepreneurship – where it is so ubiquitous as to have become a cliché. This volume demonstrates that innovation is a useful concept in scholarly analysis. And we would be wise never to ignore religious beliefs and practices whenever we assess change in human societies.

The scholars in this volume have successfully challenged the presumption that religion is invariably opposed to innovation. To argue thus is to resort to a caricatured narrative, unsubstantiated by careful scholarly examination. While religion is certainly not always innovative, in several contexts it has played an important, albeit often-unappreciated, role in initiating and facilitating innovation. The fact that the examinations in this volume are so diverse in scope, historical context and disciplinary approach strengthens the case that religion's interface with innovation is far more complex than commonly assumed.

Collectively, the original studies in this volume raise a number of questions that have considerable potential for further inquiry. Among them are the following: What are the actual dynamics of the religion–innovation nexus? Can we move beyond immediate, proximate factors present in specific instances to suggest, at least tentatively, more general conditions whereby religion can be innovative? Based on their work in early modern England, Bulman and Ingram contend, for example, that 'religious innovation … tends to occur in periods of extreme social and political upheaval'. Can this claim be substantiated by further investigation of other periods marked by significant crisis and upheaval? What roles do other notions such as *tradition* and *progress* typically play in the interface between religion and innovation? To what extent is religion-related innovation a project of renewal that recasts recurrences of the 'old' as 'new'? Or does religion operate in a process of recombining existing cultural elements or beliefs in such a way that a degree of novelty is introduced?[18] What is the role of intentionality in innovation?

The findings on religion and innovation discussed here should stimulate additional research. But will they gain traction in today's intellectual culture? Oxford theologian Alister McGrath suggests that scholarship alone may be insufficient to counter cultural mindsets shaped by entrenched master narratives.[19] Further probing of the relationship of religion and innovation needs to consider why negative stereotypes of religion persist, what purposes they serve and what forms of appropriate cultural engagement are needed.

Part 1 Religion and Innovation in Pre-Columbian Societies

1 Innovation, Religion and Authority at the Formative Period Andean Cult Centre of Chavín de Huántar

JOHN W. RICK

This chapter looks at the intersection of three major themes: innovation, religion and the Formative Period of the ancient Central Andes. I argue that the Formative is an exceptional temporal context for understanding a particular, perhaps unusual, relationship that develops between religion and innovation. Viewed from the long-term archaeological perspective, I believe it is possible to see exceptional time periods in which issues such as competition between emerging hierarchical persons and polities leverage innovation within the context of religion to promote advantage, without being necessarily concerned with the innovations beyond the immediate benefits provided.

My point is primarily to delineate the context and the nature of the innovations and to describe the degree to which we can use archaeological data to build this understanding. By context I refer to both a general and a specific temporal–spatial setting for innovation – that is, the general characteristics of this time and region that were enabling for innovation, and the local and proximate factors that led a small number of people to develop a novelty. In the case to be observed here, both scales of context are crucial and can be simply subsumed at the broader level of a time period – principally the middle-to-late (later) Formative period (ca. 1200–500 BCE) in a place – the central part of the Central Andean region (roughly what is central and northern Peru today) – and at the local level as the single (if internally complex) centrally located iconic site of Chavín de Huántar, over the same time range. Without consideration of the broader context of the Formative, the importance and durability of innovations would not be apparent. But without considering the motivations for site-specific, socially focused origins of the innovations, we would encounter no agents responsible for the actual process of innovation.

I begin with consideration of basic definitions – important because we cannot simply transfer concepts from the present day to ancient time periods without considering the nature of the later Formative period and what we know of its organization, ideology and technology. This in turn will serve to better anticipate the relationship of religion and innovation over this dynamic time period. Then I will turn to the site of Chavín to look for evidence of innovation within one particular temple system over about 600 years of time and attempt to understand those developments within the major processes of the Formative.

Definitions

Undoubtedly, the thorniest issue to be addressed is a definition of *religion*. Any archaeologist is obligated to ask the question of 'when'? – meaning, of course, some reference to sociopolitical time. To really believe that the religion of Formative farmers conforms to the same definition as that of the Church of England strains the imagination, and this perspective is all the more important for this period of major change in the structure of Andean societies. As Lars Fogelin has recently documented, anthropologists have most often seen religion as reinforcing the structure of a society as a symbolized and conservative system of meaning that pervades the life of the society in a broadly shared fashion.[1] This can be seen to conform to the broad stereotype of an emergent theocracy – an evolving, religiously based leadership system, in which the role of articulating and elaborating the linkages between population and core religious practices is assumed by an increasingly influential priesthood.[2] The coherence and conservative nature of the society is assured by the unifying force of tradition conserved in the religious continuities over time.[3]

This perspective, what I have previously described as a 'devotional' religious system, can be contrasted with an alternative perspective in which the goal of those originating and organizing the religious contexts, actions and symbols is, in fact, change, as strategized by theocratic, but differently intentioned authorities who constitute a 'manipulative' system.[4] The goal is no longer unification through devotional coherency, but rather through status, rank or power differentiation of this leadership itself and increase in economic income to the religious leadership and system. Obviously, these perspectives may be combined, and in both cases there is conformance to beliefs. But in the former, those beliefs would tend to be quite conservative, while in the latter system, the goals go far beyond reinforcement or expansion of the religious system and verge on transformation of both political and economic systems through changes justified by at least somewhat transformed beliefs. I have argued that there is stronger evidence for a manipulative nature of Chavín religion than for a broad-based devotional character. Thus in this trans-Formative time, religion might well be radical and change-producing.[5]

Chavín religion has frequently been seen as a cult, reflecting the fact that it seems to have primarily included only a fairly small membership of elite individuals, and that it is only one of a number of contemporary, geographically dispersed variants.[6] As I will argue, it also shows signs of having been a variant of a secret society – in many ways, a cult that relied heavily on restrictive control of information within a limited membership with implications for rights and privileges such as access to resources.[7]

Innovation clearly refers to the application of novel ideas or knowledge in material and behavioural realms.[8] Innovation seen from an archaeological viewpoint is a complex matter. Knowing who actually innovated and where innovations occurred is difficult to pinpoint precisely.[9] Different classes of innovation will vary in archaeological visibility. For new technical, functional, ideological or stylistic innovations materialized in durable products, documentation should be archaeologically visible. Behavioural or other non-material innovations, however, may be more difficult to establish, involving assumptions about the meaning of material or distributional data in a process of inference. Combining the two makes it clear that innovation will always involve the creation of both behaviours and materials. And it is in the richness of their evolving intentional and unintentional interactions that the greatest understandings of innovation lie.[10]

Because the long temporal view of archaeology can grapple with the longer time frames of this evolution, it is particularly capable of making up for not resolving the finest levels of temporal resolution with its time-sweeping vista. In this regard, archaeology may be able to point to particular times of change, but at the same time, to times and realms of culture that are stable and not subject to change, perhaps because stable solutions to problems have been found, or just as probably because the conditions promoting potential inventions and their implementations are not sufficient to overcome cultural conservatism.[11] Thus, identifying what aspects of cultural material and behaviour are subject to innovation, where innovations occur on the social and physical landscapes, and the temporal patterns of innovation occurrence is a tremendous advantage. The force of tradition in suppressing change, however, should not be underestimated. So patterns of non-innovation are a clear complement to viewing innovative change.[12]

The Broader Context: The Later Central Andean Formative

The central Andean region is well known for being an independent centre of state origin and appears to have seen a pristine process of the development of hierarchical authority structures. The Formative period, although defined in various ways, can best be seen as the period that runs from the earliest stages of well-defined sociopolitical inequality to the threshold of state societies.[13] The earliest Formative period, usually termed the Late Archaic, starts with the monumental construction of temple-like structures and other precocious cultural features somewhat before 3000 BCE at such well-known sites as Caral.[14] This Initial Formative period is followed at around 1800 BCE by Early, Middle, Late and Terminal Formative periods, reaching up to around year 0 BCE/CE. Monumentality of construction, in sheer volume, hits its peak in the Early Formative, also gaining a more structured architectural organization in the major temple centres. But as in the Initial Formative, we rarely see broadly shared iconic representation, evidence of long-term authority-based leadership or highly specialized craft production and long-distance exchange.[15] With the advent of the Middle Formative around 1200 BCE, but becoming particularly notable within the Late Formative beginning at 800 BCE, a new consistency emerges in highly organized patterns of monumental structures and material culture. But in many areas of the Central Andes, this ends by 400–500 BCE.[16] It is this latter span of around 800 years – what I term the 'later Formative' – that is the focus of attention here. It is a time that seems to witness considerable innovation in both material and behavioural terms and in quite direct association with what are clearly ceremonial centres and significantly changing sociopolitical organization.

The character of the later Formative is fairly well defined from a number of major research projects that have contributed data, mostly about ceremonial centres and occasionally about smaller, residential sites or their settlement pattern on the landscape.[17] Nonetheless, the view from these numerous, widely distributed highland and coastal ceremonial centres is fairly clear: there is growth and sophistication of the material technologies, architectural capabilities, and ceramic and other materials' similar but not identical iconic styles. The centres are unified in their general architectural and material culture patterns, but under close examination, it appears that each shows specific variability in patterns, styles, icons and technology. So while they are engaged in similar cultural evolution and function, they are sufficiently distinctive in their details to be understood as independent, parallel centres.[18]

That these ceremonial centres are indeed temples involved in religious rituals is not in question, but the nature and inclusivity of religious activity within them is still subject to considerable interpretation. They have been seen as oracle centres, pilgrimage destinations, locations for religious observances by very large assemblages of participants or locations primarily for interaction limited to temple authorities and elites of both local and distant residence.[19] But it is very clear that significant rituals were conducted in the very elaborate, decorated and structured architecture, involving striking costuming, extensive paraphernalia and the ingestion of a number of psychoactive plant products. There is evidence for long-distance movements of highly decorated and decorative mineral, ceramic, stone, bone and shell artefacts – in some cases of up to 1,000 kilometres. Iconic elements generally present include large felines, snakes, raptorial birds, caiman-like creatures and, commonly, human representations, often incorporating threatening elements of the aggressive animals mentioned, such as fangs, claws, talons or beaks.[20]

Strikingly, the highly decorated and elaborate objects and architecture are mostly confined to the centres. In general, the smaller sites of the period in the regions of the ceremonial centres appear to be scattered farmsteads or modest communities of rural farmers continuing to live as did their ancestors for the previous several thousand years.[21] Thus, the ceremonial centres provide a major contrast with an otherwise largely unchanging cultural landscape, one in which there is little impact from the developments in the major centres.

The Formative Centre of Chavín de Huántar

Chavín de Huántar is one of the major ceremonial centres of the Formative period, with a long history of investigation since the site was recognized as an early temple complex by the pre-eminent Peruvian archaeologist Julio C. Tello around 1919.[22] I have been leading a sizeable programme of archaeological investigations in this World Heritage site for twenty-one years, together with various Peruvian and international researchers. These include Luis G. Lumbreras, who in the 1960s and 1970s carried out his own major archaeological project in the site.[23] Tello felt that the site represented a virtual capital of a Formative period, state-like 'mother-culture' and was thus a unique base that administered the first very large political entity of the Andes. Time has clearly shown, however, that Chavín was a member of the above-mentioned set of Formative ceremonial centres, and that while it has some unique characteristics, its commonalities with other sites are of overriding importance. The site did demonstrate an iconic art style, which over the course of the twentieth century was broadly recognized in approximately contemporary sites throughout the Central Andes. Tello's 'mother culture' hypothesis initially prompted archaeologists to assume that whenever they encountered Chavín style elsewhere it came directly from, or was an imitation of that seen in, Chavín itself. It was eventually recognized that Chavín's imagery may not be the earliest versions of the style, and also that there was significant variability in the style, albeit within the mentioned strong overall similarities.[24] Rather than the origination point of the various commonalities, Chavín came to be seen instead as receiving them at a relatively late date, synthesizing them, and then serving as the centre point of their diffusion or even proselytizing in a subsequent spread of the new formulation late in the Formative.[25] Our recent efforts to re-date Chavín argue that it is neither way ahead of the rest of the region and certainly not far behind.[26] But the important issue here is that later Formative studies have from the beginning been concerned with the origins and sources of the very recognizable architecture, art and artefacts that broadly characterize the period. Both earliest and possibly later synthesized versions of material culture represent innovation; most significantly, there is both the specificity of character and design and the range of variation in subject and medium to be able to differentiate new from old.

Chavín is located in the north-central Peruvian highlands at an altitude of 3,180 metres, tellingly positioned at the point where a perennial major tributary stream joins a sizeable highland river, a meeting known in Andean traditions as a *tincu* or *tinkuy* and a quite significant landmark. Although argued to be on a particularly advantageous route across the Andes from coast to eastern lowland jungles, topographic analysis shows that any such route through Chavín would be costly in altitude change relative to optimal pathways located to the north and south.[27] It would be more accurate to describe Chavín as being in an out-of-the-way location, but nestled in a dramatic landscape of energetic rivers, towering snowcapped peaks and sweeping vistas.

What makes Chavín a member of the later Formative set, and what distinguishes it from the others? Chavín shares in almost all general characteristics, but differs at a more detailed level almost as completely. The site is made up of platform mounds or severely truncated pyramids, which have a tendency to be arranged in a U-shape configuration around circular or square countersunk plazas, a commonality (Figure 1.1). But in Chavín, a good portion of the facades of these structures are made of cut stone, a rarity at other sites. Whereas in other sites these big buildings are solid, in Chavín they are made porous by many systems of underground labyrinthine passageways known as galleries. Chavín contains more galleries than all other known Formative sites by a huge factor; there are no other complex or labyrinthine internal structures in any other Formative site. Chavín, like many other Formative

Figure 1.1 Artist's reconstruction of Chavín de Huántar at its maximum extension, between 850 and 500 BCE. A human figure serves for scale in the large square plaza on the left. Drawing by Miguel Ortiz.

centres, had extensive graphic representations incorporated into its architecture, but like relatively few others, this art seems to have been predominantly engraved and sculpted stone.

Radiocarbon dating of site areas surrounding the ceremonial centre shows that human presence goes back at least to the 4th millennium BCE, and dates from the centre itself range back to 1300 BCE.[28] The site is known to have grown through more than fifty major construction events that seem to have clustered in time, with at least one period of intensive use of the ceremonial architecture without additions or modifications.[29] The limited amount of valley bottom land available to accommodate Chavín was augmented by moving the course of the major Mosna River. This seems to be part of a pattern of willingness to confront natural risk with audacious site expansion. Risk analysis suggests that Chavín's location was subject to a number of severe natural processes.[30] The continued expansion of the temple's layout and the availability of lower risk areas nearby may mean that Chavín's leadership actively sought the challenge of surviving the dangers of natural elements, perhaps as a way of demonstrating human power as capable of countering that of nature.

Evidence for Innovation at Chavín

As mentioned previously, finding evidence for innovation in the archaeological record is not easy, nor is interpretation of the evidence straightforward. The case of Chavín seems exceptional in that we have a number of material factors, arrangements and apparent behaviours that either originate or change during the later Formative and which also appear to be unique in their presence or condition at Chavín. If one were to split hairs, it would be possible to find uniqueness in almost any archaeological assemblage or setting. Thus I will aim at a representative series of examples here, rather than a comprehensive listing. For each, I will review the type of evidence and the category of innovation involved.

Technological Innovations

In many senses these are the most interesting and easily identified ones, as well as the most unusual. In the modern world, we are not accustomed to seeing technological innovations coming from the religious sector. If anything, the more common perception is one of the rejection or suppression of technological innovations by some religions.

Pottery. Pottery was in widespread use by the later Formative, but this period witnessed the development of technical quality and diversity in form, execution, decoration, colour and many other details. The problem is that as pottery was a focal technology, it was widely exchanged. And the archaeological techniques for establishing the origin point of ceramic variants are still in the early stage of application. Doubtlessly, some of the most spectacular pottery found at Chavín was developed there and was highly sought after as an icon of Chavín cult membership. But we are not yet at the point of definitively identifying them. One particular group of decorated ceramics, however, stands out as distinctive and found mostly at Chavín, with a small amount of identical material at the relatively nearby site of Kotosh.[31] We have labelled this pottery 'Complex Stamped' for the highly graphic and intricate stamps that were used to impress designs into the surface of high-quality vessels (Figure 1.2). Since Chavín is the much larger site of the two and with much more substantial amounts of this pottery present there in the later Formative, it is likely that this variant originated at Chavín. The process of stamp preparation is complex, involving a precise carving of the original negative design, followed by the creation of a positive stamp by impression into the original, which is subsequently used to stamp pots in a repetitive fashion to form a band around the vessel. While the simple stamping of circles, apparently using a cane positive stamp, is common in later Formative pottery throughout the region, Complex Stamped pottery was distinctive

Figure 1.2 Examples of Complex Stamped Chavín pottery, the end result of an intricate Chavín innovation; the item in the lower right is a fragment of one of the stamps used to create these designs.

and technically difficult to produce because of the detail in the complex designs, capable of conveying important information about origin, meaning and identity, all probably closely tied to Chavín.

Stone tools. In general, Chavín had a relatively rudimentary flaked stone industry – utilitarian tools made out of undistinguished, local raw materials. While obsidian also was obtained from considerable distances away, it was mostly used for sacrifice (see below), and no technology of note was developed with it. Chavín, however, infrequently but regularly yields fragments of large spearheads, originally up to 25 centimetres or more in length, made out of high-quality flint raw material with a technology that in my experience is unique in the New World. This involves alternately flaking and grinding this durable material, resulting in a clean, visually impressive and distinctive outline form. The cost in production was undoubtedly immense, with the investment perhaps somewhat lessened by the development of an efficient grinding technology, perhaps through the use of imported, tough abrasives (flint is harder than steel, and not easily ground). The formal consistency evident in the fragments encountered thus far at Chavín suggests a highly focused and coherent technology likely employed by skilled and dedicated artisans, perhaps in a workshop setting. A series of fragments of one such spearhead, in fact, was found on the floor of a workshop in a location just outside the ceremonial centre of Chavín. Stone tipping of projectiles was commonplace in the later Formative, usually with points in the range of 3–5 centimetres, and thus the greater category is not an unusual one. But the raw material, execution and the resulting impressiveness of a ceremonially displayed 'mega-weapon' (although not fragile per se, these spearheads would be shattered if thrown in daily practice or use) only to be seen at Chavín creates a very different and distinctive class of material culture. In fact, these spearheads show up on the ends of elaborate spears carried by engraved figures in Chavín art. All evidence indicates that they are Chavín innovations highly associated with ritual activity and inimitable in the absence of long apprenticeship and major investment.

Graphic stone carving. Chavin is not unique in carving relatively hard stones like granite, but two forms seem to be primarily – perhaps exclusively – restricted to the site. The first are tenon heads, predominantly made of a distinctive local soft white volcanic tuff and used as decorations high on the temple walls. The larger-than-life heads seem to be carrying messages, perhaps illustrating a shaman-like transition from human, through intermediate forms, to animal-like entities.[32] They were numerous in the site. More than one hundred are known today, and this may be a small minority of the original total. Heads as decorative motifs in architecture are not unknown from the later Formative or before, but the particular way of dealing with the subject matter, and the specific placement seem distinctively of Chavín origin. More technical, and equally distinctive as a Chavín showpiece, were the large slab-like plaques of granite that were cut to precise rectangular or square forms and used to line the internal faces of the countersunk plazas of Chavín (Figure 1.3).[33] The larger series of these plaques, some still found in place in the elegantly executed Circular Plaza, weigh in the range of 200–300 kilograms and were finely carved in low relief

Figure 1.3 Example of low-relief granite plaque from Chavín's Circular Plaza, showing feline design and, particularly, the inset right angle cuts bordering the main figure and the raised frame around the figure.

on their millimetrically flat and polished faces with designs of humans and humanoids or felines. Often in pairs of sequential, identical images, the figures were carved in error-free repetition. But the clearly distinctive feature of the plaques is that they have a raised frame at the edge of the face, which requires the delicate but difficult carving of an inset angle at the base of the frame in order to countersink the background around the featured figure. This technical feat, combined with the precision of the stone carving in general, is not found outside of Chavín in the later Formative or prior to it. In fact, to this day we do not know how this was done in the absence of steel-hard metal-cutting tools, something never present in the pre-Columbian Andes. Given the concentration of these stone plaques at Chavín in a number of locations and also the presence of apparently chronologically earlier versions of plaques, I am convinced that this specific technology of carving was a Chavín innovation. It allowed for inexplicably fine images that must have been deeply impressive for even the most distinguished visitors to the site.

Combined Behavioural/Technical Innovations

Subterranean canal hydraulic technology. One of the most distinctive and truly unique features of Chavín is an elaborate and extensive network of sizeable underground water canals totalling several kilometres to date.[34] Because we rarely discover these canals unless our excavations go below the level of the earliest Chavín-period occupation surfaces, and given the inferred interconnections between known canal segments, it is clear that what we know of Chavín's canals is a small percentage of the total. The canal system greatly exceeds the needs for the rainfall/runoff/drainage function originally inferred for the first-known canals. Initially begun to restore adequate drainage for site conservation, our investigation of canals has been spurred by the incontrovertible evidence that the same network was used to bring water into the site as well. Moreover, the canals were clearly used to receive sacrificial offerings and probably for undetected personnel movement between distant parts of the site, as well as possibly for disposal of human bodies. The enigmatic canals had formal entrance staircases and highly elaborate interconnections (Figure 1.4), often with waterfall features allowing small, highly inclined, high-energy feeder canals to rush their waters spectacularly into the major trunk canals. The consistent entry of such smaller canals from the left side of the larger canals repeatedly replicates the nearby joining of the adjacent *tinkuy* pattern of small/high-energy and large/low-energy river junction mentioned previously.

Most exceptionally, we have evidence for at least three instances of pressure systems, in which supply canals were capable of elevating water a significant distance to the surface by means of a fountain or other inexplicable water presence in a form otherwise unknown for this time period. Interestingly, the trajectory of some canals, running completely underneath the major buildings of Chavín, implies centuries of pre-planning of an extensive canal system designed from the beginning to deal with the full, final architectural layout of the centre. In general, later Formative sites have only small-scale, short-trajectory canals and in no case do they have the complex hydraulic features of the Chavín system. The only reasonable conclusion is that much, if not all, of Chavín's capability with respect to canal hydrology and practical and symbolic manipulation of water was developed locally. Importantly, this does not represent, as in prior examples, a relatively limited field of knowledge and practice, but involves architecture, ritual performance, planning and extensive understanding of how to deal with water within complex constructions and over major space. Far beyond the 'craftsperson' analogy for the other technical innovations, this is more

Figure 1.4 Part of one of Chavín's underground canals, with right angles interconnecting segments, and formal entrance staircase (far left).

analogous to a 'planning department' type of organization, in which various subsets of specialists would need coordination and supervision.

Manipulation of sound and light in underground spaces. The gallery systems of Chavín, probably in great part the contexts for under-surface rituals, have features that imply certain practices that are unique, or at the very least, uniquely calculated and adapted for Chavín. Both have to do with the ducts, usually about 20–40 centimetres square in section, which connect the galleries to one another and to the outside world. They are known for providing fresh air to the galleries and, in some cases, cross-ventilating a major building by passing through a series of galleries. This also has the beneficial effect of removing excess humidity from the otherwise dank-building interior. Strikingly, the ducts are often in multiple segments, carefully aligned along an absolutely straight line, as the duct transits from the exterior and passes through various segments of one or two galleries. The straightness seems more ideal for conducting light and sound than air, and the frequent finding of small anthracite mirrors in site deposits has led to a hypothesis that the ducts could have been used to bring dramatic outside sunlight deep into the structures' interior. The fact that light projected in this way through one duct provides very effective frontal lighting to a major, 4.5-metre-high idol-like image still in its original location deep in one gallery seems to partially confirm this idea.[35] The ducts also played a role in manipulation of sound in a way that confirms the presence of a form of acoustic engineering in the site. Archaeoacoustic work by Miriam Kolar has shown that the same duct that allows light to hit the sacred Lanzón statue has a special, tapering configuration that serves as a filter, allowing only the range of tones immediately around the native voice of Strumbus shell trumpets to pass in amplified form.[36] Our excavations in a small, sacristy-like gallery setting at Chavín revealed a series of these trumpets, many of them highly decorated. The configuration of this duct is highly unlikely to be due to happenstance, indicating an intentional manipulation of sound, achieved through understandings of acoustic factors in the physical configuration of ritual space at the site. Further work by Kolar has revealed a variety of acoustic situations in the galleries that may have created conditions of disorientation for visitors listening to sounds in these spaces. These innovations are, of course, audio-visual in character and involve knowledge and experience in acoustics and light reflection. Some degree of sound generation through water movement may have also occurred in Chavín, interlinking the technologies of the canals, including pressure systems, and the acoustic properties of a variety of internal spaces.

Behavioural–Conceptual Innovations

Undoubtedly the richest innovations were in the ideational realms that created the fields of meaning for innovation in the technologies and physical settings. While much of this is difficult to infer, and for which it is particularly difficult to establish priority or uniqueness, some exploration of Chavín's evidence is worthwhile.

Sacrifice behaviours. The destruction of various forms of material culture is a world-wide ritual activity, and an unlikely place to seek specific innovation. But some aspects of Chavín sacrifice suggest an approach that is as yet not reported elsewhere in the Andes. A case in point is the handling of obsidian in ceremonial contexts. Most obsidian recovered in the centre is in the form of very small, angular and sometimes cubic fragments of larger flakes or chunks. The edges of these small fragments do not show evidence of extensive post-depositional damage that might have resulted if breakage was due to sediment reworking. To the contrary, it is apparent that the obsidian suffered a series of concerted, intentional damages that include intense and deep scratching of the glassy surfaces with a hard instrument, sometimes in organized patterns of overlain actions. The angular break-up of the material was achieved through direct smashing of the original flakes between hard surfaces in massively destructive action. And interestingly, there are also cases in which the obsidian surfaces have been etched or frosted through chemical action. This pattern of modification and destruction of a material obtained over distances of hundreds of kilometres suggests a specific, habitual and sustained sacrificial behaviour that I have not witnessed at other locations in the later Formative or before. Many highly valuable materials, including minerals, metals such as gold, pottery, carved bone and perhaps carved stone vessels and plaques were also destroyed in ritual locations. But none show the degree and complexity of destruction as the obsidian. Such activity could be propitiatory, but it could also be related to potlatch-like behaviour, in which the destructive act involved a show of indifference to the loss of the valued material for sociopolitical reasons, such as a demonstration of wealth, status or spirituality.[37] The smashing of obsidian would have had limited visibility – a more intimate character, and perhaps a very particular symbolism. But it does seem to be consistently present in many ritual locations within the centre. It may be idiosyncratic to Chavín and perhaps of little meaning itself, but it might also be a clue to the specific precepts that Chavín employed in developing distinctive ritual routines.

Human–nature relationships. The Andes is a rich area for documenting human–nature relationships and conceptual developments surrounding strong natural forces or elements. The later Formative seems to specialize in illustrating, for instance, body parts of fierce animals incorporated in human forms. Chavín, however, seems to go another step in the siting of the centre and its growth pattern. As mentioned previously, the location of the site is in a spot with an abnormally high coincidence of risk factors from landslides, hillslope subsidence, flooding and riverine erosion (Figure 1.5).[38] Areas less subject to such dangers are nearby but were ignored for constructing ceremonial architecture. The directions of architectural growth within the centre indicate the intention of not only moving towards risky areas, but also actually provoking higher levels of insecurity. The Mosna River, for example, was displaced in order to build the largest known plaza at Chavín, creating the imminent danger of the river reclaiming its accustomed course – something that did happen in the twentieth century. The reasons for accepting such a risk could be diverse, but ignorance of the problems is not tenable, given centuries of observation and experience in the

Figure 1.5 View showing major risk factors at the site of Chavín (lower central area), including pathway of major landslides (narrow descending white arrow), constantly slipping hillslope (wide white arrow), and original direction and energy impact of the Mosna River (white arrow entering from left); directions of the site's architectural growth are shown by smaller black arrows.

Formative. The perseverance in this location suggests an intentional comparison of the destructive natural forces and the human ability to overcome or, perhaps, subdue them. I am not aware of another later Formative centre anywhere near so intent on such an apparent challenge to nature. This might be part of the particular strategy of authority-building at Chavín and even an innovation specific to the site.

Likely areas for further inquiry: Psychoactive drug use, architectural design.

There are many fertile areas for further examination of possible innovations at Chavín, but here I mention only two. The first is psychoactive drug use, which is amply indicated in the representation of drug plants and side effects of the drugs, as well as in the presence of paraphernalia for drug use.[39] The emphasis on this aspect of ritual activity seems sufficiently strong to indicate that the effects of drugs were probably built into strategies of experience, coupled to the architectural contexts, ritual routines, sound, light and other stimuli involved with Chavín religion. The substances or combinations of them, dosages and timing of experiences were, in all likelihood, tuned for maximum effectiveness in achieving the desired mental states on the part of cult participants. Clearly, there would be room for considerable local innovation within what seems to be a fairly general pattern of the use of psychoactives in the Andean Formative.

Another major emphasis in Chavín's ceremonial centre is architectural configuration. It is highly likely that different architectural layouts with varying scales, inter-visibilities, decoration and other features would have been effective for specific ceremonies and their cultic outcomes.

The Role of Innovation at Chavín and the Andean Formative

Even from this condensed review of just a few features of Chavín de Huántar, it seems abundantly apparent that innovation was undertaken in a variety of fields of knowledge, production, action and belief. It now remains to make sense of why such a place in such a time would have been so driven to produce novelty, and why it took the character that it did.

First, we must recall what happened across the Formative. At its beginning, between 2000 and 3000 BCE, the indicators of significant departure from a fairly egalitarian condition are relatively few and weak, although precursors to most later Formative features do exist. But by the end of the Formative 2,000–3,000 years later, there are not only indicators of substantial status differences between social ranks, but also abundant evidence for high degrees of specialization within an increasingly differentiated population. Hierarchy was being strengthened throughout the period, with new layers of authority and leadership emerging, probably as the result of the strategizing in a myriad of local situations. In these senses, the Formative itself was a huge innovation – a new pathway undertaken, and one with a clear religious character behind much of the development. Organization in earlier societies depended in a similar way on belief systems – credibilities that fuelled local organizations – as much as they depended on energy flows and economic production.[40] But in the later Formative, such belief systems went far beyond supporting limited local authority; rather, they were supporting a progressive restructuring of the overall organization of society.

But what did it cost to achieve these changes? Since the ceremonial centres are the very crux of change, we can assume that they were a necessary cost. The physical resources necessary to build them and the labour and organizational costs were great. But the Formative is more than big buildings and their tons of stone or other materials. They reflect by all indicators newly developing organizations that continued, amplified over time, within a coherent belief system. More difficult to comprehend is the challenge represented by the newly designed concepts, convincing systems and the retraining, rerouting and storing of new information and economic products.

But the playing field of these changes was not level. There can be little question that conservative forces would mitigate wholesale change that did not parse within the pre-existing concepts and beliefs. If prior credibilities were destroyed and a whole new system built from scratch, the cost would have been great. But it is dubious that such complete and disjoint redirection would have found acceptance within any segment of the existing populations. Thus, the cost of caution and calculations of tolerability must have plagued those driven to push for change. As I have argued elsewhere, it was probably necessary to couch major change in the guise of following or even reinforcing prior concepts and beliefs.[41] The innovations reviewed in this chapter show precisely this pattern. Seen uncritically, many of these innovations might be taken as sophistications (or perversions) of traditional cultural features, when, in fact, they are part of a major restructuring.[42] Because of a more restricted audience, apparently composed of a secondary elite, rather than the overall population, there is a major emphasis on building the impressiveness of the synthetic construction that is Chavín, its decoration and the creation of a world apart by means of carefully planned investments in developing effects and contexts, often in intimate settings that could never have included large numbers of participants.

Ultimately, the success of Chavín depended on its competitiveness with other centres in drawing in the emerging elite of the Central Andes, many of whom had the choice of which cult to invest in. This is where innovation was rewarded as one of the elements of success: the ability to competitively create new, costly, inimitable and ever more impressive technologies, contexts and actions to be employed in more convincing ritual activities, in spaces that evoked another world in which social differentiation was intrinsically justified. And Chavín was the most undeniable of portals. The innovations we are able to identify cover a wide spectrum of human creativity. They are truly capable of creating 'shock and awe' but more importantly, belief and credibility. A rational decision would be to go with the cult that was most effective in creating the objects, the actions, the ideas, the images, the sensory impacts and the architecture that made this new world as real as the old one and, arguably, compatible with it. In this way, there was a major stimulus for innovation, but these 'advances' were very subject to imitation or adoption by competing cult centres. Attempting to keep the technologies, inventories of most effective rituals, formulas for psychoactive substances and many other knowledge bases secret would have been a likely strategy. Thus Chavín can likely be viewed as an elaborate form of secret society – one unwilling to widely distribute the products achieved beyond the limits of the immediate cult membership or to divulge the technology, knowledge and organization behind the physical and behavioural innovations.

From the long-term Andean perspective, it is possible to see the Formative as a time of development of religious belief systems that had everything to do with the evolution of more structured, differentiated and hierarchical societies. They sowed and cultivated the seeds of change that ultimately led to the strong, widespread Andean states, including innovations that eventually spread over geographic and social space. The purpose of most innovations we can see at Chavín was to create objects, actions and spaces to reinforce a belief-system-dependent authority structure. Yet, many of these new elements would be the underpinnings of a much broader technical change. Thus, the later uses to which the innovations were put can be considered mostly as unintended consequences. In fact, the original intent was precisely to avoid the dispersion of their use and knowledge of them beyond ranking cult members. Many elements of Chavín were fundamental in later, somewhat more secular political organizations based more on coercive control than on convincing measures. Later innovations were probably driven by different stimuli and strategies. While competition hardly disappears between political units in the Andes, it changes in character. From an admitted position of temporal chauvinism, I argue that the range, extension, creativity and originality of the belief-system-driven innovations of the Formative are an exceptional development along the human trajectory.

2 Religion and Political Innovation in Ancient Mesoamerica[1]

ARTHUR A. JOYCE AND SARAH B. BARBER

The Mesoamerican Formative was a time of profound transformation in all aspects of social life. Following thousands of years of experimentation with domesticates by mobile horticulturalists, the initial Early Formative (ca. 1800–1200 BCE) saw the establishment of sedentary communities and agriculture. Within just a few centuries, the Gulf coast Olmec and the Mokaya in the Soconusco region created politically complex societies. These precocious developments culminated in an explosion of complex, urban polities across Mesoamerica by the later Formative (400 BCE–300 CE). Current evidence indicates that intertwined innovations in religion and politics accompanied the emergence of these complex societies, although debate continues about religion and its significance in social change.[2]

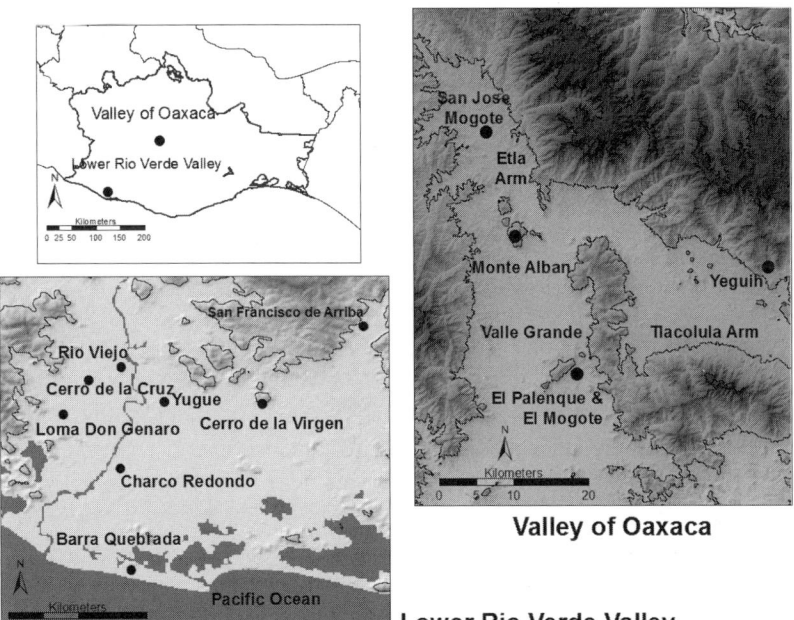

Figure 2.1 Map of the lower Río Verde Valley and the Valley of Oaxaca showing sites mentioned in the text.

In this chapter, we use an approach based on theories of power, practice and materiality to address the interplay of religion and politics during the later Formative period through a comparison of two regions in the Mexican state of Oaxaca: the lower Río Verde Valley on the Pacific coast and the highland Valley of Oaxaca (Figure 2.1). We argue that in both regions, religious belief, practice and the material items and settings in which religion was enacted were crucial to the political changes of the period. Yet our two regions had dramatically divergent later Formative histories that point to different roles for religion in political innovation. In the lower Verde, religion was a conservative force, constraining innovations that could have led to political centralization. In contrast, in the Valley of Oaxaca, we find that religion fostered innovations that would eventually give rise to a politically centralized polity with its seat of government at the city of Monte Albán. Both regions also show that religion was not necessarily a unifying factor in social change as has often been assumed, but instead could be a crucible of tension and conflict through which political innovations were produced. This comparative study leads us to consider the broader historical factors that contribute to understanding when religion can constrain or enable political innovation. We begin with a discussion of the theoretical perspective through which we approach religion and politics.

Theorizing Religion and Politics

Archaeological research in Mesoamerica has typically examined the role of religion in the integration of complex societies and the legitimation of political hierarchies. Political integration and legitimation are often viewed as necessitated by an increase in hierarchy and the scale of political control resulting from more general cultural evolutionary processes. The role of religion in these scenarios is secondary to what are considered general causal factors driving the evolution of social complexity such as warfare,[3] the control of key resources[4] and the obligations and influence gained by status-seeking aggrandizers.[5]

Our focus is on the role of religion in political innovation during the Formative period, but we take a more dynamic view of political process consistent with the theories of power, practice and materiality on which we draw.[6] Rather than viewing religion as a set of social and material relations that arise to stabilize developing political hierarchies, we view religion as a fundamental component of the complex negotiations – simultaneously social, material and spiritual – from which early centralized polities developed.[7] By innovation, we refer to the widespread implementation of novel and interconnected ideas, practices and materials. We do not, however, attach any assumptions that innovations necessarily involve progress or the unfolding of universal cultural evolutionary stages. We define political centralization as the concentration of political authority in a cohesive set of ruling institutions that typically operates from one or a small number of urban or suburban settlements, referred to in archaeology as political centres. In addition, centralization involves the expansion of political authority by ruling institutions over broad regions and large populations, generating large-scale social identities through which people in multiple communities acknowledged shared social, economic and political relationships. Participation in political relations, however, would have differed substantially among polity members.

In pre-Hispanic and early colonial period Mesoamerica, religion involved a series of sacred propositions that delineated the relationship between people and the divine world of deities and ancestors.[8] Yet religious belief, experience and practice were difficult to disentangle from most aspects of daily life including agriculture,[9] trade and exchange,[10] domesticity,[11] rubbish disposal,[12] politics[13] and identity.[14] This entanglement of religion with other dimensions of social and material life can be linked to the relational ontologies of Native Americans,[15] which blur the boundaries between the natural, cultural, material and divine worlds in contrast to their differentiation in modern Western worldviews. We cannot effectively address pre-Hispanic religion, therefore, without considering the entangled and often diffuse networks of religious belief and practice as well as the places and things that both carried sacred meanings and were fundamental to religious practice.

Although we are interested in tracing the relationship between religion, identity and political institutions and authority, we wish to avoid reifying these concepts by anchoring them solidly within the material world and human–thing entanglements.[16] Material things play an indispensable role in the constitution, stabilization and transformation of society and hence are inextricably caught up in the kind of political transitions we examine in this chapter. In ancient Mesoamerica, complex societies were co-produced, materially anchored and given a degree of stability and persistence through the work of many things linked to religion such as public plazas and buildings, carved stones, burials, bloodletters, divinities and musical instruments. Although many of these items represented social distinctions and the many institutions that were fundamental to the constitution of society, as discussed in this chapter, things were more than simply symbols of a pre-existing social reality. Rather, things were co-producers of society through their entanglements with people. It is through material entanglements such as these that the larger-scale social identities that defined a polity came to be, along with changes in political institutions and authority that resulted in political centralization.

By using terms like *entanglement*, *enmeshment* and *assembly*, we suggest that social life derives from enabling and constraining relations among people and things. In certain instances, people and things become so tightly intertwined that the possibilities for social change are severely limited unless there is a dramatic unravelling of these relations – a condition that archaeologist Ian Hodder terms *entrapment*.[17] In contrast, human–thing entanglements can also foster creativity and innovation because things have spatial and temporal properties that make them unpredictable and unstable. Rather than assuming highly integrated political formations, we explore how entanglements through which political authority and power were constituted may have been multiple, overlapping and potentially in conflict. We begin by considering the development and collapse of an incipient regional polity in the lower Río Verde Valley on Oaxaca's Pacific coastal lowlands.

Río Viejo: Religion and the Entrapment of Political Innovation

The Río Verde emerges from a narrow canyon in the Sierra Madre del Sur mountains of Mexico onto a broad coastal valley approximately 20 kilometres north of the Pacific Ocean. Archaeological evidence indicates that as early as the Late Formative (400–150 BCE), public buildings in the lower Río Verde Valley were central to the constitution of communities. Communal practices associated with public buildings, including ritual feasting, cemetery burial and collective labour projects defined local groups consisting of multiple households and perhaps entire communities.[18] The evidence for communal rituals and labour projects and the lack of indications of a strong social hierarchy suggests that the dominant locus of authority and identity during the Late Formative was communal rather than hierarchical and exclusionary.

Political developments culminated during the Terminal Formative (150 BCE–CE 250) with the emergence of an urban centre at Río Viejo that extended over 225 hectares.[19] Increased inequality is evident in mortuary offerings, domestic architecture, ceremonial caches and monumental buildings. During the Terminal Formative, collective labour projects and public rituals continued to be a focus of communal identity. Monumental buildings were constructed at Río Viejo and at least nine other sites.[20] The most impressive public buildings were located at Río Viejo, especially the site's acropolis, which was one of the largest buildings ever constructed in pre-Hispanic Oaxaca.

At outlying sites such as Cerro de la Virgen, Yugüe and San Francisco de Arriba, communal ceremonies associated with monumental public buildings and spaces continued and expanded in scale from the Late Formative, including mortuary rituals in cemeteries, feasting and the ceremonial emplacement of communal offerings.[21] Ritual offerings often consisted of hundreds of items including ceramic vessels or beads made from greenstone and crystal that were sequentially emplaced within public buildings. Taking views of indigenous ontology into account, both the emplacement of ritual offerings and the burial of human remains in cemeteries should be understood from the perspective of religious rituals designed to 'ensoul' and sustain public buildings as non-human, animate beings and as community members.[22] The interment of human bodies and ceramic vessels in public buildings can also be seen as forms of sacrifice through which people petitioned divinities for agricultural fertility and well-being.[23] In Mesoamerican creation stories, the current world was the result of a sacred covenant between humans and the divine, often forged through warfare, whereby people petitioned deities for agricultural fertility and prosperity in return for sacrificial offerings.[24] The ultimate sacrifice was that people agreed to go into the earth at death. Viewed in this light, acts of sacrifice were cosmogenic in that they re-enacted the cosmic creation and renewed the world.

The assemblages of living people and things such as ancestors, ensouled buildings, deities, ceramic vessels and greenstone beads that constituted and distinguished community came together and were centred on public buildings. For example, the construction and use of public buildings created shared connections to a physical place on the landscape, which we believe was viewed by pre-Columbian people as a living, non-human, divine being that required sustenance in the form of the dead and other items such as ceramic vessels. The interment of human bodies in public buildings in turn linked these structures to the households and families from which the deceased originated. The interment of locally made pottery entangled public buildings with the varied producers and production loci of the vessels, while imported items like greenstone created ties to the people and places from which these things were obtained, some undoubtedly distant, powerful and sacred. Feasts brought together people in commensalism, creating social bonds and obligations much like modern, indigenous fiestas do in Mesoamerica.[25]

Time and history also came together at public buildings in ways that constituted community. For example, public buildings at Yugüe, Cerro de la Virgen and San Francisco de Arriba were the product of hundreds of years of collective labour. Even after their completion, public buildings made of earthen architecture required continuous physical maintenance in the face of the elements. Public buildings also required spiritual maintenance in the form of acts of 'feeding' with the bodies of the dead and with offerings. The bones of ancestors and items interred as offerings exposed during subsequent ceremonies indexed collective rituals carried out in the past. These interred materials referenced the history of human devotion to the divine and its importance for renewing community and cosmos.

Our evidence suggests that while the kinds of entanglements that defined communities across the region were generally consistent, there were clear differences among sites in the specific materials and practices through which community identity was constituted. For example, among the Terminal Formative sites excavated in the region, there was considerable variation in site orientations and construction techniques of monumental buildings. Variation in the kinds of objects used in ceremonial caches indicates a pattern of regional idiosyncrasy in the use of public buildings.[26]

Political authority was embedded in and tightly constrained by communal entanglements centred on public buildings. Excavations in outlying communities indicate that the authority of local leaders depended in part on specialized religious knowledge, abilities and implements.[27] For example, the most elaborate burial yet discovered in the region was an adolescent male from Yugüe who was interred wearing an iron ore pectoral and holding an incised flute made from a deer femur (Figure 2.2a). This individual was likely a local elite and a ritual specialist with the ability to contact divinities and other non-human beings. Evidence that elites had specialized ritual roles also comes from a ceremonial cache in a restricted public building at Cerro de la Virgen, which included a stone mask depicting a rain deity (Figure 2.2b). A high-status house excavated at Cerro de la Virgen was spatially associated with the site's ceremonial complex. The marking of elite bodies via adornment and prestigious objects at Yugüe, as well as the elaborate architecture and special setting of the high-status house at Cerro de la Virgen, demonstrate the increasing visibility of high status among local elites. The interment of prestige goods in communal burials and offerings in public buildings, however, were practices that transformed hierarchy into

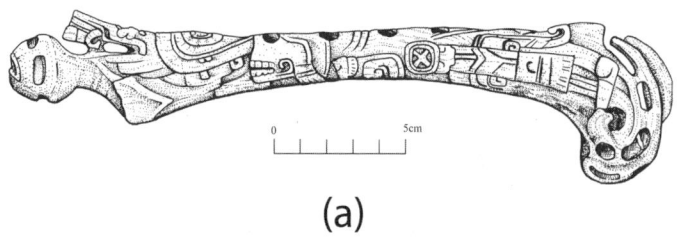

(a)

(b)

Figure 2.2 Religious objects from the Terminal Formative in the lower Río Verde Valley: (a) Carved bone flute found with a burial at Yugüe; (b) Rain Deity mask from an offering at Cerro de la Virgen.

expressions of traditional communal principles because valuables became collective resources.[28] Likewise, the interment of elites in community cemeteries upon death, simultaneously highlighted their difference from non-elites and their membership in a local collectivity. By obtaining the most powerful items through which communities met their obligations to the divine, local nobles would have become powerful actors within entanglements that constituted community. Nevertheless, it appears to us that political authority and expressions of high status were constrained by their dependence on the obligations of elites to their communities. Although the position of local elites seems to have been enhanced during the Terminal Formative, contradictions and tensions between community and authority were more acute at the regional level.

Evidence suggests that during the Terminal Formative, the rulers of Río Viejo were able to extend their influence to surrounding communities. The construction of Río Viejo's massive acropolis, which became the ceremonial centre of the site by the late Terminal Formative, would have required the mobilization of a large labour force.[29] At this time, the acropolis consisted of a platform rising at least six metres above the floodplain and supporting two large substructures both of which stood at least sixteen metres high. Based on estimates of the labour needed to construct the acropolis, we have argued that workers must have been drawn from both Río Viejo and surrounding communities.

Yet, beyond collective labour, there is only limited evidence for activities that would have continued to draw large numbers of people to Río Viejo after the acropolis was built. Despite four major field-seasons of excavation, the only ceremonial practices that are clearly visible on the acropolis are those related to ritual feasting.[30] Evidence from middens and a large earth oven indicate that both large-scale and repeated food consumption was taking place and that the feasts were not restricted to the elite. Ritual feasting would have drawn people away from ceremonial activities in their home communities. The increase in obligations of feast participants at both the local and regional levels could have taxed people's abilities to generate surpluses and led to social tensions and conflicts just as feasting can do in modern Mixtec communities in Oaxaca.[31]

The lack of human interments and offerings in the acropolis highlights a surprising difference between the acropolis and the public buildings we have examined at outlying sites. The ceremonial objects and human remains that fed and animated public buildings, and embedded history and community in places elsewhere in the region were not present on the acropolis. These sacred objects were already removed from circulation and entrapped within public buildings in local communities and could not simply be appropriated by the rulers of Río Viejo. Another difference between the acropolis and public buildings at outlying sites is the absence of direct evidence for rulers and non-royal nobility at Río Viejo's ceremonial centre. We have yet to find a noble residence on the acropolis, and there are no stone monuments with the portraits of rulers or elaborate tombs at this time as have been recorded in other regions of Mesoamerica. Instead, we see evidence for regional political authority in the distribution of the population, in the coordination required to underwrite monument construction and in the sponsorship of large-scale feasts and possibly other rituals on the acropolis.

The evidence from the lower Verde therefore suggests to us that religious belief and practice were central to the political changes of the later Formative. At this time, local community identity and authority were constituted through entanglements involving living people, ancestors, ensouled buildings, deities and ceremonial offerings. By the Terminal Formative, people from different communities in the region had begun to participate in the construction and ritual use of the acropolis and rulers of Río Viejo had gained some degree of political influence over multiple communities. At the same time, the sacred and material obligations people had in their local communities to sustain non-human, divine beings in the form of public buildings as well as their social obligations to other people created through ritual feasting together countered incentives to establish ties to regional rulers and places. The acropolis at Río Viejo along with public buildings at outlying sites must have become sites of struggle and negotiation among people in the region. The result of these social tensions surrounding religion, community and polity was that multi-community links were impeded to the degree that Terminal Formative Río Viejo challenges the limits of what might be defined as a polity. A crucial aspect that constrained the creation of multi-community relations and identities was the physical entrapment of the bones of ancestors, offerings and divine beings within public buildings in local communities. Since the Río Viejo polity collapsed probably within a handful of generations following the construction of the acropolis, it appears that these tensions were not resolved. By CE 250 the acropolis was abandoned, Río Viejo declined in size and a period of political fragmentation began.

Monte Albán: Religion as a Catalyst of Political Innovation

The semi-arid Valley of Oaxaca is the largest highland valley in southern Mexico. Archaeological research shows that by the Late Formative a centralized polity had emerged in the valley with its political seat at the city of Monte Albán.[32] As in the lower Verde, in the Oaxaca Valley religion played an important role in the initial political centralization. Although public buildings afforded a point of reference through which local and multi-community affiliations were defined, unlike in the lower Verde, they were also enmeshed in a broader process by which access to the sacred increasingly became mediated by polity rulers.

Religion and Community Prior to the Founding of Monte Albán

In the Valley of Oaxaca, the origins of the region's first centralized polity with its political seat at Monte Albán can be traced to developments centred on the earlier site of San José Mogote.[33] The Middle Formative (700–500 CE) ceremonial centre at San José Mogote was located on a massive platform built over a natural hill. Known as Mound 1, the platform rose fifteen metres high and faced a large open plaza. On the summit of Mound 1 a number of public buildings were constructed. Unlike public buildings in the lower Verde, those in the Oaxaca Valley were not locations of communal cemeteries. Instead, people were interred in their residences, which means that rituals designed to contact ancestors via their remains were spatially and conceptually disbursed in contrast to the communal pattern seen in the lower Verde. The modest nature of the dedicatory offerings associated with Mound 1 suggests that rituals of ensoulment may have been restricted to a small number of participants in contrast to similar rituals in the lower Verde.

At about 600 BCE, events centred on Mound 1 unfolded that accelerated social changes and contributed to the beginnings of hereditary status distinctions in the Valley of Oaxaca and perhaps, ultimately, the founding of Monte Albán.[34] At this time, a temple on Mound 1 (Structure 28) was burnt to the ground. Joyce Marcus and Kent Flannery argue that the destruction of the building was the result of intercommunity conflict, which would indicate that the most restricted and religiously important part of the site was penetrated by a raiding party.[35] Since the temples on Mound 1 were undoubtedly important religious structures, the destruction of Structure 28 could have triggered a crisis for the entire community by interfering with people's access to the divine. Following the destruction of the temple, major changes are evident in the use of Mound 1, probably initiated by one or more of the leading families in the community. These changes involve innovations in religion and their relationship to social status and political authority.

Immediately after the destruction of Structure 28, archaeological evidence shows that rather than rebuilding the temple, a series of architecturally elaborate high-status residences were constructed over the ruins.[36] The orientation of buildings was shifted from 8° west of north to 3–6° east of north, which would soon become the dominant orientation of public buildings at Monte Albán. In pre-Hispanic Mesoamerica there was a close association between site orientations and layouts, the movement of celestial bodies/deities and conceptions of time. Another innovation associated with these residences was the region's first formal stone masonry tombs, which shows that prominent people were now buried in special locations that differentiated them from non-tomb interments. We know from later times that living descendants directly consulted the bones of ancestors through tomb-reopening ceremonies. Tombs made the ancestors more salient to the living both as divine beings and because their bones became accessible and potent ritual objects.

A potentially more significant object from Mound 1 is Monument 3, which was discovered in a corridor between two public buildings (Figure 2.3). Monument 3 depicts a naked sacrificial victim with eyes closed and with blood emanating from the trilobe heart glyph on his chest. The individual's calendrical name or the name of his captor is also shown. There has been considerable debate concerning the age of this monument based on archaeological context and stylistic features.[37] If the radiocarbon dates reported by Marcus and Flannery correctly date the monument, then it would belong to this period and represent the earliest evidence in Oaxaca for human sacrifice, writing and calendrics.[38]

The evidence from Mound 1 indicates the emergence of the first hereditary nobles in the region and reveals that status was strongly associated with religion. After 600 BCE, elite identity and status were defined in part by the association that people of high status had with sacred buildings, which by this time may have been viewed as living, ensouled beings. Social distinction was thus created not only episodically during public ceremonies, but instead continuously through the quotidian practices of dwelling. The discovery of ritual paraphernalia in the residence, including obsidian bloodletters and an anthropomorphic effigy brazier, along with evidence for new forms

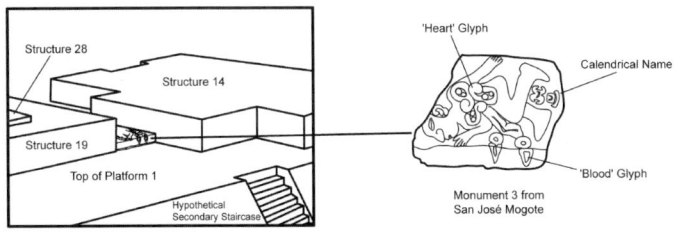

Figure 2.3 San José Mogote Monument 3.

of religious practice such as tomb rituals and perhaps human sacrifice, suggest that the inhabitants may have included ritual specialists. These are strong indications that through their roles as ritual specialists, rulers were becoming mediators between people and the divine. Entanglements that defined the San José Mogote community were now reordered such that elites as well as their houses, ancestors and ritual items were more central to the networks through which the community and perhaps a broader polity were constituted.

San José Mogote, however, did not continue as a focal point in the innovations in religion and politics that were catalysed by the destruction of the temple. At about 500 BCE, monumental construction on Mound 1 ceased and the site may have declined still further in size. Many Middle Formative sites surrounding San José Mogote also declined in size. The people who left San José Mogote and nearby communities founded a new political and religious centre at Monte Albán.[39] As discussed in the next section, the changes in religion and politics that began at San José Mogote were further extended and transformed at Monte Albán.

Religion and Political Innovation at Monte Albán

Monte Albán is located on several hills in the centre of the Oaxaca Valley. The site was founded about 500 BCE and rapidly grew into the largest community in the valley, extending over 442 hectares with an estimated population of 10,200 to 20,400 by the Late Formative.[40] One of the earliest activities at the site was the construction of a ceremonial centre located on the Main Plaza precinct, which was an unprecedented labour project (Figure 2.4). The initial version of the Main Plaza consisted of the plaza, along with the western row of buildings and much of the eastern half of the massive

Figure 2.4 The Main Plaza of Monte Albán.

North Platform.[41] The scale, accessibility, openness and symbolism of the Main Plaza indicate that it was constructed as an arena where thousands of people could participate in public rituals. Many public buildings on the plaza were ensouled with offerings, including human burials and ceramic vessels, although most were modest in scale, suggesting restricted ceremonies similar to those at San José Mogote.[42] Since Monte Albán's Main Plaza was built on the top of an imposing mountain, it is likely that Zapotecs considered the entire ceremonial precinct as a sacred mountain of creation and sustenance.

The symbolism and spatial arrangement of architecture and iconography suggest that the Main Plaza symbolized the cosmos where rituals could be performed that re-enacted and commemorated the cosmic creation.[43] During the Late Formative, the plaza resembled ceremonial centres at other Mesoamerican cities where the cosmos was rotated onto the surface of the site such that north represented the celestial realm and south the earth or underworld. The southern end of the plaza contained iconographic references to sacrifice, warfare, ancestors and the underworld as represented by two iconographic programmes (galleries of multiple carved stone monuments that are meant to be 'read' as a group and that may have constituted a narrative). The first was located in Building L-sub, which contained a gallery of nearly 400 carved orthostats (large stones set upright in the building's façade). Although they were traditionally interpreted as victims of human sacrifice, Javier Urcid has recently reinterpreted the programme as a warrior sodality carrying out autosacrifical rituals to invoke the ancestors in preparation for battle (Figure 2.5a–c).[44] The cornerstones of

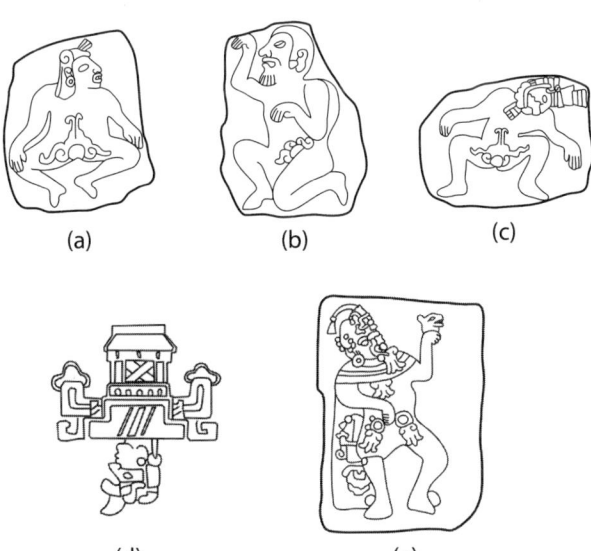

(a)   (b)   (c)

(d)   (e)

Figure 2.5 Late Formative period carved stone monuments from Monte Albán's Main Plaza: (a) Young adult from the first rank in the lower row of Building L-sub; (b) Elder with beard from the upper rank of Building L-sub; (c) Rain god impersonator from the upper rank of Building L-sub; (d) Slab depicting possible revered ancestor; (e) Monument J-41.

the programme contained short hieroglyphic texts that refer to at least three rulers, their enthronements, genealogical statements and the defeat and decapitation of an enemy. Decapitation sacrifice is also referenced by four depictions of severed heads. The second iconographic programme consisted of approximately fifty finely incised slabs that may refer to revered ancestors (Figure 2.5d). Their original location is not precisely known, although most were later reset in Building J.[45] A possible cornerstone from the programme (Monument J-41) depicts the only portrait of a ruler known for this period who is shown performing human sacrifice through decapitation while dressed in the guise of the rain deity (Figure 2.5e). In contrast to the southern end of the plaza, a frieze on the North Platform included iconographic references to sky and rain as well as Cocijo, the Zapotec rain deity.

The archaeological evidence raises the possibility that the founding and early development of Monte Albán was related to a new political and religious movement that began during the Middle Formative at San José Mogote. The archaeological and iconographic evidence indicates that cosmogenic ceremonies like human and autosacrifice as well as ancestor veneration, divination, feasting and ritual preparations for warfare were carried out on the plaza.[46] As a place of cosmic creation and renewal where the planes of earth, sky and underworld intersected, the Main Plaza was an *axis mundi* and a powerful divine entity in its own right. In particular, the ritual innovation of human sacrifice was a potent means through which the sacred covenant was activated to petition divinities for fertility and prosperity on behalf of the community. Ritual specialists who organized and led ceremonies on the plaza would likely have been equated with important actors in creation narratives, especially the rain deity. New religious beliefs and practices are indicated by the first occurrence of effigy vessels depicting deities like Cocijo, the Old God and the Wide-Billed Bird deity.

The impetus for this religious movement probably included political developments both local and macro-regional. Innovations in religious belief and practice may have been one means through which people responded to the declining fortunes of San José Mogote. Similarities in the organization of ceremonial space, religious symbolism and hieroglyphic writing suggest that people at Monte Albán appropriated religious ideas and practices from earlier political centres like La Venta in the Gulf Coast, Chalcatzingo in Central Mexico and Chiapa de Corzo in the Chiapas Central Depression.[47] The collapse of many of these political centres towards the end of the Middle Formative may have reshuffled far-reaching relationships involving the movement of goods, people and ideas. The situation was fraught with potential for innovation because the unravelling of historically important social and material relations demanded management and stabilization. What resulted was a new city, founded on an uninhabited hilltop completely dissociated from earlier spatial and social relations. In this new and very compelling location for human–divine engagement, there was both physical and conceptual space to create novel institutions and large-scale social affiliations. The rapid growth of Monte Albán suggests that people were drawn to the religious and political innovations occurring in the urban centre, rather than being coercively compelled.

The social identities of people living in and around Monte Albán were no longer defined just by affiliations with their families and communities, but were increasingly enmeshed with the political and religious actors, institutions and implements at Monte Albán, especially its Main Plaza complex. Yet, the entanglements centred on the plaza do not seem to have extended throughout the Valley of Oaxaca as a whole. Differences in ceramic styles and monumental architecture suggest that the sites of El Mogote and Yegüih were centres of independent polities.[48] Evidence also indicates that Monte Albán periodically attacked El Mogote and the nearby site of El Palenque.

Religion and the Negotiation of Political Authority

The innovations in religion and politics during the early years of Monte Albán clearly benefited the nobility and contributed to rising inequality and separation of noble and commoner identities. Archaeological evidence indicates, however, that both newer forms of hierarchical authority and more traditional forms of communal leadership vied for political influence.[49] For example, the Late Formative iconography and spatial organization of the Main Plaza complex downplayed the political authority and the ritual role of rulers. Although nobles lived near the ceremonial precinct and directed public rituals, there were few overt representations of rulers and there were no high-status residences directly facing the plaza. Other than the portrait on Monument J-41, rulers were represented solely in the hieroglyphic inscriptions on the cornerstones of the Building L-sub programme, which were probably understandable only to the literate nobility. Instead of the authority of rulers, the plaza emphasized public buildings, public spaces and cosmic symbolism including images depicting sacrifice, divination, ancestors, deities and warfare-related rituals. Communal authority was represented by the members of the warrior sodality shown performing autosacrifice on Building L-sub, arranged according to age and achieved status with higher-ranking members, including bearded elders and rain god impersonators, located on the top of the platform and lower-status members placed in the lower levels close to the plaza surface (Figure 5a–c). The Main Plaza, therefore, would have constrained the ability of rulers to monopolize religious and political authority.

The two potentially competing forms of authority – communal and noble – carried inherent contradictions and latent points of tension. Powerful nobles threatened the traditional authority of communal institutions, while the latter constrained the power of the nobility. Although only rulers were clearly associated with human sacrifice, commoners were shown performing autosacrifice and invoking ancestors. If the rain god impersonators from Building L-sub were non-nobles, as argued by Urcid, then both higher-status commoners and rulers were able to embody the deity. These data suggest that the settings in which hereditary nobles and communal organizations negotiated and contested political authority probably included public rituals and access to special ceremonial roles like rain god impersonator, as well as activities related to the preparation for and conduct of warfare.

By the Terminal Formative, however, the rulers of Monte Albán were increasingly gaining authority in the interrelated fields of religion, politics and economics. At Monte Albán, new construction projects restricted access to the Main Plaza and the building of high-status houses directly on the plaza indicate greater elite control over the ceremonial centre. At the same time, the rulers of Monte Albán increasingly forged political and economic ties with other communities in the valley through coercion and the control of social valuables. The conquest of El Palenque suggests that Monte Albán's rulers used coercion to force communities into compliance.[50] Evidence indicates that the rulers of Monte Albán also controlled the manufacture of social valuables such as fancy cream-ware ceramics and shell ornaments that were used to create debts and obligations with people in outlying communities.[51] Both cream-ware ceramics and coercive force were also enmeshed with religion. Fancy cream-wares often exhibited designs symbolizing the rain deity, and warfare was, at least in part, motivated by the need to obtain captives for human sacrifice.

Evidence from the end of the Terminal Formative suggests that tensions between communal and hierarchical forms of authority may have erupted in a political upheaval at Monte Albán.[52] At this time, both of the major iconographic programmes on the Main Plaza were dismantled and some monuments were defaced and buried under new buildings. Since these iconographic programmes probably represented communal forms of leadership, their dismantling and destruction may directly reflect the suppression of communal authority. A temple on the North Platform was also burnt, and a wall for defence and/or monitoring of access was built around parts of the site. By the Terminal Formative, the rulers of Monte Albán had expanded their influence in the Oaxaca Valley beyond the central valley area through a combination of alliance, religious persuasion and military conquest, although the nature and extent of their political control is unclear. By the Early Classic, more exclusionary and hierarchical forms of authority gained prominence over competing forms of leadership.

Conclusions

In this chapter we have considered the role of religion in later Formative political innovations in the lower Río Verde Valley and the Valley of Oaxaca. Rather than viewing religion as secondary to what are typically seen as causally prominent economic and political factors, we argue that in both regions, religious belief, practice and the material items and settings in which religion was enacted were central to the political changes of the time. In both regions, religion was at the core of the entanglements through which community, polity and political authority were negotiated and at times contested. These entanglements were focused on public buildings and spaces and assembled people from different communities and varying statuses as well as entities such as ancestors, deities, offerings, sacrificial victims, burials and feasting foods. Yet, our case studies demonstrate dramatically divergent outcomes that point to different roles for religion in political innovation depending on culturally and historically contingent circumstances.

In the lower Río Verde Valley we argue that religion was a conservative force constraining innovations that could have led to political centralization. As early as the Late Formative, public buildings were a focal node in the entanglements that constituted communities. The construction of the acropolis engaged people from multiple communities in a large-scale collective works project and created the potential for reorganizing and expanding the scale of entanglements that could have constituted a politically centralized polity. At the same time, the persistence and durability of the bones of ancestors and ceremonial offerings emplaced within public buildings at outlying sites created conditions of entrapment. The sacred and material bonds and obligations people had in their local communities to sustain non-human, divine beings in the form of public buildings, as well as their social obligations to other people created through ritual feasting, countered incentives to establish ties to people, place and authority at the regional level. The construction and use of the acropolis coupled with the physical entrapment of the bones of ancestors, offerings and divine beings within public buildings in local communities created sites of tension and conflict between local and regional collectivities and authorities. The outcome was that the multi-community links and centralized political authority that could have come to define a polity were fleeting and unstable. Río Viejo collapsed probably within only a few generations of its emergence as a political centre.

In the Valley of Oaxaca we also found that religion and, especially, public facilities were central to entanglements that constituted community and political authority. In contrast to the lower Verde, however, religion was less constraining in the Oaxaca Valley and, instead, fostered political innovations. In particular, in contrast to the lower Verde, the bones of ancestors were distributed in family residences rather than entrapped within public buildings, and rituals of ensoulment did not engage large numbers of people. The burning of the temple at San José Mogote and the broader political crisis catalysed an unravelling of religiously focused entanglements among community members, buildings and the divine. The innovations that followed at San José Mogote included the appropriation of Mound 1 by community leaders, the interment of elites in tombs, the increasing role of elite ritual specialists as mediators between people and the divine and the reorientation of the site to a new sacred axis. The result was that elites as well as their houses, ancestors and ritual implements came to be more central to the entanglements that constituted the San José Mogote community. These innovations were also the means through which hereditary status was institutionalized for the first time, setting the stage for the emergence of powerful regional rulers.

This process of innovation and reordering of entanglements continued and accelerated with the founding of Monte Albán. The Main Plaza was constructed as an *axis mundi* and mountain of creation where public rituals could be performed that re-enacted the cosmic creation. The plaza brought together people from Monte Albán and the surrounding communities for the enactment of established ceremonies like ancestor veneration and feasting along with new rituals like human sacrifice. At the same time, political and religious leadership were increasingly linked such that political authorities and institutions, both communal and hierarchical, mediated between people and the divine. What resulted was a centralized polity with Monte Albán as its political seat. Monte Albán provides a clear contrast to Río Viejo in that centralized political authority and multi-community political relations and identities were far more tenuous in the lower Verde. Like at Río Viejo, however, newer forms of hierarchical authority at Monte Albán were in dynamic tension with more traditional forms of communal leadership. During the Late Formative, these tensions were successfully negotiated by downplaying the political authority and ritual role of hierarchical rulers, while foregrounding polity identity and communal forms of authority. By the Terminal Formative, the political, religious and economic reach of the rulers of Monte Albán expanded through their increasing domination of the Main Plaza, military coercion and the control of prestige goods. Another catalytic event seems to have occurred towards the end of the Terminal Formative when tensions between communal and hierarchical forms of authority erupted in some sort of conflict. Unlike at Río Viejo, hierarchical authority at Monte Albán triumphed.

More broadly, our analysis suggests new avenues of inquiry into the relationships between religion and political innovation in ancient societies. The reasons why religion could be so constraining in the lower Verde, but leave openings for innovation in the Oaxaca Valley, have to do with historically contingent factors involving the ensoulment of public buildings, the storage of the remains of ancestors and the centrality of rulers in relation to the divine as well as the unfolding of catalytic events such as the burning of the temple at San José Mogote.

Our case studies, however, provide some clues to the kinds of entanglements that may be more binding on political innovation. It seems to us that it was the salient, material connections between people and local community in the form of the remains of ancestors and offerings ritually emplaced in public buildings that was most constraining of the creation of broader regional identities and forms of authority in the lower Verde. The presence of the bones of ancestors and communal offerings in public buildings materially anchored social memories that engaged the entire community. In the Valley of Oaxaca, we do not see the same degree of enduring material connections between people and local places. At San José Mogote and Monte Albán, there were certainly material embodiments of community in the form of public facilities, but these were linked to people largely through periodic experiences such as participating in the construction of monumental buildings and public ceremonies. On the other hand, what may have made the events at San José Mogote so catalytic was the dramatic and unexpected destruction of the temple on Mound 1 – a highly visible and seemingly durable material entity that was central to the entanglements that constituted community. Finally, as shown for both regions, religion could generate tension and conflict rather than the cohesion so often assumed in models of early complexity. Our results suggest that it may be more productive in cases of early political centralization to consider whether religion is, in fact, often a source of conflict to be overcome rather than a unifying ideology.

3 Religious Innovation at the Emerald Acropolis: Something New under the Moon

TIMOTHY R. PAUKETAT AND SUSAN M. ALT

Among the ancients, a city was never formed by degrees, by the slow increase in the number of men and houses. They founded the city at once, all entire in a day … [and it] was always a religious act.

(Numa Denis Fustel de Coulanges, 1864)

Fundamental relationships between religion and innovation, specifically as these were intertwined at the founding moments of ancient cities, are poorly understood. In the last twenty years, religion has become a focus of considerable concern in archaeology.[1] But many archaeologists assume that religion is best defined as a set of codified conservative beliefs that endure despite the actions of people and the turnings of the world. Certain archaeological approaches to religion are even ethnocentric, hung up on religions as institutions and orthodoxies, swaying analysts to ignore the unofficial, quotidian, magical and spiritual practices of people less often depicted in official art and iconography.[2]

Formal, belief-bound, institutional definitions of religion inhibit considering the religious dimensions of many kinds of relationships between people, places, things and more. This is particularly problematic in non-modern historical eras where people related to the world as if their histories, identities and futures were bound to non-human sentient beings or other animate powers.[3] In those times and places, people lived and breathed their religions daily. Their actions were infused with religious associations and metaphors that in some way referenced, invoked or presenced numinous powers. Did such entanglements underwrite the first cities?

Certainly, the first cities in their respective regions almost all came about during premodern eras when religion was not distinguished from politics, economics or society.[4] Thus it should be no surprise that, according to the classic treatise by Fustel de Coulanges (1864), the early cities of the Mediterranean were founded on religious principles, if not actually established by the gods themselves working through human beings, places or things. We can take his point further.

In the case of the indigenous pre-Columbian city of Cahokia in the Mississippi valley of North America, we find that the qualities of specific substances and landforms east of the soon-to-be city converged with other primal forces – ancestral spirits and beings/ deities of the night sky – in ways that *caused* this singular indigenous experiment in urbanism. The city developed in short order during the mid-eleventh century CE. Nothing like it had ever existed before on the continent north of Mexico, although a series of 'Mississippian culture' towns followed that, to varying extents, looked to the founding city as an archetype. In the end, Cahokia lasted but 300 years, having shrunk to the size of a small town after 1250. When finally abandoned in the fourteenth century, its occupants moved away and forgot about their former home. An astonished Euro-American lawyer was the first to take notice of its mounded ruins in 1810.[5]

As an example of early cities (if not also 'the state'), Cahokia, we argue, needs to be reconsidered as the by-product of a momentous politico-religious movement that began with the powers of the substances and landforms east of the city. One of these landforms was the site of the Emerald acropolis, an elaborate shrine complex at which we have documented an array of associations between coloured earth, mounds, special architectural constructions, upright wooden posts, human bodies and the moon immediately before and during Cahokia's founding moment at ca. 1050 CE.[6] These associations were realized through human experiences and were, we suggest, the pre-conditions for a centralization of power(s) and, ultimately, the founding of the American Indian city of Cahokia.[7] The Emerald acropolis, that is, was the material embodiment of urbanism in the making.

Ontologies

The conceptual problem of an archaeology of religion – that religion is epiphenomenal and of secondary importance until institutionalized – is rooted in a modernist ontology, which is to say a post-Enlightenment way (or theory) of being that relies on Cartesian philosophy. Priority in explanations is usually given to the mind (i.e. theoretical consciousness) over bodily experience (i.e. practical consciousness/embodied knowledge). From such modern vantage points, humans, beliefs and institutions (a.k.a. 'structures') are qualitatively distinct from non-humans, embodied practices or histories, respectively.[8] Archaeologists working in such veins reason (based on unquestioned assumptions) that human beings, beliefs and institutions were bounded entities removed from the continuous, dynamic, inter-subjective realm of physical experience, cultural practice or performance.

But from alternative ontological perspectives, people are not the sole cause of human history, beliefs do not exist except as performed continuously and institutions are only made to appear durable through physical constructions on, or 'inscriptions' of, landscapes.[9] These alternative ontologies include a host of 'animistic' or relational ways of being-in-the-world that are inseparable from people's perception, or sense, of the world and the moving forces therein.[10] For instance, to varying degrees and in different ways, many people throughout history recognized non-human and even inorganic beings, bodies and things as animate or, in some ways, powerful. They perceived dreams as real extensions of one's soul. They identified themselves vis-a-vis cosmic relationships.[11] Individual identities like those assumed to be natural today were uncommon outside Europe, especially before the Enlightenment.[12]

Such ontologies are not deep beliefs or even world views as much as they are repeated experiences in a world where forces or powers that influence the lives of people are dispersed across the landscapes of social experience. That the sun, rain, plants and animals are life-giving forces that affect human beings can be sensed during the day; that the moon and stars follow patterned movements across the sky can be seen at night. Few human beings living in such worlds would have categorically ranked people and their institutions above other beings and powers. Instead, many indigenous people sensed and yet sensed intuitively or as second-nature – without much conscious, theoretical reflection – that their personhood, agency and power were not merely theirs alone. It was, instead, shared or extended to other people, places, things, spirit guides, etc.[13] Agency and power resided at the intersections of any number of moving, animate or sensuous beings and forces.[14] Spirits, gods, ghosts, life-forces or other cosmic, causal powers might inhabit things or be presenced in landmarks, monuments or places at key moments, enabling historical change. Heavenly bodies, atmospheric phenomena, animals, caves, springs, etc. might all become entangled with the world of people. Among many indigenous Prairie-Plains peoples of the historic era Midwest, for instance, the moon was a prominent feminine being of the night associated with ancestors, the earth, crops and the underworld.

Invariably, beliefs were not understood to be conceptualizations distinct from the doing, living and being of life. That is a modern Cartesian conceptualization.[15] Native American religions were animistic, comprised of entangled relations of cosmic, human and non-human forces. They were not abstract coda cognized after the fact and then represented or professed.[16] 'We don't *believe* our religion', said a Plains Indian, 'we dance it!'[17] And the performing or doing of one's religion in such ways, unlike professing beliefs, has historical implications. Physically embodying, 'presencing' or emplacing the spiritual forces or numinous powers through practice entangled specific people, places, things and substances with the greater order of the universe. A human being might embody such powers (e.g. a shaman or priest), but so might other beings, places, objects, substances (e.g. earth) or even qualities of experiences (e.g. sounds such as thunder). Indeed, concentrations, 'bundles' or convergences of such powers define that which we ordinarily identify as religious phenomena.[18] But, depending on their qualities, especially their ability to be reiterated in practice, they shape the future terrain of human experience. They may attract people, alter residence patterns or afford certain temporalities of experience (living your life vis-à-vis lunar cycles, for instance, will engender social rhythms beyond the everyday).

Religious beliefs, practices and sacred experiences, that is, may be at the centre of significant long-term and regional, if not pan-continental, social change such as the rise of cities. Indeed, the rise of the earliest cities, states or social classes, among other things – usually framed in political-economic terms – might be productively reconsidered as collective negotiations of the sacred.[19] Such collective negotiations entail considering how peoples, places, things, substances or phenomena are co-engaged in historical developments, potentially providing, in turn, significant new insights into religion and cultural innovation generally.

A North American City and Its Shrines

The development of the indigenous North American city of Cahokia presents us with potentially profound insights into such a co-engagement process. Heir to millennia of spacious mounded ceremonial centres in eastern North America, Cahokia was an exceptionally large, planned, proto-urban and monumental complex of earthen pyramids and pole-and-thatch architecture at the heart of a region populated by tens of thousands of people.[20] It was a sprawling proto-urban complex consisting of at least 200 earthen platforms, including the third largest pyramid in the Americas, Monks Mound, in terms of volume. Most of these people were sedentary farmers of maize, native starchy and oily seed crops and squash, leading some archaeologists to infer that Cahokia was the culmination of gradual social-evolutionary processes played out in the guise of unchanging religious principles.[21]

Multiple lines of archaeological evidence, however, challenge that old scenario.[22] We now know that Cahokia was expanded abruptly in the mid-eleventh century CE to encompass three major civic-ceremonial precincts (Cahokia proper, East St Louis and St Louis) that cover an irregular area of up to 20 square kilometres within a central administrative zone (Figure 3.1).

By CE 1100, just fifty years into its existence as a city, Cahokia and the related complexes at East St Louis and St Louis sprawled irregularly across nearly 20 square kilometres of the Mississippi River floodplain and adjacent Missouri river bluffs, comprising a 'capital zone'. Site plans and excavations attest to key organizational differences between the big-three complexes, hinting that each was a distinct

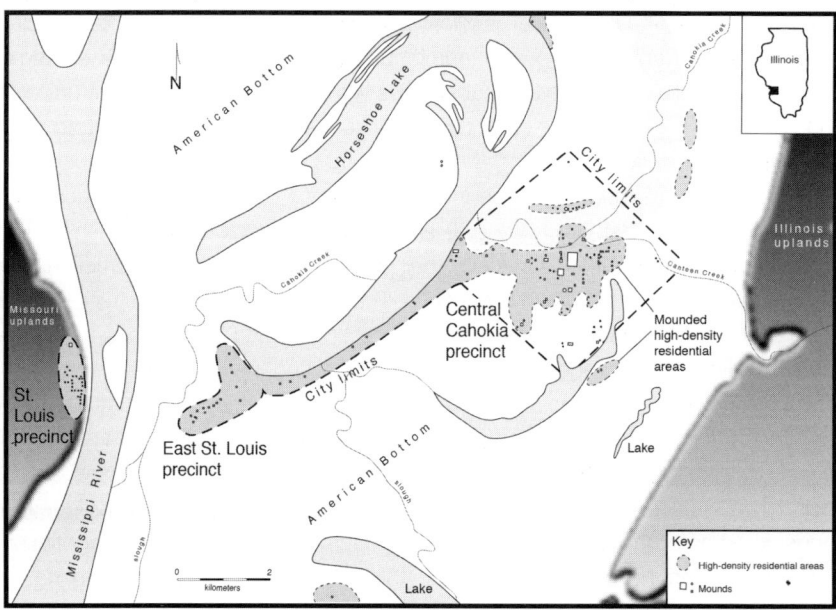

Figure 3.1 Plan map showing location of Cahokia's three precincts.

administrative or ritual-residential district. Within that whole, there were at least 191 earthen pyramids: 120 in Cahokia, 45 in East St Louis and 26 in St Louis. There were also several major plazas and a series of apparent neighbourhoods strung out archipelago-like between ancient oxbow lakes and the Mississippi River itself.

Based on counts of excavated houses and estimates of household size and building duration (calibrated by known numbers of rebuilds per fifty-year phase), estimates of maximum population sizes for the Cahokia and East St Louis complexes range from 10,000 to 16,000 and 2,000 to 3,000, respectively. St Louis could have been comparable in size to East St Louis. Combined, and taking into account several more small towns and a greater Cahokia region populated by farmers, 25,000 to 50,000 people may have routinely engaged or identified with the city during its early-twelfth-century peak.[23]

As Susan Alt has argued, the city and its hinterland farmers included sizeable immigrant subpopulations.[24] Recent isotopic evidence from Cahokia proper suggests that as much as 30 per cent of the city's population at any given point in its history was made up of people from outside the greater Cahokia region.[25] Moreover, archaeological evidence from two kinds of deposits in the very centre of the Cahokia precinct gives us some sense of the motivations underlying immigration. First, great religious festivals attended by thousands took place in the precinct's public plaza in the years immediately after CE 1050.[26] Second, in those years and later, until circa CE 1200, elaborate mortuary rites saw the periodic interment of prominent people, god-like impersonators and sacrificial victims.[27] These were theatrical spectacles that marked time and defined identity.

Following arguments by Thomas Emerson, it could be inferred that such ritual performances may have had the effect of integrating the organizations or syncretizing the practices of a diverse population. But if so, integration was not necessarily that which had been intended, but, instead, the historical by-product of the experience of Cahokian religious order: its grand spatiality, its elaborate architectural forms, its ritual medicines and its crafted objects. The result was a thick co-association of feminine powers, wooden posts, small anachronistic ancestral temples and bone baskets, crops, serpents and, probably, the moon.[28]

The moon, in fact, seems to be a prominent component of a third line of evidence related to Cahokian religion that has recently come to light from a Cahokian farming district 15–30 kilometres east–southeast of the city. Based on excavations from this 'Richland' farming complex, Pauketat recognized patterns in the orientations of and depositional patterns at two mounded sites, Pfeffer and Emerald, along with a few smaller sites. Both of the large complexes are situated at the edge of a great flat prairie open to the eastern sky. Both possess suggestive features and alignments of earthen mounds, likely among other buildings and posts. These suggestive characteristics include off-cardinal organizational axes. At the Pfeffer site, at least eight small circular mounds were arranged along a prominent natural ridge alongside a ninth mound, a small four-sided earthen platform. At the Emerald site, eleven circular mounds are arranged in three rows at right angles to a six-metre-high rectangular pyramid (Figure 3.2).

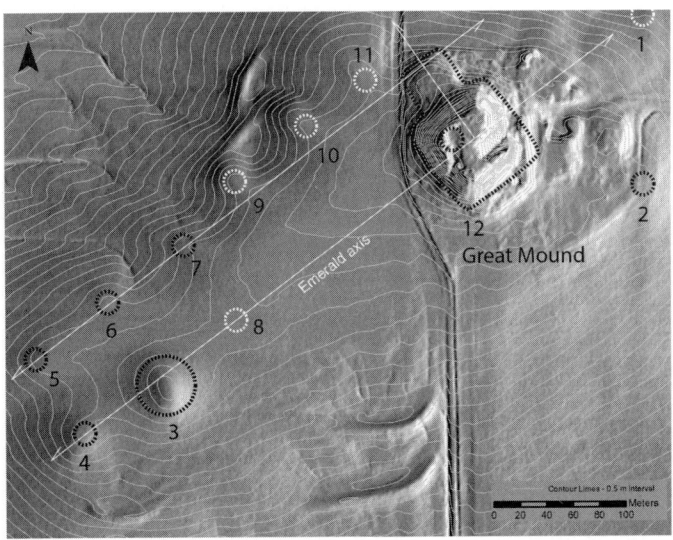

Figure 3.2 Plan map of the Emerald acropolis showing mound locations. White dashed lines indicate uncertain mound locations while black dashed lines indicate confirmed mound locations (based on airborne LiDAR scan, used with permission of Illinois State Archaeology Survey).

While the Pfeffer site's layout is difficult to reconstruct owing to modern-day site destruction, Emerald's plan is clear. The small mound rows mark a 53-degree azimuth while the large pyramid marks the orthogonal at the same time as it faces another mound in the distance. As it turns out, the angular configuration of the Emerald mounds, and probably those at the Pfeffer site, precisely mark a notable moonrise sometimes referred to as 'standstills'.[29] Standstills, or lunar maxima and minima, are phenomena caused by the 18.6 cycle of the moon as it revolves around the earth. For about one year out of every 18.6 years, the full moon appears to rise and set at maximum northern and southern extremes (beyond the solstice sunrise and sunset positions). Just over nine years later, the full moon rises and sets at minimum positions inside the solstitial envelope, meaning that there are four notable moonrises and moonsets every 9.3 years for a total of eight significant observational angles, four to the east and four to the west. The Emerald acropolis, the core of the Emerald site, appears to have been pre-aligned to the 53-degree position of the maximum northern moonrise at this latitude, correcting for declination, horizon distance and angle, and atmospheric conditions associated with lunar observations.[30]

That such a mounded complex might be aligned to a once-in-a-generation celestial event is partially explained by the history of ceremonial centres in the American midcontinent. The 'Hopewell culture' of Ohio's first through fourth centuries CE in particular witnessed the construction of great earthen enclosures aligned to lunar maxima and minima, along with other celestial and earthly orientations.[31] Previously, William Romain and others have noted that Hopewell religious associations appear to have been based in animistic practices that emphasized shamanic vision quests, powerful material qualities and the spirit journeys into the realm of the dead. However, the Hopewell world came to an end centuries before the Emerald site, and the 'Late Woodland' period that followed (ca. 400–1050 CE) weakly evinces such associations, and, then, only at key sites. For instance, lunar records might have been held in the American mid-South, notably at the Toltec site in central Arkansas, CE 700–1050.[32] But few of the other trappings of that which will come to characterize Cahokian religion (feminine powers, serpents, crops, etc.) are known until CE 1050 (see below). That is, Emerald may have been the first of a new series of complexes in the greater Cahokia region and beyond that re-established such moon-related knowledge in the American Midwest.

Indeed, Emerald may have been foundational to the city of Cahokia, a plausible preliminary observation owing to the existence – only noted in passing before our investigations in 2012 – of a formal avenue between Emerald and the city of Cahokia, 24 kilometres to the west.[33] That roadway, initially identified in the 1800s as a well-worn Indian trail, entered the hilltop Emerald complex from the southeast and exited towards Cahokia to the northwest. Given its width, circa 50 metres, it is possible that many people in formal processions frequented the Emerald complex to witness exceptional astronomical phenomena.[34] The religious entanglements that resulted would have been primary among the reasons for Cahokia at CE 1050 (if not also the subsequent widespread 'Mississippianization' of eastern North America[35]). If true, then how this happened – the specifics of human and non-human convergences – goes a long way towards delineating the causal power of religion in the emergence of urbanizing civilization.

Emerald Archaeological Project

The specifics of such convergences can be observed in the results of recent research at the Emerald and Pfeffer shrine complexes. In 2012 and 2013, the Emerald Archaeological Project undertook large-scale excavations, geophysical surveys, airborne laser scanning and on-the-ground pedestrian surveys to identify additional sites. For the present purposes of inferring if and how the religious entanglements of the upland shrine complexes underwrote the rise of Cahokia, we highlight some of the evidence detailing the timing, periodicity and scale of the Emerald and Pfeffer occupations as well as the details of pole-and-thatch building construction and closure. These data emphasize how the relationships between the Emerald and Pfeffer shrines and the moon contributed to the rise of the city of Cahokia.

Survey Data and Chronological Patterning

As of May 2013, the Emerald Archaeological Project had surveyed approximately 624 hectares across six variably sized tracts surrounding the Emerald acropolis. Within the surveyed area were sixty-seven new sites dating to the Cahokia-Mississippian period

(CE 1050 to 1350) based on surface materials. Most of these were small sites, farmsteads or short-term habitations, each seldom covering more than one hundred square metres. All but one, an outlier of the main Emerald complex, are suspected to be residential sites composed of the remains of from one to a few pole-and-thatch buildings. Most are concentrated within a 2.5-kilometre radius of the acropolis (Figure 3.3).

Extrapolating to unsurveyed areas around Emerald would produce two to three hundred more house sites in the immediate vicinity of Emerald, a significant concentration given the relatively short history of the complex: artefacts recovered from all sixty-seven sites fall within the narrow range of the middle 1000s to the early 1100s. In addition, four possible additional mounds or shrines were located on distant hills along the lunar axis or its orthogonal at distances of 1.5 to 8.0 kilometres from the central pyramid, verifying the importance of the twelve acropolis–mound alignments and suggesting that the acropolis was just the centrepiece of an entire ordered landscape in the Emerald vicinity.

From all indications, the Emerald acropolis immediately pre-dates Cahokia's urban expansion (see below), but was significantly expanded simultaneous to Cahokia's mid-eleventh-century transformation into a monumental city. Hints of construction fill along the southeastern edge of the acropolis observed during salvage archaeological excavations at the site in 2011 were complemented in our excavation blocks by overwhelming evidence of a Lohmann-phase (CE 1050 to 1100) building boom at the Emerald site.[36] A total of eighty-two Cahokian single-set-post or wall-trench style pole-and-thatch buildings or building reconstructions were identified in the 3,931 square metre area excavated during 2012 and 2013 (Table 3.1).

Based on the pottery remains, few of the buildings post-date CE 1100, and none of them post-date CE 1150 with the exception of a series of likely thirteenth-century pole-and-thatch temples atop the primary platform mound, as revealed in a project trench in 2012.[37] In short, in addition to the Pfeffer site, the Emerald complex appears to have been of primary importance immediately before and during Cahokia's rapid ascent as North America's only pre-Columbian city.

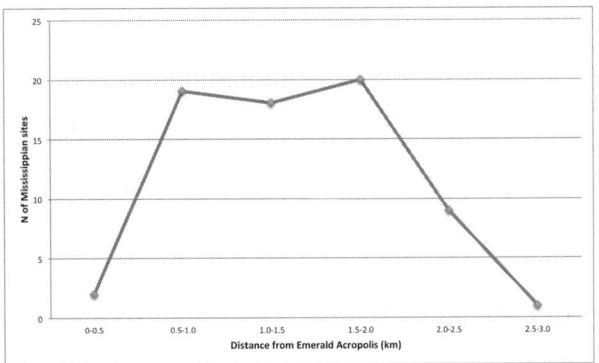

Figure 3.3 Graph showing the numbers of early Cahokia-Mississippian sites documented in the Emerald Archaeological Project survey with distance from the Emerald acropolis.

Table 3.1 Inventory of Buildings in Emerald Archaeological Project Excavations

Building form	Number of wall-trench constructions*	Number of single-post constructions*
Temple	1	6
Council house	6	0
Rotunda/sweat lodge	8	0
T-shaped medicine lodge	2	0
Rectangular domicile/temple	2	0
Other rectangular buildings	54	3
Total	**73**	**9**

*note: numbers include significant reconstructions or subsequent superimposed buildings

Construction Pulses

At Pfeffer, a new stratigraphic trench appears to confirm the previously recognized pattern of an intermittently occupied or periodically rebuilt ritual-residential complex. A one-by-four metre trench revealed a construction history involving at least three construction events, similar to the periodicity of pole-and-thatch architectural constructions known from excavations in 2000 and again in 2007.[38] The ashy silt construction fills and light and dark plaster atop one of the mound stages match those seen in the floors of special temples and pits in the earlier excavations, hinting at site-wide ritual events.

Similar mound-construction pulses were apparent in two Emerald platforms tested, and evident in the five excavation blocks opened in off-mound locations at the Emerald site, three in 2012 and two in 2013. The blocks, in addition, produced surprising evidence of dense stands of public and ceremonial architecture, including the full complement of Cahokian T-shaped medicine lodges, circular rotundas, square council houses, rectangular ancestral temples and other rectangular pilgrim or visitor housing. A large assemblage of pottery remains from one such building, temple F157, date the earliest construction at the site by association to CE 1000 to 1050, or the pre-Cahokian 'Edelhardt' phase.[39]

Pottery evidence from all of the rest, excluding buildings atop the large central pyramid, reveal the remainder to fall within the early construction (Lohmann) phase and climax (early Stirling phase) of the city of Cahokia, CE 1050 to 1150. This includes one building located beneath Mound 2 in 2013 and it includes at least six other temples. Notably, all temples are usually distinguished not only by anachronistic single-set-post walls and deep semi-subterranean floors, but also by two characteristics first observed in the remains of two temples excavated at the Pfeffer site: yellow plastered floors with formal hearths.[40] In addition, at Pfeffer and at Emerald, the temples witnessed complex closure ceremonies involving deposits of earth or ash, the incineration of substances on the old floors, the burial of the floors by waterborne silts and human re-excavations into the old temple locations that restart the entire sequence of depositional events all over again.

All nine small temples at Emerald and Pfeffer also had their long or short axes rigidly aligned to within a degree of a maximum or minimum northern or southern moonrise (Figure 3.4). The temples were not the only buildings so aligned; other constructions might have been aligned to unknown referents or were not aligned with precision. This seems to have been the case for a palimpsest of rebuilt wall-trench houses near the F157 temple. All twenty-five of these rectangular buildings lacked any indication of deeply dug floors, interior roof support posts and hearths. Moreover, none of them produced significant accumulations of domestic refuse. Even incidental potsherd or chert-flake refuse inclusions in their wall trenches were rare, unlike the situation with typical domestic houses in the greater Cahokia region. Thus it appears that little actual living took place in and around them. Given the high rate at which they were reconstructed, we interpret them as temporary shelters for intermittent ceremonial events.

Perhaps such ceremonial pulses at the site were also the occasions for a number of notable decommissioning events, especially evident in and around the temples. For instance, one single-set-post building adjacent to F157 was burnt, possibly coincidental to the incineration of ritual materials in F157's decommissioned open

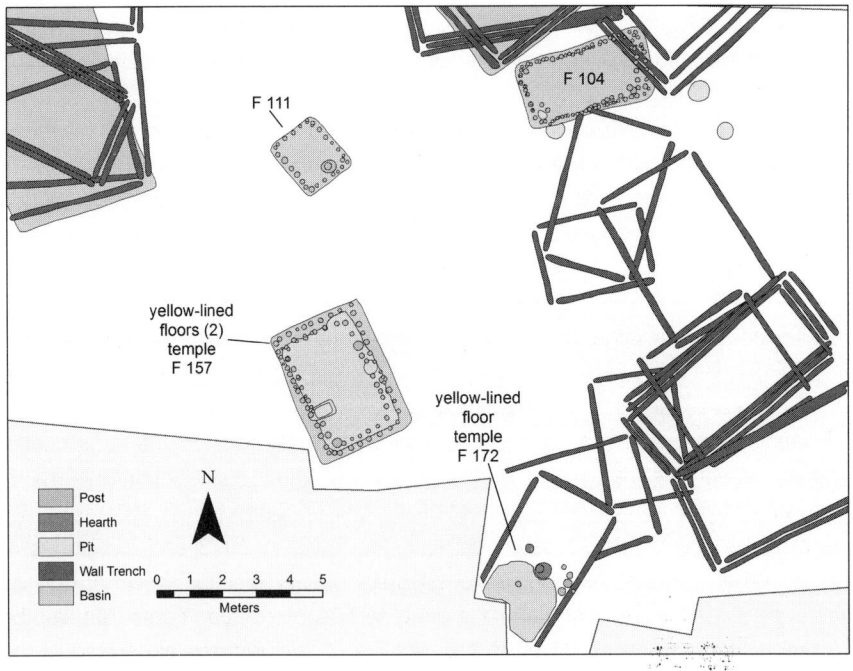

Figure 3.4 Plan map of excavation block 2 section, showing temple F157 and adjacent building outlines (F157 short axis azimuth is 067.01 degrees).

basin. Similar burnings are known from all other temples at Pfeffer and Emerald. These seem to be complemented by buildings closed with the aid of water, best exemplified not by a temple but by one of the three large square council houses excavated in 2012. Known as F110, this council house was also unusual for its oversized central roof support post, F120 (Figure 3.5). Rebuilt two times after its initial construction (with a lifespan of perhaps thirty years), the council house was probably dismantled in the early 1100s, as indicated by the chronologically sensitive pottery remains found in association. Importantly, water-laid silt appears to have marked the dismantling of this particular building, as did a human interment into the now-open central roof support post pit. There, after the two-metre-deep, half-metre-wide wooden post was pulled out of the ground, the gracile flexed remains of a human body – likely a young female – was placed in the hole. Then, those who laid her in the hole allowed her body to be covered completely with water-laid silt, possibly during a major rain event, prior to the hole being filled with earth.

Importantly, this council house was oriented to a maximum southern moonrise event. Moreover, its oversized post pit and its human offering were located along the centreline of one of the hypothesized 53-degree maximum north moonrise axes that run through the entire complex. Hence, the human interment may have been connected not only to the decommissioning and dismantling of a council house and to water from the sky but also to the moon.

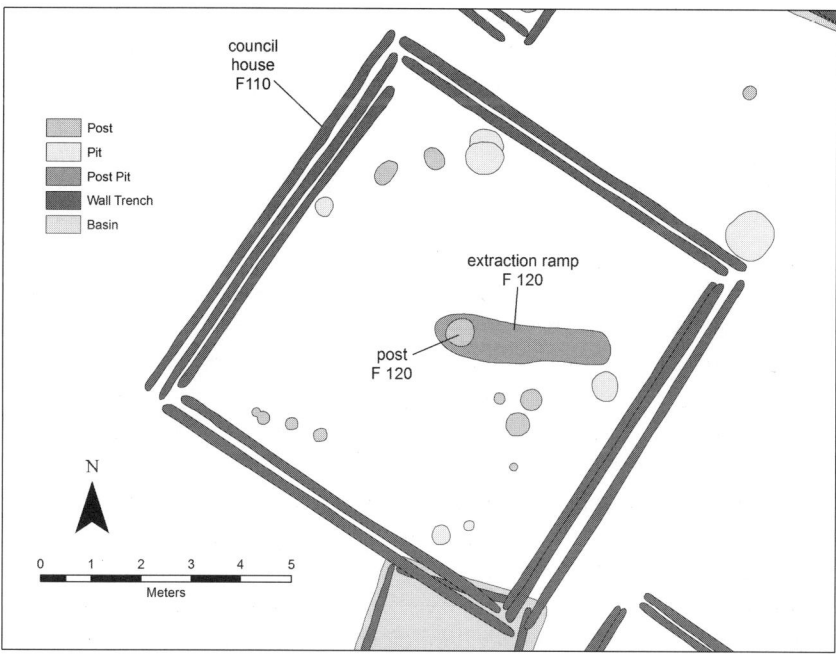

Figure 3.5 Plan map of council house F110 in excavation block 1 (northwest to southeast azimuth is 120.0 degrees).

Discussion

The multiple lines of evidence from the Emerald Archaeological Project appear to converge in single moments, buildings or pulses at the Pfeffer site and Emerald acropolis. At a small scale, for instance, a special building aligned to a once-in-a-generation lunar event possesses a special yellow plaster floor featuring a hearth and, when decommissioned, becomes the scene for a fire-and-water-assisted closure ceremony. At a larger scale, the acropolis itself, naturally pre-aligned to a maximum north moonrise, appears to have been expanded and then surrounded by pole-and-thatch ceremonial structures and short-term habitations. Presumably, the expansion signals that the acropolis embodied the fundamental relationships between earth, sky, life and the moon. The roadway seems to testify to the power of that landform, so amplified, to attract the attentions of many people moving to and from Cahokia during the phase when Cahokia's population was experiencing rapid growth.

Certainly, the discrete deposits or building associations at Emerald appear to parallel those previously noted by Emerson and others as the gist of Cahokian religion: feminine powers, wooden posts, small anachronistic ancestral temples, crops, serpents and, now, the moon.[41] It is worth highlighting the point that such bundles of powers, associations and practices do not appear to have existed as sets prior to the rise of Cahokia in the mid-eleventh century.[42] It is also worth emphasizing that the power of such entangled sets was in their performance. Elsewhere, researchers have noted that substances – yellow earth, fire, water, bones and smoke, among them – possessed potentially animate properties.[43] In fact, many Native Americans living in the eastern Woodlands and Great Plains in later centuries, including likely descendants of Cahokians, recognized such substances (especially as bundled together) to be 'witnesses', able to see that which people were doing and to communicate it to higher powers.[44] They were, in essence, portals to other worlds. Where they converged with human movements, such as at the Emerald acropolis, they connected people to the most holy of holies. Such connections would, then, define the sensibilities, identities and political proclivities of people.

Indeed, we conclude that the fundamental religious associations that generated an indigenous city at Cahokia were physically produced and sensually experienced at the Emerald and Pfeffer sites, along with the other nearby shrine complexes. First and foremost, Emerald and Pfeffer appear to have been elaborate, overbuilt and underpopulated emplacements of religious temples, council houses, medicine lodges and visitor housing. Few to no domestic habitation structures have yet been found. At least one temple at the Emerald complex pre-dates the city of Cahokia, though Cahokians very clearly enlarged the Emerald complex and built the Pfeffer shrine at ca. 1050 to 1100, or the same period over which they rebuilt Cahokia into a cosmic city. Both Emerald and Pfeffer were periodically enlarged and occupied by sizeable groups of people who may have processed into and out of the mounded, post-studded and aligned spaces of the hilltop shrines, possibly on their way to and from Cahokia.

Readily evident, nested and redundant lunar alignments provide substantial evidence that Emerald was a place where people aligned themselves to the moving cosmos, especially the moon and all of its associations. The human remains, posts, coloured construction fills and plasters, and water-laid deposits seemingly positioned people between the forces of life, death, earth and sky in palpable, sensuous ways. Human beings, celestial beings, animate forces, substances and other experiential phenomena (light and shadow) are all implicated, making Cahokian religious experience a thick sensuous convergence – possibly by definition but certainly as a demonstrable phenomenon at Emerald. Future understandings of similar developments of ancient cities, in addition to the 'Mississippian' towns and polities that followed Cahokia across the eastern United States, hinge on our recognition of the innovative potential of religion conceived not as pre-existing systems of belief but as the very terrain of social relationships.

In other words, the 'urban revolution,' as Gordon Childe once dubbed it, was very likely closely tethered to the ways of being of people who did not distinguish their beliefs from their practices.[45] Because of this, the powers resident in certain people, beings, places, things, substances and phenomena – even the moon in a night sky – might be understood as causal in the larger history of societies. That this was the case with the appearance of cities everywhere was originally inferred by Fustel de Coulanges and appears supported in the archaeology of the Emerald acropolis. There, the answers to the questions of why a city emerged are to be found in the elemental combinations of earth, sky, body and soul. Had the Emerald hilltop not been pre-aligned to a lunar standstill or had ancestral temples not been built before 1050 to provide powerful convergences of the living and the dead, perhaps there would have been no Cahokia.

Part 2 Religion and Innovation: Naturalism, Scientific Progress, Enlightenment and Secularization

4   The First Enlightenment: The Patristic Roots of Religious Freedom[1]

TIMOTHY SAMUEL SHAH

There are those who contend that the prevailing narrative of modern Western culture centres on the Enlightenment and the rise of science. These forces, they argue, have swept away the dogmatism and constraining influences of religion, especially Christianity. Key to this narrative is the view that intolerant Christianity has been an enemy of religious freedom. Consider, for example, the work of John Rawls, who has exerted a towering impact on generations of political scientists, philosophers, legal scholars, practising lawyers, public policy professionals and judges. In major works of political theory, such as *Political Liberalism*, Rawls offers a popular account of the origins of political freedom. Once upon a time, there was Christianity, which was 'authoritarian', 'expansionist' and dominated by a clerical elite with special access to the Truth and to the means of Grace. Far from making positive intellectual or institutional contributions to the historical development of political freedom, in this account, Christianity created intractable problems for freedom that only liberalism could solve. More bluntly, Christianity posed the great moral and political problem to which Enlightenment liberalism was the necessary solution.[2]

Many scholars join Rawls in making the case that the Christian church and political freedom stand completely at odds. Historian Perez Zagorin has noted that 'a Christian theory of persecution ... long antedated any concept or philosophy of religious toleration and freedom'.[3] In a recent issue of *Contemporary Sociology,* a senior sociologist at the University of Pennsylvania summarized 'the net effects of religion and faith on happiness'. What did he conclude? 'A few thousand years of horrible wars, genocide, slavery's ideology, sexual exploitation, torture, devaluing others as not human, terrorism, and organized hatred.'[4] This view encourages the belief that whatever persecution Christian communities experience they must deserve as a legitimate response to Christianity's own intolerance. New Testament scholar Luke Timothy Johnson, for example, argues that this was the real reason for Roman persecution of early Christianity: 'Rome's unusual intolerance in [Christianity's] case was a response to [Christianity's] own intolerance of diversity.'[5]

On offer in today's academy is the view that a spirit of intolerance and militant proselytization is embedded in Christianity's DNA; that doctrines of liberalism, democracy and freedom of conscience could only emerge in direct revolt against Christianity. Contrary to this prevailing orthodoxy, a significant body of evidence suggests that some of the earliest persecuted Christian communities incubated innovative doctrines of individual and institutional religious freedom, which themselves generated new concepts of political freedom.

I argue in this chapter that persecuted Christians developed a remarkably robust concept of religious freedom early in Christian history. Moreover, the evidence suggests that this concept was more than a tactical plea for tolerance in the face of Roman persecution. Early Christians, rather, made a full-throated defence of an individual right of religious freedom for all people, not just Christians. In what follows, I trace the development of arguments for religious freedom in some of the earliest Greek and Latin Fathers of the church: Justin Martyr, Athenagoras of Athens and, especially, Tertullian and Lactantius. But I also emphasize that the mere experience of persecution on the part of the church hardly made this radical conceptual innovation inevitable. On the contrary, the arguments articulating a principle of universal religious freedom arose without any real precedent, in either classical pagan thought or the New Testament writings themselves. Patristic arguments for religious freedom constitute one of the most radical conceptual innovations in human history. Long before the fabled European Enlightenment, a moral and political enlightenment occurred in Late Antiquity that was far more impressive in at least this one respect: whereas the European Enlightenment built on the foundations of earlier Christian theology and patristic thought in key respects (even when it pretended not to), the 'Patristic' or 'First Enlightenment' developed its key conceptual affirmations and innovations concerning an equal right to religious freedom with little prior precedent.

The First Christian Responses to Persecution

Whatever the claims of some scholars, Roman authorities persecuted the early Christians.[6] As the New Testament documents themselves make clear, Christians faced persecution almost from the moment they emerged as a distinct religious movement. Often, this persecution assumed a violent and, to modern eyes, an astonishingly peremptory and cruel form.

To us moderns, it seems obvious that the early Christians should have openly opposed religious persecution as wrong – not just objectionable de facto, because Christians found it oppressive and inconvenient, but wrong and unjust de jure and in principle, because it violated some kind of moral or legal principle. But this seems obvious only because we inhabit a world in which arguments against religious persecution have become ubiquitous. Religious freedom is articulated as a distinct human right in the Universal Declaration of Human Rights of 1948, and it receives protection in the International Covenant on Civil and Political Rights of 1966. Relatively few modern constitutions fail to enshrine respect for religious freedom as a basic human or civil right.

Of course, religious persecution remains astonishingly widespread in our world. But principled arguments against it – that it is a violation of conscience, a violation of religious freedom as a basic human right and an attack on human dignity, etc. – are almost as pervasive as religious persecution itself. These arguments, however, were not obvious to early Christians for two very powerful reasons: no such arguments were readily available; and the most influential early Christians were generally disinclined to argue against religious persecution in the first place.

The early Christians could not pull arguments against religious persecution off the shelf because none existed. As members of the Hellenized world of the first and second centuries, Christians had access to a vast repertoire of philosophical and religious thought, which they did not hesitate to utilize. According to the Acts of the Apostles, the Apostle Paul himself quotes not one but two Greek poets in his sermon on the Areopagus. Indeed, the idea that Christians should plunder the literary heritage of the pagans to articulate and advance the gospel became a virtual rallying cry. Church fathers such as Augustine and Jerome counselled their fellow Christians to plunder the literary treasures of the pagans for evangelical purposes.

If pagan arguments against the morality and justice of religious persecution had been available, and if Christians could have deployed such arguments to their advantage, they would have done so with alacrity. But we have no record of Christians doing this, mainly because the arguments did not exist. Nor could Christians find precedents in the other obvious place they might have looked: the Old Testament. To be sure, the Hebrew Bible denounces the Egyptian persecution of the Israelites and their subsequent liberation, and the Book of Esther celebrates a scenario whereby the Jewish people are saved from a persecutorial plot of genocidal proportions. But both the denunciation and the celebration are *de facto* and *ad hoc*, applicable to particular or proposed acts of persecution visited on one particular people, the Israelites. They neither offer nor contain any general arguments against religious persecution as wrong or unjust in principle. Indeed, the Old Testament records instances in which the Lord expressly enjoins his own worshippers to undertake what can only be described as great acts of religious persecution and even annihilation.

Even if such had been available, it is not clear the earliest Christians would have been inclined to make them. Consider the New Testament writings themselves, and in particular those documents believed to have been written by the earliest and most influential apostles: Peter, Paul and John. Even a cursory examination of the major New Testament documents demonstrates that these apostles possessed little inclination to argue against persecution and, in fact, possessed a strong tendency to accept and embrace persecution as integral to God's redemptive purposes.

The mainstream, authoritative, apostolic response to the persecution of the church fell about as far it could get from a sustained series of principled arguments against persecution. In fact, the early apostles developed a theological affirmation of persecution – as something one should choose to embrace and suffer. So strong and consistent is this affirmation that one might call it a 'preferential option for persecution'. It does not appear to be rooted merely in the well-known belief of the earliest Christian apostles in the imminence of the *eschaton* – a belief that declined with the passing of the apostolic era. The preferential option for persecution, rather, originates in at least four distinct and deeply rooted sets of theological considerations: political theology, Christology, kerygmatic proclamation and eschatology.

In one of the earliest New Testament writings, the Apostle Paul articulates a famous and compact political theology. Written circa CE 57–58, Paul's Epistle to the Romans famously instructs the Christians in Rome about the nature, origin and proper response to political authority. Paul's clear, deliberate and sweeping affirmation of authority is striking: 'There is no authority except from God, and those that exist have been instituted by God. Therefore whoever resists the authorities resists what God has appointed, and those who resist will incur judgment' (Rom. 13:1–2). Only a few years after Paul wrote these words, the Christians in Rome suffered the first great wave of persecution under Nero. Whatever Paul's precise intentions, and whatever the exact meaning of his words, there is little doubt that Romans 13 has been widely interpreted across the centuries as counsel of submission even to unjust, persecutorial authority. Presumably, many of the Christians in Rome who first read Paul's letter in the years before and during Nero's persecution would have interpreted it this way. 'Let every person be subject to the governing authorities' (Rom. 13:1). For even those authorities that persecute the church exist by the will of God. Remarkably, the apostle Peter's First Epistle – almost certainly composed during or well after the Neronian persecution, circa CE 60–96 – articulates the same basic political theology: 'Be subject for the Lord's sake to every human institution, whether it be to the emperor as supreme, or to governors as sent by him to punish those who do evil and to praise those who do good' (1 Pet. 2:13–14).

Then there are considerations of Christology. According to the earliest apostles, persecution brings Christians who suffer it closer to God through a Christological mimesis. This line of thought begins with the astonishing reflections of the author of the Epistle to the Hebrews: suffering played a kind of redemptive role even in the earthly life of Christ himself (Heb. 5:7–10). Christ himself needed to suffer in order to fully assume his role as Christ. If unjust suffering plays a necessary role in perfecting the Son of God, it presumably plays at least as necessary a role in sanctifying ordinary Christians. The early apostles pursued precisely this line of thought. Consider Peter's words: 'But if when you do good and suffer for it you endure, this is a gracious thing in the sight of God. For to this you have been called, because Christ also suffered for you, leaving you an example, so that you might follow in his steps' (1 Pet. 2:19–21). The Epistle to the Hebrews makes the same argument: 'Jesus also suffered outside the gate in order to sanctify the people through his own blood. Therefore let us go to him outside the camp and bear the reproach he endured' (Heb. 13:12–13). Through the voluntary acceptance of unjust suffering more than perhaps by any other means, Christians could achieve a radical Christological mimesis. When the persecuted imitate Christ in the voluntary acceptance of unjust suffering, according to the early apostles, they open the door to their own dynamic transformation. By embracing persecution, the followers of Christ invite Christ to make them more like Christ.

The imperative of kerygmatic proclamation also led the church's foundational teachers and texts to adopt a remarkably positive view of religious persecution.

It is not just that they emphasized that Christ's ministry and message themselves culminated in his persecution and sacrificial death. It is also that persecution figures so prominently – and positively – in their account of the birth of the church, the church's kerygma or proclamation of the gospel message and the church's missionary expansion. Persecution gave the apostles a multitude of opportunities to preach the gospel directly to various political and religious authorities. In the Acts of the Apostles, for example, persistent persecution gives Paul the opportunity to make an appeal to the emperor, which, it is believed, ultimately enables him to preach to the imperial household in Rome.

Persecution acted as an evangelistic accelerant in at least two other ways. Persecution frequently provided the occasion for spectacular demonstrations of God's overcoming power and faithfulness to his people. However vehement and determined the opposition and persecution might be, God can demonstrate that his power and faithfulness are even greater. The Exodus story supplies the archetype for this pattern. The Pharaoh's intensifying repression of the Israelites simply serves to make Yahweh's ultimate intervention and liberation all the more spectacular – for all to behold. Following the pattern, the militant persecution of Saul of Tarsus in the Book of Acts simply prepares the way for Christ's direct and dramatic intervention in which he personally confronts and converts Saul on the road to Damascus. The second way, according to the New Testament, is that persecution scatters the seeds of the gospel message across a far wider territorial ambit than would have been the case otherwise. Acts, for example, emphasizes that the martyrdom of Stephen and the first great persecution of the early church at Jerusalem greatly widened the circle of kerygmatic proclamation, both territorially and ethnically, and ultimately expanded the church (Acts 11:19–21).

Finally, considerations of eschatology also strongly counselled the early apostles towards embracing persecution. They believed that persecution was an essential part of the grand plan of God that would be fully revealed only at the end of time (Rev. 6:9–11). Another relevant eschatological consideration was that persecution was a means of testing and confirming God's chosen ones and separating them from the unfaithful – an eschatological winnowing. Suffering and public reproach constituted means whereby God confirms 'those who have faith and preserve their souls' and separates them from 'those who shrink back and are destroyed' (Heb. 10:9). Closely related to this is an affirmation of the impending reality of God's eschatological judgement. Christians need not resist or oppose persecution because God himself will swiftly and comprehensively visit his judgement on the persecutors (Rev. 6:12–17).

It is striking how often the earliest and most authoritative Christian texts comment on the issue of persecution. These texts approach religious persecution on the basis of a rich conceptual armoury – political-theological, Christological, kerygmatic and eschatological. Even while the earliest Christians experienced so much persecution and undertook so much considered theological reflection on it, they produced not a trace of a principled theological or moral argument against persecution. Of course, the reflection they did produce about persecution clearly presupposed that it *was* wrong. When the Epistle to the Hebrews enjoins ordinary Christians to embrace unjust suffering as Christ did, it presupposes that the suffering in question is precisely that – unjust. But it did not interest the author of Hebrews, or any other apostolic writers discussed above, to develop a line of reflective argument against religious persecution articulating why and in precisely what ways it was unjust. The most urgent imperative for early apostolic leaders such as Peter, Paul and John was to help their fellow Christians face the threat of unjust persecution with faith, hope and love, not explore and clarify the underlying reasons why it was unjust.

In any case, the experience of religious persecution alone hardly makes it inevitable that one will develop systematic, principled arguments against it. Many creative, considered and conceptually rich ways of responding to religious persecution exist besides systematic argument against religious persecution, as the case of apostolic Christianity in the first century demonstrates.

In looking for arguments against religious persecution and in favour of religious freedom among the early Christians, we find ourselves on unpromising ground. The earliest Christians were simply not interested in this enterprise. Indeed, one might even say that they lacked the conceptual and propositional equipment to argue for religious freedom, given the overwhelming theological reasons they offered for embracing religious persecution. If principled arguments were going to be deployed against religious persecution in Late Antiquity, they could not be pulled from the conceptual storehouses of classical philosophy or apostolic Christianity. If such arguments were going to appear at all, they would require a truly radical conceptual innovation.

Arguments against Religious Persecution in the Greek Fathers: Justin Martyr and Athenagoras

In the middle of the second century, no more than two generations after the close of the Apostolic Age, the first systematic Christian arguments against persecution begin to appear. Writing around the time of the martyrdom of Polycarp, a Greek philosopher-turned-Christian – now known to us as Justin Martyr – composed two 'apologies' in the form of traditional Roman petitions, or formal requests for redress of grievances.

As already noted, the writings of the early apostles that discuss religious persecution were addressed to the persecuted, and they were designed not to offer arguments against persecution but to provide pastoral advice to help the persecuted face the experience of persecution in light of fundamental Christian affirmations. Composed around CE 155, Justin Martyr's *First* and *Second Apologies* are the first in a series of remarkable second-century Christian documents that address not the persecuted, but the persecutors.[7] These documents – Athenagoras's *Plea for Christians* and Tertullian's famous *Apology* – are far more political than pastoral. They offer philosophical and theological arguments for the plausibility and credibility of

Christianity, but they articulate their pro-Christian arguments in a wider context of direct legal advocacy and political engagement. Addressed directly to high Roman officials, these documents have one immediate political aim: to persuade the high officials of the Roman state, including the emperor himself, to exchange their policies of arbitrary and unjust persecution of Christians for policies of just, humane and equal treatment. It is in this context of high-stakes political advocacy that an unprecedented moral and political innovation in the history of human affairs unfolds: the development of principled arguments against religious persecution and, eventually, the articulation of a positive doctrine of religious liberty for all people.

In this development, Justin Martyr unquestionably led the way. Born in Palestine around CE 100, Justin developed serious philosophical interests and eventually converted to Christianity. He travelled to Rome to found his own school for philosophical instruction. Perhaps moved by the martyrdom of Polycarp at Smyrna, which is believed to have occurred in CE 155 or 156, he most likely composed his *First* and *Second Apologies* around CE 155–157. On behalf of his 'unjustly hated and wantonly abused' fellow Christians, Justin went straight to the top, directly appealing to Emperor Antoninus himself – perhaps deliberately echoing St Paul's appeal to the emperor. Justin's appeal was audacious, too, in its comprehensiveness, addressed to the son of the emperor, the son of a previous emperor, the Roman Senate and even the 'whole people of the Romans'.[8]

Justin Martyr's arguments, however, turn out to be less bold than his choice of audience. His central point is more procedural than substantive: the Romans should not pass judgement on Christians or Christianity without a thorough and impartial investigation. He asks merely that the officials of Rome consider the Christians innocent until proven guilty. Now if a 'searching' investigation proves the Christians guilty, he acknowledges that they should be 'punished as they deserve'.[9] But a truly sound investigation must meet a very high bar. It must proceed 'in obedience, not to violence and tyranny, but to piety and philosophy'.[10] And Justin directly quotes Plato's *Republic* to remind his addressees – whose philosophical credentials he had made a point of highlighting – that 'unless both rulers and ruled philosophize, it is impossible to make states blessed' (*Republic*, V.18). Rulers, in other words, must be ruled. They must not operate by purely arbitrary standards or private *arcana imperii* understandable and accessible only to themselves, which would render them entirely unaccountable. They must be governed by the truth. And clearly here, Justin conceives of the truth not as something that is, in principle, the common property of all rational human beings. It is Justin Martyr, after all, who famously democratizes (because he Christianizes) Platonic philosophy by insisting that 'the seed of reason [the Logos]' has been 'implanted in every race of men'.[11]

Justin evidently does not believe that even the most philosophically serious investigation could convict Christianity and its adherents of the crimes widely attributed to them. And he devotes much of the *First Apology* to defending Christian teaching and practice 'on the merits', in the face of numerous Roman suspicions and accusations – for example, that Christians are guilty of atheism.

In stating his case against the Roman persecution of Christianity, Justin Martyr advances several principled lines of attack. He makes a powerful appeal to the necessity of equity and transparency in political decision-making in general and judicial procedure in particular. And he even anticipates modern liberal 'harm principle' when he suggests that the theological opinions of the Christian sect are no business of the Roman authorities. On the Christian belief in the everlasting punishment of the wicked, Justin comments that 'if any one [should] say that this is incredible or impossible, this error of ours is one which concerns ourselves only, and no other person, so long as you cannot convict us of doing any harm'.[12]

In general, however, Justin Martyr's arguments do not contain much of an account of why politically organized religious persecution as such is unjust or wrong in principle, much less articulate a positive doctrine of religious liberty. His procedural and political arguments are too general to provide such an account, because they assail arbitrary acts of governmental power rather than policies of religious persecution. Furthermore, by focusing on process and procedure, Justin arguably (though, of course, inadvertently) invites the continuation and even expansion of Roman persecution – just as long as it is less arbitrary and more thorough and transparent. If such an investigation found that Christians genuinely departed from forms of piety the Romans judged crucial to the health and survival of the Roman state, what then? Justin risked yielding to the conclusion that the persecution of Christians would be justified. At the same time, his religious arguments are too specific to provide principled arguments against religious persecution. They are designed to show that the particular persecution of Christians is unjustified, not that religious persecution in general is unjust or unwarranted. Whatever the merits of Justin's arguments, they certainly did not halt or even, apparently, diminish the Roman persecution of Christians. Indeed, Justin himself died a martyr, being beheaded, around CE 165, early in the reign of Emperor Marcus Aurelius.

With Athenagoras of Athens (circa CE 133–190), we find another Greek Father who took a serious interest in developing a multi-layered defence of Christians against Roman persecution. In about CE 175, Athenagoras wrote *A Plea for Christians*, a text modelled on the apologies Justin had written some twenty years earlier. As does Justin with his *First Apology*, Athenagoras goes right to the top: he addresses his *Plea* to the reigning Roman emperor, Marcus Aurelius, and his son, Commodus. And just as Justin had done, Athenagoras draws attention to the philosophical inclinations of his imperial addressees: 'To the Emperors Marcus Aurelius Antoninus and Lucius Aurelius Commodus, conquerors of Armenia and Sarmatia, and more than all, philosophers.'[13] As classicist Timothy David Barnes points out, Athenagoras does not refer to Commodus as 'Augustus', which strongly suggests that he is writing before Commodus was officially proclaimed Augustus in 177; he must also be writing after the conquest of Sarmatia in 175. Interestingly, this makes the text roughly coterminous with the visit of Aurelius and Commodus to Athens in the late summer of 176.[14]

Barnes suggests that all this makes for an intriguing possibility: that Athenagoras composed his *Embassy* 'as if he really did intend to present his work openly and perhaps even recite it in the imperial presence' while Marcus and Commodus were in Athens in CE 176.[15] It is probable, after all, that Athenagoras – who styled himself 'the Athenian' – was not only born in Athens but also based there throughout his life. In a direct encounter with Marcus Aurelius, perhaps Athenagoras saw an opportunity to slow or even stop the waves of Christian persecution occurring under the emperor's rule. It was early in the reign of Marcus Aurelius, after all, only about a decade before the emperor and his son made their journey to Athens, that the man who provided the clearest and greatest inspiration for Athenagoras and his work, Justin, was made a martyr.

Athenagoras builds on Justin's earlier work by recapitulating virtually all of his arguments against religious persecution. He rehearses Justin's argument that the Romans must investigate whether Christians are, in fact, guilty of any real crimes, and not punish them merely because of their identification with (or refusal to renounce) the Christian name. Like Justin, he rebuts the litany of popular charges against the Christians – atheism, cannibalism and incest.

Beyond these arguments, however, Athenagoras makes a series of striking appeals to the humanity and justice of the emperor. Essentially, he argues, that the same high level of justice that characterizes Aurelius's rule in general should also characterize his treatment of Christians. This approach may seem puzzling, especially given Justin's martyrdom. Even so, despite the great waves of Christian persecution that occurred during Aurelius's reign, some evidence suggests that the emperor's direct involvement and responsibility may have been limited. In fact, a number of second-century Christian writers wrote as if Aurelius perhaps even acted as the protector of Christians. If Athenagoras shared this view, then he can be read as urging the emperor to rein in those directly responsible for persecuting Christians. Second, even if Athenagoras was not altogether convinced of the emperor's personal innocence concerning Christian persecution, it is very possible that he sought to flatter Aurelius and Commodus. Perhaps Athenagoras reasons that, however much Aurelius may have fallen short in practice, he genuinely aspired to a higher and more philosophical statesmanship. If so, Athenagoras offers an account of his rule that is neither mere flattery nor mere criticism, but a positive, hortatory invitation to bring his political practice more fully into line with his moral and philosophical ideals.

In any case, the early chapters of the *Embassy* should be read less as a fully accurate account of the political record of Marcus Aurelius than as a window into the political ideals of Athenagoras. One principle this self-consciously philosophical Christian apologist clearly articulates is that a diversity of religious opinions and practices is natural, universal and, in some sense, acceptable, even if the religious opinions or practices in question may be 'ridiculous'. 'In a word, the various races and peoples of mankind perform whatever sacrifices and mysteries they wish.'[16] As Justin had argued with respect to the Christian belief in eternal punishment, it is not criminal to believe what others may consider erroneous or outlandish. Athenagoras goes beyond the basic observation that there is a legitimate range of religious diversity, however, to advance an explicitly political argument:

> In a word, the various races and peoples of mankind perform whatever sacrifices and mysteries they wish. The Egyptians regard even cats, crocodiles, snakes, asps, and dogs as gods. All these both you and the laws permit, since you regard it as impious and irreligious to have no belief at all in a god and think it necessary for all men to venerate as gods those whom they wish, that through fear of the divine they may refrain from evil. But in our case – and do not be misled as are the majority by hearsay – hatred is shown because of our very name. Yet names are not deserving of hatred; only wrongdoing calls for punishment and retribution.[17]

Athenagoras clearly endorses the putatively tolerant political perspective he attributes to Aurelius: 'To all these both you and the laws give permission.' As an accurate description of the Roman state, this perspective leaves much to be desired. As a window into an early form of philosophical Christianity on the vexed issue of religious persecution, however, it reveals the beginning of an argument against religious persecution more positive and robust than any of the arguments against religious persecution articulated by Justin Martyr. In spelling out this argument, it is irresistible to recall Edward Gibbon's well-known description of Roman religious policy: 'The various modes of worship, which prevailed in the Roman world, were all considered by the people, as equally true; by the philosopher, as equally false; and by the magistrate, as equally useful.'[18] This is not quite what Athenagoras is arguing, but it is very close.

Athenagoras in this passage adopts the point of view of 'the magistrate'. Whether or not actual Roman magistrates were as high-minded and expansively tolerant as Gibbon makes them out to be – and there is a great deal of evidence that they were not – the perspective of the magistrate *per se* is a special one. The properly reflective magistrate should not have a point of view that is identical, or reducible, to that of the philosophical sceptic or the superstitious masses. Rather, the magistrate should be concerned with promoting an upright citizenry, 'kept from wrong-doing'. Most useful to this objective, Athenagoras argues, is a genuine 'fear of the deity'. In order to genuinely fear the deity, however, 'it is necessary for each man to worship the gods he prefers'. Civic virtue, then, depends on the sincere and heartfelt fear of the deity. But fear of the deity can be sincere and heartfelt only if every individual is free to fear the deity he 'prefers', and not forced to worship a god he cannot believe in. In Athenagoras's account, then, the route to widespread and deeply rooted civic virtue is a policy of expansive religious toleration.

In addition to an argument for religious toleration based on an appeal to civic virtue and order, Athenagoras offers an argument for religious toleration by way of an appeal to civic equality and justice.

Individual men, admiring your gentle and mild natures, your peaceableness and humanity toward all, enjoy equality before the law; the cities have an equal share in honour according to their merit; and the whole empire enjoys a profound peace through your wisdom. To us, however, who are called Christians, you have not given the same consideration, but allow us to be driven to and fro and persecuted, though we have done no wrong; in point of fact – as will be shown in what follows – we are the most pious and righteous of all men in matters that concern both the divine and your kingdom; the crowd is hostile toward us only because of our name. For these reasons, we have dared to set forth an account of our position – you will learn from it how unjustly and against all law and reason we suffer – and we ask you to show some concern also for us that there may be an end to our slaughter at the hands of lying informers. For the penalty our persecutors exact does not affect only our goods. … No, when our property is gone, their plots against us affect our very bodies and souls.[19]

The argument here is straightforward and simple. It offers no original syllogism showing why religious toleration is a crucial ingredient in political happiness. It first premises that it was the policy of the Roman imperial government and the practice of Aurelius and Commodus, in particular, to ensure that all individuals in the empire lived 'in the possession of equal rights' and that all its cities lived in 'equal honour'. According to Athenagoras, that was policy. But Christians were conspicuously and violently excluded from it. For this, Athenagoras does not shrink from holding the emperor and his son responsible. The vision with which the passage begins – of the emperor's 'mildness and gentleness' and of his 'peaceful and benevolent disposition towards every man' – was a mirage. For if any group could suffer the kind of unjust and violent treatment Athenagoras describes, there was no genuine civic equality or justice.

Athenagoras, it must be said, does not develop these arguments. But they are there, and they are strikingly original. Marcus Aurelius may have spoken of equal rights, but before Athenagoras, no one, as far as I am aware, had ever urged a policy of equal rights for all religious groups as an essential foundation of civic order, civic virtue and civic justice. Furthermore, these original arguments accomplished something truly extraordinary and innovative: they provided a basis for opposing religious persecution in general – not only the persecution of Christians – that was rooted in considerations more solid and enduring than the niceties of judicial procedure or the interests of any particular religious sect.

The Articulation of a Right to Religious Freedom in the Latin Fathers: Tertullian and Lactantius

Tertullian, the first great church father to write in Latin, was in many respects the most brilliant creative genius – as well as the most notorious *enfant terrible* – among the early Christian apologists. In his *Apology*, Tertullian's first great work, we see the culmination of patristic arguments against religious persecution. Following the precedent set by Justin Martyr and Athenagoras, Tertullian directly addresses the Roman magistrates. And in the course of his highly aggressive polemic, he develops a full-fledged argument for religious liberty.

To refute the oft-repeated charge that Christians were guilty of sacrilege, Tertullian throws the charge back in the face of the Romans. He argues that the Roman policy of religious coercion was not a sign of their much-vaunted *pietas* – the piety the Romans boasted was the secret of their imperial success – but a sign of their lack of respect for religion and piety. 'See that you do not give a reason for impious religious practice by taking away religious liberty (*libertatem religionis*) and prohibiting choice (*optione*) in divine matters', insisted Tertullian, 'so that I may not worship as I wish (*velim*), but am forced to worship what I do not wish'.[20] In a letter written in CE 212 to the proconsul of Carthage, he argued in remarkable terms for a premodern thinker that 'it is a human right (*humani iuris*) and a natural power or natural privilege (*naturalis potestatis*) that one should worship whatever he intends (*quod putaverit colere*); the religious practice of one person neither harms nor helps another'.[21]

The fact that we should encounter these passages is truly astounding. To the extent that people have any clear knowledge of Tertullian, it is the result of reading Edward Gibbon's unflattering account of him in *Decline and Fall of the Roman Empire*. Based partly on passages from Tertullian's *On the Theater,* Gibbon paints the picture of a harsh and moralistic early Christian theologian. Tertullian occupies a special place in the *Decline*'s controversial chapter 15, 'The Progress of the Christian Religion', where Gibbon depicts him as the father and representative of the 'inflexible … and intolerant zeal of the [early] Christians'. He is the 'stern Tertullian', the 'zealous African', full of 'unfeeling witticisms'.[22] Beyond Gibbon, people might know Tertullian as the author who wrote: 'The blood of Christians is [the] seed [of the Church].'[23] These isolated bits of information yield a distorted image of Tertullian as a humourless, masochistic and puritanical church father – someone who was puritanically repelled by pleasure and morbidly attracted to suffering.

Tertullian was infinitely more complex. For one thing, he could be extremely funny. He even joked about Christian martyrdom. He poked delicious fun at the Roman tendency to blame every calamity on the Christians: 'If the Tiber rises so high it floods the walls, or the Nile so low it doesn't flood the fields, if the earth opens, or the heavens don't, if there is famine, if there is plague, instantly the howl goes up, "The Christians to the lion!"' To which Tertullian adds: 'What, all of them? to a single lion?'[24] It is worth noting that Tertullian and his fellow Christian apologists of the second century did not respond to persecution merely by heaping apocalyptic warning and condemnation on their persecutors. To the contrary, they not only joked in the face of persecution but also responded to it with extraordinary theological and conceptual creativity. Nor did they simply reactively plead for mercy. Instead, they aggressively appealed to the consciences of the Roman magistrates to recognize what they took to be universal principles of liberty and justice.

A century after Tertullian, Lactantius, known in the Renaissance as the 'Christian Cicero' because of the elegance of his Latin rhetoric and his interest in Ciceronian themes such as justice and civic responsibility, defended religious freedom in similar terms. 'Nothing is so much a matter of free will as religion', Lactantius argued in his great *Divine Institutes*. In contrast to a conception of religion as having merely to do with bodily ritual, Lactantius insisted that the proper worship of God requires both a 'full commitment' (*maximam devotionem*) and a 'blameless life'.[25]

Furthermore, because Christianity centred around the *ecclesia* – the church was literally an 'assembly', a word with inescapably political connotations – for Tertullian, Lactantius and other early Christians, defending religious freedom necessarily involved defending their right to form a distinct community accountable ultimately to God alone. As Tertullian wrote to the Roman proconsul of Carthage in CE 212, 'We have no master but God. ... But those whom you regard as masters are only men, and one day they themselves must die. Yet still this community will be undying.'[26] In other words, the freedom to which persecuted Christians bore witness was not just that of a cult's private freedom of worship. It was, rather, the freedom of a new community to organize itself independently of the political authority and to bear public witness to the death and resurrection of Jesus Christ. Messenger and message were thus indissolubly fused: an autonomous new messenger, the Christian *ecclesia*, taught and embodied a new freedom that was personal and public. To put it bluntly, persecuted Christians could bear witness to freedom because they already knew they were free. And they acted like they were free – even on pain of death.

Taking Stock of the First Enlightenment

The doctrine of religious freedom enunciated by the church's early theologians ran radically contrary to ancient practice. The 'theocratic ordering of society' widespread in the ancient world endowed 'the ruler who controls the physical apparatus of state coercion with a sacral role also as head and symbol of the people's religion', as in the claim that the Roman Caesar was *Pontifex Maximus*.[27] Occasionally, such theocratic systems adopted policies of limited religious tolerance, as in the edict of Emperor Ashoka in India that 'a man must not ... disparage [the sect] of another man without reason'.[28]

In contrast, early church teaching did not merely tactically plea for forbearance. It was a principled doctrine of 'religious liberty' *per se*. Indeed, Tertullian seems to have invented the very phrase, *libertatem religionis*. Furthermore, the early church grounded its conception and defence of religious liberty in a voluntarist and personalist view of the nature of religion. In addition, it was framed in terms of an individual power or right to adhere to the religion of one's own choice – a power and right possessed by each and every person, not just Christians. Finally, it emphasized that religious liberty has necessarily communal and public dimensions, along with interior and individual dimensions – that is, *libertas ecclesiae* as well as *libertas personae*.

The courageous, creative witness of the early persecuted church yielded important political consequences. Elizabeth Digeser, Robert Wilken and other scholars suggest that the Christian advocacy of religious freedom influenced imperial policy. By CE 310, Lactantius had joined the court of Constantine himself, and his *Divine Institutes* were recited in Constantine's presence. The result, it seems, was that the church father had such an impact that ultimately 'Constantine followed the principles and rhetoric of the Lactantian policy of religious freedom'.[29] Imperial edicts ending Christian persecution reflected early Christian thinking on religious freedom. The Edict of Milan, for example, echoed the arguments (and even the very phrases) of Tertullian and Lactantius by granting 'both to Christians and to all persons the freedom [*libera potestas*] to follow whatever religion each one wished'.[30]

More broadly, the early church's insistence on *libertas ecclesiae* created a permanent tension between two authorities or 'two sovereignties', the church and the state, and 'from this tension would grow liberty'.[31] In particular, Pope Gelasias's fifth-century letter to the Byzantine emperor asserted both the church's sovereignty and limits to the powers of government. In so doing, the pope '"desacralized" politics and ... opened up the possibility of a politics of consent, in place of the politics of divine right or the politics of coercion'.[32] Thus did the early church's distinctive principles contribute not just to the development of religious liberty but also to a new concept of political freedom – one that included incipient notions of limited government and an independent civil society not subject to the authority of the state.

Postscript: The Second Enlightenment Tips Its Hat to the First

Writing in his *Notes on the State of Virginia* (Query XVII) in about 1782, Thomas Jefferson articulated a characteristically modern and liberal formulation of every individual's right to religious freedom:

> Our rulers can have authority over such natural rights only as we have submitted to them. The rights of conscience we never submitted, we could not submit. We are answerable for them to our God. The legitimate powers of government extend to such acts only as are injurious to others. But it does me no injury for my neighbour to say there are twenty gods, or no god. It neither picks my pocket nor breaks my leg.[33]

Interestingly, all modern editions of Jefferson's *Notes* record that he made an annotation at this very point in his own private copy of the *Notes*. In his own hand, Jefferson wrote out in Latin the following quotation, roughly translated:

> 'But it is a fundamental human right, a privilege of nature, that every man should worship according to his own convictions: one man's religion neither harms nor helps another man. It is assuredly no part of religion to compel religion – to which free-will and not force should lead us; a willing mind is looked for even from him who sacrifices.' (Tertullian, *Ad Scapulam*, ch. 2)

As noted earlier, this passage contains the first articulation of religious freedom as a fundamental, natural and universal human right in the history of human thought.

This very fact clearly arrested Jefferson. The catalogue of his personal library, in the U.S. Library of Congress, identifies one item as Tertullian's *Apologeticum* and also includes *Ad Scapulam*. One can turn to *Ad Scapulam* and see for oneself that Jefferson had underlined the passage and put an X in the margin. There are no other markings in the book: Jefferson had not been reading Tertullian. It seems that sometime after he drafted the *Notes on the State of Virginia,* he learnt of the Tertullian passage. And in reading through the section on religion in the *Notes,* he decided to put the Tertullian quote where he could find it easily. According to the Library of Congress catalogue, Jefferson purchased the copy of Tertullian from the catalogue of Louis Girardin on 7 July 1814 – just about 200 years ago. This suggests that sometime between his composition of the *Notes* (roughly in 1782) and 1814, he learnt about the citation. When he finally acquired a copy of the volume, he must have rushed to look up the passage, whereupon he underlined and marked it.[34]

Jefferson must have been astounded to learn that the very idea of an individual, natural right to religious freedom – that he articulated and defended in the *Notes* and in other places – had already been articulated so clearly, so many centuries earlier. And articulated by the church father Tertullian no less, a favourite target of Enlightenment writers as a symbol of early Christian dogmatism and fanaticism. One can almost picture Thomas Jefferson, trudging up the religious freedom mountain, step by arduous step. And when he reached the top and reached his radical conclusions about religious freedom – not mere toleration – as a universal natural right, one can imagine his surprise. A North African church father was already sitting there – and had been sitting there for 1,600 years! Long before the European Enlightenment we all know about, there was another liberal enlightenment that deserves to be far better known.

5 Religion, Innovation and Secular Modernity

PETER HARRISON

The last fifteen years have witnessed a remarkable resurgence of interest in the topic of secularization. Questions related to the putative decline of religion in the modern West increasingly command the attention of scholars working across the disciplines of sociology, history, philosophy and religion. For much of the twentieth century, sociologists of religion spoke uncritically about 'the process of secularization' as if it were a given, and this general notion provided the dominant theoretical lens through which the relationship between modernity and religion was understood. Moreover, the secularization thesis was often attended by an implicit normative commitment that held the secularization process to be a 'good thing' – the final stage of an emancipatory programme that would see an end to the baneful influence of organized religion. Descriptively, religion was viewed as the enemy of social innovation; normatively, its decline was regarded as something to be encouraged. Classical secularization narratives reflected these two elements. Thus it was held not only that as Western society became less religious it became more scientifically and technologically advanced, but also that there was a significant causal connection between these phenomena. At the same time it was assumed that these developments were largely positive and that if the jettisoning of religion was the price to be paid for progress, it was a price well worth paying.

In the twenty-first century, however, standard assumptions about the inevitability of secularization, its incipient norms and the historical trajectories that have led to it have been subjected to considerable critical attention. On the part of sociologists, there has been a growing realization that the pattern of religious decline thought to characterize northern Europe does not represent some teleological end-state towards which all modern societies will inevitably progress. The influential sociologist Peter Berger, in what amounts to a retraction of his earlier commitment to the standard model of secularization, now contends that 'the world today is massively religious, is *anything but* the secularized world that had been predicted (whether joyfully or despondently) by so many analysts of modernity'. He further maintains that the 'whole body of literature by historians and social scientists loosely labeled "secularization theory" is essentially mistaken'.[1] Berger is part of a growing chorus of voices drawing attention to the disconnect between the predictions of the standard model and what is actually taking place both in the first world and in emerging economies. Some analysts have gone so far as to say that the twenty-first century will be 'God's century'.[2]

In addition to these empirically driven renunciations, new historical and philosophical accounts of secularization have also challenged aspects of the standard secularization model. Perhaps the most notable of these is Charles Taylor's *A Secular Age* (2007). Taylor wishes to question the notion that secularization is the mere absence of religion, and he denies that the secularization is somehow 'caused' by the rise of science and the triumph of reason. He also asks whether the demise of religion, or at least particular forms of religion, is a good thing.[3] Taylor's work represents a new kind of narrative about secularization – one that both scrutinizes a number of the implicit assumptions of standard narratives while at the same time rejecting the incipient triumphalism that characterizes such accounts.

There are three different kinds of secularization stories.[4] The first of these is the originating secularization narrative, articulated in the eighteenth century by Auguste Comte. This story speaks of stages of history in which religion is destined to be replaced by a more advanced form of thought – science. The second is the most influential of all secularization stories – that told by Max Weber about the disenchantment of nature. For Weber, it is not so much that religion is displaced by a secular world view. It is, rather, religion itself – and forms of Protestant Christianity in particular – that are the initial drivers of secularization. The final, and most recent, kind of secularization story is that narrated by Alasdair MacIntyre, Charles Taylor and Brad Gregory. These authors tell a more nuanced story – one that focuses more on what is lost than what is gained in the transition to modernity. In my view, it is this latter style of narrative that does most justice to the historical record. But as we shall see, in the end this rests not only on historical judgements but also on value assessments of what has transpired. Each of these stories, I submit, has important lessons for how we might think about the way religion might be related to innovation.

Auguste Comte, Sociology and the Stages of History

In this early version of the thesis, secularization is a key ingredient of a more general process of historical progress. The idea of progress is typically associated with the European Enlightenment. And while some historians have argued that progressivist notions can be found in Greek antiquity, it is clear that in Enlightenment historiography we see the first systematic attempts to view human history as progressing through fixed stages. Such histories are now referred to as 'stadial histories'. Enlightenment historians such as Dugald Stewart, Adam Smith, Giambattista Vico and Anne-Robert-Jacques Turgot typically divided the course of history into three or four successive stages such as hunting, herding, agriculture and commerce. The French thinker Auguste Comte (1798–1857), now known as the father of sociology, introduced stages of *thought* into these stadial schemes. Famously, he proposed that human history progressed through three stages – the theological, the metaphysical and the 'positive' or scientific.

In addition to his law of the three stages, Comte also explicitly sought to shape a new master science – sociology – in opposition to a religious interpretation of human affairs that invoked supernatural events and beings, and sacred times and spaces. Christian religion had offered its own account of the meaning of history, structuring it around the key events of the creation, incarnation and final consummation of all things. Theology also promoted certain social and moral values, offering a world view in which they made sense. In seeking to replace theology with sociology, Comte sought to imbue sociology with similar features – offering an alternative ideology that would also function as a source of values, albeit values that were grounded 'scientifically'. Sociology thus began, as Bryan Wilson would have it, 'as a contradiction of theology'.[5] In this respect, Comte's scheme resembled that of Karl Marx, whose theories included descriptive, predictive and normative components.

While Comte's late modern successors in the discipline of sociology have either forgotten or ignored his explicit normative commitments, significant vestiges of these remain embedded within the discipline that he helped to forge. While sociology now presents itself as a neutral and positive science, arguably both it and the master narrative of secularization bear within them an incipient anti-religious bias. As a consequence, while sociologists have made efforts to insulate a neutral and 'scientific' thesis of secularization from a commitment to the programme of secularism, in practice that has proved difficult because of what has been built into the DNA of the discipline. Accordingly, there is considerable truth in the recent assertion of historian J. C. D. Clark that 'secularization is not a process, but a project'.[6] Moreover, it is a project that is not always cognizant of its unspoken ideological commitments.

The model that Comte helped establish thus sees secularization as the outcome of inexorable historical forces in which religion is necessarily displaced by more developed modes of thinking. As we will see in the next chapter of this volume, subsequent formulations by social scientists followed a similar path, with seminal works of anthropology by E. B. Tylor and J. G. Frazer suggesting that religion was a form of primitive science, destined to be superseded by the genuine article. While anthropologists have discarded crude versions of these older evolutionary models, our modern conceptions of science and religion and our understanding of their mutual relations continue to be informed by them.[7]

It may seem that in this model of secularization, religion would necessarily be the enemy of innovation, since it represents a primitive and more static period of history. This was not, however, the case for Comte himself. He was deeply indebted to the utopian socialist, Henri de Saint-Simon (1760–1825), who also exerted a similar influence on the young Karl Marx. Saint-Simon had a relatively positive view of the historical impact of Christianity, but he believed that the time had come for a new form of universal religion that would be adopted by all nations. Theological theory, he insisted, 'needs to be renovated at various times, in the same way as physics, chemistry and physiology'. Religion could be a source of innovation, provided it remained open to the general tendency in all things towards progress. This 'new Christianity' (*nouveau christianisme*) would aim at ameliorating the social and moral condition of the poorest social classes.[8]

Comte had a similarly ambivalent view about the relationship between religion and social innovation. Theological thinking, he acknowledged, had at one time served a vital role in moving primitive human societies into a more advanced state. One factor had been the way that religion had facilitated the existence of a privileged class of individuals – a priesthood if you will – able to devote considerable time to speculative thought. Had it not been for these theological thinkers, Comte insisted, 'human society would have remained in a condition much like that of a company of superior monkeys'.[9] Human progress in its earliest stages was thus made possible by 'theological philosophy'.

It is worth noting, parenthetically, that sociologist Émile Durkheim (1858–1917) would later develop a related view about the essential functional role played by religion in early human societies. For Durkheim, religion is intrinsic to every society, since it provides the social glue that enables individuals to live together in a collective.[10] It is not so much that religion is a source of social innovation, but rather that it is a prerequisite for any kind of social reality since societies cannot exist without it. Ultimately, then, Durkheim departed significantly from Comte, since he held that without religion there could be no society, in the primitive past or the modern present. It follows that religion, at least in Durkheim's sense, can never fade away as long as human societies remain.[11] And science cannot displace religion, since it does not provide a basis for living and acting.[12]

Returning to Comte, while religion was a constructive force primarily in primitive societies, even in the more advanced period of early modernity, Comte could find some positive role for particular types of religion. Hence Catholicism could still contribute to human progress: 'Far from being merely hurtful to social improvement, as we are apt to suppose, it [Catholicism] has aided political progress for three centuries past.'[13] Yet, despite such concessions, Comte concluded that theology was now opposed to genuine scientific thinking and was destined to be rendered obsolete.[14] Or perhaps it is more accurate to say that for Comte, scientific thinking might still need to retain some of the cultic forms of the theological thinking that it was destined to displace. And this is the fundamental insight that underpins Comte's controversial idea of a secular religion of humanity. We might thus think about Comte's version of secularization as a 'Catholic' model, insofar as it seeks to retain particular cultic forms, secular saints and an ecclesiology of sorts. With the benefit of hindsight we might say that Comte was both right and wrong in his prescriptions – wrong in thinking that traditional religion would necessarily wither away, and correct in his realization that religious rituals and symbols would prove to be indispensable even in a scientific age.

Weber, Rationalization and Protestant Disenchantment

Of all sociologists, it is Max Weber (1864–1920) who is most closely associated with the secularization thesis – this in spite of the fact that he tended to talk more frequently about 'disenchantment' (*Entzauberung*) and 'rationalization' than of secularization per se. Nonetheless, Weber's ideas were to have a seminal influence on the formulation of modern secularization theory. A crucial difference between Weber and Comte lies in the fact that for Weber there was no universal historical tendency driving a single process of religious displacement. Secularization was not the inevitable outcome of a teleological historical process. Rather, secularization takes place in different ways in different religious and social contexts. Comte had been indebted to the genre of history writing known as conjectural history, which sought to make universal claims about the development of various human institutions but at the cost of replacing empirical evidence with philosophical speculation. Jean Jacques Rousseau memorably enunciated the underlying principle in his essay *On the Origins of Inequality* (1755): 'Let us begin then by laying facts aside, as they do not affect the question.'[15] Weber, by way of contrast, was far more empirically grounded and interested in specific cases and the differences between them.[16]

The celebrated case that Weber considered in detail is found in *The Protestant Ethic and the Spirit of Capitalism* (1904, 1930), which explores how a Protestant ethos might have led to the rise of Western capitalism. Weber begins this classic essay with a series of empirical observations about the apparent correlations between economic activity and confessional allegiance in Europe. His analysis suggested that the most conspicuous centres of economic activity in his own time were regions or cities that had become Protestant at the time of the Reformation. Weber made further observations about the vocational preferences of Catholics and Protestants, again arguing that the latter were more likely to be involved in commerce and industry. These observations led him to search for religious factors that might account for these apparent differences. One of these Weber identified as the 'Protestant ethic' that consisted of a particular kind of self-discipline that Weber referred to as 'inner asceticism'. This internalized value system made modern capitalism possible by motivating individuals to the pursuit of wealth beyond what they needed for their own subsistence. Hence Protestantism and, in particular, aspects of Calvinism had provided a crucial impetus for the emergence of capitalism in Western Europe.

There were a number of features of the Protestant ethic that Weber regarded as having particular significance. One of these was the Protestant attitude to work. While advocacy of hard work was by no means exclusive to Protestants, Weber spoke in this context of the rationalization of labour and of the way in which labour was invested in Protestant societies with an intrinsic value that went beyond a mere provision for life's necessities. This was accompanied by an internalized self-discipline that was extended to other areas of life. The fact that this attitude towards work was informed by an ascetic element meant that the financial rewards of disciplined labour were not dissipated on luxurious living but were either directed towards the common good, or saved, resulting in an accumulation of capital. Sentiments of the kind that Weber regarded as motivating such behaviours are easily identifiable in the moral prescriptions of leading Puritan authors. Richard Baxter (1615–91), one of the most prominent Puritan authorities in seventeenth-century England, thus wrote that 'it is for action that God maintaineth us and our abilities: work is the moral as well as the natural end of power. ... Every man therefore is bound to do all the good he can to others, especially for the church and commonwealth. And this is not done by idleness, but by labour'.[17] The more general context for these recommendations was the disenchantment of the world (to which we shall return in a moment). For Weber, these distinctive features of the Protestant ethic were crucial to the emergence of capitalism, although the modern economy now functions without the support once provided by these religious impulses.[18]

Since its articulation in the early twentieth century, the Weber thesis has been subjected to considerable criticism. It has been argued that capitalism pre-dated Protestantism; that Weber misinterpreted key elements of Calvinism; and that the apparent correlation between economic activity and Protestantism might not reflect any underlying causal relationship. Nonetheless, the thesis remains highly influential and continues to be a source of ongoing discussion. The recent Eurozone crisis, for example, might give pause to those who now regard the Weber thesis as obsolete. Noting the robust fiscal health of Protestant Norway, Denmark, Sweden and Germany compared to Spain, Italy, Portugal and Ireland, Stephan Richter wryly observed in 2012 that 'too much Catholicism is detrimental to a nation's fiscal health, even today in the twenty-first century'.[19] Also contributing to the longevity of the thesis are patterns of development in emerging new economies. Sociologist Peter Berger has recently argued that the particular constellation of values that Weber associated with the Protestant ethic can now be found in new Pentecostal movements in Latin America. Here, he suggests, we again encounter a significant correlation between a Protestant ethic and economic growth.[20]

On the broad question of religion and innovation, Weber's thesis contrasts with those of both Comte and Marx. In opposition to Marx, Weber insisted that ideas, and not simply material conditions, serve as drivers of social change. Religion, in particular, has the capacity to motivate individuals in powerful ways, and hence it has the potential to be a genuine source of social innovation. In contrast to Comte, Weber was more attentive to historical detail, grounding his theories in case studies and observations rather than in a grand, progressivist, historical narrative. For Weber, then, religion was not a single abstract variable. It was, rather, understood as having forms that differed in their transformative potential. Weber thus drew a distinction between ascetic and mystical religions and between inner-worldly and other-worldly orientations. This yielded a fourfold typology of religions. The two religious types with an other-worldly orientation had little impact on the immediate socio-economic matrix in which they were located, since their primary focus was elsewhere. Inner-worldly mystics, for their part, were not interested in transforming social institutions, but rather in existing within them. The distinctive inner-worldly asceticism of Protestantism, however, was directed towards engaging with and transforming social and institutional structures, and this accounts for the role of Protestantism in promoting economic and social innovation.[21] Weberian theory thus offers an explanation for why some religions have the potential to drive social, political and economic innovation, while others do not.

Before concluding this discussion of Weber's thought, it is worth commenting briefly on how his theories might be related to innovation in another sphere – that of the natural sciences. Broadly speaking, insofar as Protestant forms of religion are associated with a disenchantment of the world, they can also be allied with the growth of modern science.[22] While Weber himself spoke little about connections between scientific innovation and Protestantism, in the 1930s the sociologist Robert K. Merton elaborated a thesis that linked Puritan values with the great efflorescence of scientific activity that took place in seventeenth-century England.[23] Like Weber, Merton begins with empirical data – in this instance, information about the religious affiliation of members of the Royal Society of London during the 1660s. He noted the disproportionate number of Puritans in the Society, leading him to suggest that Puritan values played a major role in motivating scientific activity in seventeenth-century England. Again, like Weber, Merton identified 'the Puritan ethic' and 'value attitudes basic to ascetic Protestantism generally', as key factors motivating 'the systematic, rational, and empirical study of Nature for the glorification of God in His works and for the control of the corrupt world'.[24]

The Merton Thesis, like its Weberian parent, has been subjected to considerable scrutiny, but still commands significant allegiances.[25] Moreover, it has been further elaborated and extended by subsequent scholars.[26] Although he is still widely misinterpreted on this point, Merton was at pains to deny that Puritanism was both necessary and sufficient for the rise of natural science. Counterfactually, there might have been an ideological movement that could have provided similar support for an emerging scientific culture. It just happened to be the case that at this particular time, and in this particular place, Puritanism fulfilled this role. If the Merton Thesis has something to commend it (and I believe it does), and if we consider the emergence of modern science to be a case of innovation, we might say that we have a historical instance of religion leading to significant innovation. But as in the case of Weber's thesis concerning Protestantism and capitalism, this is not 'religion' in general, but a specific form of Christianity. Moreover, it is not the case that there is some essential or necessary relationship between this form of religion and the innovative development of modern science. It is simply that the timing and combination of factors was such that Puritanism was 'in the right place at the right time' as it were, and did make such a contribution. It is entirely possible to imagine other religious traditions that might instantiate similar values that could be equally conducive to the emergence of a scientific culture.[27] A more general point, as we will see in the next chapter, is that there are historical examples that demonstrate how scientific innovation might be underpinned by religious considerations.

Returning to Weber, and on the assumption of the broad validity of his approach, two conclusions follow. First, as already noted, the processes of rationalization do not result from the unfolding of some universal teleological process, but rather take place at different rates in different spheres and have varying outcomes. If this is so, then there are no general principles that enable us to systematically relate religion and innovation (at least if we consider the rise of capitalism to represent a case of innovation). Second, it is significant that Weber himself remained deeply ambivalent about the value of the transitions that he was describing. It is in this context that he makes his gloomy remarks about the modern predicament in which individuals find themselves trapped in an 'iron cage':

> No one knows who will live in this cage in the future, or whether at the end of this tremendous development entirely new prophets will arise, or there will be a great rebirth of old ideas and ideals, or, if neither, mechanized petrification embellished with a sort of convulsive self-importance. For the last stage of this cultural development, it might well be truly said: 'Specialists without spirit, sensualists without heart; this nullity imagines that it has attained a level of civilization never before achieved.'[28]

Whether the secular modern period was to lead in turn to 'new prophets' and 'a great rebirth' was unknown, but Weber makes it clear that he does not share the naïve optimism of stadial historians of the Enlightenment, for whom social progress was inevitable.

Nostalgic Narratives of Secular Modernity

Weber concluded his remarks about the 'iron cage' of modern capitalism by remarking that he was entering the risky territory of 'judgements of value and of faith' in a way that was not entirely appropriate for a purely historical discussion.[29] However, such judgements were certainly embedded within Enlightenment narratives of the arrival of modernity, whether they were acknowledged or not. Weber signalled his reluctance to enter that territory, but nonetheless did so, rendering a not entirely positive verdict on the developments that he was analysing. The last fifty years have seen the articulation of historical narratives that are more explicitly normative in their intention. Chief among these are three writers sympathetic to the Catholic tradition and concerned to point out that the transition to modernity and the innovations that it wrought were also accompanied by losses of various kinds.[30] That is to say, they offer accounts of the evolution of secular modernity, but question whether the 'innovations' that attend it are to be viewed in an unambiguously positive light.

Alasdair MacIntyre is best known for his defence of a virtue-based moral philosophy and for his efforts to rehabilitate an Aristotelian account of the good. His arguments rest on a particular historical account – one that describes the demise of the virtues in the early modern period and their replacement with modern understandings of morality based on either utilitarianism or Kantian conceptions of duty.[31] The former focused on the outcome of human actions, and in one of its most common forms sought to define human actions as good insofar as they contributed to the sum total of human happiness. The latter ignored the outcomes of human actions, concentrating instead on human intentions and whether or not they conform to universal principles. According to MacIntyre, these two incommensurable projects are emblematic of the more general disarray of modern moral discourse. Philosophical discussions of the foundations of morality have comprehensively failed to establish an uncontroverted rational basis for the values that we have inherited from the past. This situation has led to the natural conclusion, most forcefully articulated by Friedrich Nietzsche (1844–1900), that modern moral discourse has no coherent, rational foundation.

For MacIntyre, the best response to the chaotic state of contemporary moral discourse is to turn the clock back to the period before the crisis arose and to rehabilitate a Thomist–Aristotelian understanding of the good. This older approach, most powerfully articulated by Thomas Aquinas (1225–74), focused on the nurturing of virtues, understood as habits that promoted natural human ends. This is not the occasion for a full analysis of MacIntyre's views, which are more subtle and compelling than can be conveyed in a few brief lines. But the general point is this: in MacIntyre's understanding, events linked to the Protestant Reformation were deeply implicated in the demise of a robust tradition of moral thinking that was superior to any of the modern alternatives that arose to replace it. Events that took place in the sixteenth and seventeenth centuries thus set up the conditions for the failure of the Enlightenment's moral project. The legacy of this failure is the incoherence of contemporary moral discourse. Hence, the same events that we associate with 'innovative' developments such as the rise of capitalism and the genesis of modern science had less appealing consequences for moral discourse.

It is worth noting at this point that MacInytre's analysis intersects in an interesting way with that of Weber, who suggested that the roots of modern utilitarianism can be traced to the moral prescriptions of Puritan thinkers. On this point, Weber cites the Puritan divine Richard Baxter, who contended in the context of his arguments for the sanctity of labour that 'the public welfare, or the good of many, is to be valued above our own'. Similar impulses can be seen in the proto-utilitarianism of Francis Bacon (1561–1626) and other apologists for the new experimental science of the seventeenth century, who drew upon Protestant values to lend legitimacy to fledgling scientific projects.[32] Advocates of the religious applications of science or 'natural philosophy' thus argued that they should be devoted to 'the benefit and relief of the state and the society of man' and to the applications of 'things as may tend to a *universal benefit*'.[33] Francis Bacon also reconfigured the Christian virtue of charity so that it is no longer an infused virtue, but consists rather in acts and policies that tend to promote the social good. For Bacon, these included the practices of experimental science. Interestingly, the implications of these developments for moral philosophy had already been hinted at in the 1920s by the Christian socialist economic historian, R. H. Tawney, who lamented: 'When the age of the Reformation begins, economics is still a branch of ethics, and ethics of theology; all human activities are treated as falling within a single scheme, whose character is determined by the spiritual destiny of mankind; the appeal of theorists is to natural law, not to utility.'[34] If MacIntyre and Tawney are correct, an unintended consequence of these religiously motivated projects is the present deracinated condition of modern moral philosophy. And we might add to this the potentially alienating consequences of rampant capitalism and the potential of the natural sciences to promote the despoiling of the natural world.

A second thinker who shares MacIntyre's affinity for aspects of the Catholic tradition is Charles Taylor. His much discussed *A Secular Age* defies simple summarization, but as it relates to our present argument, it offers a major challenge to standard accounts of secular modernity, particularly those inspired by Comte. Taylor insists that modernity is not simply attained through the displacement of religious modes of thought by more scientific ones. The oft-repeated refrain that 'science refutes and hence crowds out religious belief' is simply false.[35] More generally, he wants to discount what he calls 'subtraction stories', according to which secular modernity is arrived at through a leeching away of religious impulses and institutions.[36]

Taylor has more sympathy for the Weberian narrative, however, and he offers his own account of disenchantment. This takes place *within* religion, rather than *against* religion, as proponents of Reformed Protestantism inveighed against those elements of Roman religion that they considered to be magical. The Protestant animus against magic is evident in their attempt to radically reduce the number of sacraments, in their denial of the efficacy of saintly intercessions and in their insistence that the age of miracles had long passed. But, again, disenchantment for Taylor does not consist merely in the shedding of false and irrational beliefs in intangible entities. It involves a change in the conditions of belief: 'The process of disenchantment involves a change in sensibility; one is open to different things, yet one has lost one important way in which people used to experience the world.'[37] Taylor regards the loss of this sensibility as a serious 'impoverishment', but unlike MacIntyre, who believes that key elements of the premodern condition can be rehabilitated, he is doubtful about the prospects of a re-enchanted modern world. This is the flip side of his rejection of subtraction narratives: an enchanted world could not be reconstituted by starting to believe in unseen entities again, because the grounds for the *conditions* of belief have so radically shifted.[38] Protestant religion has thus been the driver of a kind of irreversible change, and while this may have made possible an instrumental and scientific approach to the world, the impoverished experience of the sacred that has resulted from this transition may be difficult to redress.

The third and final thinker in what I call the 'nostalgic' category is Brad Gregory. His *The Unintended Reformation* shares the scope and ambition of *A Secular Age,* along with a number of Taylor's sympathies. In great detail, and with considerable sophistication, Gregory sets out to show how the religious reform movements of the sixteenth century, which had as their goal the purification and intensification of religious life, ironically gave rise to a modern world in which religious beliefs, practices and values have become increasingly marginal. The book takes aim at many targets, and one is the teleological historical model, conspicuous in Comte (but arguably intrinsic to much Protestant historiography) that identifies the historical transitions that followed the Reformation as inherently progressive. It may seem that these teleological narratives have long been discredited and hence no longer warrant serious attention. Gregory argues, however, that a contemporary form of stadial history, in which Catholicism gives way to Protestantism, which gives way to Enlightenment rationality, and which is in turn superseded by a uniform secular modernity is still very much in play. He also contends that such narratives continue to inform much of the secular scholarship of the modern academy. While social-scientific discourse presents itself as objective, disinterested and ideologically neutral, Gregory contends that it is, in fact, as value-laden as old-style confessional histories written by ecclesiastical historians.[39] Gregory's contention nicely parallels that made by MacIntyre, who argues that the putatively neutral stance of secular liberalism in the political sphere is largely illusory.[40]

Much more could be said about Gregory's multi-faceted argument, but one crucial point relates directly to our general question about religion and innovation. Speaking of the features of modernity that he is seeking to account for, Gregory notes that 'how one evaluates them – whether one finds in them cause for concern or celebration – is a matter separate from the persuasiveness of the historical analysis that purports to explain how we have arrived at them'.[41] Gregory's own assessment is not uniformly negative, but his historical argument is constantly attended by normative judgements about 'troubling' features of the modernity that he describes. Science has enjoyed 'astonishing success', but has also contributed to 'untold destruction and human suffering'. The successes of science, moreover, are inversely matched by the abject failures of philosophy and 'an increasingly rancorous culture of moral disagreement and political contestation'. These are dangerous conditions that leave us open to man-made catastrophes on an unprecedented scale. In offering the mixed evaluation of our modern predicament, Gregory has much in common with MacIntyre and Taylor.

Three elements of Gregory's case relate directly to the question of religion and innovation. First, identifying innovation might seem relatively straightforward, but as we have already seen, the task calls for normative judgements – it is not simply a matter of enumerating relevant facts. Second, in the specific case of religion and Western modernity, *religion* is too broad a concept to function as a causal agent. A number of the transitions to modernity that Gregory identifies relate to specific features of Protestant religion, but not Roman Catholicism. Third, and following on from this, it is important to distinguish the explicit and intended goals of historical actors from the unintended consequences of the historical transitions that they may have promoted. In speaking of the ways in which religious factors might have shaped history, it is thus important to distinguish between the influence of specific religious ideas (e.g. Protestant conceptions of work), and the unforeseen consequences of religious change (e.g. the pluralism that arose as an unintended consequence of post-Reformation religious disputes). Gregory thus invites us to reflect on the different ways in which religion or specific kinds of religion exert an influence on the course of history.

Conclusion

The three secularization narratives offer somewhat different prescriptions to the question of whether or how religion might give rise to innovation. That said, some general conclusions can be drawn.

First, it seems unlikely that there could be a general theory of religion and innovation. The best candidate for such a theory is an Enlightenment narrative of the kind set out by Comte, which on the face of it proposes a negative relationship between religion and innovation. Here religion is consigned to an earlier primitive stage of human development, and it is set in explicit opposition to scientific advance. It might seem that such narratives are no longer taken seriously, and certainly historians have long since abandoned teleological accounts of this kind. The Enlightenment myth of progress, however, continues to exert a powerful influence over more popular understandings of the historical roles of religion and science and informs the crude historiography of such groups as the 'new atheists'. Moreover, if Gregory's contentions about the implicitly secularist bias of modern academy are on the right track, the underlying animus of the progressivist stadial histories of the eighteenth and nineteenth centuries continues to function as a powerful, if largely unacknowledged, metanarrative for the social sciences. All that said, even Comte himself stopped short of endorsing some general theory about the relation between religion and progress, since he allocated a specific and positive role to theological thinking in the earliest stages of human development.

Second, if no general theory of religion and innovation is possible, common to each of the narratives is an allocation of an important role to religious factors in shaping the course of history. (Had Marx been included in our deliberations, he may have demurred, given his preference for materialistic rather than ideological historical explanation.) It follows that it has always been possible, and remains possible, for religious factors to have a positive influence on social innovation. The specific case of Protestantism and modern science would present itself as an obvious example. What both Weberian and nostalgic narratives suggest, however, is that in the absence of some general theory, the question of religion and innovation is one that has to be addressed on a case-by-case basis within specific historical contexts.

Third, and finally, the categories *religion* and *innovation* are too imprecise to serve as variables in any fine-grained historical analysis. This relates not merely to the difficulties of constructing some general theory about their relationship, but applies even when looking at more narrowly focused historical cases. Most of the narratives we have considered concentrate on Christianity, and within Christianity, Western Christianity, and within Western Christianity on either Protestantism or Catholicism, and, at times, even some specific variant of Protestantism such as Puritanism or Pentecostalism. Arguably, the diversity within religious traditions is too great to warrant speaking of *religion* in general as having some kind of unitary historical force.[42]

As for *innovation*, the problem here is different and concerns how to distinguish a relatively neutral category such as *change* from the more loaded term *innovation*. It is apparent from our 'nostalgic' narratives, and to some extent also from Weber, that what counts as innovation – and whether innovation should be viewed in a positive light – comes down to a value judgement. It is not merely a matter of historical or sociological analysis. Indeed, it is an interesting historical curiosity that prior to the seventeenth century, *innovation* had significantly negative connotations. Positive change was spoken of as 'reformation' or 'renovation', both of which denote the recapturing of positive elements of a lost or forgotten past. The valence of *innovation* changes over the course of the seventeenth century. It follows that the teleological historical narratives that begin to be formulated from the eighteenth century onwards not only purport to tell a story that highlights modern innovation. They also embody a quite new attitude to novelty that accords a positive status to innovation and the factors conducive to it.

6 Religion, Scientific Naturalism and Historical Progress

PETER HARRISON

The idea of progress has long been associated with the European Enlightenment. Over the course of the eighteenth century, a number of prominent French *philosophes* enthusiastically announced the inauguration of a new era of human advancement in which the achievements of the moderns would far outstrip even the most impressive accomplishments of past civilizations. Religion and science were allotted specific roles in the standard version of this story: religion represented the stultifying forces of conservatism, while science was the embodiment of moral and material progress. The philosopher, mathematician and political theorist Nicolas de Condorcet thus declared in his *Sketch for a Historical Picture of the Progress of the Human Spirit* (1795) that 'the triumph of Christianity was the signal for the complete decadence of philosophy and the sciences'. Escaping the bondage of religious ideas and institutions – and in particular those of Catholic Christianity – was a precondition for the progress of society, and Condorcet and his fellow *philosophes* applauded this process which they believed to be well in train.[1] This contrast between science and religion was to become commonplace in progressivist readings of Western history for the next two centuries. Chemist and amateur historian John Draper wrote in his influential *History of the Conflict between Religion and Science* (1874) that 'faith is in its nature unchangeable, stationary; Science is in its nature progressive; and eventually a divergence between them, impossible to conceal, must take place'.[2] To a significant degree, this view of things also informed early-twentieth-century histories of science. George Sarton, often regarded as the founder of the university discipline of history of science, announced that scientific activity 'is the only one which is obviously and undoubtedly cumulative and progressive'. Science is 'the most revolutionary activity of our mind'; it dispels 'the superstitious relics of the past' and 'scandalizes faithful hearts'.[3] Science, in other words, is the predominant source of innovation in society, while religion is just the opposite.

In recent years, historians have challenged this narrative in various ways. The idea of a perennial feud between science and religion seems not to be borne out by the historical evidence. It is now clear that for long periods of time, religious institutions were among the chief sponsors of scientific activities; that key scientific figures were conventionally religious and saw no conflict between their faith and their science; that religious assumptions often provided the foundation for scientific ideas; and that religious arguments provided social legitimation for science. Moreover, few, if any, historians now subscribe to the theory, common to a number of eighteenth- and nineteenth-century thinkers, that history progresses through specific epochs from a more 'primitive' religious stage to a more 'advanced' scientific stage. It is also worth noting that the boundaries between what we would now call *science* and *religion* were rather less distinct in the past than they are today. In the light of these considerations, when called upon to characterize the historical relations between science and religion, most contemporary historians now speak of 'complexity': there is no overarching story; rather a series of different relations, some positive, some neutral, some negative, but all of which are very much context dependent.[4]

Despite the best efforts of this generation of historians, the idea that religious sensibilities are necessarily inimical to a scientific approach is persistent and widespread. For many who subscribe to the conflict model, the problem is one of simple logic – the admission of supernatural causes and explanations is incompatible with a scientific approach that necessarily deals only with the natural. Jerry Coyne, a professor of biology at the University of Chicago, puts the argument this way: 'Science and faith are fundamentally *incompatible*, and for precisely the same reason that irrationality and rationality are incompatible. They are different forms of inquiry, with only one, science, equipped to find real truth. ... Their ways of understanding the universe are irreconcilable.' He goes on to relate these differences to possibilities for human progress: 'And *any* progress – not just scientific progress – is easier when we're not yoked to religious dogma.'[5] The logic of this position seems to prevail over any apparent historical counter-instances. Thus, unwelcome countervailing examples drawn from the past can be dismissed as instances in which the relevant individuals were either self-deluding – not understanding the contradictory nature of their deepest commitments – or as dissemblers who, aware of the inherent contradictions in their religious and scientific pursuits, were insincere in their professions of piety.

The putative irreconcilability of science and religion that drives this distorted version of history ultimately boils down to a contrast between *naturalistic* and *supernaturalistic* approaches. Naturalism, understood as the view that 'there are no non-natural or unnatural, preternatural or supernatural entities', is usually taken to be a basic premise for scientific investigation and, prima facie, is at odds with a religious understanding of the world.[6] In the late nineteenth century, 'Darwin's Bulldog' Thomas Henry Huxley declared: 'Historically, indeed, there would seem to be an inverse relation between supernatural and natural knowledge.' The progress of humanity, he maintained, was 'accompanied by a co-ordinate elimination of the supernatural from its originally large occupation of men's thoughts'.[7] According to this persistent nineteenth-century view of things, the innovative potential of the sciences lies in their commitment to naturalism, while religion is necessarily hamstrung by its appeal to vague entities that inhabit a mysterious region conveniently quarantined from rigorous scientific investigation. The former approach is said to be warranted by virtue of the results that it yields. As one account of the merits of naturalism puts it, the approach of the natural sciences 'is justified in virtue of the consistent success of naturalistic explanations and the lack of success of supernatural explanations in the history of science'.[8] In short, naturalism is the key to scientific success and social progress, and in this respect, science is diametrically opposed to religion.

The logic of this position needs to be challenged, as well as what might seem to be an obvious alignment between naturalism and science on the one hand, and supernaturalism and religion on the other. By focusing on a few specific cases in the history of Western science, one can make a good case that religion – monotheistic Western religions in particular – can actually promote naturalistic approaches to the world; that the very distinction between natural and supernatural (which is a logical presupposition of naturalism) is indebted to theological discussions; and that the idea of nature as an intelligible and lawful realm that is susceptible to scientific investigation is indebted to religious notions of creation. In sum, the logic that drives distorted readings of the historical record is simply mistaken. It also follows that historical arguments that propose a simple alliance between science and progress, while attributing to religion an essentially conservative or inhibitory role, may need to be revised.

The Ionian 'Naturalists' and the Beginnings of Science[9]

It is not uncommon for surveys of the history of science to begin with the pre-socratic philosophers of ancient Greece and, in particular, Thales of Miletus (c.629–555 BCE). What distinguishes Thales from his forebears is said to be his disavowal of mythical and supernatural accounts of the operations of nature. Instead, Thales proposed naturalistic explanations. In his *Science and Technology in World History*, for example, David Deming informs us that 'Thales is largely regarded as the first scientific thinker because he was the first to invoke naturalism'. Kiempe Algra agrees that what distinguished the contributions of Thales's disciple Anaximander (c. 610–546 BCE), was that the 'explanatory factors are no longer more or less anthropomorphic gods[;] … the approach is *naturalistic*'.[10] Pythagorean thought was similarly characterized as explaining things in terms of 'the intrinsic nature of the objects in the world, and not through the intervention of unknowable supernatural agents'.[11] Other surveys offer comparable accounts: Thales and the Ionian natural philosophers 'were the first to believe that the universe could be understood using reason alone rather than through mythology or religion'. Rather than offering 'myths that were usually irrational, subjective, specific and dogmatic', the early Greek philosophers 'tried to give rational impersonal answers that could be subjected to criticism and query'. What set early Greek science apart was that it sought to explain things 'in terms of impersonal forces and natural physical processes rather than the activities of purposeful supernatural agents'.[12] And so on.

Not only do these accounts pit a naturalistic and innovative (proto-)scientific approach against a mythological or religious mindset, but in a larger historical frame, a number of them also attribute the subsequent decline of these early scientific activities in the first centuries of the Common Era to the rise of various religious cults and to the eventual triumph of Christianity. These developments brought an end to scientific progress and the 'Dark Ages' ensued. One writer has it that 'no significant advances were made in rational philosophy or the sciences for nearly a thousand years'. Another suggests that the Christian commitment to scripture was 'a discouragement to scientific endeavors and these languished for a thousand years'. Yet another speaks of 'the closing of the Western mind', which saw independent reasoning and rational thought replaced by 'mystery, magic and authority'. The influential historian and philosopher of science Karl Popper sums up these positions in his observation that the method of science was born among the ancient Greeks, that it was 'suppressed by a victorious and intolerant Christianity' and was finally revived following the Renaissance.[13]

In spite of the number of witnesses to this version of history – some of whom are distinguished historians – there are difficulties with this narrative. For a start, it is by no means clear that the inception of presocratic Greek philosophy represents a decisive transition from a mythological or theological frame to a naturalistic and 'scientific' one. Even a cursory glance at the fragmentary writings of the presocratic 'naturalists' reveals an approach to the world that is far from naturalistic. One of Thales's best-known remarks is that 'all things are full of gods'. Anaximander is reported as having said that 'the unlimited heavens are gods' and that a divine lawmaker governs the operations of the natural world.[14] Anaxagoras (b. c 500 BCE), the first philosopher to offer a proper explanation of eclipses and who enjoyed notoriety for his impious and materialistic views about the heavenly bodies, asserted that the universe is governed by a quasi-divine principle, the *nous* (mind or intellect).[15] This idea informed subsequent Greek assumptions about the rationality and intelligibility of nature.

None of this is suggestive of a decisive break with mythological or religious understandings of the world. Indeed, the putative naturalism of these figures, as Werner Jaeger remarked many years ago, is the consequence of modern scholars 'seeing their own likeness' in the natural philosophy of the presocratics.[16] Cambridge historian David Sedley has more recently suggested that there has been 'a serious misperception of the Presocratic agenda'. 'That the world is governed by a divine power', he concludes, 'is a pervasive assumption of Presocratic thought'.[17] Much of the misperception has to do with a misreading of myth and an unwarranted assumption that myths function as a primitive form of science. Myths were understood as bearers of important philosophical truths and were thus not regarded as incompatible with more 'scientific' accounts.[18]

It is true that some of the presocratic philosophers – Heraclitus and Xenophanes – criticize the capricious anthropomorphic deities of Homer and Hesiod. But in the case of Xenophanes, this critique is offered in the service of a different kind of theology, one which sees the fickle and immoral deities of the poets displaced by a transcendent God who orders the cosmos: 'God is one, supreme among gods and men, and not like mortals in body or in mind'. This god 'moves all things by the will of his mind.'[19] It is likely that these theological conceptions influenced later thinkers such as Heraclitus, Anaxagoras and Aristotle, each of whom, albeit in different ways, proposed a single source of divine order in the world.[20]

One reading of these developments, then, is that what we encounter in early Greek attempts to understand the natural order is not a progressive displacement of theology by a naturalistic science, but a conception of nature that already encompasses what to us are 'supernatural' elements. It is also possible to discern a natural philosophy that develops in tandem with new theological conceptions that, in turn, reinforce particular systematic conceptions of the ordering of the cosmos. There is certainly no simple inverse relation between scientific and theological explanations, but a rather more complex situation in which, in some cases, a different kind of theology comes to provide the premises for a rational account of the natural world. Arguably, something similar will be true of the relations between theology and science in the early modern period.

Before moving on to the case of the Latin Middle Ages, it is also worth addressing briefly the question of whether the inception of Christianity impeded the development of scientific thought in the first millennium of the Common Era, as is often asserted. The situation is complicated and much has been written, more generally, about the decline of the Roman Empire and the role of Christianity. It is certainly true that early Christian thinkers had different priorities from those of the Greek philosophers. That said, Christian antipathy to pagan learning, while undoubtedly present in certain quarters, has been exaggerated.[21] Specifically in relation to the nexus of science, religion and naturalism, the early Christians were far less likely to believe in a multiplicity of deities, in astrology and magic, in the divinity of the heavens and in the idea of an immanent world soul than their pagan counterparts. In the ancient world, Epicureans, Jews and Christians were exceptional in not believing in the divinity of the heavenly bodies, and the scepticism of the last two groups was motivated by theological considerations. The comparatively restricted scope of the supernatural beliefs of the first Christians thus led to their being bracketed together with the Epicureans, who were notoriously sceptical about the significance of the traditional deities.[22] Educated pagans such as Celsus and Simplicius were thus scandalized at the impiety and atheism of Christians in relation to the gods.[23] So it is possible to speak of a theologically informed desacralization of nature of a kind that is likely to provide a metaphysical basis for the pursuit of a systematic and rational account of the operations of nature. What we encounter here is not an alliance of naturalism and science over against religion, but rather a situation in which certain forms of religious thought promote a kind of naturalism.

Naturalism and the Supernatural in the 'Dark Ages'

While it is still possible to encounter in some scholarly writings references to the 'Dark Ages', along with the idea that nothing much of intellectual worth happened in the West between the fall of Rome and the Renaissance, this is no longer a view that attracts much support among historians of the period.[24] Most scholars now have a sense of the quite remarkable philosophical, scientific and technological achievements of the period. Beyond general claims about the intellectual achievements of the Middle Ages, two significant developments warrant our attention. The first concerns the appearance of a formal distinction between the natural and the supernatural. Without such a distinction, the very idea of naturalism does not make much sense, and most modern understandings turn on precisely this distinction. Second is the way in which, having made this distinction, medieval thinkers began working in a mode that was self-consciously naturalistic, to the point where this approach became embodied in the institutional structure of the medieval universities.

To return to the presocratic philosophers for a moment, it is striking that for these individuals nature (*phusis*) seems to encompass the totality of all that there is. This included gods, heavenly bodies, human beings, animals, plants and material objects. It is partly for this reason that their natural philosophy did not exclude treatment of the gods. Aristotle was critical of this all-inclusive conception of nature, proposing that while natural philosophy was competent to deal with nature, there was something beyond. The realm of mathematics, while not enjoying the independent status accorded by the Pythagoreans and Platonists, nonetheless seemed to deal with what could be abstracted from nature. But the realm of theology or 'first philosophy' was concerned with what was eternal, atemporal and self-subsistent – God – upon whom to some extent nature depended.[25] There is already in Aristotelian philosophy (and Platonism as well for that matter) an understanding that there is something beyond nature. However, various elements of Greek thought militated against the kind of sharp natural-supernatural distinction with which we are now familiar. Aristotle, for example, had contended that, like God, the world was eternal. Plato had proposed that the world was the product of the demiurge's fashioning of pre-existing materials, suggesting that there was always something besides God, and also providing for intermediate entities between God and terrestrial beings. Neoplatonists suggested that the world was the result of emanation from 'the One', and thus not wholly distinct from divine being. For this reason the standard contrasts were between nature and convention, natural and artificial, or natural and 'violent', rather than between nature and supernature.

The Christian doctrine of *creatio ex nihilo*, in which a transcendent deity creates the world from nothing, offers the possibility of a much more clear-cut distinction between natural and supernatural. While this doctrine emerged as the orthodox Christian view from about the third century, the natural–supernatural distinction was not fleshed out in detail until the thirteenth century, when Christian thinkers began to grapple with the legacy of Aristotelian philosophy. One important element of the context was the question of how Aristotle's understanding of the operation of causes might be made consistent with the Christian doctrines of creation, providence and miracles.[26] In what was to become the standard theology text of the Middle Ages, the *Four Books of Sentences*, Peter Lombard observes a distinction between causes that are simultaneously in both God and the creatures, and those that are in God alone. When changes take place in nature, these are typically brought about by the joint activity of God and the relevant creatures (whose causal powers arise from the capacities that God has implanted in them). However, God can act independently of creaturely causes, when things take place as the consequence of his actions alone. As Lombard explains, some events are said to come to be 'naturally' ... but the others (are said to come to be) 'beside nature' [*praeter naturam*], the causes of which are only in God.[27] In Thomas Aquinas, this same category, 'the praeternatural', comes to be the more familiar 'supernatural' [*supernaturalis*]. While the expression *supra naturam* (above nature) has appeared in patristic writings from the fourth century, only in the twelfth century does the terminology of the 'supernatural' come into common usage.[28]

Medieval thinkers with an interest in the natural world found this distinction particularly useful in distinguishing two forms of knowledge. One was the knowledge of nature gained simply through a consideration of natural causes alone. As Lombard put it, it is through an examination of *natural* causes that 'the course of nature makes itself known to men'.[29] The other form of knowledge concerned causes that were to be attributed solely to God – 'hidden in God' is the phrase that Lombard uses. These could not be known from the course of nature, but were revealed in scripture. A number of scholastic thinkers, among them Albert the Great, Siger of Brabant, John Buridan and Nicole Oresme, proposed that it was possible to speak of natural events 'according to nature' (*de naturalibus naturaliter*). When dealing with specific Aristotelian texts, for example, Albert (*c.* 1200–80) declared that 'since I will discuss natural things, I am not concerned about the miracles of God'.[30] That is to say, Albert advocated a mode of explanation that explicitly ruled out miraculous divine interventions. Siger of Brabant (*c.* 1240–80), admittedly a more radical figure than Albert, advocated a similar approach to natural philosophy: 'But the miracles of God do not now concern us, since we will discuss natural things naturalistically.'[31] This was an approach that, for the purpose of the exercise, discounted the possibility of divine intervention. This stance, which resembles what we would now call 'methodological naturalism', was predicated on the newly emerged understanding of the natural–supernatural distinction. Methodological naturalism, of course, is now taken to be one of the distinguishing features of modern science.

To some degree, this twofold approach to knowledge was reflected in the structures of the medieval universities. While it is often assumed that the main business of medieval universities was instruction in dogmatic theology, in fact, relatively few students progressed to the higher Faculty of Theology. Indeed, a number of universities did not even teach theology. The basic teaching in universities was conducted in Faculties of Arts, and the masters who taught there enjoyed a considerable degree of independence in their choice of subject matter. By the end of the thirteenth century, there was an established curriculum, centred on the recently translated works of Aristotle. Study in the Faculty of Arts was effectively insulated from the teaching of theology, and its subject matter consisted largely of material that was accessible irrespective of religious commitments. Inevitably, there were boundary disputes relating to the jurisdictional scope of the arts and theology faculties, but even these could have consequences that favoured the development of fruitful speculations about the natural world.[32]

In sum, modern naturalism is premised on a sharp contrast between natural and supernatural that was clearly articulated for the first time in the Middle Ages. Moreover, it was the medieval universities – religious foundations that represent one of the oldest continuing institutions in the West – that provided a venue in which naturalistic approaches to the world could be practised. It is reasonable to argue that these institutions and the principles that they embodied made possible a genuinely new approach to the natural world that, in turn, provided some of the foundations upon which modern science was constructed.

Naturalism and the Rise of Modern Science

There are two key elements to the modern understanding of scientific naturalism and upon which its successes are predicated. One is a sharp distinction between supernatural and natural along with an admission of explanations that refer only to the latter. The other is the belief that nature's operations can be described in terms of exception-less laws of nature. The naturalist philosopher David Papineau thus characterizes philosophical naturalism as a commitment to the view that all natural phenomena are physical and that all natural events are explicable, in principle, in terms of the laws of physics.[33] As we have seen, the first element – the distinction between natural and supernatural, along with an accompanying practice of a form of methodological naturalism – is a product of the Middle Ages. The idea that there are inviolable laws of nature, usually mathematical in form, first arises in the seventeenth century.[34]

It is often assumed that a commitment to laws of nature will be inconsistent with belief in the possibility of direct divine action in the world. Certainly, this assumption meshes neatly with definitions of naturalism that seek to attribute all events to the operations of natural laws. However, for those early modern thinkers who authored the idea, laws of nature were, in fact, directly identified with divine activity. René Descartes (1596–1650), who first proposed the modern idea of laws of nature, conceives of them as rules that could be derived from the nature of God. The laws were eternal and immutable because they shared these predicates with their divine author. In *The World*, an early work completed in 1633 but not published until after his death, Descartes articulated three fundamental laws of nature, which, he says, were 'imposed' on nature by God.[35] In his *Discourse on the Method*, he similarly attributes the origin and content of laws of nature to God: 'I showed what the laws of nature were, and without basing my arguments on any principle other than the infinite perfections of God, I tried to demonstrate all those laws.'[36]

While English natural philosophers such as Robert Boyle and Isaac Newton questioned the method by which Descartes had derived his laws of nature, they nonetheless accepted the basic premise that laws of nature were to be understood in relation to God. For these Anglophone natural philosophers, natural laws were imposed on nature by God and were an expression of the divine will. Boyle observed that when God created the world, he 'establish'd those *Rules of Motion*, and that order amongst things Corporeal, which we are wont to call the *Laws of Nature*'. (Boyle preferred to speak of laws of motion, presciently believing that speaking of laws of nature might lead to the false assumption that the laws were somehow inherent in matter.[37]) The Preface to the second edition of Newton's *Principia* sets out a similar conception, explaining that the laws of nature come 'from the perfectly free will of God, who provides and governs all things'. The reference here to 'free will' is significant, because it suggests that God had a range of alternative ways of ordering the natural world, from which he chose just one. It followed that to determine what particular order God had willed for the creation, it was necessary to investigate it empirically – as the Preface to the *Principia* puts it, not by 'using untrustworthy conjectures, but … by observing and experimenting'.[38]

Accompanying this new idea of laws of nature was an understanding that God was the primary, or even the sole, causal agent in nature. Natural things were not thought of as bearing within them their own causal efficacy (as had been the case with Aristotelian natural philosophy). In the case of gravitational attraction, for example, Richard Bentley, who corresponding with Newton on the theological implications of his theories, claimed that 'gravity, the great basis of all mechanism, is not itself mechanical, but the immediate *fiat* and finger of God, and the execution of divine law'.[39] Newton was himself less explicit about this although there is good reason to think that he shared this view.[40] Certainly, subsequent Newtonians were unambiguous. William Whiston, who succeeded Newton in the Lucasian Chair of Mathematics at Cambridge, contended that the operations of nature are nothing but the effects of divine power 'acting according to fixt and certain laws'.[41] Samuel Clarke, the philosopher-theologian who represented Newton in the controversy with German philosopher G. W. Leibniz, agreed 'that Order and Disposition of Things, which they vulgarly call the *Course of Nature*, cannot possibly be any thing else, but the *Arbitrary Will and pleasure of God* exerting itself and acting upon Matter continually'. Given this view, the difference between natural and supernatural was merely a human convention, since God was the immediate cause of all 'natural' effects. Clarke could thus declare that

> absolutely speaking, in *This strict and Philosophical Sense*; either nothing is miraculous, namely, if we have respect to the Power of God; or, if we regard our own Power and Understanding, then almost *every thing*, as well what we call natural, as what we call supernatural, *is* in *this Sense* really miraculous; and 'tis only *usualness* or *Unusualness* that makes the distinction.[42]

The upshot of all this was that the natural/supernatural distinction, forged during the Middle Ages, was now understood as merely a manner of speaking, since all events, considered in terms of their causes, were regarded as immediate acts of God. Natural events were simply supernatural events under another description. This conception of the laws of nature persisted for almost 200 years. The two most authoritative philosophers of science of the nineteenth century advocated it. John Herschel wrote in his influential *Preliminary Discourse to the Study of Natural Philosophy* (1830) that the laws of nature were nothing other than 'the constant exercise of his [God's] direct power in maintaining the system of nature'.[43] Three years later, the Cambridge polymath William Whewell agreed that all efficient causes in the universe arose directly from divine agency. Science, he proposed, 'discloses the mode of instrumentality employed by the Deity'. The knowledge and agency of God, he went on to say, 'pervade every portion of the universe, producing all action and passion, all permanence and change'. Laws of nature were thus simply the rules that God used to govern his own acts.[44]

In sum, the laws of nature as they were originally conceived, far from displacing divine activity from the world, actually made it foundational. The intrinsic *powers* of things, on the basis of which medieval scholastic philosophers had been able to carefully distinguish natural and supernatural causation, were replaced by a single layer of efficient causality that was directly identified with divine action. This certainly gives the lie to the assumption that 'supernaturalism' is a kind of 'science stopper', since supernaturalism underpins the modern conception of laws of nature (and this was explicitly acknowledged by the major players). Because this particular understanding of laws of nature was premised on the collapse of the medieval natural/supernatural distinction, however, it opened up the possibility of an asymmetrical naturalism that seemed viable even in the absence of a supernatural counterpart. In other words, laws that *God* had imposed on nature could become laws *of nature* without remainder. Regularities, and the power to instantiate them, were no longer located in the Divine will, but were vested in nature itself. A number of nineteenth-century naturalists made this move. They would also rewrite history to elide the original theological derivations of both the natural/supernatural distinction and the notion of laws of nature.

Science, Naturalism and Historical Progress

In his famous presidential address to the 1874 British Association meeting in Belfast, the prominent physicist and popularizer of science John Tyndall (1820–93) insisted that the practice of science called for 'absolute reliance upon law in nature'.[45] But unlike his predecessors, Tyndall did not seem to think that this stance called for theological assumptions about the source of those laws. On the contrary, he held that it was precisely because nature was lawful that reference to theology was superfluous. The orderliness and causal determinism of nature was taken as a given and not in need of further justification. This was a metaphysical claim, grounded in a set of assumptions about the inherent powers and qualities of 'nature', and not itself a scientific theory that could be supported by observation and experiment. Accordingly, its plausibility rested on neither observation nor argument, but on what would become an oft-repeated story about a gradual progression in human history from an anthropocentric supernaturalism to a scientific naturalism. Moreover, because as a matter of historical record the modern conception of laws of nature *had* emerged from a set of theological commitments, it was necessary to provide an alternative history.

Tyndall thus began his Belfast address with speculations about how 'primeval man turned his thoughts and questionings betimes towards the sources of natural phenomena'. He proposed that the 'rule and governance of natural phenomena' were at that time attributed to 'supersensual beings'. Contrasted with this superstitious approach was the naturalism of Democritus, Epicurus and Lucretius, which Francis Bacon revived in the seventeenth century after a long hiatus during the Christian Middle Ages.[46] Overlooking the whole tendency of early modern thought that had attributed nature's regularities to divine ordinances, Tyndall, instead, equated supernatural activity with 'caprices of the gods' that were inimical to the conduct of genuine science. The history of science was thus reconstructed in terms of an ongoing conflict between naturalists (who sought regularities) and supernaturalists (who could see only capricious divine interventions). Regularity was characteristic of a naked 'law in nature'.[47] In other words, Tyndall quietly ignored the actual history of the natural/supernatural distinction and elided the logical relations between divine qualities and the laws of nature that had long provided the basis for the intelligibility of nature.

Tyndall was by no means the only late-nineteenth-century scientist to adopt this stance and support it with fanciful historical reconstructions. Thomas Henry Huxley, Joseph Hooker, Henry Maudsley, Herbert Spencer, Francis Galton and others adopted a similar stance. It was Huxley who identified their creed as 'scientific naturalism', and he, too, offered a history of this commitment.[48] Huxley maintained that 'from the earliest times of which we may have knowledge, Naturalism and Supernaturalism have consciously or unconsciously competed and struggled with one another'. Those who focused on naturalism, he contended, have been rewarded with the provision of 'the conditions of a civilized existence' and 'a progressive revelation of reality'.[49] Naturalism, understood in this exclusionary way, was to be endorsed not because it could be justified on the basis of philosophical argumentation, but because history showed that it alone yielded material and moral benefits. Naturalism was the engine of human progress, and its merits were proved by its fruits.

One of the models for these alternative histories was John Draper's *History of the Conflict between Religion and Science* (1874), mentioned at the beginning of this chapter and which Tyndall had used as one of the key historical sources for his Belfast address. The other classic work that pitted science against religion was Andrew Dickson White's *History of Warfare of Science with Theology in Christendom* (1896). Like Draper, White spoke in terms of an overarching historical pattern that he described as 'the conflict between two epochs in the evolution of human thought – the theological and the scientific'. His book also argued that in any particular era, human progress was inversely proportional to the attention paid to 'supernatural agencies'.[50]

Recent histories of the relationship between science and religion have tended to identify Draper and White as progenitors of the 'conflict myth', and this is largely true in relation to the specific evidence that they enlist. But the authors of these remarkably successful books were drawing upon a general historiography that goes back to eighteenth-century Enlightenment theories of history. Of particular importance was the structuring of history proposed by the positivist French philosopher Auguste Comte (1798–1857). As we saw in the previous chapter, Comte proposed that history inevitably progresses through three successive stages: the theological, the metaphysical and the scientific (or 'positive').[51] While subsequent thinkers differed with Comte about specific details of the programme, the idea that history moves through progressive stages became a common feature of a number of historical accounts of the nineteenth century. In virtually all such accounts, religion (or at least certain forms of religion) was associated with a relatively primitive phase of human history, and one that was destined to disappear. Karl Marx famously maintained that religion acted as a palliative for human alienation. Once society had progressed sufficiently towards a classless state, religion would prove to be unnecessary. While Marx gave economics a key role in the onward march of history, others found a prominent place for science. British pioneer of anthropology E. B. Tylor (1832–1917) proposed that myth was a primitive form of science, suggesting that cultures evolve from a stage of primal religion to monotheistic religion, and eventually to science. In his classic *Golden Bough*, Tylor's successor J. G. Frazer (1854–1941) set out a similar stadial scheme in which societies move through magical and religious stages before maturing into a scientific stage. Evolutionary theory gave a great boost to these versions of history, since it was often interpreted in progressivist terms. Human history could thus be seen as coextensive with a directional biology. For John Draper, the progress of human history rehearsed an earlier process of organic evolution: 'From point to point in this vast progression there has been a gradual, a definite, a continuous unfolding, a resistless order of evolution. … By degrees, one species after another in succession more and more perfect arises, until, after many ages, a culmination is reached.'[52] The histories sketched out by scientific naturalists to support their own metaphysical commitments thus meshed neatly with dominant trends in late-nineteenth-century history, biology and social science.

Few, if any historians, now subscribe to the idea that history moves through progressive stages, yet this idea, allied with a mistaken understanding of the historical relations between science, religion and naturalism, is a powerful myth that continues to inform present understandings of the historical role of religion, and of the springs of human innovation and progress.

Conclusion

The broad question of whether religion is a source of innovation is not one that can be answered simply. It depends, obviously, on which religion we are talking about, and even more generally on what counts as religion. As for notions like *progress* and *innovation*, to some degree these call for normative judgements of a kind that seldom command universal consensus. A further complication concerns whether the innovations in question are unintended consequences of particular religious developments, for such consequences might actually be at odds with the values and intentions of the relevant agents. Partly for these reasons, I have not sought to offer a global answer to the question of whether religion promotes scientific innovation. A large part of what I have attempted to do is show that some standard arguments to the contrary, when considered on their own terms, fail. There is a powerful and influential nineteenth-century narrative about progress that seeks to identify *religion* with supernaturalism and regressive conservatism on the one hand, and to equate science with naturalism and progress on the other. There are good historical reasons to regard these associations as fundamentally mistaken. Monotheism, and certain forms of Western Christianity in particular, have often served as agents for the disenchantment of nature. Not only does this make these traditions an ally of non-doctrinaire scientific naturalism, but, arguably, these forms of religion provided the metaphysical foundations upon which that naturalism was constructed.

7   Religion, Enlightenment and the Paradox of Innovation, c. 1650–1760

WILLIAM J. BULMAN AND ROBERT G. INGRAM

Enlightened Englishmen knew that innovation was a bad thing. As late as the 1750s, Samuel Johnson defined *innovation* as 'change by the introduction of novelty', while *novelty* was 'newness; state of being unknown in former times'. Tellingly, for both terms Johnson used illustrative quotations from the inventor of Anglicanism, Richard Hooker (1554–1600), on the dangers of novelty. 'They which do nothing', read one passage from Hooker's *Laws of the Ecclesiastical Polity* (1593), 'but that which men of account did before them, are, although they do not amiss, yet the less faulty, because they are not the authors of harm; and doing well, their actions are freed from prejudice or novelty'.[1] *Innovation* and *novelty* remained pejorative terms in eighteenth-century England because intellectual innovation and novelty were thought to have produced the internecine religious wars of the mid-seventeenth century. Thereafter, even revolutionaries denied that they were innovators, because innovation was thought to lead to bloodshed and disorder. And because zeal was the single most potent source of novelty, the Enlightened English knew it had to be curbed. They knew, in other words, that there was a direct and potentially destabilizing relationship between religion and innovation, a relationship to which they needed to put an end. The English Enlightenment, considered from this perspective, was an attempt to prevent zeal from ever again disturbing the peace of civil society.[2] This attempt to root out the sources of destructive novelty, though, was doubly ironic in its results: it ended up producing an entirely new species of religiously inspired innovation.

The origins of this development lay not in the mid-seventeenth century but further back, in the Reformation, a movement meant to ground religious truth on something solid and irrefutable: *sola scriptura*. Rather than revealing and recovering a secure set of truths, though, the Reformation unexpectedly and wholly unintentionally generated an ever-expanding set of competing truth claims about (and eventually, for and against) Christianity in Europe.[3] In seventeenth-century England, an intra-Protestant war erupted over them. The Civil Wars (1642–51) proved to be the bloodiest conflict in British history before the First World War.[4] In the post-bellum period, elites of all ideological persuasions proposed new epistemological foundations for truth. A few proposed rationalistic metaphysics as that foundation, but their contemporaries largely rejected their overtures.[5] Instead, most tried to ground truth on history, since it was something that existed not in the mind's eye, but in the recoverable record of what they called 'matters of fact'. The identification and description of golden moments in the past was the primary site of intellectual contestation in the century after the Revolution of 1649. In England, the Enlightenment was, above all, about the competitive use and interpretation of the past, and in particular, the religious past. It was a historiographical moment rather than a metaphysical one.[6] Historical research and discourse, the most literally backward-looking forms of scholarship and polemic, led paradoxically to innovation, and became far greater solvents of traditional belief and practice than had metaphysics. This was true despite the fact that in England, Enlightened historiography was mostly produced not by unbelievers or heretics, but by the orthodox establishment. The solutions Enlightened histories offered to the problem of civil peace were neither predominantly liberal nor narrowly secular; nor were they inherently irreligious.

Instead, the practical upshot of historical inquiry in the eighteenth century was one to which both the establishment and its enemies contributed. History demystified the world, and in particular, the world of religion. When contemporaries tried to corroborate even revealed truth with historical evidence, they became unwitting or, in some cases, unwilling agents of secularization. The revolutionary era had made English engagés more acutely aware than ever before that their own religious commitments (or lack thereof) constituted a choice among many available forms of religion (and irreligion), all of which could be embraced by sane and intelligent (if erring) people. It was with this awareness that they posed, answered and tackled in practice the question of civil peace that the previous century had bequeathed to them. This tended to mean that Enlightened solutions to the riddle of public religion were defended (and alternative solutions refuted) with recourse to both immanent critique and purportedly minimal, shared epistemological, and ontological, assumptions, like those made by the critical historians of the eighteenth century. In this way, elite secularity supplied a second guiding question for the English Enlightenment: How could plans for moving forward be defended, evaluated and implemented in a manner that people of widely varying types and degrees of belief and unbelief could possibly be expected to accept? The need to answer the question of civil peace under conditions of secularity accounts for the familiar turn in Enlightened argument away from the theological, the demonological, the providential and the revealed, and towards the useful, the natural, the rational, the civil, the moral, the peaceful, the cosmopolitan and the human.[7] Talking about religion in this way rendered it more 'worldly' than ever before, as Samuel Johnson and his contemporaries would have said. This was the great innovation – the great novelty – of eighteenth-century English intellectual life, one that emerged not from secular sources but from religious ones. It was a novelty that itself would eventually father a notable feature of modern life: the state's functional monopoly on the truth. For when even history proved incapable of reconciling or arbitrating between competing truth claims, into the breach would step Leviathan.

This chapter focuses on the central but often ignored contribution of religious leaders to the Enlightenment. In late-seventeenth- and early-eighteenth-century Europe, members of the religious establishment were central to the Republic of

Letters and, in particular, to the cutting-edge historical culture that was the essential terrain of Enlightenment.[8] This was no less true in England than in the rest of Europe. Indeed, many of the Enlightenment's central developments emerged directly from pastoral projects, religious polemic and technical scholarship on the Bible and the traditions of the church. This meant that many of the most important concepts and normative concerns of the early Enlightenment derived from concepts that were originally designed to solve religious problems, in a world where theology was still widely considered to be the most advanced form of intellectual activity. It was the fire of religious zeal and its episodically disastrous effects on early modern European society that were most responsible for posing the basic question that defined the Enlightenment and led to its signature, secularizing achievements: how was it possible to reorganize civil and political society in order to avert the chaos and bloodshed of religious war? But it was Christianity itself – and the priestly order at its helm – that many English Protestants believed to be uniquely capable of articulating, furnishing and establishing the patterns of earthly behaviour that would ensure a perpetual civil peace. In all these ways, Christianity underpinned the Enlightenment imperative of progress, despite being ostensibly hostile to the very notion of progress itself.

This chapter sketches the relationship between social, political, intellectual and theological innovation in England from the mid-seventeenth to mid-eighteenth centuries. It emphasizes the ways in which the putatively modern, liberal notion of religious toleration and the secularization of thought and practice emerged unexpectedly, even paradoxically, from within religious debates. The chapter first provides an overview of the ways in which contemporaries initially responded to the religiously inspired chaos of the mid-seventeenth century. In particular, it shows how two interrelated innovations originated as schemes for preventing future religio-political conflict in England. It then follows the long-term trajectory of this development from the Glorious Revolution of 1688–9 onwards with reference to a few specific examples. It illuminates how the innovatory post-revolutionary religious settlement itself spawned intellectual and theological developments that further contributed to a process of secularization. In its final section, the chapter suggests that the account of religion and Enlightenment offered here has a wider applicability beyond the shores of the British Isles, and might even shed some light on the general relationship between religion and innovation.

The English Civil Wars and Revolution provoked many innovations, but among the most lasting and important were the Enlightenment and what is often called 'Anglicanism'.[9] The restoration of the monarchy in 1660 brought a modicum of political stability, but it addressed neither the fundamental religio-political problems that had led to war, nor the series of novel problems the Revolution itself had spawned. During the quarter-century reign of Charles II, the political nation fiercely debated how best to solve them. From these debates emerged what many consider to be the first political parties. Tories touted themselves as defenders of monarchy and an episcopally governed Church of England, while the Whigs touted themselves as defenders of Protestant Nonconformity and more limited government. In a world where religious energies drove politics forward, the re-established church was bound to play a pivotal role in the conflicts of the day.

After the bloody spectacle of mid-century, the English could no longer ignore the problem of religion on earth. Elites of all ideological stripes wondered whether there was any way to break the bond between zeal and chaos when ordinary people seemed to agree less and less on the nature of God and his plans for the world. What sort of religion would be at once acceptable to all and a prop to authority? To find out, it seemed essential to think about doctrines and rites with keen attention to their necessity, functions and side effects. It also often seemed prudent to pay little heed to the work of God or Satan on earth. Hardly anyone did this to cast doubt upon divine or diabolical agency: the idea was to bracket theological conflict in order to address shared concerns. And hardly anyone who sought out common ground in this way meant to be impartial: the idea was to more successfully peddle the partisan. Students of religion in the late seventeenth century were not friends to all mankind. They offered peace on their terms. But in so doing, they helped give birth to a modern conception of religion. One of the signature achievements of the early English Enlightenment was the development of sociological, anthropological and materialist conceptions of religious history, the exposure and denunciation of religious imposture, and the espousal of civil and natural religions.[10]

One of the new answers to the problem of civil peace posed by the conflicts of mid-century was Anglicanism itself – or in less contentious terms, the Restoration Church of England.[11] The post-bellum church, the largest and most complex institution in English society, is usually thought to have been the most reactionary force of the age. In fact, the later seventeenth century was a moment in which brittle reaction had no place. After the restoration of the monarchy in 1660, the church self-consciously transformed itself in order to play a pivotal role in a new era. It claimed to stand in a middle position between Rome and the Reformed churches of the continent; it combined essentially Reformed but anti-Calvinist theology with a worship centred on ritual. No longer confident of the abiding support of a state that had recently abandoned it and daily threatened to forsake it again, the church took comfort in the civil and spiritual benefits of a style of ministry and worship that could prosper without the aid of the magistrate's sword. Its leaders prized diligent catechizing, measured preaching, restrained polemic, a creed of virtue and a clericalism that pretended to humility. The pastoral and ideological agenda of conformist Anglicans was a response both to the horrors of war and rebellion and to the intellectual and ideological challenge posed by their enemies. They offered a solution to the theological and pastoral problems that had caused the English Revolution and a series of conformist arguments supported with new intellectual and scholarly resources. In short, they argued on functional grounds that the technologies of ancient Christianity and natural religion were perfectly suited to the task of post-bellum social reconstruction.

The Church of England innovated by resurrecting the primitive and the primordial in an altered form.

In order to properly understand the relationship between the Church of England and the innovations of the early Enlightenment, it is first necessary to recognize that the nurseries of the ministry, the universities of Oxford and Cambridge, were not scholastic backwaters, as learned observers since Thomas Hobbes and John Locke have generally assumed. Instead, the universities that the clerical elite attended were thoroughly humanistic in their pedagogy and, indeed, served as the nerve centres for cutting-edge humanistic inquiry in late-seventeenth-century England.[12] Future divines followed the same undergraduate curriculum as their classmates destined for secular careers, and in their advanced studies, church leaders pursued the same broad humanist ideal of 'general learning' that inspired their lay counterparts. While generations of scholars have contended that Anglicanism had a special affinity with the Scientific Revolution and the 'new philosophy', it was in fact within the world of late humanism that conformist Anglicans defended their faith and made their most important intellectual contributions. Their theology was less a domain of scholastic or metaphysical reflection than a muddled scholarly terrain where history, antiquarianism, philology and other humanist disciplines collided, with potent polemical and intellectual results. Above all, the Church of England constructed its identity and made a claim to intellectual distinction by writing about the past. Enlightenment and apologetics grew out of the same soil.[13]

Within historical culture, one of the great achievements of the early Enlightenment was the emergence of a post-sceptical, critical methodology and epistemology.[14] This technical advance enabled substantive innovations. Since the appearance of Paul Hazard's pioneering work in the early twentieth century, the late-seventeenth- and early-eighteenth-century 'crisis of the European mind' has been associated with a profound relativization.[15] This development was in many ways the product of imperial and missionary expansion, which put Europeans in contact with an astonishing global religious diversity.[16] This exposure in turn provoked nascent social-scientific interpretations of religion and an attendant-creedal minimalism. This finally made possible two of the great Enlightenment manifestos on religion, the anonymous *Traité des trois imposteurs* (1719) and David Hume's *Natural History of Religion* (1757).[17] But the Enlightenment view of religion did not point exclusively or even predominately in a radical or heterodox direction, despite the assumptions of Hazard and most historians since. This should come as no surprise when so many Enlightened travellers were missionaries and colonial servants, and so many home-bound scholars studied religion in this way to wage intra-confessional warfare. The empirical basis for the nascent social science of the early English Enlightenment was in large part the result of evangelicalism, imperialism and confessionalism.

Conformist Anglican reflections on the social life of religion, in particular, became centrepieces of the nascent sciences of religion, society and politics that emerged from the world of late humanism in England. Universalized notions of religious corruption or 'priestcraft', modern understandings of the sacred and the profane, and new theories of natural and civil religion all resulted in part from clerics' extension of central aspects of English post-Reformation polemic and the Anglican claim to a *via media* – in particular, the discourses of 'popery' and 'puritanism' – to the study of paganism, Judaism and Islam. Indeed, over the course of the seventeenth and eighteenth centuries, as the English developed extensive comparisons between corrupt Christianities and non-Christian cults, anti-popery and anti-puritanism were transformed into 'Enlightenment Orientalism'.[18] Here there were a series of direct connections between the learned world of the Reformation era and some of the key concepts, theories and ideologies of the Enlightenment. Religious belief and practice were not only important subjects for innovative scholarship in this period, but also crucial occasions for it.

Hugh Trevor-Roper's classic argument for 'the religious origins of the Enlightenment' still garners support from many historians of England, but their work remains dependent upon Trevor-Roper's erroneous assumption that the religious 'liberalism' of the English Enlightenment was inherently allied with nascent political liberalism and, in particular, with perhaps the central tenet of political liberalism: religious toleration.[19] In other words, they continue to take it for granted that in late Stuart England, intellectual innovation could only have an antagonistic relationship with predominant conceptions of religious truth and order, and that, accordingly, those who championed religious conformity could only be forces of intellectual ossification. In fact, throughout this period there existed a symbiotic relationship between early Enlightenment historical culture and the invention and perpetuation of traditionalist, ritualized and clericalist – often styled 'high church' – forms of Anglicanism. The church's entire pastoral agenda was envisioned, expressed and defended with a novel set of scholarly and conceptual resources. Central strands of later Stuart Anglicanism amounted to a re-invention of early Stuart Laudianism and a strikingly innovative form of Protestantism, but one conceived as the recovery of both a lost, pristine form of Christianity and universal forms of civilization. With recourse to sophisticated historical and philological methods, proponents of this religious style argued on functional and often ecumenical grounds that priestly ritual, preaching and catechizing were eminently capable of promoting piety, morality and civil stability. The new intellectual repertoire of the post-bellum Church of England did not provide a rhetorical platform for a familiar cause. It prevented most of the church's leaders from holding on to the past in any meaningful sense. Their ideas about history, nature, civilization and humanity influenced the way they envisioned their pastoral and social roles, and thereby conditioned their religious and political behaviour. That behaviour, in turn, shaped the way in which the leading clergy formulated their ideas. Anglicanism and Enlightenment were born together.

That Anglicans were able to do all this did not, of course, imply that they were closet materialists or secularists. They continued to wed their pastoral mission to an evolving theological framework, but they did so in a largely non-systematic manner that did not contradict their more pragmatic and materialistic arguments. They insisted that their style of Christianity, like many other religious forms in world history, was an unusually effective solvent of civil peace; but they also insisted that it offered something that many other religions, including a purely civil religion, did not: salvation. The intellectual innovations that were central to the defence of conformist Anglicanism in the late Stuart period were, however, subject to subversive forms of creative adaptation. In seeking to defend their faith in the new age, they had transformed its epistemological underpinnings. Both their scholarly inventiveness and their new ideological platform enabled and encouraged new challenges to their position in society.

In the end, the innovations of Anglicanism and the early Enlightenment in post-Civil War England were parts of a single innovatory phenomenon: Anglican Enlightenment. The central technology for this innovation was the learned culture cultivated within the church. When the prominent churchman William Warburton assailed Hume's *Natural History of Religion* (1757) nearly a century after the monarchy's restoration, this species of Enlightenment was alive and well.[20] Like early Enlightenment figures, Warburton grappled with the problems of the mid-seventeenth century and proposed solutions that were unintentionally secularizing.

Much, though, had changed between the Restoration era and the 1750s. The Glorious Revolution (1688–9) had ushered in a new kind of religious settlement, one its proponents claimed would forestall the religiously fuelled wars of the past. During the reign of Charles II, the fresh memory of violent rebellion and the fact that the king's main political ambition seems to have been his own political survival had helped to stanch revolutionary impulses. But Charles's Roman Catholic heir, James II (r. 1685–9), was, unlike his brother, a conviction politician, one bent upon crushing the established Church of England and removing the civil disabilities imposed upon both Catholics and Protestant Dissenters. A sufficient portion of the English political nation – supported by a Dutch army – pushed back against James's efforts. He fled to the continent and abandoned his throne to his son-in-law and daughter, William and Mary.[21] Some called it an abdication, others a deposition; most subsequently called it the Glorious Revolution. The abrupt change in monarchs presented churchmen with a stark dilemma: adhere to their previous oaths to James II or conform to the new Williamite regime. Around 400 clergy and five bishops joined Archbishop William Sancroft in refusing to swear the required new oaths, but most clergy conformed, if grudgingly and with reservations. Yet, the widespread acceptance of regime change did not put an end to the dilemmas Anglicans faced after the Revolution. Instead, regime change itself catalysed further political and religious innovations, not the least of which was the Toleration Act (1689), the centrepiece of the post-revolutionary religious settlement.

The original plan had been for Parliament to take up two bills simultaneously: one concerning toleration within the church (usually termed 'comprehension'), and the other concerning toleration outside it.[22] The first bill meant to widen the door into the established Church for Protestant Dissenters, and the second, to deal with recalcitrant Dissenters for whom even the comprehensive terms on offer were too restrictive. As it turned out, William III's political bungling doomed the comprehension bill, and the Toleration Act passed into law as a stand-alone legislation. The effects were profound and unintentionally transformative: the Act deprived the Church of England of its functional monopoly on public worship and at once legally confirmed and condoned England's religious pluralism. To be sure, Roman Catholics and anti-Trinitarians remained unprotected under the terms of the Toleration Act, while the Test and Corporation Acts (1661, 1673) continued to disbar Protestant Dissenters from public office. But the margins of publicly unacceptable heterodoxy constricted slowly during the early eighteenth century, while the practice of 'occasional conformity' to Anglican rites and the repeated parliamentary indemnity acts gradually eroded the Test and Corporation Acts' effectiveness.[23]

Even the extension of toleration to Protestant Dissenters failed to resolve many of the questions over which the mid-seventeenth-century wars of religion had been fought. What sort of church should the Church of England be? What roles, if any, should its priests play in English society? What should be the content of its doctrine? What should be the relation of established church to state? These remained live issues, and the potential danger that attended their irresolution could be seen in the Convocation controversy of the late 1690s, the Sacheverell crisis of 1709–10, the Bangorian controversy of 1717 and the rampant anti-clericalism of the 1730s, all of which were deeply fractious instances of religious conflict.[24] Well into the eighteenth century, the post-revolutionary religious settlement remained a political innovation in search of intellectual – and, primarily in the context of the times, a theological – justification.

The pursuit of an authoritative intellectual justification for the Revolution settlement lay at the heart of post-revolutionary religio-political debates, which themselves constituted the core of later English Enlightenment thought. John Locke looms large in the historiography of these matters. Toleration, he noted in his *Letter Concerning Toleration* (1689), is 'the chief characteristical mark of the true church', an institution which existed to promulgate 'true religion'. That true church was 'not instituted in order to the erecting of an external pomp, nor to the obtaining of ecclesiastical dominion, nor to the exercising of force'. Rather, it was a 'voluntary society of men, joining themselves together of their own accord, in order to the public worshipping of God, in such a manner as they judge acceptable to him, and effectual to the salvation of their souls'. In the internal affairs of the true church, the civil magistrate had no right to meddle – even by requiring adherence to 'speculative' articles of faith – nor should the church, even if established by law, itself have the power of civil compulsion. Yet, Locke reckoned, there were limits to what could and should be tolerated. Popery was intolerable, not on account of its theology, but because it was a 'secret evil', which claimed a 'peculiar prerogative' that was 'opposite to the civil rights of the community'. Neither, he continued, should 'atheism' be condoned, since the 'promises, covenants and oaths, which are the bonds of human society, can have no hold upon an atheist'.[25] Locke's objections to both popery and atheism, then, had to do with the political implications putatively to be derived from popish and atheistic first principles, not necessarily with the first principles themselves.

For many, Locke's advocacy of toleration, limited as it may seem in hindsight, stands as a prominent milestone on the road to Western liberalism's triumph.[26] Whatever the merits of that particular argument, Locke's relatively irenic and ecumenical conclusions were certainly idiosyncratic for the time. Yet, what perhaps most distinguished his work on toleration was its method of argument. For while the tumultuous events of the previous five decades in English history formed the backdrop of his work, they were not explicitly at its front and centre. This was decidedly not the case in the works of most polemicists of the period, especially those who were Anglican divines. At one end of the clerical spectrum, men like Charles Leslie (1650–1722) blamed the seventeenth-century 'troubles' on religious nonconformists who had challenged the Church of England and its clerics.[27] Others like Benjamin Hoadly (1676–1761), at the opposite end of the spectrum, blamed the 'troubles' on the seventeenth-century sacerdotalists whom Leslie and his allies adored.[28] Leslie and Hoadly certainly made divergent arguments about the church, but they nevertheless shared a form of argument: their claims were not grounded in abstractions but in the Christian and English pasts. That rhetorical standard remained normative through most of the eighteenth century.[29]

Even Warburton – who attempted a more ahistorical mode of reasoning that defended the *status quo* but would, he hoped, avoid the sort of scholarly wrangling about the past that had characterized English religio-political debate since the Reformation – came to his preferred approach by way of history. For while much of Warburton's thinking in his celebrated *Alliance between Church and State* (1736) was guided by Locke, he only wrote the *Alliance* after closely studying the Earl of Clarendon's celebrated *History of the Rebellion and Civil Wars in England*, a work he compared closely to English state papers from the period.[30] His aim in this work was clear from its subtitle: *the Necessity and Equity of an Established Religion and a Test Law demonstrated, from the Essence and End of Civil Society, upon the Fundamental Principles of the Law of Nature and Nations*.[31] He hoped, in other words, that by reasoning deductively he could reconcile the fact of religious pluralism with the Church of England's legal establishment and with the Test Acts, both of which he took to be concomitants of legalized religious toleration. While Warburton did from time to time reference historical events, his analysis throughout the *Alliance* was mostly grounded in abstraction.

Civil society, Warburton contended, was 'invented for a Remedy against Injustice'. Civil society's laws, however, were necessarily only partially sufficient to protect against the injustice endemic to the state of nature, for they only restrained people 'from an open violation of Right'. Civil society therefore required some other 'coactive Power that has its Influence upon the Minds of Man to keep Society from running back into Confusion'. Religion was that coactive power, one whose interests, properly understood, coincided with the state. The wholly natural alliance between church and state was one whose 'Fundamental Article is that the Church shall apply all its influence in the Service of the State; and that the State shall support and protect the Church'.[32] While Warburton was agnostic about which religions proved the best allies of states, he did provide a set of specifications. For any such alliance to work, the state had to ally itself with a religion that acknowledged the being of a God, his providential care over human affairs and a clear distinction between moral good and evil.[33] But religion, Warburton insisted, was more than simply 'a kind of divine Philosophy of the Mind'; indeed, religions of 'pure Ideas' never lasted. Instead, religions required a dedicated priestly office along with the 'open Profession' and performance of articles of faith and a common liturgy in order to prevent 'Enthusiasm' and 'a childish unmeaning Superstition'. The priests' job was to 'preside, direct and superintend the Acts and Offices of Religion, lest any Thing childish, prophane or superstitious should (as it certainly would, if left to everyone's fancy) obtrude themselves into them'. The priests' duty to ensure orthodox liturgical practice was important because salvation was at stake: 'Purity of Worship is the immediate End of Religious Society and Salvation of Souls the ultimate End thereof', Warburton reckoned. For all of this to happen, though, a religion allied with the state needed simultaneously to be wholly independent of the state and to be that state's subordinate partner.[34] In the absence of any 'coactive Power of the Civil Kind', religious societies needed the power to excommunicate those members who obstructed or objected to their ultimate ends. At the same time, the state, in order to uphold its end of the alliance, needed to enforce test laws. Indeed, states had to resort to 'restraint' and 'punishment' on behalf of established religious societies.[35] All of these conditions, of course, attended in post-revolutionary England, which meant that Warburton's scheme validated the church-state alliance as it then stood. Both his conclusions and his mode of reasoning simultaneously excited and repelled the Leslies and Hoadlys of his day. His Erastian sacerdotalism was, at the very least, an anomalous stance.

If Warburton's method and conclusions in the *Alliance* seemed idiosyncratic to many at the time, the argumentation and theses of his next major work, *The Divine Legation of Moses Demonstrated* (1738–41), struck his contemporaries as downright bizarre.[36] There Warburton took on a problem central to the English Enlightenment: the origins of religion. In particular, he aimed to defend orthodox Christianity – and the role of the Christian religion's priests – 'On the Principles of a Religious Deist'.[37] This involved not the abstract reasoning that had characterized the *Alliance*, but a deep engagement with the sources of ancient Jewish and early Christian history. Warburton claimed essentially that he could more ably interpret Judeo-Christian history than his polemical opponents. And he did this, in part, by re-reading biblical history with the aid of a novel theory of language.

Freethinkers had long argued that religions first emerged as ways for the elite to control the lower orders, with the promise of a future state of rewards and punishments a crucial means of that control. In this, deists and other thinkers thought they had pinpointed the origins of 'priestcraft', and during the late seventeenth and early eighteenth centuries, Christianity itself was often pilloried as 'priestianity'. Furthermore, freethinkers noted that because there was no mention of an afterlife in the Hebrew scriptures, its inclusion in later Judeo-Christian thought must have been a priestly addition. Conventionally, orthodox Christians tried to rebut this charge by reading the Old Testament in such a way as to find indications, however veiled, of a promised future state of rewards and punishments. Warburton chose a different polemical strategy, accepting the freethinking claim that Moses had, indeed, never conveyed from God nor himself had promised to the Jewish people any hope of a future life. Instead, he contended that God's providential interventions in the life of the Jewish people had made such promises wholly unnecessary. And, while the 'double-doctrine' of future rewards and punishments had been hinted at through 'types' in the Old Testament, God had only revealed that doctrine in 'the Fullness of Time'. This, Warburton reckoned, proved conclusively that the Mosaic religion must necessarily have been of divine origin since it contained within it no promises of an afterlife.

Contemporaries recognized Warburton's *Divine Legation* for both its brilliance and perversity. And while Warburton himself might have been confident that he had destroyed the deistical argument, most others at the time were less certain. Nearly two decades later, however, when Warburton took on Hume's *Natural History of Religion*, he criticized Hume – 'a Veteran of the dark and deadly trade of Irreligion' – using more conventionally orthodox historical arguments.[38] Hume's now-familiar claim was that 'theism' could not 'have been the primary religion of human nature'; instead, humans were first polytheists.[39] Indeed, 'idolatry', he continued, was a kind of natural state of affairs in religion, the state to which theism itself reverted periodically throughout history. This line of argument turned on its head both freethinking and orthodox Christian arguments. Freethinkers had long argued that monotheism had been the original natural religion, one whose original purity had been corrupted by priests.[40] Orthodox Christians, by contrast, largely held the view expressed in Warburton's influential rebuttal of Hume, in which he argued that the 'Bible tells us, that the first man did not gain the principles of pure Theism by a knowledge of letters or the discovery of any art or science, but by Revelation'. For Warburton and other orthodox Christians, the miracles against which Hume had a 'childish prejudice' were among the variety of ways that God had revealed 'true religión' to the world; revelation was, in other words, a source of historical truth, one that could be verified.[41] For Hume, by contrast, historical research had rendered irrelevant the claims of both freethinkers and of orthodox Christians like Warburton. Historical inquiry, in the hands of Hume and later in those of someone like Edward Gibbon, had not identified 'true religión'. It had discounted the possibility that there even was such a thing.

The later English Enlightenment's primary fault line, then, lay between those who thought that history confirmed God's revealed truth and those who reckoned that it did not. The opposing camps spoke past one another, but they argued in precisely the same mode and covered much the same terrain. Not surprisingly, natural theology's apologetical popularity waxed during the late eighteenth and early nineteenth centuries, while historical apologetics' popularity waned, until revived – or, perhaps, revised – by John Henry Newman and others.[42] For pre-Darwinian natural theology offered a possible way around history even more than it had during the early Enlightenment.[43]

Equally unsurprisingly, toleration's limits expanded during the nineteenth century. The repeal of the Test and Corporation Acts (1828) and the legal emancipation of Roman Catholics (1829) were not unforced errors but acknowledgements that historical research had not resolved – and most likely could not resolve – Reformation-spawned religo-political problems. By the 1820s, the most common theological style was not a historicized monotheism but an a-historicized theism. The nineteenth-century version of English toleration recognized this and marked the surrender of the Lockeans to the Humeans. And while the English Church remained established, it did so not because its doctrines were true, but because the state found it useful as a civil religion, if a non-obligatory one. Anglican Enlightenment did not begin with modern toleration but, rather, collapsed into it. This happened because the various forms of circumscribed toleration inherent in Anglican Enlightenment had themselves been corroded, again and again, by the historical scholarship originally meant to bolster that Enlightenment. Secularization was the product of Anglican Enlightenment's failure, not of its design.

———————————

The details in the story told here have been English ones, but the story itself resonates more widely.[44] Like the Reformation and the Renaissance, the English Enlightenment was characterized by activity that aimed to prevent innovation and to encourage integration but achieved precisely the opposite, on both fronts. It was an example of what we might call early modern innovation: a process in which creativity resulted from attempts to eradicate novelty. This was precisely the opposite of the modern, scientific perspective, which is inherently reflexive and progressive. The signature characteristic of early modern innovation – in the Reformation, in the Renaissance and in the Enlightenment – was the employment of *ad fontes* tools or procedures. Innovation resulted from attempts to produce and evaluate testimonies to pre-existent and unchanging truths and facts, with recourse to tools originally developed by late Renaissance humanists. These *fontes* included the past (in historiography and memorialization) and revelation (in biblical scholarship and natural philosophy), both of which yielded insights about divine and natural law. Fundamentally, the technology of early modern innovation was *historia*, in the Herotodean sense of empiricism.[45]

What distinguished the Enlightened form of early modern innovation was its symbiotic relationship with secularity.[46] The pastoral and ideological vision of conformist Anglicans in the post-Civil War period was founded upon a deep awareness that the style of Christianity they preferred was not only one of many pious and true forms of worshipping Christ, but a choice in a world in which there existed many pious 'religions' that served similar purposes, as well as various forms of unbelief cherished by many learned men. Anglican divines were instrumental in authorizing the novel notion that 'religion' and 'true religion' were not the same thing. They re-invented Anglicanism in this period in order to preserve and enhance their privileged position in England society as it underwent transformative changes. Because they had to defend their religio-political programme in multiple registers, in a manner that contemporaries of differing forms of belief and unbelief could accept, their arguments came to give primacy to the civil benefits of what they also believed was a saving faith.

Early modern innovation was an inherently unstable procedure that automatically produced divergent results, at least when it was combined with the interests and institutional horizons of practitioners, which it inevitably was. There is, nevertheless, a close relationship between early modern and modern innovation. Indeed, some of the most striking innovations of the Enlightenment were reflexive, in the sense that they resulted from self-conscious attempts to study and overcome the inherent instability of early modern forms of innovation. These attempts included various forms of religious minimalism and the establishment of clearer and more reliable historical and scientific procedures. This sort of innovation had a more integrative purpose (and often, a truly integrative function), and it is the sort of innovation that had the most long-term significance. This activity was certainly akin (and related) to the movement towards 'experimentalism' in the sciences.[47]

The story recounted in this chapter also suggests a series of basic contextual factors that appear to be conducive to moments of religious and intellectual innovation. Religious innovation, for instance, tends to occur in periods of extreme social and political upheaval. In particular, it tends to occur when the contemporaries who experience crisis attribute it to the destabilizing effects of religious zeal or to problems that they understand in moral or theological terms. Broader forms of intellectual innovation are also likely in these moments: when contemporaries associate religion with significant social problems, religion becomes a natural source for potential solutions to these problems, and religious experts are positioned as pivotal problem solvers. Other historical factors, however, seem necessary to reinforce these dynamics and enhance their broader importance. Religion is likely to be central to intellectual innovation in societies where religious elites are an authoritative presence in both intellectual and political life, because this increases the extent to which their work shapes the way in which a society grapples with pressing social problems. As a corollary to this, religion is likely to be an important source of intellectual innovation where religious thought is conducted in idioms (like historical writing) that are both prized in the scholarly world and central to the way civil society conceives of social and political problems.

Finally, the arguments on offer in this chapter make it clear that scholars ought to be particularly aware of the paradoxical, counter-intuitive ways in which religion and innovation can find themselves in a mutually sustaining relationship. The anti-modernity, counter-Enlightenment and self-destruction that seem to characterize so many religious movements ought not to be allowed to shroud their innovatory and productive impulses and dynamics. The very notion that religion is in an inherently antagonistic relationship with modernity, Enlightenment and secularization is itself an illusion. Religious vitality becomes central to narratives of modernity when we realize that even modern secularism was and is produced not by secularists alone, but by a complex series of dialectics.

8 Remembering the Reformation, 1817 and 1883: Commemorating the Past as Agent and Mirror of Social Change

THOMAS ALBERT HOWARD

The world is fast approaching a momentous date: 31 October 2017, the quincentennial of the Reformation, the date of Martin Luther's famous 95 Theses – the headwaters event for all Protestantism. Countries, social movements, churches, universities, seminaries and other institutions shaped by Protestantism face a daunting question: how ought one to commemorate the Reformation 500 years after the fact? Like the bicentennial of the American Revolution in 1976 or the marking of the 500th anniversary of Columbus's voyages in 1992, observing 2017 will bring into public view long-standing scholarly debates, interpretations and their revisions – along with lingering confessional animosities and more recent ecumenical overtures. For Western Christianity, a moment of historical recollection on this scale has not presented itself in recent times.

The occasion also invites curiosity about how past commemorations of the Reformation have been observed. In Protestant German-speaking lands, a rich tradition of publically remembering the Reformation stretches back to the first centenary 'Reformation jubilee' (*Reformationsjubiläum*) in 1617. Indeed, 1617 is generally credited with inaugurating the modern custom of centennial celebrations in general.[1] Martin Luther's birth and death dates, respectively, 1483 and 1546, have also been ritualistically and ceremoniously commemorated over the centuries, in German-speaking lands and beyond.

In the sprawling literature on commemoration and social memory, one frequently encounters the refrain that acts of public remembrance have as a principal aim the stabilization of group identity. The retrospective gaze helps a group (in our case, German Protestants) remember who they are and extend its identity into the future. As John Gillis writes, 'The core meaning of any individual or group identity, namely, a sense of sameness over space and time, *is sustained by remembering; and what is remembered is defined by the assumed identity.*'[2] Put differently, acts of commemoration seek to shore up collective identities, to 'stop time' to ensure appropriate uniformity between past and present.[3] Without shared referents in the past, group identities would be fleeting and fragile – or disappear. Identities, in other words, must be continually activated by rituals of memory and commemoration, or else they will peter out and the past that once gave substance and energy to identity will become what the great memory theorist Maurice Halbwachs once called 'dead memory'.[4]

In many cases, such motivations for commemorations are no doubt accurate. But I want to argue for something quite nearly the opposite: that major commemorative events can also serve as catalysts and shapers of social innovation and change. This point will be made by examining two key 'moments' in the modern history of Reformation commemorations: (1) the 300th anniversary of the Reformation in 1817 as commemorated in the states of the newly formed German Confederation (1815) and (2) the 400th anniversary of Luther's birth in 1883 as commemorated in the newly founded German Empire (1871).

Earlier commemorative years, such as 1617 and 1717, took place as profoundly religious events in the confessionally divided Holy Roman Empire. But in the wake of the Enlightenment in the late eighteenth century and the disruptive revolutionary-Napoleonic years (1789–1815), new, distinctly modern historical forces took root and grew in central Europe: namely, liberalism, nationalism and a new historical consciousness often designated with the umbrella term *historicism*.[5] These new forces did not displace older religious motives for commemoration. What is interesting, in fact, is precisely how powerful religious elements retain their salience in nineteenth-century commemorations, while at the same time mutating in ways that accommodate, and even foster, innovative modern ideas and sensibilities.

1817: The First Modern Centennial of the Reformation

Prior to its collapse in 1806, the Holy Roman Empire had witnessed numerous commemorations of key Reformation events. In 1617 and 1717, Luther's attack against indulgences was marked; in 1630 and 1730, the Augsburg Confession (1530) was remembered. And, of course, the birth and death dates of Luther and other key reformers received wide, public ceremonial attention. While differences in these events abound, their commonality is most striking. They were planned and experienced as profoundly religious events expressing the realities of the confessionally divided nature of the Empire. Lutherans in Saxony, for example, saw the first Reformation 'jubilee' in 1617 as an opportunity to assert their custodial rights over the memory of the Reformation against an assertive Tridentine Catholic Church, and also against Reformed-Calvinist Protestants. Calvinists, too, wanted to commemorate 1517 in 1617, but they sought to observe it as a pan-Protestant celebration, not a specifically Lutheran one. After the official recognition of Calvinism in the Empire with the Peace of Westphalia (1648), Calvinists, incidentally, became less interested in observing 1517 and focused on other dates more directly relevant to their confession.[6] The year 1717, therefore, was a decidedly more *Lutheran* affair than 1617.[7] Anabaptists and other religious minorities, as one might surmise, simply had no interest in 1517, for the Protestant state-supported churches presented to them just as much of a stumbling block as the Roman Catholic Church. In short, prior to the nineteenth-century

Reformation, centenary commemorations were by and large confessional affairs, promoted by state churches for the primary purpose of reflecting on Luther's 'recovery' of religious truth and the political protection of that truth given by the arm of the various states in the Holy Roman Empire.[8]

By 1817, however, important changes were afoot that affected Reformation commemorations, enabling their retrospective gaze not only to serve the past but also to reflect and shape social and intellectual currents in the present. These changes did not happen overnight, but it is fair to generalize that a number of developments and events in the eighteenth century precipitated a metamorphosis in the memory of the Reformation. Some of these changes can be attributed to the revolutionary-Napoleonic watershed years after 1789, to be sure, and with them the turbulent rise of a novel, bourgeois ethos. But others go back to developments earlier in the eighteenth century. Four developments, in particular, gaining momentum prior to 1817, merit spotlighting.

First, the trickle of Enlightenment sensibilities, some already evident at the 1717 commemorations, had become a gushing stream by 1817, greatly affecting views of the Reformation. While Enlightenment figures (*Aufklärer*) certainly did not speak with one voice, many converged on a stadial view of human history – the view that history was not simply the arena of sin, death and salvation, but a forward-moving enterprise, capable of discernable development and progress.[9] For those who subscribed to such views, Luther could still appear a restorer of proper religion, but in doing so he also became a catalysing agent advancing the human story away from superstition and darkness (medieval Catholicism) towards reason and light (modern Protestantism). In figures such as Johann Lorenz von Mosheim (1694–1755) and Johann Salomo Semler (1725–91), moreover, the stirrings of a less confessional, more objective or scientific (*wissenschaftlich*) approach to the Reformation became more pronounced.[10] For such men, the creedal correctness of Lutheranism might not be beside the point, but they emphasized the form, not the content, of Luther's challenge to the papacy. Just as Luther had taken on the authorities of his day, so contemporary scholars should challenge authorities – indeed, even orthodox Lutheran ones – if they were beholden to tradition bereft of reason's illumination. 'The true Lutheran', as Gotthold Ephraim Lessing summed up this sentiment, 'does not take refuge in Luther's writings, but in Luther's spirit', equating it with conscience and reason and pitting it, when necessary, against the 'yoke of tradition'.[11]

Second, the evangelical renewal movement of Pietism exerted a significant influence on assessments of the Reformation throughout the eighteenth century – indeed, it was among Pietists that the word *Reformation* first began to designate a discrete period of church history. While one rightly resists making an overly sharp distinction between Lutheranism and Pietism in the eighteenth century, Pietists were less inclined to confessional rigidity when interpreting the Reformation and more open to thinking about its ethical and affective aspects. Leading Pietist scholars focused attention on the vital, introspective piety of Luther and contrasted that with the doctrinal rigidity and state control of the Lutheran churches of their times. Many also made distinctions *within* Luther's own life, extolling the young Luther as 'liberator' and pitting that image against the mature, wizened Luther as 'statesman and church builder'.[12] Pietist-inflected interpretations and evocations of the Reformation, radiating especially from the university town of Halle, gained ground in the late eighteenth and nineteenth centuries.[13]

Third, the late eighteenth and early nineteenth century is well known as the crucible period during which historicism (*Historismus*) was born. Historicism is a notoriously slippery concept, in part, no doubt, because scholars have used it as shorthand to signify such a massive and multifaceted shift in modern German and Western thought – what Friedrich Meinecke called 'one of the greatest intellectual revolutions that has ever taken place in human thought'.[14] Its representative figures such as the philologist Friedrich August Wolf, the jurist Friedrich Carl von Savigny or the historian Leopold von Ranke looked primarily to the past and to the category of 'development' (*Entwicklung*) to understand any human phenomena – not least the French Revolution, which had given practically all Europeans an acute sense of historical rupture and change.[15] The 'turn to history' in German thought brought with it renewed and copious attention to the Reformation as a watershed moment in the not-too-distant past. What is more, a causal link existed, many scholars felt, between the Reformation's challenge to authority in the sixteenth century and the liberal, modernizing impulses of their present.

Finally, early currents of German nationalism influenced assessments of the Reformation in the nineteenth century. Incubating in the thought of a few eighteenth-century thinkers and popularized as a result of the French Revolution and Napoleonic wars, nationalism had a marked impact on the jubilee of 1817 and, indeed, on practically all commemorations during the nineteenth century. Johann Gottfried Herder (1744–1803) portrayed Luther as a German hero, the repository of a noble past and the herald of a bright future for the German-speaking peoples of central Europe. 'Become once more [Luther] the Teacher of thy nation, its Prophet, its Pastor', Herder exclaimed.[16] With a handful of others, Herder inspired the Idealist-Romantic notion that each nation possesses a 'soul' or 'spirit' (*Geist*), which at times manifested itself in a 'great man', larger-than-life geniuses, who embody this spirit in their very being, albeit while contributing to the spiritual commonweal of humanity. For the English, it was Shakespeare; for Italians, Dante; and, for Germans, Luther.[17] The image of Luther as the harbinger of the German nation stirred to life towards the end of the eighteenth century and became more broadly popular after the Battle of Nations near Leipzig in October 1813 – an event that effectively threw off the Napoleonic yoke and intensified nationalist sentiment, especially among the young and intellectual classes.[18]

The intertwined fate of Napoleon and the German people, in fact, provides the crucial, immediate context for understanding the Reformation commemorations of

1817, which were observed in late October and early November as had been the custom going back to the seventeenth century. As Thomas Nipperdey has famously written: 'In the beginning was Napoleon. His influence upon the German people, their lives and experiences was overwhelming at a time when the initial foundations of a modern German state were being laid.'[19] In his quest for European mastery, Napoleon's actions had precipitated the massive reorganization of ecclesiastical and political arrangements, resulting in the humiliation of Prussia at the Battle of Jena in 1806 and the cessation of the Holy Roman Empire in the same year. Under Napoleon's yoke, currents of liberalism and nationalism fanned to life, reaching a crescendo as a consequence of the aforementioned Battle of Nations. Regrettably, however, in the view of nationalists, no robust, pan-German state emerged after Napoleon's defeat. Instead, the German people had foisted upon them the unwieldy German Confederation, a sop to nationalist sentiment but in reality an integral part of the reactionary scheme hatched by Count Metternich and other architects of Restoration at the Congress of Vienna (1814–15). In short, the peace settlement of Vienna sought to put the lid on German liberalism and nationalism and to restore the *Ancien-Régime* principles of throne and altar.[20]

But neither liberalism nor nationalism complied. In fact, they dramatically burst onto the scene in October of 1817 when German students from several different universities convened at the Wartburg Castle to commemorate the fourth anniversary of the Battle of Nations *and* the 300th anniversary of the Protestant Reformation. This was one of two defining events of 1817. The other was the establishment of the Prussian Union Church (*Unionskirche*), a government-orchestrated effort to merge the Lutheran and Reformed churches in Hohenzollern lands to create one harmonious, Reformation-heritage (*evangelisch*) church – an example imitated by other territorial churches. Examining more closely the Wartburg student rally and the Prussian Union Church, followed by sampling the content of celebratory addresses and sermons (*Festpredigt*) from 31 October to 2 November 1817, will shed a broader perspective on the 300th anniversary of the Reformation as a departure from past centenaries and as an agent of historical change.

Frustrated by the conservative settlement at Vienna in 1815, nearly 500 young men – all members of university fraternities of *Burschenschaften* – met at the Wartburg Castle on 18 and 19 October 1817. Many had fought in the wars against Napoleon, and they desired to rekindle the exalted nationalist-liberal sentiment that they had felt in 1813. In the 'Wartburg Rally Declarations', the students summarized their aims: national unity, constitutional freedom, a liberal pan-German government and the elimination of the vestiges of feudalism.[21] The site where Luther translated the New Testament into German in 1521–2 seemed an apt symbolic location for such a gathering. Amid the drinking, singing and nostalgia for the recent past, speeches were made in which students exhorted one another to long for the German nation, to love freedom, to transcend particularism and to defy the reactionary political climate. With reference to Luther setting fire to the papal bull condemning him, students staged a book burning of works deemed 'un-German' by their ideological standards. At root, the enthusiasms of the Wartburg rally reflected the students' sense of betrayal. The nationalist-liberal longings of 1813 had been stifled by the political settlement of 1815, and the students desired to use the Reformation's tercentenary of 1817 to bring the spirit of 1813 back to life. 'Four long years have gone by since the battle', one student exclaimed; 'the German people entertained bright hopes, but they have all come to nothing; everything is different from what we expected'.[22]

For those who experienced Wartburg, it was an intoxicating event, and in the judgement of historians, a key moment in shaping German national sentiment.[23] A heady blend of nationalist hopes, historical awareness and Protestant conviction permeated the rally. In the judgement of the Wartburg celebrants, the Reformation had inaugurated an expansive understanding of spiritual freedom (*Geistesfreiheit*) and inwardness (*Innerlichkeit*). Just as the Prussian General Gebhard von Blücher had defeated Napoleon in 1813, so Luther had earlier defeated papal tyranny and superstition, long-standing impediments to freedom. The freedom envisioned by the students, however, was not the licence often associated with Western liberalism, but a freedom that manifested itself in the hope for the progressive national unity and statehood of the German people. This sensibility pervaded the *Jubelfeier* of 1817.[24]

The ruling elite of Prussia envisioned a different sort of unity, but one that, nonetheless, dovetailed with nationalist goals: the unity of the two Protestant confessions into one united evangelical church or *Unionskirche* – something unthinkable in earlier, more confessional epochs. In part, the drive towards union arose from the king's personal religious motivations. In the years preceding the union, Friedrich Wilhelm III (r. 1797–1840) had taken an interest in the episcopal structure of the Church of England and in the liturgies of the Orthodox and Catholic churches. In comparison, his churches in Prussia seemed poorly organized and liturgically too variegated. What is more, the Reformed king had previously married a Lutheran wife from Mecklenburg, and had found it frustrating that they could not share communion together.[25]

Yet, the decision for union did not emanate from the king's whims alone; other intellectual and political exigencies came into play. To a number of Prussian ministers, the Church Union represented a welcomed opportunity to overcome confessionalism and thus achieve a more progressive understanding of religion, one more in line with the outlook of the Enlightenment and German idealist philosophy.[26] Furthermore, the union was recognized as a matter of *raison d'état*, of bringing religion 'into harmony with the direction of the state', as Minister Karl von Altenstein put it. It would help achieve national unity after the Treaty of Vienna (1815), which had greatly increased Prussia's size, population and religious diversity. In particular, government officials thought that a centrally administered, united state church would foster greater understanding between Prussia's eastern Lutheran provinces and the newly acquired provinces of the Rhineland and Westphalia, which contained numerous Reformed communities.[27]

The dual goals of diminishing intra-Protestant confessionalism and consolidating (Prussian) national unity gained wide support, not least from the likes of the philosopher Hegel and the theologian Schleiermacher, who energetically championed union from the pulpit and university lectern alike.[28] The actual process of church union got underway fully in September of 1817.[29] In anticipation of the tercentenary celebration of the Reformation in October, the king issued a proclamation on 27 September 1817, in which he deplored Protestant divisions, argued that only externals still divided the two churches and commended reunification as an act of deep religious significance. The king made it clear that the Reformed did not have to become Lutheran, nor Lutheran Reformed, but that from their separate identities a new 'evangelical' church would develop. The king then set an example for his subjects: on 31 October he celebrated the Reformation by attending a service in Potsdam that combined Lutheran and Reformed elements. During the communion, he received the bread from the Reformed court preacher, the cup from a Lutheran pastor.[30] Shortly afterwards, the king issued a medal to commemorate the event: Luther and Calvin graced one side, and a symbol of Mother Church appeared on the other, clutching her two sons to her bosom.[31]

The drive towards Protestant union was not limited to Prussia. It spread to other German states as well, including Baden, the Palatinate, Saxony-Weimar, Hanau, Waldeck-Pyrmont, Anhalt Brandenburg, Waldeck, Rhine-Hesse, Hildburghausen, Hesse and Anhalt-Dessau.[32] A variety of particular circumstances accompanied these unions, but practically all drew inspiration from the lofty rhetoric of the Reformation's tercentenary and the example of Prussia. What is more, practically all were top-down affairs, influenced and orchestrated by church and state bureaucracies and carried out under the banner of national interest.

Not everyone was pleased with this arrangement. In the judgement of more traditionally confessional Lutherans, the top-down, coerced unity by the state, was anathama – a betrayal of what Luther desired, not its fulfilment. No one evinced greater displeasure than the Kiel pastor Claus Harms (1778–1855), who took it upon himself in 1817 to pen his own 95 theses against the Prussian union, publishing them alongside Luther's original 95, which he called the 'cradle and diapers in which our Lutheran church lay'. As a diehard confessional Lutheran, Harms was exasperated with the direction of events in 1817, which offers strong testimony about how this jubilee departed from previous ones. Harms interpreted unionism as a worrisome manifestation of various eighteenth-century currents of thought, which he grouped under the catch-all rubric 'rationalism'. In his judgement, such rationalism had pitted progress, the autonomous conscience and the imperatives of theological conciliation against the time-tested truths of an older, creedal Lutheranism. A sampling of Harms's theses provides a window onto his concerns:

2. Doctrine in relation to faith and behavior is now construed in such a way so as to conform to the needs of man. This is why now protest and reform have to be repeated.

3. With the idea of a progressive reformation (*fortshreitenden Reformation*) – as this idea is defined and how it is brought up – one reforms Lutheranism into paganism and Christianity out of the world.

9. We could call belief in reason our age's pope, our antichrist. …

43. When reason touches on religion, it throws out the pearls and plays with the husks, the empty words.

77. To say that time has abolished the dividing wall between Lutherans and Reformed is not clear talk. At issue is: who has fallen away from the faith of their church, the Lutherans or the Reformed? Or perhaps both?[33]

The publication of Harms's theses on 31 October 1817 lit a tinderbox of controversy. Over sixty pamphlets were published by those weighing in either for or against Harms. Even Friedrich Schleiermacher could not let the matter rest, but came out strongly against Harms's theses in February of 1818.[34] In the ensuing decades, the controversy did not die down. In fact, an attempt to impose a new uniform liturgical book (*Agenda*) throughout Prussia resulted in the further disaffection of large numbers of so-called 'Old Lutherans', led by the Silesian pastor Johannes G. Scheibel (1783–1843). Their opposition, in turn, often met with the retaliation from the state. Under Minister Altenstein, in fact, some pastors were even imprisoned and coerced 'union services' were held in the presence of Prussian troops! The situation seemed so bleak by the 1830s that many Old Lutherans resorted to emigration – to Canada, Australia and the United States.[35]

But let us return to 1817. In the celebratory sermons and addresses of this year, themes of historicism, nationalism and bourgeois liberalism cropped up repeatedly. Again, these did not entirely displace older confessional themes, but the disparity between 1617 and 1717, on the one hand, and 1817, on the other, is striking.

The Enlightenment theme of historical progress, in particular, stands out in 1817. The Reformation might have been a religious event that sought to return Christianity to its sources, but the net, salutary effect of this retrospective vision was to inaugurate a new vision of historical progress and freedom. The Reformation, thus understood, became a stepping stone (*Vorstufe*) to the modern world, a premonition (*Vorboten*) of modern enlightenment. In this vision, the Roman Catholicism was less a false church (though perhaps that too) than a massive historical impediment to progress, a dungeon of ignorance and supersitition that vexed and oppressed the human spirit.

In Berlin both Schleiermacher and the pastor August Ludwig Hanstein (1761–1821) interpreted the Reformation as humanity's collective step in the right direction. As dean of Berlin's theological faculty, Schleiermacher gave an address on 3 November 1817, in which he praised the Reformation for introducing the critical spirit into theology, without which it would slip back into Catholic dogmatism, itself a species of 'Jewish' priestcraft.[36] Luther's acts in the sixteenth century represented for Schleiermacher 'the complete overthrow of the superstition of arbitrary works and external merit'. While Catholic universities fell prey to papal authority, Protestant universities 'were ennobled by freedom of teaching and learning'.[37] Significantly, Schleiermacher also sympathized with the political aspirations of the students who met at the Wartburg Castle.

In a series of before-and-after scenarios, August Hanstein made his case for the progressive character of the Reformation. 'The Reformation brought instead of the word of man, the word of God; instead of constrained interpretation, free inquiry into the Holy Scripture; instead of dark, blind faith, the rational clarity of free conviction; instead of the coercion of conscience under priestly power, the freedom of the spirit and heart under a concience under God's power.'[38]

Indeed, numerous homilies and orations in 1817 sought to connect the Reformation with the birth pangs of modern reason, political liberalism and/or bourgeois society. It was frequently pointed out that all of the major reformers – Luther, Melanchthon, Zwingli and others – hailed not from aristocratic but middle-class backgrounds.[39] K. H. L. Pölitz of the University of Leipzig captured a broadly felt sentiment in the title of an address he gave on 30 October 1817: 'The similarity between the fight for civic and political freedom in our age and the fight for religious and ecclesiastical freedom in the age of the Reformation.' The right of religious and ecclesiastical freedom in the sixteenth century, and the right of civil and political freedom in the nineteenth, Pölitz opined, first originated as ideals championed by 'educated individuals of of the third estate'.[40] The Berlin theologian and biblical scholar Wilhelm Martin Leberecht de Wette (1780–1849) went further still, contending that the Reformation contained the seeds of practically every sort of modern freedom – and not least the freedoms championed by students at the Wartburg demonstration. 'The spirit of Protestantism', de Wette argued, 'necessarily brings the spirit of freedom and the independence of the people (*das Volk*); Protestant freedom leads necessarily to political freedom'.[41]

Not only did the Reformation anticipate modern political ideals, but its influence had also improved the material and social circumstances of life. In contrast to Catholicism, which inclined society to accept autocracy, sloth and social squalor, Protestantism – so many argued – encouraged civic virtue, domestic manners and bourgeois respectibility. Adumbrating Max Weber's notion of a Protestant ethic, Gottfried Erdmann Petri of Zittau, for example, argued that the Reformation, by reshaping everyday habits, led to improved social and moral conditions. 'Wherever Protestantism triumphs', he proclaimed, 'the conditions of ethics, of the industry of businesses, and of domestic life receive a better form'.[42] Respect for law and order, industriousness, proper care for the poor, beneficial trade and better education all coincided with the spread of Protestantism, he continued. The Erlangen pastor Carl Georg Friedrich Goes (1762–1836) reasoned similarly. 'A good [Protestant] Christian [is] a good citizen (*Bürger*).' A sense of 'vocation and duty' (*Beruf und Pflicht*) followed in the wake of the Reformation; through its influence, the Lord brought 'blessing and prosperity to bourgeois life and activity'.[43]

The well-ordered Protestant bourgeois life received praise not only in addresses and sermons, but also in the many illustrations of Luther's life, which became legion around the time of the tercentennial. Popular artists such as Friedrich Camp, Carl Alexander von Heideloff, Heinrich Bornkamm, Johann Erdmann Hummel and Gustav König painted episodes from Luther's life. These illustrated key turning points in the Reformer's career – his decision to become a monk, the attack on indulgences, the burning of his letter of condemnation, his appearance at the Diet of Worms, his translation of the Bible at the Wartburg Castle and his peaceful death (*sans* the Catholic administration of the sacrament of extreme unction). In these popular paintings, the apocalypticism and confessional polemics (hallsmarks of earlier illustrations) took a backseat to emphases on bourgeois respectability and a well-mannered society. A popular image, for example, was that of 'Luther as family father', in which the mature Luther played the piano (or engaged in some other domestic activity) in the company of well-behaved, admiring family members.[44]

Significantly, it was only at this time that images of the 95 Theses being posted on the Castle church door in Wittenberg became widespread. This image had several variations. Often the artist depicted a young student proxy-posting the theses while Luther and other scholars in the foreground led a discussion, with citizens of Wittenberg looking on. Sometimes Luther was portrayed posting the theses himself; an early instance of this scene appeared in 1817 in a cycle of Luther's life by the artist Georg Paul Buchner. Alongside the image of the reformer burning his bull of excommunication and his defiance of Charles V at Worms in 1521, the image of the 95 Theses formed a kind of mental tryptich for the post-Enlightenment liberal spirit of the times: Luther had first shown that reason cannot always trust tradition and authority.[45]

To say that themes of bourgeois respectibility, liberalism, nationalism or historical progress permeate the tercentenary jubilee is not to say that older confessional themes disappeared altogether. As we have already seen, the orthodox pastor Claus Harms took strong exception in 1817 to the 'rationalism' and 'unionism' that he felt was subverting Luther's pure religious teachings. He was not alone, but was joined by others such as Adam Theodor Lehmas of Ansbach, Berlin's Gottfried August Hanstein and Phillip Friedrich Pöschel of Augsburg.[46] Channelling the stricter orthodoxy of the early modern era, but also in touch with the awakening movement (*Erweckungsbewegung*) and the political conservatism of their day, such figures sought to focus on doctrinal purity above all else – and on Luther's teachings on justification and the Eucharist, in particular.[47] Nonetheless, the fact that such voices were perceived and regularly perceived themselves as a protest movement against more dominant trends suggests that the Reformation centenary of 1817 no longer functioned strictly as an effort to stabilize confessional Protestant identities. It had become the vehicle through which newer ideologies, alongside the modification of older ones, could express themselves and, through the power of public memory, shape the future course of German history.

1883: Martin Luther and the German Empire

The tercentenary celebration of 1817 set in motion an 'epidemic' of Reformation commemorations. Leaving aside the birth and death dates of key reformers besides Luther, mention ought to be made of the 300th anniversary of the Augsburg Confession in 1830, the 300th anniversary of Luther's death in 1846, the 200th anniversary of the Peace of Westphalia in 1848, the 300th anniversary of the Peace of Augsburg in 1855 and the 350th anniversary of Luther's challenge to indulgences in 1867.[48] The nineteenth century also witnessed the designing and erection of numerous monuments (*Denkmäler*) to Luther and the Reformation. The foundation stone for the first of many Luther statues was laid in Wittenberg in 1817 by no less a person than Prussia's king Friedrich Wilhelm III. His successor, Friedrich Wilhelm IV, used the occasion of the renovation of the Castle Church there in 1856–7 to put up bronze doors engraved with Luther's 95 Theses.

But such actions were a mere prelude to 1883: the 400th anniversary of Luther's birth, an epic jubilee, the first after the founding of the German Empire in 1871. As was true in 1817, religious and, particularly, Protestant-confessional motivations and motifs were not in short supply in 1883. But what strikes one is how the memory of Luther at this time was put in the service of newer movements and developments: in a major key, imperialist nationalism and in a minor key, the new scholarly ethos of historicism. The latter is evidenced in fresh efforts to achieve a greater historical understanding of Luther and the Reformation. The former is seen in the fact that the remembered Luther comes across less as a restorer of religious truth than as *the* hero of the German nation, indeed the quintessential, primal German man – a liberator of the 'teutonic mind' from Rome, the author of practically every major German achivement and no less the creator of a new ideal of humanity.[49] The Luthermania of 1883, as the historian Thomas A. Brady once quipped, amounted to a 'belated birthday for the new German Reich'.[50]

The tone of the Luther jubilee of 1883 was set from above. The Emperor Kaiser Wilhelm I issued an order on 21 May 1883, encouraging all churches in the German Empire to mark the 400th anniversary of Luther's birth festively. The selected dates were 9, 10 and 11 November, a Friday through Sunday. On Friday, church bells were to be rung; on Saturday, activities in educational institutions should take place; and on Sunday, special commemorative worship services were to be held.[51]

In cities and towns across Protestant Germany, a spate of events took place during these dates. These included parades and torch-lit processions; academic orations; the distribution of commemorative medals and medallions; the singing of hymns, particularly 'A Mighty Fortress'; the unveiling of more monuments and busts of Luther; the publication of pamphlets and histories; encomiums to secular powers for their past and present protection of Protestantism; the laying of foundation stones for new churches; and, of course, countless sermons reflecting on Luther's life and the broader significance of the Reformation.[52] To be sure, a jumble of themes and emphases are apparent in these events. But among the most conspicuous in 1883 was the refrain that Luther was a German hero, a powerful early manifestation of German culture and national identity, which, finally, had rendezvoused with political destiny in 1871. German Protestants in 1883, as Hartmut Lehmann has written, collectively felt that 'Luther's heritage demanded ... nothing less than the completion of Germany's unification'.[53] 1871 made good, in other words, on potentialities unleashed in 1517, which, in turn, were celebrated in 1883.

Such a triumphalist, nationalist sentiment appeared nowhere clearer than in an address, 'Luther and the German Nation', given in Darmstadt by the Prussian historian Heinrich von Treitschke. Bewailing the fact that German Catholics, still reeling from Bismarck's *Kulturkampf*, could not rightly appreciate Luther's legacy, Treitschke identified the Wittenberg reformer as 'the pioneer of the whole German nation', as a man possessing 'the power of independent thought that typifies the German character', and as someone 'with all the native energy and unquenchable fire of German defiance'. In throwing off the 'foreign [Roman] yoke', Luther had united Germans in a quest for freedom and in the conviction 'that no one can sit in judgment over the human conscience but God alone'. Luther's impact, as humble in its beginning as extensive in its outcome, had both spiritual and incipiently nationalist implications: 'The actual setting free of Germany was the direct outcome of an internal conflict waged in an honest German conscience. Luther drew from his very humility sufficient strength to endow him with utmost boldness.'[54]

An untiring champion of German political unification under Prussian leadership, Treitsckhe praised Luther for liberating the state from 'ecclesiastical despotism' and setting in motion the possibility of state sovereignty. According to Treitschke, 'The emancipation of the State from the tyranny of church control nowhere brought with it so rich and lasting a blessing than in Germany, for nowhere had the old Church been more closely interwoven with the State than in the Holy Roman Empire and in the many ecclesiastical princedoms supported by the imperial power.'[55]

With many others in 1883, Treitschke traced the achievements of the German language, literature and education back to the 'little monk' of Wittenberg. 'Goethe alone has rivaled him in his command over language', Treitschke noted; 'but, notwithstanding this eloquence, [Luther] remains the most "popular" of all our writers'. His works 'show deep thought, close compression of material, compelling argument, and an immense prodigality of magnificent words, so that the reader seems to hear the heartfelt accents of the preacher himself'. In translating the New Testament at the Wartburg Castle, 'we received our literary language at a definite moment of time and at the hands of a single man'. In doing so, Luther allowed 'that God might speak German to the German nation'.[56]

What was good for language and literature was also good for education. By dignifying the vernacular and allowing conscience to trump traditional authorities, Luther had set in motion forces salutary for German higher education. These forces bore fruit especially in the eighteenth-century Enlightenment at the reform university of Halle, epitomized there by the polymath Christian Thomasius, the first scholar to lecture in the vernacular and one keen to appeal to conscience over custom in championing an enlightened cosmopolitan. But whether at Halle or elsewhere, Treitschke emphasized, 'all the leaders of this new learning were Protestants. The new [enlightened] ideal of humanity (*neue Ideale der Humanität*) could proceed only from the autonomy of conscience'.[57]

In short, the German Empire in 1883 possessed a historical hero worthy of its present-day aspirations. But not only that. Luther, in fact, towered above other national heroes. There was something primal, commanding, awe-inspiring about this determined monk. In breaking with the church, he had unwittingly and incipiently forged 'Germania'.

If a pungent imperialist nationalism was one aspect of Treitschke's talk, the Prussian historian also gave indication of the new scholarly historicism of the nineteenth century. Great strides in 'historical science', he observed, had made possible a more penetrating understanding of Luther and the Reformation. Many other addresses from 1883 made this point. The young Adolf Harnack, for example, held an oration on 'Martin Luther and his Significance for the History of Scholarship and Education', in which he argued that Luther, although no great scholar himself by modern standards, had through his defiance helped conquer medieval obscurantism and thereby paved the way for the rise of 'free inquiry'.[58]

Conclusion

It is not always easy to disentangle religious elements from other aspects of nineteenth-century commemorations. The powerful inertia of older confessional realities certainly persists in 1817 and 1883, and, indeed, in practically all of the many commemorative occasions of the nineteenth century.

At the same time, if one compares the activities and events of these two jubilees with earlier ones, those in 1617 and 1717, it is clear that far from simply seeking to reify older Protestant ideas and identities, the commemorations of the nineteenth century stand out as mirrors and agents of newer developments – particularly, as I have argued, of liberalism, nationalism and historicism, among the defining ideologies of the nineteenth century.

Thus understood, we need to take with a grain of salt the claim that acts of commemoration aim primarily at stabilizing identity and/or seeking to preserve continuity between past and present. That is certainly true – and perhaps more often true than not. But the Reformation of jubilees of both 1817 and 1883 also indicate that acts of commemoration can be enlisted to reflect, shape and introduce novel forces into history. They were not simply conduits or transmitters of the old, but definers and harbingers of the new. In this sense, we might view these jubilees not unlike the sixteenth-century Reformation itself: a series of acts motivated by the desire of retrieval and restoration that, in the final analysis, left a legacy of profound change, disruption and innovation in human history.

9 Secularization and Religious Innovation: A Transatlantic Comparison

DAVID HEMPTON AND HUGH McLEOD

It has become a cliché in recent years that there is a 'God Gap' between a more 'religious' United States and a more 'secular' Western Europe. This has become a focus of sometimes bitter debate among three of the main schools of thought in the sociology of religion, namely the advocates of 'rational choice', 'multiple modernities' and the 'secularization thesis'.[1] It has also been the subject of numerous newspaper articles, many of them highly polemical. It is often assumed that the contemporary differences have deep historical roots. Moreover, historians and sociologists of American religion often suggest that churches have flourished in the United States because American Christians have been more innovative than their European counterparts in their response to the threat of secularization. The latter, it is argued, have been fatally constrained by an over-close relationship with the state, by a more rigid social structure or by fear of the 'modern'. However, there has been little comparative historical research testing these assumptions against the evidence from both sides of the Atlantic, and having due regard to the differences between European countries and between American regions.[2]

This chapter, drawing on the results of a conference held at Harvard Divinity School in May 2014, has three main aims: first, to provide a more systematic comparison between the religious histories of the USA and Western Europe from the late eighteenth to the late twentieth centuries; second, to ask whether American Christians have indeed responded to the threat of secularization in more innovative ways than their European counterparts and, if so, in which ways and for what reasons; and third, to ask to what extent European Christians have been held back from productive innovation either by the limits imposed by the state, or by the rigidities of European social structures or by fear of militant anti-clericalism – or, indeed, for other reasons. We have chosen six areas where we think these questions might be usefully asked: church, state and money; evangelicalism and evangelism; new religious movements that have reinterpreted Christianity in more fundamental ways or which have gone beyond the boundaries of Christianity; gender; popular culture; and the formation of new kinds of congregations.

Church, State and Money

Here we are on well-trodden ground. Numerous scholars have argued that the separation of church and state enacted at the federal level in 1791 and later followed by each of the individual states marked an innovation of fundamental importance, which set the infant United States on a different religious path from Europe.[3] The First Amendment to the United States Constitution included not only a 'no establishment' clause but also a 'free exercise' clause. It must be remembered that however liberal the American Constitution, at the local level religious minorities, notably Catholics and Mormons, could face discrimination and, sometimes, violence. This was not only because the great majority of the people were members or adherents of one of the Protestant denominations, but also because political and economic power was disproportionately concentrated in the hands of those belonging to a small group of churches, notably the Episcopalians, Presbyterians and Congregationalists, which until well into the twentieth century were regarded as constituting an informal 'Establishment'.[4] By the beginning of the twentieth century these ranks were supplemented by large numbers of upwardly mobile Methodist and some Baptist congregations.[5]

With these qualifications, it remains true that even the most powerful and prestigious of the American churches were in important respects differently situated from the 'established churches' of Europe. First, they enjoyed a degree of freedom that those latter churches lacked since the privileges arising from establishment came at a heavy price in terms of state controls. And second, they could not count on any financial support from the state, so they had to find other ways of raising money. Here we have a striking example of innovation. Eric Baldwin's work on the industrial centre of Lowell, Massachusetts, shows that nearly every Protestant church founded in the city in the years before the Civil War created an incorporated body to own its building, which then sold dividend-yielding shares.[6] The church building became literally a for-profit enterprise. In the short term, this strategy was highly successful, since the considerable sums raised in this way permitted an impressive wave of church-building in the early years of the city's growth. Unfortunately, there is no form of fundraising that is free from potentially harmful side effects. This method of raising money forced the churches to place a high priority on maximizing the income from pew rents in order to maintain the necessary level of profit. John Bennett in his research on English pew-renting in the nineteenth and early twentieth centuries showed how much higher these rents often were in the USA than in England, and how American churches often adopted a business approach to the pricing of seats that was rare in England.[7] The changing composition of the population in the later nineteenth century, which brought the immigration of large numbers of Irish and French Canadian Catholics, meant that there were not enough Protestant 'customers' to maintain the business, and many churches were forced into bankruptcy.

In the early nineteenth century, the established churches of Western Europe could generally count either on direct financial support from the state, such as the state salaries for the parish clergy in France, or other assured sources of income, such as the ownership of large amounts of land in Spain or the church rate, which paid for the maintenance of church buildings from local taxation in England. With the growth of Dissenting and anti-clerical movements in the nineteenth century, however, these were always under threat. For example in Spain, church property was expropriated by Liberal governments in the 1830s and 1840s, and in England the church rate, having long been uncollectable in towns with numerous Dissenters, was finally abolished in 1868. But even where the state continued to pay the clergy or support the church in other ways, the support given was seldom generous and came with strings attached. For example, in France new parishes could not be created without the permission of the state, which was seldom granted. So in Europe, as much as in the USA, churches of all kinds, established or Dissenting, had to find new ways of raising money, in order to pay for the new buildings and the additional clergy that a fast-urbanizing continent required and to support the many charitable enterprises prompted both by compassion for the urban poor and by fear of revolution.[8] As in the USA, one of the most popular ways of doing this was not innovative at all, namely the quest for wealthy patrons, whether drawn from 'old', often aristocratic, money, or from the 'new' money accumulated in the era of industrialization. Generosity of this kind often arose from the piety of the donor, but political considerations also played a part. Generous donations tied the church to the political agendas of its benefactors, and sometimes brought subsequent retribution – as, for instance, in Barcelona's Tragic Week of 1909 when anti-clerical gangs roamed the city attacking convents and other religious buildings.[9]

The main alternative to the seeking of patrons was the raising of large numbers of small donations, whether through pew-rents, collecting money at the door (the method favoured in the mainly working-class Catholic congregations of late-nineteenth-century America) or the holding of bazaars, intended to attract the general public, as well as church members. Simon Green has emphasized the importance of these among the churches of late Victorian Yorkshire – and, indeed, the fact that these churches depended much more on this method than on the relatively scarce wealthy benefactors.[10] Roger Ottewill in his work on Edwardian Congregationalism in England has shown that the tried-and-tested medium of the bazaar could also offer scope for innovation, as ingenious new ways of attracting customers were devised.[11] More generally, Stewart J. Brown's work on the established churches of England and Wales demonstrates the immense energy with which they approached the task of Christianizing the whole nation, especially in the period from the 1840s, when the worst abuses of the previous era had been largely addressed, until the end of the nineteenth century when new problems ranging from the growth of religious 'doubt' to intensified class conflict were presenting themselves.[12]

Probably the most important innovation in Europe in the late nineteenth century was one that might not seem like an innovation at all, namely the church tax. This seems to have been first introduced in the German state of Oldenburg in 1852 and to have been adopted more generally by the German states in the late nineteenth century, as well as in Scandinavia.[13] It was administratively simple since it was collected as part of income tax. Those who wished could opt out, but in doing so, they would forfeit the right to church marriage and burial and the baptism of their children. It assured a regular and reasonably predictable income for the church. Germany and Scandinavia thus offer the clearest test cases for the frequent complaints by sociologists of the rational choice school that financial support from the state made established churches complacent and their clergy lazy.[14]

The main liability inherent in this approach was not so much an unwillingness to innovate as an overly close identification with the state. On the one hand, this can lead to a view of the church as an official body, necessary, respected, but hardly loved. On the other hand, during times of rapid political change or among social groups alienated from the state, the 'people's church' is apt to be reviled as merely a 'state church'. Clearly, over-close ties between state and church have been a major factor, though by no means the only factor, in the anti-clerical movements, which have played such a large role in European history since the French Revolution of 1789. Of course, even where ties between church and state are lacking, close links between churches and particular political parties can be a source of both strength and weakness. The recent links between American evangelical churches and the right wing of the Republican Party are an evident example.[15] Overall, the harmful effects of links between church and state have been not so much in inducing complacency on the part of the clergy as in limiting the options open to the church. There was a clear example of this in France where the separation of church and state in 1905 proved to be a blessing in disguise for the Catholic Church, which entered a period of revitalization. The loss of state subsidies forced Catholics to undertake a massive fundraising drive, but they were now free to reorganize the church according to the needs of the times. And lay Catholics were challenged to respond to the apparent crisis by contributing their energies as well as their money to the revival.[16]

If establishment has sometimes placed constraints on innovation, the same can be true of separation. One of the more striking examples of American religious innovation was the decision of the Roosevelt administration during the Second World War to ignore the First Amendment and to engage in a massive programme of building places of worship and supplying religious literature and chaplains to those enrolled in the armed forces. The support of the Christian and Jewish faiths was deemed essential to the morale of the fighting forces and so, in spite of the (quite limited) opposition, Roosevelt went ahead. Michael Snape has argued that we have here one of the roots of the post-war 'religious revival' and the reputation of the 'greatest generation' who fought in the Second World War as more devout than their predecessors or any succeeding generation.[17] With over sixteen million personnel enlisted in the military and with remarkable commitments to the provision of chaplains, the building of chapels and the circulation of Bibles, a persuasive argument can be made for a state-led revival of religion in the armed forces during the Second World War, which was sustained in the immediate aftermath of war by the impact of the Cold War and a renewed enthusiasm for foreign missions. Ironically, by comparison with Britain where denominational differences were respected in the supply of chaplains, American state-led religiosity probably achieved more purchase than anywhere in Europe, while at the same time, American military personnel serving in Europe perceived themselves as more religious than their European counterparts, especially the French.

Evangelicalism and Evangelism

One major reason for the contrast in religious styles between Europe and America lies in the differential impacts of evangelical Protestantism in Europe and the United States. Although there were significant pockets of evangelical strength in eighteenth- and early-nineteenth-century Europe (most notably in parts of England, Wales, the Scottish highlands and the northern part of Ireland), evangelicalism, with its rhythms of revivalism, grew much more strongly and for longer in the United States. Even Methodism, which originated in England, achieved its most striking growth rates in the United States, and that was also the case for the Baptists and other popular evangelical traditions. It is hard to account for the different cultural styles of American religion since the mid-eighteenth century without paying close attention to the enduring strength and cultural mobilization of different varieties of evangelical Protestantism.[18] Moreover, the evangelical tradition in the United States has shown a remarkable capacity to adapt to cultural change, create new church and parachurch organizations, exploit new technological innovations, produce bestselling literature, modernize its praise and worship, evangelize, sustain long-term and short-term missions around the world, insert itself (not always successfully) into political discourse, create massive world relief organizations such as World Vision, and attract money from the fruits of American capitalism.

Throughout much of the eighteenth and nineteenth centuries, a good case can be made for a shared transatlantic tradition of personnel, styles and innovations. But decidedly from the end of the nineteenth century onwards, the British and American evangelical traditions began to diverge in significant ways, especially with the growth of Pentecostalism and Fundamentalism in the United States.[19] Moreover, Heather Curtis has shown that even when American and British evangelicals created common ventures, such as the widely circulating *Christian Herald*, the American version was more commercially orientated, more innovatory, more successful in fundraising, more 'sensational' in content, more engaged in international relief (helping starving peasants in Russia, orphans in India and Armenians within the Ottoman Empire) and, ultimately, more widely disseminated and culturally influential.[20] Curtis and David Bebbington agree that whatever may be said about the shared traditions of transatlantic evangelicalism, the American version has been paradoxically both more commercially innovative and more conservative in its politics and theology. That combination proved far more successful in the long run.

One field in which American Christians, and specifically evangelical Protestants, have been richly innovative is evangelism. Itinerant open-air preaching was a method already common in Britain before George Whitefield's famous visit to the American colonies in 1740.[21] But most of the evangelistic innovations in the nineteenth and twentieth centuries achieved their greatest influence in the United States. One example is the camp meeting, which was widely adopted in 'frontier' areas during the Second Great Awakening in the years around 1800.[22] The scattered nature of the population suggested the idea of a centralized meeting lasting for several days, at which preaching would be combined with various forms of entertainment as well as with more general socializing. The brief time available to those preaching at these meetings encouraged them to preach with an urgency that might be less necessary in a settled community, and their often earthy style was well suited to the tastes of many among the audience. It also appealed to some of the miners and potters who attended the famous camp meeting at Mow Cop in the English Midlands in 1807, which provoked the condemnation of the Wesleyan Conference. Some of those present would be among the founders of Primitive Methodism, which would be the most working class and the most receptive to revivalism of the major English denominations.[23]

Revivalism made an impact in many countries in the nineteenth century, especially in Britain and Ireland, but nowhere was its scope and depth more apparent than in America.[24] It was there too that a new figure emerged in the early nineteenth century, the professional revivalist, who had studied and perfected the conditions and techniques whereby large numbers of people might be expected to experience conversion. The most influential exponent was Charles Finney, whose controversial evangelistic methods seemed to work and were enthusiastically adopted not only in the United States but also in Britain. Finney's novelty was to treat revivalism as a science, whereby the use of particular methods could be expected to produce particular results.

Subsequent American evangelists have been adept at harnessing new media and aesthetics for the purposes of evangelism. Dwight L. Moody and Ira D. Sankey, in the 1870s and 1880s, introduced the popular formula by which an evangelist worked in tandem with a singer. Billy Sunday took the art of preaching as a form of popular theatre to new lengths – something Aimee Semple McPherson would take even further. Billy Graham used celebrity testimonies, especially by athletes, and his well-known role as informal adviser to a number of American presidents as part of his pitch for the gospel. Although such evangelistic techniques were closely associated with American Christianity, they proved equally effective when translated abroad. Uta Balbier has shown that Billy Graham's English and German revival crusades in the 1950s were spectacular triumphs for the evangelist, complicating our notion of a divide between American and European religious mentalities.[25] Nevertheless, Graham was unable to repeat the triumphs of his 1954 campaigns in Berlin and London when he returned in 1966 to find a less enthusiastic reception, owing in part to the unpopularity of the Vietnam War and shifts in European youth culture.

American evangelism also had distinct cultural advantages in other ways. Here one can compare the use of the radio by Christians in the USA and Britain. With the advent of broadcasting in the 1920s, many Christians in both countries were interested in the new possibilities, though others were less positive, fearing, for instance, that listening to religious programmes on the radio would become an alternative to attending church, or that there was something irreverent in the idea of broadcasting church services. The main difference was in the extent of regulation in Britain, where the BBC held a monopoly for the greater part of the twentieth century. BBC radio and television, working in cooperation with representatives of the main Christian churches, provided plenty of religious programmes, but they eschewed direct evangelism, as well as speakers from outside what they regarded as the mainstream.[26] There were some parallels with the situation in the USA where the two main networks, the CBS and NBC, for long held a dominant position, and consulted the Federal Council of Churches on religious broadcasting. But a much wider range of kinds of religious broadcasting, and more of it of an explicitly evangelistic and evangelical kind was available in the USA. There were numerous smaller radio stations with a mainly local following. This opened the way for stations with a specifically Christian mission as well as for other stations to allow evangelical preachers to have paid for time.[27]

An overriding concern with evangelism and a constant readiness to experiment with new methods of reaching potential converts has led to further initiatives in the post-war years that have only in a more limited way been adopted elsewhere. One example is that of the sports ministries, which have become highly visible in recent years, but which have their origins in the 1940s and 1950s. The two connected ideas were that sport was itself a field for evangelism, which might require specific methods, and that Christian athletes could provide role models for youth, and if they talked about their faith, people would listen. The latter idea was not new: it goes back to the late nineteenth century with the preaching tour of international cricketer, C. T. Studd.[28] Sport ministries in post-war America, however, were organized on a much bigger scale.

The unique phase in American history that lasted from about 1967 to 1972 saw the emergence of a more remarkable innovation, the Jesus Movement. This was based primarily on the West Coast, especially in San Francisco and Los Angeles, and was partly the work of professional pastors and evangelists with a mission to the counter-culture and partly the work of young people from within the counter-culture. These years saw the emergence of a plethora of Christian communes, underground papers and beach missions, many of which were ultimately absorbed into Pentecostal and other evangelical congregations.[29]

So far we have been talking mainly of Protestants, and, indeed, it is American Protestants who have had a striking record of evangelistic innovation, partly because they have been less constrained by fears of violating the rules of propriety. In this respect, the established churches of Europe may have cast a shadow even on many of those outside. For example, by the second half of the nineteenth century, English Nonconformists increasingly followed the Anglican taste for Gothic architecture and in spite of differences in theology and, often, politics between Anglican and Nonconformist clergy, the ideal of the clergyman as a socially respected, well-educated gentleman was one that many Nonconformist ministers, and perhaps even more the lay elite, found attractive.[30]

Within the Catholic Church, however, new methods more often began in Europe and then crossed the ocean, often carried by European priests. Catholic evangelism was usually not aimed at winning new converts but at rekindling the religious enthusiasm of the lukewarm and bringing back those who had 'lapsed'. Here the tried-and-trusted method was the 'mission' delivered by a priest belonging to one of the religious orders, such as the Redemptorists, Jesuits or, in the USA, the Paulists. This method was used extensively in France during the Restoration, when mission priests laboured to bring back the many people who had become detached from or totally alienated from the church during the revolutionary and Napoleonic periods.[31] Similar methods, though without the political subtext, were being employed in American cities at the end of the nineteenth century.[32] Another attempted innovation by Western European Catholics were the Leagues of the Sacred Heart established in Belgium, Germany and France towards the end of the nineteenth century. The aim was to encourage Catholic men to fight against liberalism, socialism and secularism by coming together in public processions to parish celebrations of the Eucharist. Although the numbers of Catholic men who joined the Leagues of the Sacred Heart were not inconsequential, especially in Belgium and Germany, this innovation was in essence a way of tapping into traditional Catholicism by binding together priests, men and Catholic rituals, which ultimately proved incapable of mass realization. The Leagues of the Sacred Heart showed at once the residual power of Catholic parish loyalties in Europe and their limitations for staging a revival of traditional Catholicism.[33]

New Religious Movements

While a powerful evangelistic drive, impelled both by the desire to save souls and by the imperatives of congregational and denominational survival in conditions of fierce religious competition, has pointed the way to many evangelistic innovations, America has also provided a rich soil for the growth of new forms of religion. Although increases in religious diversity are often cited as contributors to secularization for encouraging the privatization of intractable religious differences, David Holland has pointed out that new religious movements in the United States have often emerged as vocal opponents of secularism and secularizing tendencies.[34] The way new religious movements positioned themselves with respect to the legal protections of the constitution, however, shows that their self-interest could on occasions be aligned with those advocating secularist causes and on other issues with those advocating greater state responsibility for religious instruction. The balance sheets in these exchanges are hard to tally.

Of course, a large number of the most important religious denominations in the USA had their origins in seventeenth-, eighteenth- and early-nineteenth-century Britain. That includes not only Congregationalists (now part of the United Church of Christ), Baptists, Quakers and Methodists, but also the premillennial dispensationalism of John Nelson Darby, which has come to be seen as a peculiarly American form of belief. But since 1850, the only major new religious movement to emerge in Britain has been the Salvation Army, novel in many of its methods, including, especially, the important role of women, but conventionally conservative evangelical in its theology.[35] Germany in the late nineteenth and early twentieth centuries saw a number of new movements, all of them small, and most of them further removed from orthodox Christianity, such as Anthroposophy.[36]

No part of the western world can compare with the United States as a generator of new religious movements, which have either radically reinterpreted Christianity or moved in completely new religious directions. In terms of numbers, the most important of the nineteenth-century movements have been those of the Mormons, Seventh-day Adventists and Jehovah's Witnesses. But there have been many others, including, most notably, Transcendentalism, Spiritualism, Theosophy, Christian Science and related currents of New Thought. Many of these movements had a keen interest in the health of body and mind and a faith that illness and disability could not only be cured, but that they could also be prevented by changes in diet or physical exercise.[37] In a number of these movements, women were prominent among the founders, and this perhaps reflected the higher status of women in American than in European societies and the wider scope open to them whether in education, the church or moral reform movements. Some of the same tendencies were reflected in America's nineteenth-century Freethought movement, which, though small by comparison with, for example, that in France, had a significant presence not only in cities but also in Midwestern and Western states, and included, besides the celebrated Robert Ingersoll, several women among its leading speakers.[38]

Among the most significant developments in the twentieth-century history of Christianity was the rise of Pentecostalism, first in the United States and then spreading rapidly around the globe. Like the earlier new religious movements, Pentecostalism would find greater success in the United States than in Western Europe. Randall Stephens has documented the early similarities between the Pentecostal communities in the United States and Great Britain, for example, but notes their quick divergence in terms of numbers, institutional diversity and willingness to engage with the cultures of their respective locations.[39] American Pentecostalism used media more successfully, connected more deeply with other aspects of popular culture, (including country and rock music), grew out of stronger strains of pre-existing Methodist, Holiness and healing traditions, and found more compelling ways of combining supernaturalist claims with the pragmatic necessities of everyday life. Over time, the numerical strength of American Pentecostalism, as with earlier Methodism, was substantially greater in the United States than in Western Europe.[40]

The most important religious or quasi-religious movements to emerge in Europe in the nineteenth century were mainly of a more secular kind. One example was Comte's Religion of Humanity, which had gained an international influence in the third quarter of the nineteenth century, most notably in Latin America, but also in other parts of Europe and in the USA.[41] The most important example, however, would be socialism, which was often described by believers as 'my religion', and which won a large and fervent following, first in Germany and then in most other parts of the industrializing world towards the end of the nineteenth century. Socialists devised many ways of strengthening the bonds uniting those in the movement and of spreading the good news – often drawing on methods pioneered by the Christian churches, where many of them had been active and committed believers.[42]

Gender

Some of the most interesting ideas about the relations of men and women in the nineteenth century were to be found in the utopian communities that flourished in some parts of the USA in the early part of the century, and which offer another example of the rich variety of new possibilities that the New World offered. But their influence on the wider society was very limited. One of the most influential innovations at that time was one that has for so long been completely taken for granted that it no longer appears innovative: the explosive growth in the Roman Catholic Church of women's religious orders. These offered women a highly active role in teaching or care of the sick, combining a celibate life among other women with the possibility of exercising considerable responsibility within an expanding and obviously important area of society. Though the numbers of Catholic priests grew in the nineteenth century, the growth in the number of women's religious orders was considerably greater both in Europe and in the USA. The 'sisters' as much as the 'fathers' were key players in the powerful Catholic parishes that developed in many parts of Europe and America in the nineteenth century, embracing all aspects of the life of the people and aspiring to enclose them within a Catholic world.[43] Here the main impetus came from the post-1815 religious revival in Europe, which saw a programme of reconstruction by the Catholic Church in a bid to repair the damage done by the French Revolution and by Napoleon, and a return to the church by many members of the higher social classes. The hub of the revival was initially France, but its impact was also felt across Catholic Europe and in the USA.

Europe would also be the centre of the Ultramontane movement, with its focus on the papacy and a renewed emphasis on the miraculous and on all those aspects of Catholic tradition that the Enlightened Catholics of the later eighteenth century had sidelined.[44] This fed into a great expansion of the religious orders, as well as another central feature of nineteenth-century Catholicism, namely mass pilgrimage, often to the sites of recent Marian apparitions. Ruth Harris's study of the most famous of these at Lourdes has highlighted the crucial role both of local women of the lower social classes in establishing the site of Bernadette's visions as a place of pilgrimage, and of women from the higher social classes, often Parisian, in organizing and staffing the pilgrim trains that brought hundreds and thousands of the sick, the devout and the curious to this place of miracles.[45]

So far as the United States was concerned, the most influential innovations were those that took place within the Protestant churches. The USA was far ahead of Europe in the development of the women's suffrage movement, and here, as later in England, Quakers and Unitarians were especially important. But American women in the major evangelical denominations were also ahead of their counterparts in Europe in taking on public roles. Especially important were the later stages of the Second Great Awakening, when women preached and led mixed-sex prayer meetings in addition to holding positions of leadership in the anti-slavery movement.[46] The World Anti-Slavery Congress in London in 1840 was overshadowed by bitter conflict between an American delegation that included women members and the British organizers who said that only male delegates would be accepted.[47] Ann Braude has shown that a characteristic organization of nineteenth- and twentieth-century America was the religiously based reform movement, organized by women independently of the male-dominated denominational structures.[48] She also shows, however, that women's organizations within the denominations ran into difficulties because of conflicts with these hierarchies. Of the larger Christian denominations, the Congregationalists were for long the most open to ordaining women. The first ordination of a Congregationalist woman in the USA took place in 1853, whereas British Congregationalists waited until 1917. Both as a symptom and as a cause of the greater emancipation of American women in the nineteenth century by comparison with Europe, one of the key factors was the earlier development of women's higher education. Again, the important role of both the Second Great Awakening and anti-slavery is apparent: the pioneer of higher education for both sexes was Charles Finney's Oberlin College in Ohio in 1833. The same decade saw the foundation of several 'female seminaries' notably Mount Holyoke.[49]

The late nineteenth and early twentieth centuries also saw a multiplication of Christian organizations aimed explicitly at men. These included organizations for specific social groups that the church was thought to have neglected. For example, the YMCA was originally intended especially for young men of the lower middle class working in large draper's shops in central London.[50] The Church of England Men's Society was directed specifically at working-class men. The Holy Name Societies that were very popular among Catholic workingmen in the USA were particularly strong in areas of public employment with a large Catholic presence, such as the police, the fire brigade and the postal service. The YMCA originally focused strictly on prayer and Bible study, but over time developed a wide-ranging social, educational and recreational programme. The CEMS had a primarily social and recreational role, but Tine Van Osselaer argues that there were a growing number of men's religious organizations in Western Europe as well as the United States that attempted to foster a distinctly masculine form of piety and thus presumably were proof against the charge that religious worship was defined, and defined negatively, by the numerical predominance of women.[51]

Popular Culture

American cultural historians often approach the comparative religiosity of American and European popular culture by emphasizing the relationship between consumer culture and market capitalism. Many have pinpointed the United States as a nation of particularly aggressive synchronization between the market and the church. Religion has been incorporated (actively or involuntarily) into television shows, movies, radio programming, mainstream music, holiday practices, cheap consumer goods and descriptions of American industrial progress. Scholars such as R. Laurence Moore also contend that American religions have long borrowed the commercial practices of the day in order to 'sell God' and attract adherents. Moore points to the colourful cast of 'American originals' that employed market strategies in their religious work. From the antics of the wildly charismatic Lorenzo Dow in the late eighteenth century to the current sales of 'WWJD' t-shirts, Moore's characterization of American religion highlights the importance of consumer culture to the nature of religious practice.[52] Bethany Moreton has also explored how the connections between Wal-Mart, the world's largest corporation, and the evangelical Christian ethos that flourished in post-Second World War America worked to form an enormously pervasive Christian pro-business and pro-capitalism sentiment in many regions of the United States.[53] These trends also draw upon earlier conceptions of the Gospel of Wealth that gained popularity during the Progressive Era, which promoted an understanding of Christianity and monetary gain that were mutually affirming, rather than problematic. Moreover, it is not just the ability of American religion to infiltrate popular culture that is significant, but also the ways in which aspects of popular culture are sacralized that produce a particularly close affinity between religion and culture. Whether it is the ways in which new spiritualities work underground to create a common religious and spiritual language at the grass-roots level, as Catherine Albanese has it, or the ways in which religion and popular culture are brought together around clothing, media, uses of the internet, styles of Bible production or even the construction of religious sentiment at holiday festivals, it is hard to resist the conclusion that American religions are deeply situated within consumerist dimensions of popular culture.[54] Such patterns are not entirely absent in Europe where Catholic pilgrimages, processions, healing sites and community festivals are more generally popular than attending mass and confession. But, overall, there is a difference in scale and ubiquity. In the United States more so than in Western Europe, the connections between religion, again, particularly Protestantism, and popular consumer culture have been strong and enduring.

Colleen McDannell shows that the concept of secularization itself presupposes a separation between the sacred and the secular that is simply not helpful when engaging the ways in which religion is experienced through braided material culture. For example, throughout its short history, Mormonism has been particularly successful at resisting the separation between the sacred and the secular. Underscoring the continuities across the Atlantic, American Mormons utilized English organ designers and choir directors, mounted extensive transatlantic advertising and public relations campaigns, and promoted similar models of church-owned businesses. Moreover, Mormons have been relentless proponents of the fusion of spiritual and material culture through their restoration of multiple historic sites, their use of movies, pageants and displays to showcase Mormon history and the Mormon message, and their enthusiastic embrace of heritage religion as a way of melting conventional divisions between past, present and future, and between the sacred and the secular. Even the potentially damaging effects of the wildly successful stage musical, 'The Book of Mormon', were skilfully turned around by an aggressive 'I am a Mormon' advertising campaign milking the publicity and straddling the Atlantic.[55]

Congregations

Church life developed in a fundamentally different direction in the United States from that which had existed for many hundreds of years in Europe, because, according to Grace Davie, the basic unit was the congregation rather than the parish. Congregations, she argues, are flexible and potentially mobile. They can and often do relocate when their members relocate – and, of course, American cities are notoriously prone to frequent and sometimes quite sudden changes in the population of whole neighbourhoods. The idea of the congregation also implies a degree of internal democracy, though, of course, American denominations vary in their polity. The parish, on the other hand, is essentially territorial, and often tied up with local residence over several generations. It is also often seen as a hierarchical concept, the parish being a unit within a diocese or other larger controlling authority – though this too varies, since in some parts of Europe, such as Scotland, the right to elect the parish minister has long been regarded as one of the foundations of the national church. Territoriality applies especially to the rural parish, but it can, with qualification, be applied to many urban parishes too – though it has been decreasingly so over the last fifty years as large-scale migration from other parts of the world has fundamentally changed the social geography of many cities. According to Davie, the persistence of older models of church organization in the face of drastic social changes, reflects a lower level of adaptation to the modern world in European than in American churches.[56] One aspect of that is the propensity of Americans to change their religious affiliations, while in Western Europe change is less common than simply stopping altogether. Admittedly, these arguments need some qualification. Many of the British colonies in North America started with a parish system, and only gradually did the modern situation of a diversity of congregations, varying in social status as well as in theology and forms of worship, become the norm. But the biggest anomaly is presented by America's largest denomination, the Roman Catholic Church. It remains to this day thoroughly hierarchical: it is the bishop and not the congregation, or even the parish priest, who calls the tune. And the organization has always been by parish, whether territorial or ethnic, though since Vatican II the bitter divisions between progressives and traditionalists have in the USA, as in Europe, led many Catholics to choose the parish that best suits their own preferences in liturgy, theology and politics, rather than the one that is, strictly speaking, their own parish church.

Another area where American Christians, in this case, evangelicals, have been credited with an important innovation is the 'megachurch', a term that came into wide use around 1990 to describe a long familiar phenomenon. A 1971 debate in the leading American evangelical paper *Christianity Today* on the pros and cons of 'big churches' – that is, those with a membership of several thousands – reveals their already looming significance.[57] From the USA the idea has been exported to other parts of the world including Europe, but more especially Australia, Africa and some Asian countries, such as South Korea and Singapore. While being built around a charismatic preacher, the essential idea of these churches is that size permits a wide range of specialized ministries, designed to meet the specific needs of almost any identifiably distinct element of the population, from singles to seniors, from engaged couples to the recently divorced, as well as immigrants from various parts of the world. They also provide recreational opportunities, though that is nothing new. There are parallels with the 'institutional churches', which flourished in Britain and the USA in the late nineteenth and early twentieth centuries – with the difference that these were most strongly championed by liberals and moderate evangelicals.[58] Reformatting themselves as social as well as spiritual centres, these early growth-oriented evangelistic churches sought to reach as many of 'the lost' as possible. However, American megachurches, mostly unlike the large churches of nineteenth-century Britain, are focused instrumentally on growth by whatever means possible. Church growth institutes, books, conferences, workshops, tips and networks all combine to create the idea, as in American business culture, that bigger is indeed better. They produce economies of scale, allow for diversified ministries of all kinds, promote a congregational evangelistic ethic and 'count' attendance, members, baptisms and seekers/converts with a remarkably disciplined accountability. Throughout their history, megachurch outcomes have not always delivered on their evangelical aspirations. Many have gone out of business. In other cases, as H. Paul Douglass showed in his studies of American city churches in the 1920s, the number of people at churches like Chicago's Olivet Institute who took advice from the church's counsellors, left their children at the day nursery, attended clubs for teenage boys and girls or exercised in the gym far exceeded the number attending services.[59] Nevertheless, despite representing a small minority of American congregations, American megachurches are now home to a sizeable minority of American churchgoers. In this respect, the pattern in the USA is distinct from that in Western Europe and more akin to that in other parts of the world.

Conclusion

American Christians have, indeed, been more innovative than their European counterparts in certain areas and at certain times. Most obviously, the USA has, at least since the mid-nineteenth century, provided more fertile soil for radically new interpretations of Christianity that have gone on to gain an international following. Even within a more conventionally evangelical or liberal framework, sectarian Protestantism has also developed on a scale, and in a profusion of different forms, far exceeding that in even Britain or the Netherlands, the only European countries that might compete in this field. American evangelicals have been especially innovative in the field of evangelism, while both American and British liberal Protestants have been especially innovative in areas of social witness. In Catholicism, however, the most important initiatives have come from continental Europe, and often from France. As in several other cases, the political context was important. The very strength of anti-clericalism obliged Catholics to be inventive in finding new ways of defending and propagating the faith. The biggest constraints on innovation have come not from the state but from denominational hierarchies and, especially in the Catholic case, the papacy. Over the course of the nineteenth and twentieth centuries, numerous initiatives by Catholic priests and the laity have fallen to papal veto, one of the many major casualties being the French Worker Priest movement, effectively closed by Pius XII in 1954. But when the pope gave them a chance, there were enterprising Catholics ready to take it, the classic example being Leo XIII's encyclical *Rerum Novarum* (1891), which legitimated the rapid development of Christian Trade Unions, first in Germany, and soon in France, Belgium and other countries.[60] In 1936, the encyclical was still being used by priests in Detroit to justify the strikes in the automobile industry.[61]

To return to our original questions: American Christians have been on balance more innovative than their European counterparts. But whether this has in itself made them more resistant to secularization is more open to question. For most of the twentieth century, the three sections of American society most resistant to the secularizing trends were Catholics, the South and Mormon-dominated Utah.[62] The American Catholic Church brought in some significant innovations, for example the ethnic parish, but on the whole, it was the strength of inherited loyalties, often reinforced by powerful ethnic identities and the experience of discrimination by the Protestant majority, that ensured the solidarity of the Catholic community. The evangelical-dominated South was the most religiously conservative section of the nation, and the one in most respects resistant to innovation. Indeed, innovation is often a response to a perceived crisis, and it may seem unnecessary where the church is a central social institution and religion is an integral part of popular culture. Innovation may be the necessary means to survival, and even a measure of success, in less favourable circumstances, whether in western Europe or in America's relatively 'secular' West and North-East, and it may be there, rather than in the 'Bible Belt', that we should look to measure the results of American religious inventiveness.

10 Christian Transnationalists, Nationhood and the Construction of Civil Society

DANA L. ROBERT

At the turn of the twentieth century, the juggernaut of modernity rolled through the world, crushing tradition in its path. The combination of Western technology, trade, education and colonial power challenged premodern cultures and local hierarchies. Science undercut the explanatory value of religions. Technology outran the human capacity to control it. The First World War and its ripple effects dislocated millions of people and rearranged social and political structures throughout the world. The war accelerated the need for a new world order, and individual nations and peoples anxiously searched for their place in it.

Paradoxically, one of the chief resources that equipped people to deal with modernity was missionary Protestantism. On the one hand, the missionary movement rode the wave of Western colonialism and global capitalism that destabilized traditional cultures worldwide. On the other hand, recent studies have demonstrated the importance of Protestant missionaries for the spread of modern democratic ideals such as human equality. In a seminal article published in the *American Political Science Review*, sociologist Robert Woodberry made a startling claim: 'Statistically, the historic prevalence of Protestant missionaries explains about half the variation in democracy in Africa, Asia, Latin America and Oceania and removes the impact of most variables that dominate current statistical research about democracy.'[1] By providing Western education, literacy, printing presses, access to international networks and training for voluntary group activity, the Protestant missionary movement created the conditions for civil society, regardless of whether people actually converted to Christianity. In addition to its clear impact on reframing local institutions, missionary Christianity created a rich matrix of global conversations about human equality. Leading scholar of international relations Walter Russell Mead writes that 'the very concept of a global civil society comes to us out of the missionary movement; apart from a handful of isolated intellectuals, no one before the missionaries ever thought that the world's cultures and societies had or could have enough in common to make a common global society feasible or desirable'.[2]

Conversionary Protestantism was a major source of social innovation in the period of global modernization that swept the world at the beginning of the twentieth century. But exactly how can the trail of innovation be traced from the missionary school and printing press, to the 'common global society' referenced by Mead? I argue that one way to trace religious innovation from the microcosm of the mission school to the macrocosm of global discourse is to examine the construction of nationalism by early Protestant leaders in Asia, Africa and Latin America. Via the construction of modern national identities, Protestant elites sought a place at the table for their own people in an idealized new world order. Global Protestant networks created a class of articulate intellectuals who crafted new ethnic or national narratives that cohered with an overarching framework of what in the 1920s was called 'internationalism'.

Among Christian intellectuals, nationalism and internationalism remained in dynamic tension: modern national progress was inseparable from visions of an international world order marked by racial equality, peace and justice. YMCA leader and head of the Chinese National Christian Council Yu Rhizang identified the global citizenship that lay at the heart of Christian transnationalism. In a speech delivered at an international missionary conference in 1928, Yu declared:

> I am a Chinese nationalist; but I do not belong to any political party. At the same time I am an internationalist and a Christian. I am speaking this evening in the spirit of being concurrently a nationalist, an internationalist and a Christian; and I am confident that I am receiving a most hearty response from this company of world-citizens. It is this spirit of great harmony which I am strongly persuaded will help us to understand, sympathize and co-operate with one another, and which must prevail if we ever hope to achieve a better world-order.[3]

Previous generations of scholars have caricatured non-western Christian intellectuals as 'liberal elites', disconnected from their own cultural roots. In light of recent scholarship on religion and globalization, a more appropriate label would be *Christian transnationalists*. This nomenclature accomplishes several things. First, it places them into the growing literature on religious internationalism and transnationalism, the dawning recognition by historians that world religions are carriers of globalization.[4] Christianity, in particular, was the transnational religion *par excellence* in the period of modernization. Second, the idea of Christian transnationalism retains a focus on 'missionary' or 'boundary crossing' Protestantism as a source of social innovation. Christianity was not the only vision for international community in the early twentieth century. Secular socialism, for example, was closely akin to global Protestant discourse in its emphasis on human community. But the Christian vision foregrounded individual human rights within the collective, based on the idea of human equality as a God-given right.[5] Third, the concept of Christian transnationalism affirms that the emergence of modern nationalism was not only political or economic, but a matter of constructed cultural identities. While religious choice can be political, the most profound social impact of self-selected religious identity is often at the level of 'culture making', including affirmation of values. And finally, the term Christian transnationalism references the paradox that modern nationalism was a constituent part of internationalist discourse in the early twentieth century, and not separate from it. Nationalism was inseparable from Christian visions of a peaceful and just new world order. The dialectic between nationalism and internationalism is implied in the scholarly term 'transnationalism'.

How did Christian transnationalists negotiate the terrain between national identity and commitment to international community? Comparison of prominent Christian transnationalists from three different parts of the world illustrates how they crafted local identities into a global vision of human unity that laid the foundations for what they hoped would be a new world order. Putting these stories in dialogue with each other reveals something important that is missed in narrow historiographies written by area specialists. In such accounts, Christian transnationalists are treated as modern individualists, rather than as part of a broader movement shaped by missionary Christianity. Each has been interpreted in a silo, judged against national histories. Because their ideals typically did not come to fulfilment in their own lifetimes, they have often been seen as failed, Western-leaning elitists. So, for example, the ideals of Christian transnationalists were unable to stop the Second World War, or to prevent the militarization of Islam or to eliminate racism or apartheid. Yet, collectively, they demonstrate the innovative force of religious ideals for social change. Christian transnationalists constructed nationhoods within an internationalist conscience that transcended cultural particularities.

Inazô Nitobé, Internationalism and Japanese Bushido

After centuries of self-imposed isolation, including the outlawing of Christianity, no country embraced modernization as rapidly as Japan. In 1853, Commodore Matthew Perry steamed into Edo Bay and demanded that the Japanese open themselves to Western trade. Japanese leaders quickly realized their vulnerability relative to the technological superiority of the West. Thus, in 1868, modernizers overthrew the Shogunate and centralized the government under the titular rule of the Meiji Emperor. In less than twenty years, Japan had moved from an agricultural nation of over 200 different administrative units, to a centralized government system that built railroads, favoured industrialization, standardized currency and banking, raised a national army and eliminated the traditional privileges of the hereditary landed nobility. In 1889, a new constitution set up an elected bicameral legislature under a constitutional monarchy. Japan entered the high-stakes world of modern imperial powers when its army defeated China for control of Korea in 1895, defeated Russia in 1905 and was one of the victorious Allies during the First World War.

Christianity re-entered Japan as a side effect of its effort to modernize and to coexist with Western powers. With feudalism abolished, a generation of samurai found itself ill-equipped to face the future. As the former warrior class sought new outlets for leadership in service of Japan, a few allowed their children to be taught English and other Western subjects. The first Japanese Protestants were young men from the samurai class who had entered schools founded by Westerners and encountered the gospel there. Regional 'bands' of young Christian students coalesced around Christian teaching and Western learning, which they synthesized with the disciplined Confucian ethics inherited from their samurai backgrounds. For them, Christianity represented not only spiritual solace during a time of social upheaval, but also a personal pathway into the larger world of Western philosophy and knowledge. Although Christianity made little headway in Japan at large, the earliest Protestant converts exercised an influence upon Japanese international relations and civil society far out of proportion to their small numbers.

Scion of a displaced northern samurai family, Inazô Nitobé (1862–1933) was one of the first Japanese to learn English. He was deeply attracted to English literature, but also eager to continue the family tradition of land management. Nitobé was sent to the new Sapporo Agricultural College led by William C. Clark, the president of the Massachusetts Agricultural College.[6] Sapporo was built and run like a miniature New England boys' preparatory school. Along with other students in his class, Nitobé signed a Covenant of Believers in Jesus.[7] In 1884, he moved to the United States for further study. He attended Johns Hopkins University and then earned a doctorate in agricultural economics from a German university. The most personally meaningful aspect of his student days was becoming a Quaker and finding a life partner.[8] He observed in 1926 that 'only in Quakerism could I reconcile Christianity with Oriental thought'.[9] He met his future wife, Mary Elkinton, a Philadelphia Quaker, when he went to advise the Women's Foreign Missionary Association of Friends about opening mission work in Japan. The Nitobés moved to Japan in 1891, and Inazô embarked on a distinguished career as an educator, first at Sapporo Agricultural College, and then at Kyoto University and the University of Tokyo. In 1918, Nitobé became founding president of the Tokyo Women's Christian College. With the support of his wife, he encouraged the founding of girls' schools in Japan. His life task was to be a 'bridge across the Pacific'.[10] Recalled Nitobé, 'I said that I wished to be a bridge across the Pacific Ocean, a bridge across which Western ideas could flow without obstacle or impediment to Japan, and over which oriental ideas could find entrance to America'.[11]

As Japan began its imperial expansion around the Pacific Rim, tensions grew with the West. Missionaries worked to increase mutual understanding between Japan and the United States, especially in California where fear of Asian immigration led to laws against the naturalization of Japanese immigrants and then against land ownership. In 1911, to increase mutual respect between Japanese and Americans, the Carnegie Endowment for International Peace appointed Nitobé as the first exchange professor from Japan to the United States. In this capacity, he lectured at multiple universities and published *The Japanese Nation: Its Land, Its People, and Its Life*.[12] On the other side of the Pacific, he introduced American studies to Japan with lectures on 'The Foundation of the American Nation'.

In 1920, Nitobé's reputation as Japan's most famous 'internationalist' was solidified when he was appointed Under-Secretary-General to the new League of Nations. In this challenging role, he frequently gave speeches supporting international cooperation and peaceful conflict resolution. He hosted international delegations, and founded the International Committee on Intellectual Cooperation – the forerunner to the United Nations Educational, Scientific and Cultural Organization (UNESCO). The seven years of his appointment witnessed escalating tensions in US–Japanese relations. First had come Woodrow Wilson's refusal to approve the only resolution proposed by Japan for inclusion in the League covenant – that of racial equality. Second was the refusal of the United States to join the League. And finally, the *coup de grace* was the passage of the Oriental Exclusion Act of 1924. This discriminatory law eliminated Japanese immigration to the United States.

As a result of this anti-Japanese legislation, Nitobé refused to visit the United States for many years. This national humiliation was a significant factor in turning the tide towards increasing militarism and anti-Americanism in Japan. In efforts to alleviate the tension between the United States and Japan, internationalists, including Japanese missionaries and YMCA activists, founded the Institute of Pacific Relations in 1925. In its early years, this influential NGO sponsored discussions of US–Japanese relations, research in Asian Studies and advocacy for peace. By 1929, Nitobé had become a director of the Japanese branch and, with other Japanese Christian transnationalists, supported pro-American attitudes in Japan.[13]

Nitobé spent his career advocating a peaceful internationalism consistent with his Quaker faith and building modern Japan from his vantage point as a Western-leaning intellectual. His position became increasingly untenable when militarism came to define Japanese nationalism. By the 1930s, the Japanese military was using intimidation and assassination to suppress civilian leadership, and Nitobé was forced into a humiliating apology after criticizing the military in private. In February 1933, Japan withdrew from the League of Nations after its invasion of Manchuria was greeted by unanimous condemnation. Nitobé's awkward and idealistic stance has been debated by historians as alternately pro-Japanese colonialism and pro-Western. Despite the internal contradictions, Nitobé's writings show that he retained his belief in a synthesis of local and global to the end of his life. He refused a definition of nationalism based on aggressive militarism or isolationism. He wrote in the *Osaka Mainichi* in 1933:

A good internationalist must be a good nationalist and vice versa. The very terms connote it. A man who is not faithful to his own country cannot be depended upon for faithfulness to a world principle. One can serve best the cause of internationalism by serving his country. On the other hand, a nationalist can best advance the interests and honour of his country by being internationally minded.[14]

The Christian roots of Nitobé's ideals were evident throughout his political career. In the final months of his life, he delivered a speech at the Institute of Politics in Williamstown, in which he framed 'world community' in biblical Pauline terms as one body with many members, and many members united into one body. The 'diverse gifts of nations' showed their interdependence in multiple ways – economically, through international NGOs, labour organizations, diplomatic channels and the like.[15] Nitobé concluded his speech by comparing the symbiotic relationship between internationalism and nationalism to the incarnation of Jesus Christ, who was both universal God and a Jewish man: 'Jesus Christ himself was not only the son of God, not merely a son of man and as such a cosmopolite, but a son of Judea and a patriot of the highest order.

How he mourned and lamented over Jerusalem!' Despite the dashing of many of his dreams, Nitobé maintained hope in the spiritual and physical unity of the world, and the 'day when cooperation will rule the conduct of races and nations'.[16]

One of the clearest expositions of how Nitobé's Christian transnationalism incorporated nation-building was his book *Bushido: The Soul of Japan* (1899). Nitobé showed the continuity between *Bushido* and Christianity, and thus illuminated a unique path for the Japanese nation in blessing Asia.[17] In his introduction, Nitobé revealed how the progressive missionary theology of fulfilment guided his interpretation of Japanese culture. He wrote: 'I believe in the religion taught by Him and handed down to us in the New Testament, as well as in the law written in the heart. Further, I believe that God hath made a testament which may be called "old" with every people and nation, – Gentile or Jew, Christian or Heathen.'[18] In other words, just as Jesus came not to destroy but to 'fulfill' Jewish law and culture, so too it was with Japanese culture. Japanese culture was not a negative barrier to the Christianization of Japan, but a positive pathway towards it. His exposition of 'fulfilment theory' allowed Nitobé to chastise foreign missionaries who failed to appreciate the positive qualities of Japanese civilization, and to show at the same time how the future of Japan was moving towards Christianity: 'Ignoring the past career of a people, missionaries claim that Christianity is a new religion, whereas, to my mind, it is an "old, old story," which, if presented in intelligible words – that is to say, if expressed in the vocabulary familiar in the moral development of a people – will find easy lodgment in their hearts, irrespective of race or nationality.'[19] *Bushido* had died with the end of Japanese feudalism and the launch of modernity. But its deeper identity and traditional moral values of justice, benevolence, courage and the like lived into the modern era, as transformed by the gospel.

Nitobé ended his book by asking whether the *Bushido* spirit would ultimately find itself in the peaceful idealism of Christianity or the violent materialism of Nietzsche's will to power. That his own hopes lay in the former were reflected in the closing words of the book – a quotation from the Quaker poet John Greenleaf Whittier. Like a flower that had bloomed, the fragrance of *Bushido* hung in the air, and blessed mankind. And the 'traveler ... pausing, takes with forehead bare, the benediction of the air'.[20]

The publication of *Bushido* unleashed forces beyond Nitobé's control. The book became an international bestseller, with twenty-five English editions as well as translations into Japanese and at least ten other languages. According to Cyril Powles, 'through Nitobé's interpretation, *Bushido* achieved the status of a unitary explanation for Japan's success at modernization'.[21] Especially after 'little' Asian Japan defeated 'big' European Russia in 1905, British and Americans – including President Theodore Roosevelt – turned to *Bushido* to gain insight into the Japanese character. Major criticisms of the book included missionary worries that it valorized Confucian values to the extent that it undercut missions. Ultimately, *Bushido* was charged with helping to shape a 'new religion' of the Japanese military who applied its universalizing concepts to emperor worship.[22]

Contemporary scholars have typically seen Nitobé's Christianity as an irrelevant overlay to the book.[23] But if one takes seriously Nitobé's Christian commitments, they become the key to understanding his contribution to global civil society. *Bushido* hangs together as a synthesis of the old and new, framed by Christianity as a global public ethic. Just as Nitobé experienced Christianity as transformative of his personal identity as a Japanese, so its universal vision could transform the warlike qualities of the Japanese nation into a peaceful world citizen. To Nitobé, the particularity of Japanese national identity coalesced against the backdrop of Christianity as international network, and the world of nations. *Bushido* was the vision of a Christian transnationalist.

Silas Molema and 'Bantu' Nationhood

Unlike the self-confident Japanese, black South African Christian leaders in the post-First World War period found themselves on the losing side of history. After the founding of the Union of South Africa in 1909, black and mixed-race Africans were increasingly denied civil and human rights in the land of their birth. The result of the rapprochement between the Dutch and the English was the unification of white rights at the expense of black, Asian and mixed-race South Africans. The Natives' Land Act of 1913 stripped Africans of the right to own land in most of the country; overnight, thousands in the former Boer Republics became homeless. Even blacks who could afford it were denied the right to rent in 'European' areas; much of the African population was squeezed into 7 per cent of the land. In 1920, to suppress pressure for individual voting rights and representation in Parliament, the Native Affairs Act set up powerless advisory 'tribal' councils – thereby controlling black leadership by reinforcing political communalism. The Urban Areas Act of 1923 controlled black movement to and from urban areas, and prevented black South Africans from settling in cities. In 1926, the Colour Bar Act restricted Africans and Asians from holding skilled jobs in mining and other industries. These laws, among others passed during the 1920s, limited the social, economic and political advancement of Africans and condemned generations to virtual serfdom as underpaid wage labourers for white farmers. Because the British Parliament gave the Union of South Africa local autonomy, or dominion status within the British empire, there was little political will from Great Britain to support black and Indian protests against mistreatment by the white minority. In the period after the First World War, while resistance to colonialism gained traction in much of Asia, opportunities for black South Africans shrank.

The first South Africans to resist the tightening noose of race-based laws were mission-educated Christian leaders. In the 1910s and 1920s, just as Asian Christian transnationalists argued that a global ethic of human equality be applied to their developing nation-states, their South African counterparts called for racial equality as constitutive of the new Union of South Africa. Silas Modiri Molema (1891–1965) was a Morolong from a royal Tswana family. He attended the pre-eminent missionary schools in South Africa – Methodist Healdtown, and then the Lovedale Institute of the United Free Church of Scotland. Before its takeover by the apartheid government in the 1950s, Lovedale educated many of the most important South African religious and cultural leaders. In 1914, Molema's parents sent him to Glasgow University to medical school. The outbreak of the First World War trapped him in Glasgow for the duration. After his return to South Africa in 1921, Molema became a prominent medical doctor in his hometown of Mafikeng, near the border with Botswana. He treated blacks, Asians and whites in his medical practice and was an active leader in the Wesleyan Methodist Church. Dr Molema joined the South African Native National Congress (the future African National Congress) shortly after his return from Scotland. Although his large medical practice limited his time for politics, Molema attended the All-Africa Convention, held in the 1930s to oppose government laws that moved South Africa closer to the system of apartheid, or 'separate development'.

In 1943, Molema worked on the Atlantic Charter Committee of the ANC. The Atlantic Charter had been written in 1941 by President Franklin Roosevelt and Prime Minister Winston Churchill to agree upon the shape of a new world order once the Allies defeated Germany. South Africa was one of twenty-six signatories to the 'Declaration of United Nations' that adopted the Atlantic Charter in 1942. Because the document included the 'self-determination of nations', it stoked black South African aspirations. The United Nations was founded in 1948, partly as an outgrowth of the Atlantic Charter. The same year also saw the election of the Nationalist Party and the advent of full-blown apartheid in South Africa. Shortly afterwards, Molema was elected treasurer-general of the African National Congress. The apartheid government banned him from political participation in 1953, after he participated in the Defiance Campaign.[24] As a senior Motswana intellectual, Molema was an important contributor to the constitutional process that brought into being the independence of the nation of Botswana in 1966 – although, sadly, his death in 1965 meant that he did not live to see it.

Molema's transnationalism can be seen most clearly in his groundbreaking book *The Bantu Past and Present* (1920).[25] This was one of the first histories written by a black South African. From the perspective of the global Christian discourse of the early twentieth century, *The Bantu* is a masterful argument for the nationhood of the Tswana peoples. As does Nitobé in *Bushido*, Molema argues for the continuity of his people's cultural identity from the early to the modern era, renewed but not obliterated by Christianity. And just as Nitobé wrote *Bushido* to explain and justify Japanese culture to a Western audience, Molema wrote *The Bantu* to identify an ancient but now oppressed people who deserved British protection. Both Nitobé and Molema employed the tools of modern ethnographic and historical scholarship to claim a place for their own people at the table of nations. Both carried the hereditary burden of leadership, as each descended from a landed aristocratic family that found its traditional lifeway pushed aside by centralized modern governments. Writing in English provided a way for Molema to preserve the memory of oral cultures. Christianity – and the skills of literacy and education it represented – provided a path forward for the preservation of the nation. Throughout the text, Molema expresses gratitude to the missionaries who supported the 'native' ability to move forward in the modern world – especially through education and agitation for human rights.

The genealogical approach Molema employed reflected the legacy of orality – of traditional Tswana knowledge, in which the ancestors were kept alive through being remembered by their descendants. Molema wrote history because he was aware that while oral memories faded away, modern nationhood required a written legacy. The first part of the book laid out his dual genealogy as an African and a Christian. He classified Southern Africans into linguistic and cultural families, but with particular focus on his own people, the Batswana. His recitation of Tswana history took them through the terrors of nineteenth-century war and dislocation caused by the *mfecane* of the Ndebele and the invasion of their lands by Dutch Boers. At critical moments, the Batswana regrouped – often with the assistance of missionaries and under the leadership of Christian chiefs. The Tswana genealogy showed a brave and resilient people who adapted to changing circumstances and who employed Christianity as a tool for their survival as a people.

The second genealogy that Molema transcribed was that of the missionaries. Beginning with Johannes Van der Kemp of the London Missionary Society, Molema traced his spiritual lineage through missionaries of the Wesleyan Missionary Society, down through the Scottish tradition of Moffatt, Livingston and James Stewart of Lovedale. The importance of the missionary legacies lay in their evangelistic and educational work among the Bantu. In addition, Molema underscored the vital point that missionaries have been 'in South Africa at any rate, the political champions of the Bantu. For them they have interceded and conferred with Governments from the beginning of missionary work to this day'.[26]

In his contemporary context of a global Christian discourse, Molema claimed his identity as a Christian Morolong by interweaving the dual genealogy of Tswana and missionary history. Not only did he frequently cite missionary sources in praise of important African Christian leaders, but he also recounted historical turning points in which missionary Christianity energized the Bantu peoples. The complementarity of missionary and Bantu history reached its peak in the modern African. Molema structured his history to repeatedly defend the products of cultural and ethnic mixing. His praise of multi-racialism, and his appreciation for the merger of Bantu and Christian genealogies was not a product of 'confusion', but a protest against the racial separatism and ethnic essentialism being imposed upon black South Africans by the proto-apartheid white government of the Union of South Africa. It was also consistent with the inter-racial commitments of the early ANC. To Molema, the strength of Bantu nationhood within a modern nation state did not lie in a mythic racial purity, but in hybridity itself.

One of the most important points made by Molema in *The Bantu* was that a moral social order was continuous with the best of African culture. Christianity and modern virtues did not represent a break with traditional moral order. Rather, in echoes of the fulfilment theory so prominent in missionary discourse, Molema argued that modern civilization acquired through education and Christianity did not destroy ancient Bantu culture. It sharpened, perfected, broadened and purified it:

> As the current moral ideas were to be found among the ancients, so surely are they found among the primitive Bantu. Love, Obedience, Justice, Truthfulness, Benevolence, Forgiveness, Purity, Temperance, Humility, Honour, Industry, Fidelity, Friendship, Patriotism, etc., all these and other 'First Principles' of moral law were and are recognised by the Bantu. In so far as the cognition of these moral ideas is concerned, they had arrived spontaneously or intuitively where other nations – civilised or uncivilized – had arrived.[27]

Molema's defence of the innate worth of the black African was a biting reprimand to the paternalism of missionaries and other whites who assumed they had no morality, and by implication were not a civilized people. The values of Christianity were those of the ancients, including the Bantu.

Drawing upon Immanuel Kant's theory of ethics, and upon the philosopher Epictetus, Molema affirmed that the 'problem' with the utilitarian Bantu morality was that it extended only to one's own tribe. The 'greatest good' was traditionally affirmed for the local, rather than the universal.[28] And how, for the Bantu, would the universalization of values be achieved? To answer that question, Molema left his discussion of philosophy and returned to his historical and ethnographic approach. He quoted from a speech by the great Christian chief Moshesh (Moshoeshoe) of Lesotho when he invited missionaries to evangelize them.

> Rejoice, ye men of Mokare and ye sons of Mokhatshahe ! ... We are told that we have all been created by the One Being and we all spring from one man. Sin entered man's heart when he ate of the forbidden fruit, and we have sin from him. These men (the missionaries) say that they have sinned; and what is sin in them is sin in us also, because we come from one stock, and their hearts and ours are one thing.[29]

The essential Christian message as received by the great Christian kings of southern Africa was knowledge of the oneness of humanity under one God. The 'good news' of human unity, even in its common sinfulness, had profound implications for the expansion of morality as already practised by the Bantu – expansion beyond the limitations of tribe, to the multi-cultural realities of the contemporary age.

By the time Molema published *The Bantu* in 1920, there was widespread frustration over the failure of the victorious Allies to follow through on Wilson's Fourteen Points. Talk of self-determination of nations had failed to deal with the entrenched racism within nations like South Africa and the United States. The South African Native National Congress sent a delegation to Prime Minister Lloyd George in 1919 that appealed unsuccessfully for British assistance in countering the onslaught of segregationist legislation. These and other efforts by African leaders to effect white decolonization were unsuccessful, although they laid the groundwork for future efforts at African unity. Molema's anger at the failure of Wilson's internationalism can be seen in his later chapters. Because of his faith in the liberal tradition of British protection for the civil rights of South African blacks, the refusal of the Paris Peace Conference to stand up for racial equality was a bitter disappointment – especially after four years of sacrifice and death of black South Africans who supported the British cause during the First World War. Molema condemned Western liberalism as 'an astounding platitude'. 'The Western world went to the Peace Table at Versailles with professions of "Morality," "Liberalism," "Justice," "Making the World free for Democracy," and so forth, and there at the Peace Table the Western World made a blot which will go down into history as a fine example of Western Liberalism and Altruism and their idea of "Brotherhood of Nations"'.[30] Despite the best efforts of the delegate from Japan, the Treaty of Versailles refused to affirm racial equality between East and West. Shockingly, South Africa's leading internationalist General Jan Smuts had told the peace conference that South Africa was to be a white country. It was no wonder, therefore, that Molema went on to mock Wilson's Fourteen Points. For the Bantu, there was no morality, justice or Christian virtue in the Fourteen Points; they were nothing but a 'superior swindle'.[31]

Despite the failure of both British liberalism and the post-war international community to address racial injustices, Molema remained a committed Christian transnationalist. In January of 1921, he attended the quadrennial meeting of the Student Christian Movement of Great Britain and Ireland. Molema was one of a hundred internationals who joined over 2,000 British and Irish delegates for the four-day conference in Glasgow. The subject of the meeting was 'Christ and Human Need'. The tone of the conference, and its all-European cast of speakers, was paternalistic towards colonized nations and assumed that Europe maintained control 'in trust' until such nations were 'ready' for self-government.[32] Regardless of the patronizing tone of the papers, Dr Molema took inspiration from the vision of Christian community he experienced at the conference. He referred to his attendance in an address to the 'missionary meeting' of the Wesleyan Church synod a few years after his return to South Africa. In his speech to fellow Methodists, Molema claimed human equality and community as the 'Christian ethical ideal': 'Jesus Christ emphasised the brotherhood of man, or the unity of human nature, and taught universal association and equality of man with man.'[33] While issues of race relations were important political questions, the special contribution of the Church to racial justice was its fundamentally spiritual and moral approach to the need for peace and goodwill. 'It is therefore possible, by divine grace, and loyalty to ourselves, and the God in us, to transcend the many barriers of class and race, most of [ ] our making, and to realise our ideal in practical life.'[34]

In his speech to the Wesleyan synod, Molema argued for the inseparability of races from each other. Christianity taught that human society was a 'spiritual organism'. In an organism, injury to one part was an injury to the others. Natural law showed that the organism must advance together and serve the larger community, or else the entire society would regress. By referencing both Christianity and natural law as sources for the understanding of society as an organic whole, Dr Molema charted a path forward for the seamless integration of traditional African values of community with internationalism, to argue for a peaceful civil society marked by respect for individual persons and racial and cultural equality. This distinctively Christian vision was neither radical nor separatist. Although Molema grudgingly endorsed segregation as a temporary expedient, he eschewed racial separatism as both 'inefficient' for the future development of South Africa and opposed to the core values of Christian community.[35]

As conditions for blacks and Asians in South Africa failed to improve, later generations pushed aside the peaceful integrated vision of community put forth by Molema and other black Christian intellectuals of his era. By the 1930s, some adopted the materialist and conflictive ideology of Marxism, or the warlike and confrontational readings of traditional African cultures. Molema himself became more politically radical after the onslaught of full-blown apartheid in 1948. But in the context of the 1920s, his viewpoints put him squarely into the centre of internationalist discourse, alongside other Christian transnationalists, who similarly applied a global Christian ethic to the building of their own modern and multicultural nation states, amid visions of a new world order.

Philip Hitti, Syrian Nationalism and Democratization

During the course of the nineteenth century, Protestant missionaries established schools and printing presses among key population centres in the Near East, including Jerusalem, Beirut, Istanbul, Cairo, Urmia and Tabriz. They founded the first modern educational systems in the Ottoman Empire, pioneered the education of girls, and printed and promoted vernacular literatures, including Bible translations.[36] Although the largely Muslim populations resisted Christian conversion, students sought modern education in upper-level mission schools such as Robert College in Constantinople (Istanbul) and the Syrian Protestant College (now American University of Beirut). The missionary presence had its largest impact among Christian minorities. Nationalist movements were fed by Western education and expanding vernacular literacy. Arab cultural nationalism was first articulated by Christian intellectuals, graduates of the Syrian Protestant College.[37]

By the late 1800s, European colonialism and the weakening of the thousand-year-old Ottoman Empire had caused bitter backlashes against its Christian minorities. As the Ottoman Turks retreated in the face of Allied military pressure during the First World War, they massacred ethnic minorities in their wake. An estimated one million Christian Armenians died in what has been called the first modern genocide. The Paris Peace Conference debated how to organize the territories newly freed from Turkey. In 1919, Article 22 of the League of Nations covenant launched the mandate system, whereby former Ottoman and German territories were organized into proto-nations under the jurisdiction of Allied powers. Former Ottoman territory was ultimately split into Palestine, Transjordan (later Jordan), Syria, Lebanon and Iraq. Syria and Lebanon were placed under French administration, and the British retained control of Palestine and Jordan.[38]

As the meaning of nationalism became an urgent issue for people of the Near East, Western-educated Christian intellectuals played key roles in situating their peoples within the new internationalist framework. One of the most influential of these was the Maronite Christian Philip Hitti (1886–1978), the father of Arab studies in the United States. Like Nitobé and Molema, Hitti was educated in mission schools and introduced to the broader world by his Protestant connections. In 1895, Philip, a small boy from a village near Beruit with a compound arm fracture that had grown gangrenous caught the attention of a passing missionary, who insisted he be taken to the hospital at the Syrian Protestant College. After two operations Hitti survived, but was deemed unsuited for farm work. Under the sponsorship of missionaries, he studied to be a teacher.[39] Hitti won scholarships and in 1908 earned his B.A. at the Syrian Protestant College, where he began to teach. In 1911, he was selected to represent his college at the Constantinople meeting of the World Student Christian Federation. His address, 'Characteristics of Syrian Students', made a strong impression at the conference.[40]

Over the next several years, Hitti attended additional Christian student conferences in the United States and took the opportunity to visit east coast colleges. He enrolled at Columbia University for a year of study, deciding over other universities because of the presence in lower Manhattan of a Maronite community. With the outbreak of the First World War, Hitti was trapped in the United States. He began teaching Syriac at Columbia and earned his PhD. His dissertation was a groundbreaking study on the history of the Arabs, a project that finally came to fruition in 1937 with his *History of the Arabs*, the founding work in the field and since printed in multiple editions.[41]

After the war Hitti took his bride and infant back to his alma mater in what was now the new nation of Lebanon. There he introduced the subject of Arab history and became the first non-missionary to hold a full professorial rank.[42] In 1926, he was recruited to Princeton University to fill a new position in Semitic literature. Over the next twenty years, Hitti painstakingly worked to establish what became the first department in the United States to teach Arabic studies, Arabic language and Islam. In his own words, his early work was considered 'very peripheral' to the life of the university.[43] Princeton's department of Near Eastern Studies eventually claimed a solid footing when during the Second World War, American soldiers were posted to North Africa, and the State Department recognized the need to train Americans in Arabic. As the pioneer in his field, Hitti raised the funds to train the first generation of Arabists and Islamic scholars in the United States. His former students filled high positions in the State Department and populated the emerging academic posts at other institutions. At the founding of the United Nations, Hitti testified against the founding of a separate state of Israel.[44]

As with Nitobé and Molema, Hitti's first significant scholarly work was to write a history that defended the nationhood of his own people. Shortly before moving to Princeton, he published *The Syrians in America*, an act of self-definition for the people inhabiting what was becoming the country of Lebanon. As long-term Ottoman subjects, the peoples of the coastal region near the Mt. Lebanon region lacked a modern national consciousness. Traditionally, they had defined themselves by clan and by religion. Although they spoke Arabic, Christians did not feel comfortable being called Arabs because of the implication that an Arab was a Muslim. At the same time, they needed to identify commonalities that transcended their sectarian backgrounds. According to Eric Hooglund, nineteenth-century missionaries popularized the use of the geographic expression 'Syrian' to denote the people among whom they worked.[45] The nomenclature spread and became the common term used for immigrants from the region, the vast majority of whom were Christian prior to the First World War. Amid the new internationalism, the geographic term 'Syrian' took on a sharpened cultural identity.

It was left to first-generation Christian intellectuals like Hitti to infuse the geographic expression Syrian with the concept of modern nationhood. As did Nitobé with Samurai identity and Molema with Bantu identity, Hitti used history to claim strong roots of ethnic and moral qualities, continuous over centuries to the present. This ethnic and regional identity was not dependent on Islam, as it was formed prior to the Arab invasions. The opening page of Hitti's book stated that Syrians were neither Turks nor Arabs. Nor were they to be confused with Assyrians from modern-day Iraq. They were, rather, an Aramaic-speaking people descended from the 'Phoenician-Canaanite tribes who entered Syria about 2500 BC,[46] the Aramean Israelite hordes who arrived about 1500 BC, and the Arabs who drifted, and still drift in, from the desert and who gradually pass from a nomadic to an agricultural state'.[47] Syria's uniqueness also lay in its religious innovation, as the birthplace of Judaism and of Christianity, and a home for Islam. 'Nowhere else has such human achievement been squeezed into so narrow a space as in Syria'.[48]

One of the main purposes of Hitti's history of Syrians was to defend them as a benign, yet often misunderstood, diaspora of people, who fit comfortably into the United States. Their roots in Phoenician maritime mercantile culture gave them legitimacy as a mobile people on the go, familiar with pluralistic situations. Syrians were not dangerous autocrats, nationalists or adherents of a foreign religion; rather, they were family-loving, sober, chaste and industrious people, and largely members of ancient Christian faiths. They held sacred the 'sanctity of womanhood and the inviolability of home life'. Syrians were not radicals, being interested neither in trade unionism nor in socialism.[49] Hitti stressed the apolitical nature of the Syrian people, whose lack of dangerous radical tendencies made them blend in easily. In short, Syrians had all the qualities of good Americans, including being easily assimilated through attendance at public schools.

One of the most interesting arguments put forward by Hitti in the early 1920s was the synergy he saw between Christianization and Americanization:

> Between the ideals of the Republic and the Christian religion there is an identity of spirit. Both insist on the sacredness and worth of the individual human being. Both agree that for the individual to seek self-fulfillment, it is necessary that he should forsake his exclusive, egocentric self and find a larger and freer life in the service of the whole of which he forms a part.[50]

Both Christianizing and Americanizing were psychological processes of opening narrow sectarian boundaries to a larger identity that allowed for individual choice. To Hitti, the unity behind a modern nation was not based so much on race, language or geography, as on the psychological 'desire on the part of a group of men to live their lives together, and to work together, with a common purpose toward a common end'.[51] The role of the church, the sense of Christian community, was to unify different peoples into a common national consciousness.

Philip Hitti's commitment to nation-building extended across the decades and ranged across the changing terrain of inter-war internationalism. His conviction that modern Christian community was a model for civic engagement fed his personal concern as an immigrant for both Syrian (Lebanese) nationalism and Americanism. At the same time, he used his scholarship to advocate for the historical unity of Arab culture as both Christian and Muslim. For the later Hitti, Arab linguistic and cultural unity became a large umbrella under which persons of diverse sects could find themselves at home. The tension between Hitti's early Syrian nationalism and his later pan-Arabism was similar to the creative tension felt by other Christian transnationalists between their own ethnic/cultural nations amid a larger modern world of hoped-for egalitarianism and diversity. Broadly Christian values were for Philip Hitti the foundation of modern civilization. Thus his legacy is debated even today. In an age of growing Islamic nationalism, internet sites question whether Hitti is a trustworthy guide. He defended Arab states against the founding of Israel, but he was not a Muslim. Although he was the father of Arabic studies, he was a Lebanese Christian who spent most of his career in the United States. The apparent contradictions in his life and career can partly be resolved when reflecting upon Hitti as a Christian transnationalist who argued that ethnic nationalism, within the internationalist framework, should be a force for building a democratic civil society.

Towards a Global Civil Society

The construction of nationalist narratives by Christian intellectuals roughly a century ago demonstrates how Protestant Christianity functioned as a source of innovation during the early-twentieth-century period of globalization and modernization. Examination of the lives and early writings of Christian transnationalists Inazô Nitobé, Silas Molema and Philip Hitti reveals how they capitalized on Protestant missionary networks as a generative source for constructing their own nationhood, within the bigger dream of a global new world order after the First World War.

The case studies of Nitobé, Molema and Hitti suggest that Christian transnationalists shared a community of global discourse. All three men were early adopters of modern ideas of individual rights that came through their education in mission schools and attendance at international mission and Christian student conferences. Their personal sponsorship by mission-minded mentors and friendship with global-minded Christians broadened their perspectives beyond their own local cultures. Their mastery of English and entrance into the world of Western scholarship enabled each man to bridge cultures – to advocate for Western liberal values vis-à-vis his own people, and to advocate for the integrity of his own culture vis-à-vis the West.

One fascinating parallel among the men's nationalist narratives was the argument that their own cultural traditions were, if interpreted properly, appropriate bases for the building of civil society. From the latent democracy of the Batswana, to the ethical values of the Japanese samurai, to the pluralistic tolerance of the Syrians, the interpretation of each culture stressed its fulfilment in peaceful or democratic civil society. Christian visions of human unity lay beneath the cultural bridging that characterized the careers and the writings of each man. Nitobé and Molema were quite explicit about the transformative power of Christianity for their own peoples. Hitti came from an ancient Christian tradition, but he harnessed Protestantism as a vehicle for modernizing it. Throughout his life he was proud of the label 'Orientalist' in the older missionary sense of someone who edited texts and appreciated and interpreted eastern traditions, and he disliked his fellow countryman Edward Said's negative redefinition of it.[52]

The boundary-crossing character of Christian transnationalism made later generations look upon it with suspicion. Japanese militarists felt that the Quaker Nitobé was not supportive enough of Japanese militarization, even as they used his writings to justify martial virtues. The ANC Youth League that embraced the Marxist struggle in the 1940s judged men of Molema's generation as too accommodating towards inter-racialism. Hitti's support for cultural and religiously pluralistic pan-Arabism means that thirty years after his death, the militant Islamic blogosphere accuses him of undercutting Islam and pandering to the West. All three have been accused of being idealistic liberals who failed to embrace revolutionary change.

Yet, in his day, each overcame nearly insurmountable obstacles to merge his local cultural context into a cosmopolitan intellectual framework. In the midst of profound social changes, each wrote a national narrative that functioned as an apologetic for the existence of his own people, as contributing members to the modern community of nations. As bridges between East and West, North and South, local past and global future, Christian transnationalists pointed towards a global civil society marked by democracy, peace, multi-culturalism and equality among all peoples.

Part 3 Religion, Progress and Innovation in the Contemporary World

11 Sin, Guilt and the Future of Progress

WILFRED M. McCLAY

Those of us living in the developed countries of the West find ourselves in the tightening grip of a paradox, one whose shape and character have so far largely eluded our awareness. It is a paradox manifested with particular vividness in the strange persistence of guilt as a psychological force in modern life. Guilt has become an ever more powerful and potent element in contemporary society, even as the language for it has faded from discourse, and the formal means of recognizing it as such, let alone obtaining absolution for it, have become ever more elusive.

This paradox has set up a condition in which the phenomenon of rising guilt becomes both a by-product of, and an obstacle to, the phenomenon of civilizational advance. What this means is that the very real achievements of the West are in danger of being countervailed and even negated by an ever-growing weight of guilt, which poisons our social relations and hinders our efforts to live happy and harmonious lives. Hence the need for a fuller understanding of the dynamics that ironically link progress and guilt, along with a tentative answer to the question of what can be done about their ominous linkage.

Why do I call it a 'strange' persistence of guilt? Simply because the modern evolution of guilt has not followed the script that had been written for it. Things were not supposed to happen this way. Prophets such as Friedrich Nietzsche were utterly confident that with the modern Western world's general abandonment of the metaphysical framework that previous generations had regarded as obligatory, the moral reflexes that went along with that framework would eventually wither and die along with them. Chief among these outmoded reflexes would be the experience of guilt, an obvious vestige of irrational fear promulgated by oppressive, life-denying institutions erected in the name and image of a punitive deity.

Indeed, Nietzsche had argued in *On the Genealogy of Morality* (1887), a *locus classicus* for the modern understanding of guilt, that the very idea of God, or of the gods, originated hand in hand with the feeling of indebtedness (the German *Schuld* – guilt – being the same as the word for debt, or plural *Schulden*).[1] The belief in God or gods arose in primitive societies, he speculated, out of dread of the ancestors and a feeling of indebtedness to them. This feeling of indebtedness grew and expanded its hold, in tandem with the expansion in the concept of God, to the point that when the Christian God offered itself as 'the maximal god yet achieved', it also brought about 'the greatest feeling of indebtedness on earth'.

But 'we have now started in the reverse direction', Nietzsche asserted. With the 'death' of God, meaning his general cultural unavailability, we should expect to see a consequent 'decline in the consciousness of human debt'. With the cultural triumph of atheism at hand, such a victory could also 'release humanity from this whole feeling of being indebted towards its beginnings, its *prima causa*'. Atheism would mean 'a second innocence', a kind of regaining of Eden with neither God nor Satan there to interfere with and otherwise corrupt the proceedings.[2]

It need hardly be said that nothing of the sort has yet happened; nor does there seem to be much prospect of its doing so in the near future. Indeed, a younger contemporary of Nietzsche's, Sigmund Freud, offered a dramatically different prophecy, one that seems to have been more fully borne out. In his grand and gloomy *Civilization and Its Discontents* (*Das Unbehagen in der Kultur*), Freud declared the tenacious sense of guilt to be 'the most important problem in the development of civilization'. In fact, he continued, it seems that 'the price we pay for our advance in civilization is a loss of happiness through the heightening of the sense of guilt'.[3]

Such guilt made for an elusive quarry, however. It was hard to identify and hard to understand, since it so frequently dwelt on an unconscious level, and could easily be mistaken for something else. It often appears to us, Freud argued, 'as a sort of *malaise* [*Unbehagen*], a dissatisfaction', for which people seek other explanations, whether external or internal. Guilt turns out to be crafty, something of a trickster, and a chameleon, capable of disguising itself, hiding out, changing its size and appearance, even its location. And yet it manages to persist and deepen, even despite all such protean transformations.

Whatever one finally thinks of Freud – and I count myself among the respectful unbelievers in a great many of his fanciful creations – this seems to me a very rich and insightful analysis, and a useful starting place for considering a subject largely neglected by historians: the steadily intensifying (though rarely visible) role played by guilt in determining the deep structure of our lives in the twentieth and twenty-first centuries. Such an analysis cannot, for obvious reasons, be reduced to quantifiable data, and it admittedly runs the risk of veering onto the circular path of the non-falsifiable, a Freudian *spécialité de la maison*.

Yet, it has a ring of truth to it, both as a diagnosis and as a symptom of the condition it diagnoses. It suggests that what W. H. Auden claimed for Freud over seventy years ago remains equally true today: even if he was 'wrong and at times absurd', he stands for 'a whole climate of opinion/under whom we conduct our different lives'.[4] By connecting the phenomenon of rising guilt to the phenomenon of civilizational advance, Freud was pointing out an unsuspected but inevitable by-product of progress itself, a by-product that has proved to be among the most dangerous enemies of progress. He was also posing a problem that will only become more pronounced in the generations to come, one for which his own invention of psychoanalysis was no solution, but which remains an issue of critical importance.

Thanks in part to Freud, we live in a therapeutic age. And nothing illustrates that fact more clearly than the striking ways in which the sources of guilt's power and the nature of its would-be antidotes have changed for us. Freud sought to relieve in his patients the worst mental burdens and pathologies imposed by their oppressive and hyperactive consciences, which he renamed their superegos, while deliberately refraining from rendering any judgement as to whether the guilty feelings ordained by those punitive superegos had any moral justification. In other words, he sought to release the patient from guilt's crushing hold by disarming and setting aside guilt's moral significance, and redesignating it as just another psychological phenomenon, whose proper functioning could be ascertained by its effects on one's more general well-being. He sought to 'demoralize' guilt by treating it as a strictly subjective and emotional matter. After all, since the superego was for him nothing more than the introjection of socially impermissible aggressive impulses, it was not exactly a product of sweet Kantian reasonableness, let alone the deposit of God's law written on the heart.

Health was the only remaining criterion for success or failure in therapy, and health was a functional category, not an ontological one. It was a matter of managing a tolerable equilibrium among the competing elements in the psyche – less a state of peaceable harmony, or the optimal flourishing of an organism realizing its *telos*, than the achievement of an uneasy truce or stalemate between intrinsic antagonists, a condition sufficiently pacified to allow for mature and rational behaviour, and perhaps even the occasional faint and fleeting glimpse of something resembling happiness. And the non-judgemental therapeutic world view whose seeds he planted has come into full flower in the mainstream sensibility of modern America, which, in turn, has profoundly affected the standing and meaning of the most venerable of all our moral transactions, and not merely matters of guilt.

Take, for example, the various ways in which *forgiveness* is now understood. Forgiveness is one of the chief antidotes to the forensic stigma of guilt, and as such has long been one of the golden words of our culture, with particularly deep roots in the Christian tradition, in which the capacity for forgiveness is seen as a central attribute of the deity itself. It glistens with a hundred admirable qualities, and its purity and moral prestige seem beyond challenge. To forgive others is taken to be a sign of a full and munificent and sacrificial heart, and, moreover, a heart that wisely recognizes the fleeting nature of life and the universal weakness of all human beings, very much including oneself. For Christians, the willingness to forgive has an even deeper source: the simple acknowledgement that we should be willing to extend to others, in a spirit of gratitude, the same forgiveness that God has graciously extended to us.

In the face of our shared human frailty, forgiveness expresses a kind of transcendent and unconditional regard for the humanity of the other, free of any admixture of interest or punitive anger or puffed-up self-righteousness. Yet, forgiveness rightly understood does not deny the reality of justice. It is not a mindless erasure of all standards. It cannot be understood as strictly an emotional or a subjective matter. To forgive, whether one is forgiving trespasses or debts, precisely means suspending all the just and legitimate claims we have against the other, in the name of the higher ground of divine love and human solidarity. That is why forgiveness, if properly understood, is both costly and rare. It affirms justice even as it suspends it.

Scan the self-help shelves of bookstores today, however, and you will find something very different. There is a lot of interest in forgiveness, but embodied in books bearing such titles as *Total Forgiveness*, and *Forgiveness: How to Make Peace With Your Past and Get On With Your Life*, and *Choosing Forgiveness: Your Journey to Freedom*, and *Forgiveness: The Greatest Healer of All*.[5] Dozens of websites devote themselves to the subject, including a website called 'Forgive for Good' by one Frederic Luskin, PhD., director and co-founder of the Stanford Forgiveness Project (and author of *Forgive for Good: A Proven Prescription for Health and Happiness*), who declares that 'forgiveness is for you and not for anyone else'.[6] Even the respected journalist Gregg Easterbrook has posted an article on the Beliefnet website entitled 'Forgiveness Is Good For Your Health'.[7]

I do not mean to disparage these writings in a blanket way or label them as utterly wrong. There is a great deal to be said for any effort to release the soul from captivity to hateful emotions and to encourage the more noble and expansive side of our natures. But the shift in emphasis is notable. In the new acceptation, forgiveness is all about the *forgiver* and his or her well-being. And the motivation sometimes borders on the suspect. As Luskin puts it, in arguing for the health-giving benefits of forgiving, 'Remember that a life well lived is your best revenge. ... Forgiveness is about personal power.'[8]

This puts a rather different cast on the idea that the forgiving heart 'rises above' that which wounded it. In seeing forgiveness as a locus of power, even a means of revenge, we have come a long way from Shakespeare's Portia, who spoke so memorably in *The Merchant of Venice* about the unstrained 'quality of mercy', which 'droppeth as the gentle rain from heaven' and blesses both 'him that gives and him that takes'.[9] And an even longer way from Christ's anguished cry from the cross: 'Forgive them, for they know not what they do.'[10] And perhaps even further yet from the most basic sense of forgiveness, the cancelling of a monetary debt or the pardoning of a criminal offence, in either case, a very conscious suspension of the entirely rightful demands of justice.

We still value forgiveness. But we are very confused about it, and in our confusion, we may have produced a situation in which forgiveness has, in fact, very nearly lost its moral weight as well as its moral meaning, and been translated into an act of random kindness whose chief value lies in the sense of release it brings us. Like the similar acts of confession or apology, and other transactions in the moral economy of sin and guilt, forgiveness is in danger of being debased into a kind of cheap grace, a waiving of standards entirely, standards without which such transactions have no meaning. Forgiveness only makes sense in the presence of a robust sense of justice. Without that, it is in real danger of being reduced to something passive and automatic and empty – a sanctimonious way of simply moving on.

There are similar problems with many of the key concepts relating to the understanding of guilt in our day – a transformation of them into floating signifiers without any clear connection to the objective moral antecedents to which they once corresponded. As I have tried to establish, this state of affairs arises partly out of the influential therapeutic view that the experience of guilt does not involve any genuine moral issues but rather the interplay of psychic forces that do not relate to anything morally consequential. One might call this position an assertion of the fundamental *unreality* of guilt.

But that is not the only thing that confuses us. There is another factor at work, one that can be called the *infinite extensibility of guilt*. This proceeds from a very different set of assumptions and is a surprising by-product of modernity's proudest achievement: its ever-growing capacity to comprehend and control the physical world.

In a world in which the web of relationships between causes and effects becomes ever better understood, in which the means of communication and transportation become ever more efficient and effective, and in which individuals become ever more powerful and effective agents, the range of our potential moral responsibility, and, therefore, of our potential guilt, expands to literally infinite proportions. In an ever-shrinking and ever more interconnected world, it is theoretically possible for every person to go anywhere that he or she wants to go and to be made literally, or at least virtually, present to any other person, in ways that promise to become ever more vivid and high-definition in the future. In such a world, where there are few intrinsic limits to what I can do, there is almost nothing for which I cannot be, in some way, held accountable. I can see pictures of a starving child in a remote corner of the world on my television and know for a fact that I could travel to that remote place and relieve that child's immediate suffering – if I cared to.[11] Whatever donation I make to a charitable organization, it is never as much as I could have given. I can never diminish my carbon footprint enough, or give to the poor enough, or support medical research enough or otherwise do the things that would render me morally blameless.

Colonialism, slavery, structural poverty, water pollution, deforestation – there's an endless list of items for which you and I can take the rap. The demands on an active conscience are literally as endless as an active imagination's ability to conjure them. And indeed, as those of us who teach young people often have occasion to observe, it may be precisely the most morally sensitive individuals who have the weakest common-sense defences against such overwhelming assaults on their over-receptive sensibilities – assaults that may amount to little more than propagandizing and manipulation, particularly when questions of environmental sin and consumerism are at stake.[12]

So excessive is this propensity for guilt, particularly in the most highly developed nations of the Western world, that the French writer Pascal Bruckner in a courageous and brilliant study, *The Tyranny of Guilt* [the French title is slightly different: *La tyrannie de la penitence*], has identified the problem as 'Western masochism'. The lingering presence of 'the old notion of original sin, the ancient poison of damnation', Bruckner argues, holds even secular philosophers and sociologists captive to its logic, so that 'the more [they] proclaim themselves to be agnostic, atheists, and free-thinkers, the more they take us back to the religious beliefs they are challenging'. As a consequence, most of modern Western thought is little more than a 'mechanical denunciation of the West', in which 'remorse has ceased to be connected with precise historical circumstances' and has, instead, become 'a dogma, a spiritual commodity, almost a form of currency', manifested in the non-stop 'duty of repentance'.[13]

But Bruckner's analysis is not fully adequate. The problem goes deeper than a mere question of alleged cultural masochism arising out of vestigial moral reflexes. It is, after all, not merely our pathologies that dispose us in this direction. The pathologies themselves have an anterior source in the very things of which we are most proud: our knowledge of the world, of its causes and effects and of our power to shape and alter those causes and effects. The problem is summed up with unforgettable concision in T. S. Eliot's famous question: 'After such knowledge, what forgiveness?'[14] Unless one takes the position that guilt is to be banished in toto from the human condition – a position that would require banishing all moral awareness from the human condition as well – one will have to face the fact that in a world of ever-growing knowledge, there is no easy way of deciding how much guilt is enough and how much is too much.

I have spoken of two factors – the 'therapeutic' unreality of guilt paired with the crushing hyper-abundance of it – that would seem to be diametrically opposed. How can something illusory also be something omnipresent? Are we guilty of nothing – or everything? In practice, however, the two tend to reinforce each other. The utter disproportionality of the latter leads to its being managed by means of the former. Not knowing how to cope with the monumental scale of our infinitely extensible guilt, we dissolve it into a Woody Allen joke. But what cannot be laughed entirely out of existence is a tenacious sense of moral incompleteness and a weighty sense of moral burden, a burden that all of us, except perhaps the sociopathic, share to a greater or lesser extent. And as Freud knew, this sense can hide for a very long time in the dark, moving the chess pieces around the board with its invisible hand.

This brings us back to my opening assertions. Notwithstanding all claims about our living in a post-Christian world devoid of censorious public morality, we, in fact, live in a world that carries around an enormous and growing burden of guilt and yearns – sometimes even demands – to be free of it. About this, Bruckner could not have been more right. And that burden is ever looking for an opportunity to discharge itself. Indeed, it is impossible to exaggerate how many of the deeds of individual men and women can be traced back to the powerful and inextinguishable need of human beings to feel morally justified, to feel themselves to be 'right with the world'. One would be right to expect that such a powerful need, nearly as powerful as the merely physical ones, would continue to find ways to manifest itself, even if it has to do so in odd and perverse ways.

A very curious story, full of significance for these matters, appeared in a 9 March 2008 *New York Times* op-ed column by Daniel Mendelsohn, aptly titled 'Stolen Suffering'.[15] Mendelsohn, a Bard College professor who has written a book about his family's experience of the Holocaust, tells of hearing the story of an orphaned Jewish girl who trekked 2,000 miles from Belgium to Ukraine, surviving the Warsaw ghetto, murdering a German officer and taking refuge in forests where she was protected by kindly wolves. The story was given wide circulation in a 1997 book, and its veracity was generally accepted. But it was recently discovered to be a complete fabrication, created by a Belgian Roman Catholic woman named Monique De Wael.[16]

Such a deception, Mendelsohn argued, is not an isolated event. It needs to be understood in the context of a growing number of 'phony memoirs', such as the notorious child-survivor Holocaust memoir *Fragments*, or *Love and Consequences*, the putative autobiography of a young mixed-race woman raised by a black foster mother in gang-infested Los Angeles.[17] These books were, as Mendelsohn says, 'a plagiarism of other people's trauma', written not, as they claim to be, 'by members of oppressed classes (the Jews during World War II, the impoverished African Americans of Los Angeles today), but by members of relatively safe or privileged classes'. Interestingly, too, he notes that the authors seemed to have an unusual degree of identification with their subjects – in fact, a degree of identification approaching the pathological. Ms De Wael for example declared, rather astonishingly, that 'the story is mine … not actually reality, but my reality, my way of surviving'.[18]

Mendelsohn draws pertinent conclusions from these stories, about how we have lost a sense of reality and have been taken in by the claims of 'empathy' in our culture. Perhaps even profounder inferences may be drawn from this strange phenomenon. There have always been stories about 'stolen valor', about those who inflate their standing with others by boasting of wartime exploits that never occurred. And it is not hard to understand the motive behind such fraudulence: the desire to be thought a hero, and identified with heroic virtues. But this is different.

What these authors are appropriating is *stolen suffering*, and the identification they are pursuing is an identification, not with certifiable heroes, but with certifiable victims. It is a particular and peculiar kind of identity theft. How does one account for it? What is motivating it? Why would comfortable and privileged people want to identify with victims? And why would their efforts appeal to a substantial reading public? Or, to pose the question even more generally, in a way that I think goes straight to the heart of our dilemma – how can one account for the rise of the extraordinary prestige of *victims*, as a category, in the contemporary world?

I contend the explanation is traceable back to the extraordinary weight of guilt in our time, the pervasive need to find innocence through moral absolution and to discharge one's moral burden somehow, and the fact that the conventional means of finding that absolution – or even of keeping the range of one's responsibility for one's sins within some kind of reasonable boundaries – are no longer generally available. Making a claim to the status of certified victim, or identification with victims, however, offers itself as a substitute means by which the moral burden of sin can be shifted, and one's innocence affirmed. Recognition of this substitution may operate with particular strength in certain individuals, such as these authors. But the strangeness of the phenomenon suggests a larger shift of sensibility, which represents a change in the moral economy of sin. And almost none of it has occurred consciously.

In the modern West, that moral economy remains deeply tied to the Judeo-Christian tradition. And the fundamental truth about sin in the Judeo-Christian tradition is that sin must be paid for or otherwise discharged. It can neither be dissolved by divine fiat, nor repressed, nor borne forever. In the Jewish moral world in which Christianity originated, and without which it would have been unthinkable, sin had always to be paid for, generally by the sacrificial shedding of blood. Its effects could never be ignored or willed away. Which is precisely why, in the Christian context, forgiveness of sin was specifically related to Jesus Christ's atoning sacrifice, his vicarious payment for all human sins, procured through his death on the cross, and made available freely to all who embraced him in faith. Forgiveness has an enormously high standing in the Christian faith. But it is grounded in fundamental theological and metaphysical beliefs about the person and work of Christ, which are in turn traceable back to Jewish notions of sin and how one pays for it. It makes little sense without them. Forgiveness, or expiation, or atonement – all of these concepts promising freedom from the weight of guilt, are grounded in a moral *transaction*, enacted within the universe of a moral *economy* of sin.

But now, in a society that retains its Judeo-Christian moral reflexes but has abandoned the corresponding metaphysics, the moral economy of sin is rendered inoperative and its transactions ineffectual. Can a credible substitute means of discharging the weight of sin be found? One workable way to be at peace with oneself and feel innocent and 'right with the world' is to identify oneself as a certifiable victim – or better yet, to identify oneself with victims. This is why the Mendelsohn story is so important and so profoundly indicative, even if it deals with a rather extreme case. It points towards the way in which identification with victims and the appropriation of victim status has become an irresistible moral attraction. It suggests the real possibility that claiming victim status is the sole sure means left of absolving oneself and securing one's sense of fundamental moral innocence. It explains the extraordinary moral prestige of victimhood in modern American and Western societies.

Why should that be so? The answer is simple. With moral responsibility comes inevitable moral guilt, for reasons already explained. So if one wishes to be accounted innocent, one must find a way to make the claim that one cannot be held morally responsible. This is precisely what the status of victimhood accomplishes. When one is a certifiable victim, one is released from moral responsibility, since a victim is someone who is, by definition, not responsible for his condition, but can point to another who is responsible.

But victimhood at its most potent not only promises release from responsibility, but also an ability to displace that responsibility onto others. As a victim, one can project onto another person, the victimizer or oppressor, any feelings of guilt one might harbour, and in projecting that guilt, lift it off one's own shoulders. The result is an astonishing reversal, in which the designated victimizer plays the role of the scapegoat, upon whose head the sin comes to rest, and who pays the price for it. By contrast, in appropriating the status of victim, or identifying oneself with victims, the victimized can experience a profound sense of moral release, of recovered innocence. It is no wonder that this should have become so common a gambit in our time, so effectively does it deal with the problem of guilt. At least individually and in the short run, though at the price of social pathologies, in the larger society that will likely prove unsustainable.

All of this creates enormous problems, especially in our public life, as we assess questions of social justice and group inequities, which are almost impossible to address without such morally charged categories coming into play. Those categories also come into play powerfully when the issues in question are ones relating to matters such as the historical guilt of nations and their culpability or innocence in the international sphere. Such questions are ubiquitous as never before.

In the words of political scientist Thomas U. Berger: 'We live in an age of apology and recrimination.'[19] He could not be more right. Guilt is everywhere around us, and its potential sources have only just begun to be plumbed, as our understanding of the buried past widens and deepens. Questions of guilt and innocence and absolution and expiation and atonement may have been largely banished from our intramural discussions of private morality, on broadly therapeutic grounds of their being 'too judgmental', but they proliferate everywhere else, even as the public authority of traditional religious institutions has declined. Nowhere is one more likely to find such concerns expressed than in matters relating to foreign affairs and international relations, particularly in the moral responsibilities attaching to the conduct and results of wars.

Gone is the amoral Hobbesian notion that war between nations is merely an expression of the state of nature. The assignment of responsibility for causing a war, the designation of war guilt, the assessing of punishments and reparations, the identification and prosecution of war crimes, the compensation of victims and so on – all of these are thought to be an essential part of settling a war's effects justly, and are part and parcel of the moral economy of guilt as it now operates on the national and international level. This surely represents moral progress of a high order.

But the standards have been so steadily and rapidly raised, and the demands of justice are at one and the same time very demanding, even insistent, and ever more difficult to satisfy, which creates a whole different set of problems.

Berger's study of post-war settlements engages precisely these issues by examining how governments in post-1945 Austria, Germany and Japan have dealt with the aftermath of the Second World War. How can such states come to terms in an honest way with their pasts, and achieve some appropriate measure of post-war justice without crippling themselves and remaining mired either in the past or in utter denial? Or by the same token, how can such states achieve internal and external reconciliation without choosing to forgive the unforgiveable, and thereby betray the call of justice for those who suffered from historical wrongs? How does one strike the proper balance between justice and reconciliation, not only as a moral question, but also as a political question? The record of these three countries suggests that this is, in fact, a very difficult balance to achieve. Justice is not always possible without incurring costs that most political societies are, as a practical matter, simply unable to pay.

The heightened moral awareness that we now bring to international affairs is something new in human history, stemming from the growing social and political pluralism of Western democracies and the unprecedented influence of universalized norms of human rights and justice, supported and buttressed by a robust array of international institutions and non-governmental organizations, ranging from the International Criminal Courts to Amnesty International.

In addition, as Berger shows, the larger narratives through which nations organize and relate their history, and through which they constitute their collective memory, are increasingly subject to monitoring and careful scrutiny by its constituent ethnic, linguistic, cultural and other subgroups, and are responsive to demands that those histories reflect the nation's past misdeeds and express contrition for them. Never has there been a keener and more widespread sense of particularized grievances at work throughout the world. And never have such grievances been able to count on receiving such a thorough and generally sympathetic hearing from scholars and the general public. Indeed, it is not an exaggeration to say that one could not begin to understand the workings of world politics today without taking into account a whole range of morally charged questions of guilt and innocence. Such factors are now as much a part of historical causation and explanation as are such standbys as climate, geography, access to natural resources, demographics and socio-economic organization.

There is no disputing the fact, then, that history itself – particularly in the form of 'coming to terms with' the wrongs of the past, and the search for historical justice – is becoming an ever more salient element in national and international politics. We see it in the concern for past abuses of indigenous peoples, colonized peoples, subordinated races and classes and the like, and we see it in the ways that nations relate their stories of war. Far from being buried, the past has become ever more alive with moral contestation.

All of this might seem, as I have said, to represent a form of moral progress, a progress just as certain in its way as the scientific and technological progress of modernity. Perhaps the most impressive example of sustained collective penitence in human history has come from the government and people of Germany, who have done much to atone for the sins of Nazism. But how much penitence is enough? And for how long? When can we say that the German people – who are, after all, an almost entirely different cast of characters from those who lived under the Nazis – are free and clear, have 'paid their debt' to the world and to the past, and are no longer under a cloud of suspicion? Who could possibly make that judgement? And will there come a day – indeed, has it already arrived? – when the Germans have had enough of the Sisyphean guilt, which, as it may seem to them, they have been forced by other sinful nations to bear, and begin to seek their redemption by other means? After all, our age's heightened universal moral standards apply universally, which is to say that they are like weapons on a pivot, which tomorrow may be whirled around and trained to devastating effect upon the very ones who are wielding them today. Those who stand in judgement can, and should, be held to the same standards they impose. Who are they to stand forever in judgement of the Germans, Japanese, whomever? The mirror of guilt points back at them too.

Who, after all, has ever been pure and wise enough to administer such post-war justice with impartiality and detachment, and impeccable moral credibility? What nation or entity at the close of the Second World War was sufficiently without sin to cast the decisive stone? The Nuremberg and Tokyo war crime trials were landmarks in the establishment of institutional entities administering and enforcing international law. But as Berger points out, they also were of questionable legality, reflecting the imposition of *ad hoc*, *ex post facto* laws administered by victors whose own hands were far from being entirely clean (consider the irony of Soviet judges sitting in judgement of crimes their own regime committed with impunity) – indeed, victors who might well have been made to stand trial themselves, had the tables been turned, for the firebombing of Dresden, or the bombing of Hiroshima and Nagasaki, or dozens of other massively destructive acts.[20]

Or consider whether the infamous Article 231 in the Treaty of Versailles, assigning guilt to Germany for the First World War was not, in the very attempt to impose the victor's just punishment on a defeated foe, itself committing an act of grave injustice, the indignity of which surely helped to bring on the catastrophes that would follow it. Certainly, the unintended consequences of that treaty are illustrative, like none other, of the high stakes involved in the work of post-war settlement and the need to bring to it a special kind of prudential wisdom. And perhaps one of the lessons it teaches is that the assignment of guilt, especially exclusive guilt, to one party or another may satisfy the most urgent claims of justice or the desire for retribution, but may fail utterly the needs of reconciliation and reconstruction. As Elazar Barkan bluntly argued in *The Guilt of Nations*: 'In forcing an admission of war guilt at Versailles, rather than healing, the victors instigated resentment that contributed to the rise of Fascism.'[21] The work of healing, like the work of the Red Cross, has a claim all its own, one that is not always compatible with the utmost pursuit of justice (although it probably cannot succeed in the complete absence of such a pursuit). Nor does such an effort to isolate and assign exclusive guilt meet the needs of a more capacious historical understanding, one that understands, as Herbert Butterfield once wrote, that history is 'a clash of wills out of which there emerges something that no man ever willed'.[22] And, he might have added, in which no party is entirely innocent.

So, once again, we find ourselves confronting the paradox of sin that cannot be adequately expiated. The deeply inscribed algorithm of sin demands some kind of atonement, but for some aspects of the past, there is no imaginable way of making that transaction without creating new sins of equivalent or greater dimension. What possible atonement can there be for, say, the institution of slavery? It is no wonder that the issue of reparations for slavery surfaces periodically, and probably always will, and yet, it is simply beyond the power of the present or the future to atone for the sins of the past in any effective way. Those of us who teach history and take seriously the moral formation of our students have to consider what the takeaway from this is likely to be. Do we really want to rest easy with the idea that a proper moral education needs to involve knowledge of our extensive individual and collective guilt – a guilt for which there is no imaginable atonement? That this is not a satisfactory state of affairs would seem obvious. What to do about it, particularly in a strictly secular context, is another matter.

As Berger's account suggests, therefore, there may be an intrinsic conflict in post-war settlements between the quest for justice and the path to reconciliation and healing. Sometimes the latter course may result in opportunistic decisions that come to seem genuinely shameful in retrospect. David W. Blight's magisterial *Race and Reunion* dealt with just such a conflict, in the wake of the American Civil War, arguing that the sectional reconciliation of North and South, though miraculous after such a bloody conflict, was achieved at the expense of the freed slaves, whose rightful demands for simple justice and dignity would have to wait a century before being fulfilled.[23] Such a conflict reminds one of Max Weber's famous distinction between the ethic of conviction (*Gesinnungsethik*), which provides the guidance and motivation for abolitionists and saints, and the ethic of responsibility (*Verantwortungsethik*), which circumscribes the prudential decisions of Abraham Lincoln and other wise political leaders. The tension between the two may be more intense, and more complex, than ever.

Berger sees repeated examples of what he calls 'the tragedy of transitional justice', a pattern of accommodation and half-measures that he finds to have been acted out to a greater or lesser extent in the Austrian, German and Japanese responses to their respective post-war rehabilitations.[24] It would be wrong to say that Berger looks upon such responses approvingly; he calls them 'tragic'. But he insists upon realism in appraising the facts and finds that in all such instances, the requirements of large-scale social change proved simply too daunting. The purging from power of old elites, for example, proved impractical in situations where their expertise and experience was indispensable for the rebuilding of shattered economies.

And national narratives might be allowed to fudge the truth for the sake of national self-respect, as in post-war Austria, which long described itself as Hitler's first victim, a half-truth at best, rather than his ardent accomplice, closer to the fact of the matter. (This state of affairs changed dramatically, with the revelations about former UN Secretary-General and Austrian President Kurt Waldheim's possible involvement in Nazi war crimes.) It seems that the sheer passage of a certain amount of time is required for societies to have the ability to engage fully with the moral implications of their own past, without being overwhelmed by guilt, or succumbing to the grip of a 'fight or flight' mechanism. In the meantime, 'transitional justice' is the best that can be reasonably expected, however morally unsatisfactory it may seem by universalistic standards.

All this sounds reasonable. But it is never reasonable to expect reasonableness in others, particularly when deep moral passions are engaged. One should expect that the act of repressing our awareness of those universalistic standards, and of our moral accountability to them, for the sake of a fragile 'transitional justice', will not be easy to sustain. 'Sooner or later', says Berger, 'we are all going to be sorry'.[25] He is right about that too.

Again, the question arises whether and to what extent all of this has to do with our living in a world that has increasingly, for the last century or so, been run according to secular premises, using a secular vocabulary operating within an 'immanent frame' – a mode of operation that requires us to be silent about, and forcibly repress, the very religious frameworks and vocabularies within which the dynamics of sin and guilt and atonement have hitherto been rendered intelligible. I use the term *repression* here with some irony, given its Freudian provenance. But even the irreligious Freud did not envision the 'liberation' of the human race from its religious illusions as an automatic and sufficient solution to its problems. He saw nothing resembling a solution. Indeed, it could well be the case, and paradoxically so, that just at the moment when we have become more keenly aware than ever of the wages of sin in the world, and more keenly anxious to address those sins, we find ourselves least able to describe them in those now-forbidden terms, let alone find moral release from their weight.

So we return again to the paradox that a sense of sin lingers, and even intensifies, at the very moment that the vocabulary for it wanes and even disappears entirely. But the loss of that vocabulary has not happened without resistance and ambivalence, and even apprehension. Even its critics are not always sanguine about its departure from the scene. Over four decades ago, the psychiatrist Karl Menninger published a spirited book with the provocative title, *Whatever Became of Sin?*, which clearly seemed to play on a more general apprehension about the passing of the older language.[26] Written in a lively and accessible style, it attracted considerable attention and quickly became a bestseller, endorsed by figures as widely different as Princeton theologian Seward Hitner and advice columnist Ann Landers. It was, especially, a favourite of clergymen who were grateful to see an eminent physician say anything affirmative about their increasingly embattled occupation.

It was also a rather confused book. But that was a part of its appeal. Its betwixt-and-between argument perfectly mirrored the larger confusions and perplexities of its historical moment. Menninger was insistent upon the triumph of the therapeutic while deeply worried over the unfortunate effects likely to arise out of that triumph.

On the one hand, he believed that it was an incalculably good thing that ancient religious strictures against so many harmless, all-too-human behaviours – such as masturbation, a subject to which he devoted a great deal of his attention and passion – were being set aside, and that those behaviours were no longer labelled sinful and were at last being dealt with in a sensible, humane and generous manner. Yet, after first establishing the primacy of the therapeutic and commanding ancient religious sensibilities to bow before the altar of disenchanted Midwestern scientific sensibleness, he went on to worry that things might go too far and that the loss of religious sanctions, as opposed to the mere loosening of them, would lead to the loss of all effectual moral judgement. The result was a strikingly bifurcated book.

For Menninger did not want the therapeutic revolution in human moral sensibility to lead to a disappearance of the very concept of sin itself. Such a loss, he thought, would be both regrettable and dangerous, precisely because the concept of sin was more accurate and more morally effective than the alternatives – more accurate in its account of the actual behaviour of human beings, and more effective in connecting that behaviour to concepts of guilt and individual moral accountability, both of which he believed were essential to living a responsible human life.

When treated as a wise and civilized way of understanding human behaviour rather than as a self-righteous bludgeon used to beat on others and keep them in subjection, sin had an essential place in the moral ecology of modern life. Psychiatry could not, he thought, ever replace the functions of the clergy entirely in such matters. Only religious figures had the ability to preach to the multitudes and provide a basis for spiritual renewal and moral leadership, and for resistance to our all-too-human propensities towards selfishness and violence. Menninger might have added that only religious systems have the ability to provide mechanisms for redemption and the absolution of sin, the transactional process that needs to operate hand in hand with the awareness of guilt.

Menninger had hold of a far greater and profounder theme than he realized, and a far greater one than he had the intellectual wherewithal to address effectively. But Andrew Delbanco's perceptive and insightful *The Death of Satan: How Americans Have Lost the Sense of Evil* (1995) put it much better, perhaps because the passage of twenty-two years had allowed what was incipient in Menninger's time to become settled custom in Delbanco's own:

> We live in the most brutal century in human history, but instead of stepping forward to take the credit, the devil has rendered himself invisible. The very notion of evil

seems to be incompatible with modern life, from which the ideas of transgression and the accountable self are fast receding. Yet despite the loss of old words and moral concepts – Satan, sin, evil – we cannot do without some conceptual means for thinking about the universal human experience of cruelty and pain. … If evil, with all its insidious complexity, escape the reach of our imagination, it will have established dominion over us all.[27]

So there are always going to be consequences attendant upon the disappearance of such words, and they may be hard to foresee, and hard to address. Consider one of the hottest theological disputes currently raging (at the time of this writing) within the Church of England, concerning proposed changes in the wording of the baptismal liturgy. These changes would have the effect of eliminating mention of 'Satan' and 'sin', and, instead, relying entirely on the concept of 'evil'. For example, parents and godparents at a christening service would no longer have to 'repent of the sins that separate us from God', or 'reject the Devil and all rebellion against God', and the clergy would no longer describe following Christ as 'dying to sin'. Instead, they would be asked only to 'reject evil in its many forms' and to reject 'all that destroys'. 'Repentance' becomes 'turning away'. The explicit goal is wider popular accessibility, by means of a liturgy that uses 'the language of East Enders', rather than that of Shakespeare, in services.[28]

Critics such as former Bishop of Rochester Michael Nazir-Ali are appalled. They are calling the new liturgy a dumbed-down resort to 'easily swallowed soundbites', and argue that the new service 'is more like a benediction from the Good Fairy than any church service'.[29] Be that as it may, the current Archbishop of Canterbury Justin Welby has taken a favourable view of the proposed reforms. And despite the fierce opposition they have engendered, they seem likely to survive at least as officially sanctioned alternatives to the current language.

Bishop of Wakefield Stephen Platten, who chairs the Anglican church's Liturgy Commission, has insisted that the proposed changes do not represent a 'dumbing down' of the liturgy, and, arguably, he is right. But that is because the changes are more serious than he acknowledges, not merely verbal simplifications but theological and moral innovations (as verbal simplifications nearly always turn out to be on closer examination). In forsaking the concept of sin and in the banishing of Satan, the revisions seek, instead, to offer a demythologized and abstract state of moral earnestness as the model for the Christian life. Such a grounding, or non-grounding, may well be more acceptable to the sensibilities of educated people living in a naturalistic, secular and therapeutic era. But it is one that sacrifices a great deal of the tradition's force and concreteness and severs a living and enduring connection to the most ancient and venerable of Christian rites in the process.

This particular story raises in a different form the question that Menninger's title proposed so arrestingly: what, in the new arrangements, can accomplish the moral and transactional work that was formerly done by the concept of sin? If, thanks to Nietzsche, the absence of belief in God is 'the notional condition of modern Western culture', as Paula Fredriksen argues in her study of the history of the concept of sin, doesn't that mean that the idea of sin is finished too?[30]

Yes, it would seem to mean just that. After all, sin cannot be understood apart from a larger context of ideas. So what happens when all the ideas that upheld sin in its earlier sense have ceased to be normatively embraced? Could not the answer to Menninger's question be something recalling the famous cry of Nietzsche's madman: 'Sin is dead and we have killed it!'?

Sin is a transgression against God, and without God how can there be such a thing as sin? So the theory would seem to dictate. But, as Fredriksen argues, that theory fails miserably to explain the world we actually inhabit. Sin lives on, it seems, even if we decline to name it as such. We live, she says, in the web of culture, and 'the biblical god ... seems to have taken up permanent residence in Western imagination ... so much so that even nonbelievers seem to know exactly who or what it is that they do not believe in'.[31] In fact, given the anger that so many non-believers evince towards this non-existent god, one might be tempted to speculate whether their unconscious cry is 'Lord, I do not believe; please strengthen my belief in your nonexistence!' Such was Nietzsche's genius in communicating how difficult an achievement a clean and unconditional atheism is – a conundrum that he captured by asserting, not that a God does not exist, but that He is dead. For the existence of the dead constitutes, for us, a presence as well as an absence. It is not so easy to wish that enduring presence away, particularly when there is the lingering sense that the presence was once something living and breathing.

What makes the situation dangerous for us, as Fredriksen rightly observes, is not only the fact that we have lost the ability to make conscious use of the concept of sin, but that we have also lost any semblance of a 'coherent idea of redemption' – the idea that has always been required to accompany the concept of sin in the past, and tame its harsh and punitive potential.[32] The presence of vast amounts of unacknowledged sin in a culture, a culture full to the brim with its own hubristic sense of world-conquering power and agency, but lacking any effectual means of achieving redemption for all the unacknowledged sin that accompanies such power – this is surely a moral crisis in the making, a kind of moral-transactional analogue to the debt crisis that threatens the world's fiscal and monetary health. The rituals of scapegoating, of public humiliation and shaming, of multiplying morally impermissible utterances and sentiments and punishing them with disproportionate severity are visibly not on the increase in our public life. They are not merely signs of intolerance or incivility, but signs of a deeper moral disorder, an *Unbehagen* that cannot be willed away.

Where then does that leave us? The progress of our scientific and technological knowledge in the West, and of the culture of mastery that has come along with it, has worked to displace the cultural centrality of Christianity and Judaism, the great historical religions of the West. But it has not been able to replace them. For all its achievements, modern science has left us with at least two overwhelmingly important, and insoluble, problems for the conduct of human life. First, modern science cannot instruct us in how to live, since it cannot provide us with the ordering ends according to which our human strivings should be oriented. In other words, it cannot tell us what we should live for, let alone what we should be willing to sacrifice for or die for.

And second, science cannot do anything to relieve the weight of guilt on our souls, a weight to which it has added appreciably, precisely by its rendering us able to be in control of, and therefore accountable for, more and more elements in our lives – responsibility being the fertile seedbed of guilt. That growing weight seeks opportunities for release, seeks transactional outlets, but finds no obvious or straightforward ones in the secular dispensation. Instead, more often than not we are left to flail about, seeking some semblance of absolution in an incoherent post-Christian moral economy that has not entirely abandoned the concept of sin, but lacks the transactional power of absolution or expiation without which no moral system can be bearable.

So what is to be done? One conclusion seems to me unavoidable. Those who have viewed the obliteration of religion, and particularly of Judeo-Christian metaphysics, as the modern age's great and signal act of human liberation need to reconsider their dogmatic assurance on that point. Indeed, the persistent problem of guilt may open up an entirely different basis for reconsidering the enduring claims of religion. Perhaps human progress cannot be sustained without religion, or something like it, and specifically without something very like the moral economy of sin and absolution that has hitherto been secured by the religious traditions of the West.

Such an argument would have little to do with conventional theological apologetics. Instead, it would draw from empirical realities regarding the social and psychological makeup of advanced Western societies. And it would fully face the fact that, without the support of religious beliefs and institutions, one may have no choice but to accept the dismal prospect envisioned by Freud, in which the advance of human civilization brings, not happiness, but an ever-mounting tide of unassuaged guilt, ever in search of novel and ineffective, and ultimately bizarre, ways to discharge itself. Such an advance will steadily diminish the human prospect, and little by little render it less and less sustainable. It will smother the energies of innovation that have made the West what it is and will fatally undermine the spirited confidence needed to uphold the very possibility of progress itself. It must therefore be countered. But to be countered, it must first be better understood.

12 Religious Innovation and Economic Empowerment in India: An Empirical Exploration

REBECCA SAMUEL SHAH[1]

Max Weber's *Protestant Ethic and the Spirit of Capitalism* is associated with the claim that ascetic Calvinism inadvertently brought into being the modern capitalist system of rationalized and organized profit seeking. While some see Weber as offering a triumphant story of the power of Protestant faith to foster economic betterment, many ignore the fact that his *Protestant Ethic* concludes on a profoundly pessimistic note concerning the prospects for faith in the modern world. In bringing about the capitalist system, Weber concludes, the world-transforming faith of Calvinist Christianity acted in effect as its own gravedigger. For once the capitalist system of organized profit seeking emerged from the cosmos and ethos of Calvinism – once the economic train left the religious station, as it were – it became an unstoppable engine of comprehensive societal transformation, including cultural, political and social, as well as religious change. Though Calvinism birthed capitalism, the capitalist system turned the grand cosmos of Calvinism into the 'iron cage' of modernity – a disenchanted world with little room for Calvinist faith, or any ethical or religious spirit whatsoever. One cannot serve both God and mammon, Weber surmises, and it is clear that the entire system of modern life is structured to serve one and not the other.[2]

But is it true? Much rides on the question. If it is true, the implications for our understanding of modernization, secularization and religion are profound. As Alasdair MacIntyre has suggested, if the capitalist system stifles faith or squeezes it into the margins of modern life, then whatever 'religion' might remain has nothing of the public, authoritative and comprehensively transformative ambition characteristic of premodern Christianity. No religious revival, no recovery of religious *élan*, can change this intrinsically and profoundly constraining structural context.[3] Moreover, if the modern capitalist system, in effect, becomes a force that acts on religion but cannot be acted on by it, then it becomes an impenetrable and unstoppable driver of modernization and secularization, just as Max Weber, the young Peter Berger, Bryan Wilson, Steve Bruce and other sociologists of religion have insisted.[4] If religion appears to penetrate public debate and political forums and contests such as electoral campaigns but cannot penetrate and influence the economic sphere to any appreciable degree, then claims of a religious resurgence or comeback in the world are doomed to be superficial. At worst, if economic change is the core driver of modernization and secularization, and economic dynamics remain essentially unaffected by religious forces, then, in the long run, secularization remains as valid and predictive an account of religion's ultimate place in the modern world as ever.

On the other hand, is it possible that religion remains powerful enough to re-enchant the iron cage of capitalism? Is it possible that people of vital religious faith can pursue economic activity for purposes other than economic accumulation, narrow self-interest and personal gain? In the context of modernity, can people of vital religious faith operate according to a different business ethic, one that is meaningfully oriented to religious goals and principles such as charity, justice, self-denial, thrift and stewardship? If religious faith can be a driver of modern economic enterprise rather than merely its hapless victim, then it has a fighting chance of remaining a vital force and engine of change and innovation in the modern world.

Economics and religion have been pitted against each other for most of the twentieth century, in large part as a result of the work of intellectuals like Marx, Weber and Durkheim. These thinkers elevated the role of economics in almost all aspects of our everyday life. Economics influences when we get married, how many children we have, how to think about what home to buy and where to send our children to school.

In part because economic considerations undeniably permeate many non-economic activities and relationships, economics as a discipline has become imperialistic. It assumes its analytical categories of cost, preferences, employment and opportunities are universally applicable across all social sectors of society. Economists attempt to emulate the style and elegance of physics in order to discover the laws of economics. It is no surprise, therefore, that most economists assume that people will follow the law of utility maximization and choose the best possible combination of goods and services to enable them to achieve the most satisfaction regardless of non-economic factors or beliefs. Most of these economists also believe that since profit maximization is the guiding principle underlying most firms, most entrepreneurs will undertake actions and make decisions that maximize profits at any cost.[5]

Given the tendency of people and firms to optimize their own utility and profit, it is hard for us to imagine any other way to understand human behaviour. We have become accustomed to regarding the pursuit of self-interest and individual gain as an indispensable part of human activity. The origins of this prevailing form of self-interest and individualism that we now take for granted can be understood by looking at the changing interpretation of *calling* since Martin Luther first took the word previously used only in the priestly or monastic context and applied it to all worldly duties. In addition, Calvin's teachings on predestination, grace and salvation introduced qualities of self-control and discipline once required of a medieval monk into the lives of every Christian in the world. But such qualities of self-control and discipline were realized most fully only insofar as the individual pursued his God-given calling.[6]

From seeing callings as the tasks required by God to 'establish the heavenly reign of God upon earth', the concept was reduced to performing particular jobs and activities. And a division of labour based on social order was born. With the innovation of identifying callings as employment and activities, Christians were strongly urged to do *their own* work and not to interfere with another's business. The tendency to value individual interest as against collective activity and even charity to one's neighbours slowly began to gain a foothold in Western society. As economic historian R. H. Tawney suggested, an individual pursuit of salvation made more sense to those for whom personal prosperity was attainable.[7] Thus, the earlier vision of a group of Christians working together to build the church and establish a heavenly kingdom on earth was transformed into one in which individuals worked diligently, yet independently, to secure their own separate salvation.

With a focus on employment and gainful activity came a revolution in the attitude towards wealth and riches. There was an increasing openness to wealth and the accumulation of riches. Riches became a positive good. And once riches and wealth accumulation had become an acceptable and even expected fruit of one's labours, it was not long before a separation between religion and calling took place. A Christian was advised '*not only* [to] *mind heaven but also his calling*'. A person's calling was now seen as something distinct from direct, religious service to God. People were told to labour in their 'secular' callings for six days of the week and to dedicate the seventh day to the Lord.

Weber was saddened by the end of the glorious age when faith and capitalism were so intimately intertwined in search of the Kingdom of God. Thereafter, 'the religious roots died out slowly, giving way to utilitarian worldliness'.[8] Weber detested the economic culture and creeping materialism that took the place of true Christian calling and he remained deeply pessimistic because he was persuaded that modernity had made religious and ethical lives impossible. 'Since asceticism undertook to remodel the world and to work out its ideals in the world, material goods have gained an increasing and finally an inexorable power over the lives of men as at no previous period in history'.[9]

Given Weber's 'melancholy of modernity'[10] and the apparent triumph of modern-day capitalism in shaping our lives and the ways in which we think about our lives, it is nearly impossible to believe that religious faith could re-enchant the iron cage and provide a new conception of enterprise and enable the entrepreneurs to seek innovative ways of understanding success and creating value.

If, like Weber, we believe that the behaviour acquired from beliefs endogenous to Protestantism gave rise to modern capitalism, should we not, then, be open to studying the religious behaviour of Christian entrepreneurs today to determine whether their religious faith has been able to unlock the door of the iron cage and give them the freedom to live differently? Can the same religious faith that provided the disciplined and rational workforce necessary for modern capitalism also work today to shape the fundamental values of Christian entrepreneurs?

On the basis of field research in India,[11] I contend that certain Christian theologies, churches, networks, moral frameworks and practices make it possible – at least under some conditions – for poor micro-entrepreneurs to break out of Weber's iron cage of capitalist modernity and make religious faith a powerful source of economic and social innovation. To support this claim, I will provide an analytical overview of some of the different mechanisms whereby religion can promote economic betterment among the very poor and marginalized Dalits (outcastes) in India. Furthermore, I hypothesize that the faith of some poor micro-entrepreneurs leads them to generate innovative practices that yield significant benefits for themselves and their families. Certain forms of Christian faith can sometimes be an engine of palpable economic innovation and progress today.

Dalits and Outcastes

A promising approach to understanding the economic and social innovations that Christianity can generate is observing what happens when individuals convert to Christianity in entirely non-Christian contexts such as India. One such dramatic and under-studied class of cases comes from Dalit (outcaste) communities. 'Dalit' literally means 'broken', and it is used to describe people who are traditionally regarded as 'untouchable' or 'outcaste' according to the Hindu caste system. Dalit status is a matter of irrevocable, hereditary membership, conferred by birth. Dalits are often employed in jobs that are seen as ritually polluted and unclean, such as road sweeping, tanning, cleaning and rag picking.

In 1955, India passed a stringent anti-discrimination law, the Untouchability Act, to forbid discrimination against Dalits. A recent report revealed, however, that untouchability in both public and private spheres remains widespread, especially with respect to religious discrimination. On the basis of a four-year study of 1,655 villages in Gujarat, researchers found that discrimination was almost universal. Dalits were restricted from entering the village temple, touching religious articles that were in use for worship by Non-Dalits and participating in religious festivals. In nine out of the ten measures of religious restriction, the probability that Dalits would be discriminated was 90 per cent or greater. Clearly, religious discrimination against Dalits is 'incredibly widespread'.[12]

Although there is little doubt that the caste system and the consequent outcaste status are derived from Hinduism, it is well known and firmly established that Muslim and Christian Dalits are treated as socially distinct and utterly inferior communities by their own co-religionists.[13] Caste rules and customs perpetuated by the upper-caste groups ensure that social contact with outcastes is minimized. In some cases, certain upper-caste Christians maintain their social distance from Dalit Christians by prohibiting inter-caste marriages and imposing severe sanctions on those who violate this prohibition. Segregation extends to the religious sphere where upper-caste Christians tend to favour the mainstream churches such as the Church of South India (CSI), Church of North India (CNI), the Lutheran Church and the Marthoma Syrian Church. While the presence of a central hierarchy in the Roman Catholic Church in India, which often deliberately flouts caste prejudice in episcopal appointments, helps to reduce caste stratification in the Church's leadership, Dalit Catholics are more likely to attend Mass at different times than upper-caste and middle-class non-Dalit Catholics.

Mass Conversion Movements in India from 1870 to 1933

An ambitious mass movement survey conducted by Methodist missionary Jarrell Wascom Pickett in collaboration with the Institute of Social and Religious Research between 1930 and 1931 revealed that most Dalits interviewed had converted to Christianity for its intrinsic impact on their dignity, identity and overall well-being. They did not generally convert for short-term material gain, as many Hindu critics of conversion at the time (including Mahatma Gandhi) claimed, and as many Christian missionaries feared. Frequently denied a dignified status, Dalits embraced Christianity because they believed it would improve the overall quality of their lives. Pickett and his colleagues found that Dalit converts often experienced a higher quality of life that included better health, education and material prosperity, but material benefit was not generally the sole or primary motive for conversion *ex ante*. In most cases, rather, the motive lay in the Dalit belief that Christianity embodied a life of dignity and hope for a future free of degradation and subservience. Pickett's survey of converts indicated that many Dalits hoped that conversion would offer them an identity rooted in a personal faith in a loving God rather than in an identity dependent on the recognition of higher castes. In the words of one of the converts: 'I wanted to become a Christian so I could be a man. None of us was a man. We were dogs. Only Jesus could make men out of us.'[14]

At the same time, though most interviewees did not appear to have converted to Christianity for the sake of short-term material advantages, Pickett's study also suggested that conversion to Christianity yielded wide-ranging developmental benefits. For example, the survey found a strong positive correlation between the length of time parents had professed to be Christian and the attainment of literacy by their children. In Guntur, located in present-day Andhra Pradesh, 73 per cent of children whose parents were born in Christian homes were literate, compared to a 35 per cent literacy rate for children born in homes in which the parents converted only after the eldest child had entered school (at around age six).

Religious Innovation and Economic Empowerment among the Dalits in Twenty-first-Century India

Whatever the influences that shaped the past, the question remains: How conducive is religion to economic and social innovation today when conditions are different? Findings from a number of recent projects I have directed that investigate the role of religion in the economic and social outcomes of very poor Dalit micro-entrepreneurs from various faith traditions in Bangalore, India, shed light on this question. Indeed, they demonstrate to a degree the continuity of the positive effect of religion on this otherwise marginal class of people from the time of the mass conversion movements in 1870 to present-day India.

What made this research even more significant for understanding the effects of religion on the economic and social outcomes of the poor was that I unexpectedly discovered that 23 per cent of our Indian sample – seventy out of three hundred women – had identified themselves as 'converts'. These women were all converts from Hinduism and belonged to independent Pentecostal churches.

As part of the research, I studied the relationship between religious practices, beliefs and choices of the poor and the extent to which religion can promote the economic well-being of the poor by restraining consumption and enhancing savings, investing in future-oriented behaviours and connecting people with religious networks that build family, community and hope for the future. In particular, I hypothesized that under certain conditions, some forms of religious faith, practices and identities are associated with greater self-control, thrift, a sense of agency and empowerment, and participation in supportive religious networks and communities.

Methodology

Divya Shanthi Christian Community Association, (DSCA) is one of the largest and most well-established community development organizations working in northern Bangalore. Its micro-finance programme began in 1999 and has grown from about a hundred to some 4,000 clients in 2013. DSCA serves and employs people from all faith backgrounds. The basic DSCA micro-finance product is a 'canonical' group loan. *Sangams* or self-help groups of ten to fifteen women are formed, and the women are jointly responsible for the loans of their group. Each group has a president who serves as the liaison with Divya Shanthi and who works with a DSCA social worker to organize group meetings and to collect the loan repayments. Divya Shanthi and its partner organization, The Bridge Foundation, provide loans to individual *sangam* members. These loans, ranging from 1,000 to 25,000 rupees, must be repaid in fifty weeks, and DSCA charges an interest rate of 12 per cent. Loans that are taken from the collective savings of the *sangam* group members are charged at a 2 per cent interest rate and must be paid back in twelve weeks. If all the group members repay their loans on time, the group becomes eligible for larger additional loans.

I interviewed 300 female microcredit clients from the service area of DSCA, which is situated in a roughly 1.5-kilometre-square area and includes Bagalur, Lingarajapuram and Williams Town, along with a few surrounding urban settlements within a mile of the main road. The areas were selected because of the established presence of DSCA in these urban poor settlements for the past forty years. Because of the organization's long and trusted presence, I have interviewed numerous people connected to the organization about earnings, family life, and faith and faith practices in more than ten years of research without raising eyebrows – something that is not a given, partly because Bangalore's slums are not without sectarian tensions. These areas were also selected because they are not makeshift camps or communities but permanent settlements with houses constructed of bricks and mortar and with established water and electricity supplies. Eligibility to participate in the study was determined using the following criteria: the respondents must (a) be female; (b) be aged between eighteen and fifty-nine; (c) have resided in the same dwelling for at least two years; (d) have a valid form of identification and proof of residence such as a ration card, voter card or electricity bill – this is a mandatory requirement to be part of the DSCA loan programme; (e) be the main breadwinners of the family; and (f) have children and/or grandchildren living with them.

Women make up an overwhelming majority (98 per cent) of the microcredit clients at DSCA. Female self-help groups have higher repayment rates than male ones. On the basis of previous research for Boston University's Charismatic Modernity project, I also found that female clients are more willing to talk openly about their faith and their family than their male counterparts. This is in part due to a prevailing cultural pattern in southern India: men are often less involved in the religious affairs of a household and leave religious responsibilities to the women of the home. Also, men are less likely to talk openly about family issues because they are often less involved in the daily running of the household and their children's lives. Furthermore, a significant number of female clients in our sample are single – because they are either informally or formally separated/divorced from their husbands, or because they are widows.

I excluded from the research those groups that do not exhibit a mix of religious backgrounds. In fact, it is DSCA policy that a *sangam* may not be formed solely on the basis of faith (i.e. Christian-only or Hindu-only groups) or on the basis of caste. Urban and semi-urban micro-entrepreneurs in places such as Bangalore are ideally situated to provide a wide variation in the content and intensity of religious beliefs, traditions, identities and practices. I focused on studying micro-entrepreneurs in Bangalore city because unlike the rural poor, urban poor populations are highly diverse ethnically, linguistically and religiously. At the same time, all of our subjects from various religious traditions were comparable because they are all participants in micro-enterprise programmes. The project to some extent served as a quasi-experimental study of how people from very different religious backgrounds respond to the same treatment of microcredit.

The findings of our study and the unexpected initial results from our subsample of converts constitute a compelling 'plausibility probe'. Because these studies were based on observational data, I could not control for a variety of confounding variables. Our three waves of interviews over three years, however, demonstrated patterns in the change in behaviour, savings and consumption that make it plausible to believe that the religious practices, attitudes and identities I explored may well have a positive impact on the economic well-being of poor micro-entrepreneurs. Furthermore, they demonstrate that it is plausible to believe that under some conditions religion can be instrumental in empowering the poor to achieve some social and economic betterment.

Tithing: A Religious Tradition as a Source of Innovation

What we know about poverty is that it depresses, discourages and debilitates the poor to the extent that they are unable to make rational choices about their future.

In 1955, Robert Strotz was the first economist to study what became known as 'dynamically inconsistent' consumption patterns – inconsistent because a person's actual behaviour will most likely not be consistent with his optimal behaviour. Optimal behaviour is choosing a present plan of consumption and spending that will maximize one's future utility. In many cases, however, instead of seeking to make a greater investment in the present to gain a greater reward in the future, people choose to 'precommit' their future to gain a greater reward in the present. The poor may be particularly prone – and vulnerable – to 'dynamically inconsistent' consumption patterns.[15]

Recent research also suggests that poverty psychologically debilitates the poor to the point of making them qualitatively less able to make rational choices about their future. Poverty is emotionally and mentally depleting. Economists Sendhil Mullainathan and Eldar Shafir contend that the poor avoid thinking about the future or investing in practices and behaviours that might yield long-term benefits because they lack the cognitive resources or mental energy to gather and process information. They also maintain that the poor lack the willpower or emotional energy to exercise self-control and make responsible choices about their lives and livelihoods.[16] Confirming Mullainathan and Shafir's insights, Douglas Bernheim, Debraj Ray and Sevin Yeltekin argue that poverty damages self-control and limits the capacity of the poor to invest in their future.[17]

If this is true, then the chain of causality is viciously circular: poverty suppresses self-control and rational planning, which in turn begets greater poverty. That this vicious circle might be operating is evident in the research of MIT economists Abhijit Banerjee and Esther Duflo who studied consumption and income generation patterns of the poor – defined as those living on less than $1 a day – in thirteen countries. In India, for example, an average of 5 per cent of a poor person's income went towards the purchase of non-food items (e.g. alcohol and tobacco) and snacks, and 14 per cent of the median family income went towards spending on festivals and family events.[18] Psychologically limited in their ability to save and spend responsibly, the poor become poorer, which further undermines their ability to save and spend responsibly.

While a vicious cycle of fear, hopelessness and lack of self-control can lead to unproductive behaviour and lock the poor into a poverty trap, development economist Duflo suggests that hope might help launch the poor out of poverty and into more future-oriented patterns of expenditure and saving. In her 2012 Tanner Lecture on Human Values, she describes how millions of poor micro-entrepreneurs have been lifted out of poverty in Bangladesh. Duflo does not attribute this exclusively or even primarily to the mechanism of micro-enterprise development (MED) programmes themselves. After all, recent research and the mixed experience of MED in a number of countries suggest that MED organizations can even inadvertently exacerbate cycles of over-consumption and over-indebtedness among the poor by making it possible for MED clients to assume more and more loans – often at exceedingly high interest rates – in an increasingly futile effort to escape debt. Instead, Duflo believes that the presence or absence of hope may have a direct and decisive impact on the ability of the poor to make effective and responsible decisions and investments concerning their future. What she implies is that the injection of credit may help lift poor entrepreneurs out of poverty, and that such assistance in and of itself can help foster a sense of hope and optimism. Duflo also implies, however, that unless the poor overcome a scarcity mentality and acquire a sense of hope for the future, such external assistance may not be sufficient.[19]

Our study explored how some beliefs and practices embedded in the Christian tradition and some of its biblical sources, such as tithing and fasting, may help drive economic progress and innovation today. On the basis of our findings, I suggest that the poor who commit a significant proportion of their income 'to God' (i.e. poor entrepreneurs who tithe on a regular basis) exhibit a form of religiously motivated hope. Hope, in particular, religiously motivated hope, can help the poor alleviate their debilitating anxiety and a mentality of scarcity, invest in the future and move out of poverty. By hope, I do not mean an inchoate optimism or feeling that things might turn out well. Moreover, hope is not merely imagining a future that one aspires to be a part of, but which one cannot do anything to realize. I suggest that religiously motivated hope rests on a profound and active belief in the power of the transcendent to influence and empower one's life in the here and now. Although the poor are economically impoverished, I know from ample survey data, as well as our own fieldwork, that they are rich in the kinds of religious beliefs that might ground a concrete sense of hope about the future.[20]

All respondents in our survey were asked to state whether they gave money regularly or intermittently. A 'regular' giver was defined as someone who tithed or engaged in voluntary religious giving at regular intervals once a week, once a month, twice a year or once a year. An 'intermittent' giver was defined as someone who felt no obligation to give money at regular intervals and voluntarily contributed money only if she was able to do so. Nearly eight out of ten converts to Christianity engaged in regular voluntary religious contributions. These contributions were made as soon as they received their monthly wage or every Sunday during church. In most cases, converts reported tithing 10 per cent of their income. The 45 per cent of Hindu women who reported giving financial contributions on a regular basis did not have a set amount of money that they contributed.

According to our data, over 50 per cent of converts to certain forms of indigenous Pentecostal Christianity[21] reported giving voluntary weekly financial contributions to their churches. Not only that, in most cases converts reported giving 10 per cent of their income. In contrast, on average only 10 per cent of Hindu women reported giving weekly financial contributions to their temple or religious community, and most of these women did not give a fixed or significant amount. Approximately 6 per cent of Catholics reported giving voluntary weekly contributions to their religious communities (a majority of 53 per cent of Catholics reported paying their fixed monthly subscription to their local parish church in lieu of tithes or voluntary contributions). None of the Muslim women reported that they gave on a weekly basis (consistent with the Islamic tradition of the yearly *zakat*). Most interviewed converts also had written records of their weekly and monthly financial contributions.

It may seem counter-intuitive that some of the poor women entrepreneurs in our study follow the restrictive practices of tithing and fasting. An overwhelming majority of converts to Christianity (94 per cent) in our study participated in fasting and prayer

Table 12.1 Percentage of Micro-Entrepreneurs Who Tithe/Give *Zakat* According to Frequency and Religious Tradition for 2011, 2012 and 2013

2011						
	Once a week	Once a month	Once a year	Twice a year	Do not give money	Sample size (n)
Hindu	7	11	23	4	55	108
Muslim (*zakat*)	5	12	60	10	12	58
Catholic	8	59	10	0	24	51
Mainline Protestant	33	50	0	0	17	12
Convert	53	43	0	1	3	71

2012						
	Once a week	Once a month	Once a year	Twice a year	Do not give money	Sample size (n)
Hindu	15	9	25	10	41	108
Muslim (*zakat*)	0	2	62	26	10	58
Catholic	6	59	14	8	14	51
Mainline Protestant	25	50	0	0	25	12
Convert	52	35	7	0	6	71

2013						
	Once a week	Once a month	Once a year	Twice a year	Do not give money	Sample size (n)
Hindu	8	6	41	0	45	108
Muslim (*zakat*)	0	0	67	26	7	58
Catholic	22	41	24	0	14	51
Mainline Protestant	17	50	8	0	25	12
Convert	55	34	10	0	1	71

Source: India Data collected for the Templeton Foundation-funded Tithing and Thrift among the Enterprising Poor Project (2013) and the Holy Avarice Study (2013).

meetings at least once a month. In some ways, the pressures on faith are far more acute for the poor than for those with ample resources. For the poor entrepreneurs who are struggling to provide for their families month to month, the pressure to make any profit at any cost can even be greater and leave even less room for the influence of religious faith. No doubt, it would have been easier for the women to save the money they tithed to purchase food or medicines or to spend more time with their families than in prayer meetings.

Over the last few decades, there has been an increasing turn among major economists towards highlighting the inconsistency between deterministic models of rational choice and human behaviour. Nobel Prize-winning economist Amartya Sen, for example, has suggested that any theory of welfare must be based on more than individual utilities and must assume a broader view of the dimensions of human well-being. In his 1979 Tanner Lecture, Sen maintains that the assessment of human welfare must go beyond the assessment of utility, the fulfilment of basic needs and the provision of income. It must take into account the intrinsic value and importance of individual choice and freedom. In short, human development is coextensive with the expansion of 'human capabilities'. This expansion enables people to enjoy and pursue what they value and have reason to value.[22]

Remarkably, Sen's approach was in some respects anticipated by important ideas in Catholic social thought, which were powerfully and influentially re-articulated during and immediately after the Second Vatican Council in the 1960s. Catholic social teaching had suggested strong links between freedom and development. According to *Gaudium et Spes* ('Joy and Hope'):

> Human freedom is often crippled when a man encounters extreme poverty, just as it withers when he indulges in too many of life's comforts and imprisons himself in a kind of splendid isolation. Freedom acquires new strength, by contrast, when a man consents to the unavoidable requirements of social life, takes on the manifold demands of human partnership, and commits himself to the service of the human community.[23]

And in the 1967 papal encyclical *Populorum Progressio* ('On the Development of Peoples'), Pope Paul VI explicitly states that 'man is truly human only if he is the master of his own actions and the judge of their worth, only if he is the architect of his own progress'.[24]

Unfortunately, Sen's revolutionary understanding of the importance and value of freedom is limited by its exclusive focus on individuals. While Sen redirected the goal of human development and poverty reduction away from income generation alone to understanding development in terms of the freedoms we have to enjoy 'valuable beings and doings',[25] his approach anchors development primarily in enhancing the substantive freedoms of individuals. Other-oriented concerns are important only insofar as they affect the quality of an individual's own life. As moral philosopher Martha Nussbaum insists, the goal of development is primarily to serve the autonomy or capabilities of the individual as an end in himself or herself. Each person 'has just one life to live, not more than one', she argues. And 'the food on A's plate does not magically nourish the stomach of B'.[26]

In our research, it was striking and significant that the women who tithed and fasted on a regular basis went beyond possessive individualism and merely enhancing their own individual material well-being and autonomy. By participating in the life of the community around them through religiously motivated giving and meeting together for prayer and fasting, the women enhance their own spiritual life as well serve the needs of others. An individual becomes more herself because of her connection and mutual relationships with the community she serves. Serving others through the sacrificial giving of tithes or praying for one's neighbours during healing meetings enhances the well-being of each person and the community as a whole. The religious practices of tithing and fasting in this context offer the convert an opportunity to fulfil a deep yearning for a spirituality that binds her to the transcendent as well as to a community that treats her with dignity, equality and respect.

I found that women who converted to Christianity and who tithed most frequently – once a week – were the most likely to accumulate durable assets. Our data for home ownership in the slum revealed that regular tithers were more likely than irregular or intermittent tithers to own a home. In 2013, 60 per cent of the regular tithers in our sample owned a home. This is significant because home ownership can make a decisive difference in the present and future economic well-being of the poor.

Tithing operates as a proxy for hope because like hope, tithing is oriented towards the future. By agreeing to tithe regularly, a majority of the converts to Christianity in our study have committed to giving up a significant proportion of their income and are forced to look beyond circumstances and towards the future. Tithing and the hope that emerges from this innovative practice drive the poor to transform the reality of their present context by changing the way

Table 12.2 Percentage of Micro-Entrepreneurs Who Own or Rent Their Homes

	2011		2012		2013		Sample size (n)
	Own	Rent	Own	Rent	Own	Rent	
Hindu	38	62	35	65	29	71	108
Muslim	6	90	12	88	12	88	58
Catholic	51	49	43	57	43	57	51
Mainline Protestant	42	58	75	25	75	25	12
Convert	57	43	60	40	60	40	70

Source: India Data collected for the Templeton Foundation-funded Tithing and Thrift among the Enterprising Poor Project (2011, 2012 and 2013) and the Holy Avarice Study (2012, 2013).

they spend their money or the type of investments they make to secure a better future. Thus, even though it runs against the grain of the iron cage of economic selfishness, the faith-based economic behaviour of tithing (or radical giving) may actually represent a demonstrably beneficial innovation more consistent with true economic self-interest.

Hope may well help launch the poor into a virtuous cycle in which they become more confident about themselves and the future, enabling them to plan more responsibly, save more carefully and negotiate and earn higher salaries. Extra money earned and saved encourages them to earn even more and to save more and to make durable investments, as in buying a home or a refrigerator. While fear and hopelessness can lock a family into a poverty trap, hope can help them reach a tipping point in which small initial investments soon yield more productive and future-oriented patterns of expenditure and saving.

Many of the poor converts I interviewed were hopeful about the future because they felt that God 'loved them and cared for them personally' and had 'a special plan for them'. By investing in the construction of a house, the converts give their families a chance to build a secure future. Armed with the official title, the owner can use the home as collateral for loans to expand her business, to send her children to college or to pay for another house. It is what economist Hernando de Soto calls turning 'dead capital' into resources that can generate additional capital and obtain credit.[27]

The strong correlation between tithing and asset accumulation confirmed the rationale behind our hypothesis that tithing fostered both self-control and a sense of accountability to a higher authority. Tithing promotes the habit of voluntary self-control. Among other things, the commitment of a significant portion of one's income to God and one's religious community means that less of one's money is available for potentially wasteful, present-oriented consumption. More deeply, tithing inculcates the habit of seeing all of one's money as a loan from God, to be saved, invested or spent in ways that are responsible and pleasing to him. Thus, à la Weber, tithing fosters a culture of self-restraint – of 'inner-worldly asceticism' – that shields the poor from myopic overconsumption.[28]

The rationale behind our hypothesis, however, was not only that tithing betokens a sense of accountability, but also that it expresses a sense of security and hope about the future. While tithing reflects the belief that one is ultimately accountable *to* God for the responsible stewardship of one's financial resources, it also reflects the belief that all of one's resources come *from* God, who is a faithful provider. By widening the circle of security beyond the family, tithing encourages the poor to trust in God as their ultimate security and provider. According to our findings, the result is that the poor are more likely to escape the prison of present-oriented consumption, which often results from an overwhelming sense of scarcity and the anxious belief that they must spend today because they may well have little or nothing to spend tomorrow.

Empowerment and Identity

In his 2007 American Economic Association presidential address Nobel Prize-winning economist George Akerlof argued that what often motivates people in their economic and other choices is not necessarily a desire to maximize their utility as traditionally understood in economic theory, but rather a desire to preserve their dignity as well as to be a certain kind of people. Akerlof believes that one of the most important economic decisions a person can make may be the decision about what kind of person he or she should be. When the poor are excluded from the opportunity to make decisions about their identity, they are excluded from the opportunity to make the most basic choices about the quality of their lives and the lives of their families and communities. Furthermore, decisions that affirm or deny a person's identity also affirm or deny a person's agency.[29]

Economists Hanming Fang and Glenn Loury build on Akerlof's insights by emphasizing the ways in which identity choice is a 'social event'. A person's identity is shaped by his or her interactions with people within a community, not merely through the individual's assertion of his or her values and experiences. People who interact frequently, who live in close proximity to each other and who share similar social experiences and engage in similar activities may end up embracing similar identities. To the extent, therefore, that a few members of the community may have a negative self-image or a negative identity, other members within the same and relatively closed community are likely to embrace and sustain a negative collective identity as well. Furthermore, people who are pessimistic about themselves and their circumstances and who are socially isolated tend to feel victimized, and are less willing or able to take risks to improve their lives and more likely to participate in dysfunctional behaviour (such as alcoholism or drug abuse). Such behaviour can sustain and reinforce the group's isolation from the mainstream population, which, in turn, can lead to its abandonment and to further destructive behaviour.[30]

Over 60 per cent of the Indian women in our pilot study reported that they experienced domestic violence at some point in their lives. It is not uncommon to interview a successful micro-entrepreneur who is married to an abusive, alcoholic husband who is regularly unfaithful. Domestic violence, alcoholism and marital infidelity are three of the most common problems women in our Indian sample face. Data from surveys I conducted in South Sudan and Peru also suggest that many poor women in these contexts face similar problems.

Poverty can be a closed system, yet access to religious networks and communities may open a door out of the closed world of domestic violence. The Indian National Family Health Survey (NFHS), one of the largest surveys of women and children in the country, reported that only one out of four women surveyed who had been a victim of domestic violence sought outside help. Religion constitutes the most significant background differential of those seeking help. In India, overall, 32 per cent of Christian women are likely to seek outside help, compared to 24 per cent of

Hindu women and 22 per cent of Muslim women. As we see from Table 12.3, our data in India echo these findings. According to an average of responses over three tranches of interviews, 63 per cent of the converts to Christianity in our study had experienced domestic violence. Of the converts who experienced domestic violence, 57 per cent reported their abuse to a pastor or a member of a pastoral team. This is in stark contrast to clients from Hindu, Muslim, Catholic and mainline Protestant backgrounds. No Muslim woman I interviewed told anyone, even a family member, about the domestic violence she suffered, while only 19 per cent of Catholic women and 25 per cent of mainline Protestants did so.

Strikingly, converts were more likely to tell their pastor about instances of domestic violence than members of their own family. It appears that the impact of religious leaders (who are men) may have an empowering impact on women who experience domestic violence, because the men who victimize them are more likely to listen to other men than to women counsellors or social workers. In our pilot study in India, male pastors from the local Pentecostal churches regularly visited the homes of converts to offer prayer and counselling, and this appeared to shame some abusive husbands into curbing their violent behaviour.

A number of scholars who have studied Latin American Pentecostalism, such as David Martin and Elizabeth Brusco, have argued that conversion to Pentecostalism is strongly associated with a radical reorientation of males towards the family. This shift has been especially dramatic in the Latin American context, in which some men who convert to Pentecostalism exchange lives of womanizing, alcohol, festivals and soccer

Table 12.3 Percentage of Micro-Entrepreneurs Who Sought Help to Stop Domestic Violence

	Never told anyone	Told a family member	Told a Pastor/ Pastoral Team	Told a Parish Priest (Roman Catholic)	Told a Priest at the temple (Hindu)	Told the Imam or person at the mosque	Percentage of women interviewed who ever experienced domestic violence
Hindu	90	7	3	0	0	0	56
Muslim	100	0	0	0	0	0	59
Catholic	73	8	0	19	0	0	51
Mainline Protestant	75	0	25	0	0	0	33
Convert	43	0	57	0	0	0	63

Source: India Data collected for the Templeton Foundation-funded Tithing and Thrift among the Enterprising Poor Project (2013) and the Holy Avarice Study (2013).

clubs for lives of dedicated domesticity. This reorientation carries with it inevitable economic benefits: money formerly spent on prostitutes and drink is channelled to the needs of the family. More profoundly, family lives disordered by untamed machismo are transformed into more harmonious and productive social units.[31]

Also underscoring the importance of female empowerment and identity is another of our findings. Women converts to Christianity were more likely to be empowered enough to work outside of the home. Ninety per cent of converts in our study worked outside the home compared to 75 per cent of Hindus and 71 per cent of Muslim women. I also found that on average, converts to Christianity (76 per cent) were more likely than other women to negotiate with their employers about the number of hours they worked. While such negotiations did not always yield the desired results, the converts were sufficiently self-confident and empowered to make the attempt in the first place, despite their gender, income level and low-caste status.

Conclusion

Terms such as *hope*, *self-control* and *dignity* – words with an unmistakable religious resonance and valence – have moved to the centre of discussion on economics and poverty alleviation. With the rise in behavioural economics and broader notions of human development and deprivation, it is no longer unusual for prominent economists to address these topics in their lectures, books and professional journals. It is striking, however, that these concepts appear to float freely from any reference to or grounding in religious tradition or community. Indeed, while there is a growing openness to the economic importance of issues of identity, dignity, hope and self-control, there has not been a parallel openness to the economic importance of religion per se or of specifically religious beliefs, practices and communities.

There are arguably, however, signs of a growing recognition of religion's potential importance for economic and social development. Religion's influence on development extends beyond the simple existence of religious ideas, beliefs and values. Religion has been shown to influence economically relevant skills, productivity and patterns of behaviour. Social scientists Robert D. Woodberry and Timothy S. Shah call attention to the role and developmental impact of conversionary Protestant missionaries, who spread a variety of portable skills such as literacy and mass printing, largely because their theology led them to believe it was of crucial importance to equip people to be able to read the Bible.[32] Woodberry demonstrates historically and statistically that such Protestant missionaries were a crucial catalyst in initiating the development and spread of religious liberty, mass education, mass printing, newspapers, voluntary organizations and colonial reforms, thereby creating the conditions that made stable democracy and long-term economic development more likely. Statistically, the historic prevalence of Protestant missionaries explains about half the variation in democracy in Africa, Asia, Latin America and Oceania, and removes the impact of many variables that dominate current statistical research on democracy and development. Similarly, others have shown how conversionary Protestant communities have fostered a sense of empowerment and promoted economic improvement among some groups of poor people in India, both early in the twentieth century and today.[33] Conversely, according to economist Timur Kuran, some religious institutions, such as religious inheritance laws and religious trusts, have exerted a long-standing adverse effect on the development of Middle Eastern economies.[34]

In addition, the potential of religious perspectives to provide an expansive and more realistic notion of the human person and human development has become a growing theme in the work of some prominent economists and development theorists. According to Denis Goulet, it is laudable that development economists look beyond the bounds of rational choice to push economists to situate economic behaviour within human communities. It is also valuable that welfare and behavioural economists have introduced more realistic assumptions about human behaviour, choices and relationships. But this does not go far enough for Goulet. In his view, economics must find a way to recognize the religious yearnings and aspirations of human beings. If modern economics continues to yield an understanding of human development that ignores the role of religion, governments and development institutions will persist in acting as 'one-eyed giants' who 'analyze, prescribe, and act *as if* man could live by bread alone, *as if* human destiny could be stripped to its material dimensions alone'. According to Goulet, development is more human and more developed when people are called to '*be* more' rather than simply '*have* more'. The goal of development should be to satisfy the needs of 'all in man and all of men'. For Goulet, there can be 'authentic development' only when there is a 'societal openness to the deepest levels of mystery and transcendence', and when this yearning for mystery and transcendence is recognized and satisfied.[35]

Seeing religion as constitutively important for the self implies that any understanding of human development must be viewed in material as well as spiritual terms. Writing to oppose orthodox economic theories that exclude the role of spiritual and social factors in economic development, and in opposition to the assumption that material factors always dominate human behaviour, Glenn Loury has argued that what often drives and animates people is their spirit and will. These are the factors that give meaning to their lives. Human beings are 'spiritual creatures, generators of meaning, beings that must not and cannot live by bread alone', according to Loury. And 'the exercise of human agency' and 'processes of persuasion, conformity, conversion, myth construction and the like are open-ended' and 'at best only weakly constrained by material conditions'.[36]

The case for religious innovation in human development is even more compelling when we see that what sets religious networks and organizations apart – what gives them a comparative advantage in serving the poor – is the impact of their interventions on the internal constraints faced by the poor. What are they? The lack of hope and of aspirations constrains and limits the poor's ability to harness available opportunities and resources to improve their lives. A rigorous longitudinal study of the child sponsorship programme of Compassion International, a Christian international child sponsorship programme, shows that the organization increased the number of years of schooling and school completion rates by 1.5 years and 7.7 per cent, respectively. Indeed, the study found large, statistically significant impacts on years of schooling; primary, secondary and tertiary school completion; and the probability and quality of employment. The study suggests that what may distinguish Compassion International's programme from comparable interventions is its emphasis on raising children's self-esteem, aspirations and hope for the future.[37]

The example of women who were active participants in conversionary Protestant communities in our study further illustrates this point. These communities tend to be characterized by a high emphasis on religious faith and the virtues and attitudes associated with it such as hope, self-control and self-esteem, and were most likely to exhibit an empowering, pro-developmental package of practices, choices and beliefs – what I and other scholars have referred to as 'spiritual capital'.[38] It could be assumed that easier access to credit would by itself enhance the hope, dignity and agency of the poor women entrepreneurs in our sample who could at last have effective control and access to a means to support their family. Easier access to credit, however, may increase the risk of clients using additional loans to meet immediate needs rather than to make future investments. Recent studies suggest that microcredit can exacerbate cycles of over-indebtedness by making it easier for the poor to assume more loans than they can afford.[39] It was crucial for the women to exercise self-control and to have a concrete sense of hope about the future to enable them to overcome the internal constraints that exacerbate and sustain poverty. Furthermore, our study shows that poor people who convert to religious traditions and religious communities that emphasize and foster the greatest number of these religious beliefs and practices will have important developmental advantages. In particular, they will be more able to accumulate durable economic assets over the long run, more able to resist the temptations of present-oriented consumption, more able to save money, more able to negotiate higher wages, more able to be empowered in the face of domestic violence and more able to absorb unexpected economic shocks.

It is important to note that both external and internal constraints are important sources of poverty. Our research seeks to explore how attitudes, beliefs and identity choices that are internal to the psychology of the poor can help or hurt them as they seek to exploit external economic opportunities.

It is unwise and probably impossible to study spiritual or quasi-spiritual values such as hope, dignity and self-control without grounding these values in the concrete spiritual traditions, communities and choices of the poor themselves. As economists and development practitioners increasingly speak of hope, the dangers of temptation and the problem of diminished self-control, it is evident that we are dealing with issues that go beyond the material. Furthermore, there is ample evidence that religion – including religious belief, practice, observance and active participation – plays a fundamental role in the lives and well-being of many poor people around the world. Religion is clearly an important source of meaning and fulfilment and also provides innovative resources that can – if properly tapped – alleviate poverty.

13 Century of Progress? Chicago after Daniel Burnham

PHILIP H. BESS

Make no bad plans; rather make good plans. Big ones, yes! But with lots of room for communal and individual actors

Daniel Burnham

As a professor of architecture who teaches urban design in a Catholic university, I approach religion and innovation differently from other contributors to this volume. To consider certain features of their interplay, I offer here a research and design project entitled *After Burnham: Religion, Innovation, and the Future of Humanist Urbanism*. From within Catholic religious, intellectual and artistic traditions, *After Burnham* seeks to advance a tradition of classical humanist urban design historically grounded in sacred sensibilities; to which (with characteristically Catholic 'both-and' intuition) I add that the desired end of both classical humanist urbanism and *After Burnham* is also a secular common good.

The centrepiece of *After Burnham* is *The Notre Dame Plan of Chicago 2109*, a visionary 'counter-project' engaging Daniel Burnham and Edward Bennett's 1909 *Plan of Chicago*, in part to update the latter but also to critique what contemporary architecture, urban design and planning have since become. Imagining Chicago at the bicentennial of the Burnham Plan, *Chicago 2109* embraces but goes beyond the economic and environmental frameworks within which cities today are typically analysed and understood, and proposes that classical humanist urbanism and Catholic social teaching can together increase our general understanding of cities, better locate the modern metropolis in both nature and sacred order in ways symbolically legible and humane, and better help human beings to flourish. Such achievements might entail innovations, but would represent progress.

Chicago and Daniel Burnham

Chicago is renowned for many things: for the Great Fire of 1871, as the birthplace of the skyscraper and Prairie School Architecture, as Hog Butcher for the World, as a city of hustlers and entrepreneurs, of working-class neighbourhoods and the domain of Al Capone. In the second half of the twentieth century, Chicago was known as 'The City That Works', for the Mayor Daley and a supporting cast of colourful political characters, for the spare architectural modernism of Mies van der Rohe, for Mike Royko, Michael Jordan and 'Iron Mike' Ditka, for the University of Chicago's many Nobel Prize-winning economists, for great middle-linebackers and undistinguished quarterbacks, for a public lakefront that is (or should be) the envy of the world and for the unmatched enchantment of Wrigley Field and the confounding futility of its occupants. But above all and with good reason, Chicagoans have always regarded themselves proudly, almost unreflectively, as modern. In Chicago, it is a tradition.

Less widely known but, nevertheless, embedded in Chicago's consciousness is the 1909 *Plan of Chicago* by Daniel Burnham and Edward Bennett. Most Chicagoans know of 'The Burnham Plan' and have some sense that it was important, but why it was important (and might still be) is more elusive. The epigram most often associated with both Daniel Burnham and the *Plan of Chicago* is Burnham's 'Make no little plans. They have not the magic to stir men's blood … Make big plans…'. – to the spirit of which, for better and for worse, succeeding generations of Chicagoans on the make have imagined, if not professed, themselves faithful. But although Burnham loved big plans, and loved being a big actor on a big stage, he was also shaped by, and ultimately came to understand himself as a participant in, a long humanist urban tradition that understood human flourishing – something that included but was more encompassing than commercial success, convenience and entertainment – as the highest purpose of cities. Human flourishing is what the ancient Greeks would have called the *telos* of a good city, what a good city is *for*. And on the subject of human flourishing, Burnham, though not a philosopher, appears more nuanced, reflective and insightful than his critics (and even many of his supposed admirers) have given him credit. Consider this short passage from the *Plan of Chicago*, where Burnham writes that 'while the keynote of the nineteenth century was expansion, we of the twentieth century find that our dominant idea is conservation. The people of Chicago have ceased to be impressed by rapid growth or the great size of the city. What they insist asking now is, How are we living?'[1] The keynote of nineteenth-century Chicago was, indeed, expansion, as it grew from a frontier outpost of less than 500 inhabitants in 1833 to a city of 2.2 million by 1910, reaching 3.6 million in 1950, before regional growth shifted to the suburbs and the city began to decline in population.

There is perhaps no better account of nineteenth-century Chicago than environmental historian William Cronon's *Nature's Metropolis: Chicago and the Great West* (1992), a gripping story and a landmark in a larger long-term cultural project to understand, recover from and advance beyond the ruthless application of Cartesian rationality – that is, modernism – to commerce, human settlements and their adjacent landscapes.[2] *Nature's Metropolis* occasions for many readers 'a-ha' moments of clarifying insight: that cities and landscapes are not autonomous and competing entities but mutually defining and mutually dependent; that a city is best understood as part of an agrarian–urban unit; that human beings are not outside but rather part of nature; and that it is part of *human* nature to make a variety of settlement types, including cities – which means cities, even understood rightly as artefacts, are in an important sense *natural*.

Nineteenth-century Chicago was both a milestone and a paradigm of the industrial era and a precursor of today's emerging global cities, a modern mega-city that arose almost overnight in the premodern centre of a continent, a city that harnessed (uneasily and incompletely) the forces of modernity to transform its pre-existing Western landscape at a scale and speed without historic precedent. Chicago in the nineteenth century became an inland economic giant, a continental nation's centre for the sale and distribution of grain, lumber and meat by virtue of its geographical location, its status as a rail hub and the entrepreneurial genius of its citizens.

Cronon details all this in meticulously documented accounts of the economic and environmental history of Chicago and its hinterlands in the latter half of the nineteenth century. His chapters are framed by an introduction describing Chicago's premodern geography and pre-European inhabitants, and a conclusion foreshadowing subsequent efforts by Chicagoans in the late nineteenth and early twentieth centuries to figure out what to do with the wealth they had created, how to contain if not repair the environmental damage they had caused, how best to govern themselves and how best to live. And in that conclusion, *Nature's Metropolis* raises questions both philosophical and existential about nature, human nature and human settlements that historians *qua* historians cannot answer.[3]

In correctly identifying human beings as both part of and transformers of nature, Cronon perforce raises a number of related questions: about human exceptionalism and obligations of stewardship (and stewardship's further implications) arising necessarily from contemplating our collective human powers and capacities; about the meaning of human flourishing and the complex relationship between human flourishing and both environmental and economic sustainability; about urban teleology (i.e. the nature and purpose of cities); and about urban form and how urban form relates to both cities and human flourishing.

Strictly speaking, none of these subjects are the domain of environmental historians, but proper to theologians, philosophers and architects. Happily, however, there is a long and living Western religious, intellectual and artistic tradition of classical humanism (Figure 13.1) that addresses each of these issues: a religious tradition as old as the Bible; a moral and intellectual tradition as old as Aristotle's *Nicomachean*

Figure 13.1 Classical Humanist Urbanism. Left: *The Ghent Altarpiece* (1432, detail), Paradise as New Eden and New Jerusalem. Centre: The World's Columbian Exposition, Chicago (1893). Right: Proposed City Hall and Plaza, *Plan of Chicago* (1909). All images in the public domain.

Ethics and *Politics* and Augustine's *City of God*; and an artistic tradition theorized by Vitruvius in our oldest extant architectural treatise from classical antiquity, the *De architectura* (or *Ten Books on Architecture*). But of special interest here, it is a tradition brought to bear upon Chicago by Daniel Burnham: initially through his role as chief architect of the World's Columbian Exposition of 1893, and more comprehensively in the 1909 *Plan of Chicago*.

The *Plan of Chicago* is both noteworthy and exemplary for several reasons in addition to its attempt to address the challenges of the modern megalopolis with the language of classical architecture and urban design. There is the regional scope of its multiple practical proposals; its ambition (both civic and environmentally prescient) to preserve metropolitan Chicago's forests and Chicago's enhanced lakefront for public use; and its proposal for a civic realm of beautiful buildings and spaces for a population gathered from all over the world, to foster among them solidarity and affection for Chicago as a city where they and their fellow citizens and their descendants could flourish – which Burnham over time had come to regard as the *primary* task of classical humanist architecture and urbanism. Although the *Plan of Chicago* was sponsored by an organization of Chicago businessmen, Burnham envisioned Chicago not simply as a place of commerce but as both quotidian and (implicitly) sacramental home. And this intuition – I call it an intuition because the intentions and implications embodied in Burnham's actual design work are sometimes clearer than their verbal articulation – had much to do with Burnham's proposal for a city hall, civic centre and streetscape scaled to symbolically balance (and constrain) the sheer physical presence of Chicago commerce.

Daniel Burnham's Religious Sensibilities

Kristen Schafer and Judith McBrien, separately, have documented and are documenting the effects of Burnham's Swedenborgian Pietism upon his architectural vocation, which both of them regard as under-studied but significant.[4] Their findings (of which I am persuaded) notwithstanding, there is virtually no formal presence of religion per se in the Burnham Plan. A reason for this is suggested in the following passage from the *Plan of Chicago*, in which Burnham is writing about the place of 'public and semi-public buildings' and their role in the most desirable formal arrangements of Chicago suburbs:

> In each town plan spaces should be marked out for public schools, and each school should have about it ample playgrounds. … Next to the school, the public library should have place … the landscape setting … generous and the situation commanding. The town-hall, the engine [i.e., fire] house with its lookout tower, the police station with its court of justice, and the post-office, all naturally form a group of buildings that may be located about a … public square, so as to form the suburban civic center.
>
> There was a time in the older portions of the country when church and churchyard occupied the chief place in the town; and today enterprising real

estate dealers [sic] find it to their advantage to give to one or more religious denominations building sites. But so numerous are the sects into which Christianity has divided itself, and so diverse are the nationalities to be provided for, that the suburban church building rarely offers to the eye any relief from the monotonous ugliness of the airless street which it helps to frame. Also, the old churchyards, with their serried ranks of slate headstones, their cypresses and weeping willows, and their rows of tombs, made a direct appeal to the deepest feelings of the human heart; but the disorder of the modern town cemetery would seem to carry the idea of turbulence even to the grave itself. Perhaps in the coming times, the spirit of unity will draw people together in religion as well as in business, and such a syndication of religious effort will prevail as shall find expression in permanent buildings devoted to the moral advancement of all the people. The day of the splendid cathedral may never dawn for this country, but certainly in every community there will be buildings for the help of the unfortunate, and the amelioration of those desperate conditions that form the reverse side of great prosperity.[5]

What inferences might we correctly draw then regarding the place of religion in Burnham's *Plan of Chicago*? Several, I submit:

- that (per Schafer and McBrien) Burnham understood both his own life and his work as an architect and city planner at least in part as religious vocation;

- that he recognized attention to the poor as a duty with at least some religious significance (for he inserts this observation into his narrative in the context of reflections upon religion and *formal* order);

- that Burnham recognized religion as a historically unifying communal force that makes 'direct appeal to the deepest feelings of the human heart';

- that because he recognized that America's religious pluralism had rendered religion's historic unifying communal force problematic, Burnham simply punted (by declining to address) the challenge of how religious belief could or should find formal and public expression consistent with (a) the truth claims of Chicago's multiple religious communities, (b) the aspirational order of American civil society embodied in the phrase *e pluribus unum* and (c) America's own constitutional legal framework that was arguably designed to acknowledge and address both 'a' and 'b'; and more controversially;

- that the absence of any clear place for religion in the *Plan of Chicago* – in spite of Burnham's own religious sensibilities (and presumably those of many of his peers) – was a harbinger of both modernist and hyper-modernist urban form to come; and that, by ceding the public realm to commerce and government alone, Burnham unintentionally advanced theories of both urbanism and religion that would banish religion (and its claims about overarching sacred order) from the visible public realm of cities to an invisible private realm of the spiritual.

Burnham and Large-Scale Baroque Urbanism

There is arguably another manifestation of religion in the *Plan of Chicago*, more than an emanation or penumbra, and germane to the issue of religiously inspired formal innovation. But it is indirect. In order to address the issue of formal hierarchy at the scale of the modern city – and to some extent the formal challenge of the modern city *is* the challenge of scale – Burnham adopted a distinct dialect of the classical humanist language of urban design: the tradition of large-scale baroque urbanism.

It is impossible to do justice here to baroque sensibility, its grandeur, subtleties, uses and abuses. But for my purposes, suffice it to say that the origins of baroque urbanism are in the late sixteenth-century Catholic Reformation, specifically in the urban interventions in Rome by Pope Sixtus V. As part of a strategy to confirm Rome as the jurisdictional and spiritual centre of the Christian Church, Sixtus V initiated the making of several long, broad avenues that cut through the heart of medieval Rome, employing them to connect the major pilgrimage churches in Rome (and their relics) and offering to religious pilgrims both convenience and a demonstration of the ancient Christian character (and authority) of the Catholic Church.

This intervention, at this scale, was something new in the history of Western urbanism, and it depended absolutely on both the secular power and the religious authority of the Roman pontiff. Moreover, it transformed the historic centre of Rome into the essentially baroque city it is today, save for Paris and a comparatively adolescent Washington, DC, unrivalled in its *baroque-ness*. As this urban design strategy began to be employed in capital cities elsewhere in Europe – especially in France, in late-seventeenth- to early-eighteenth-century Paris; most extravagantly at Versailles; and again in mid-nineteenth-century Paris (which yielded what many today regard as the most beautiful city in the world) – and in European colonies worldwide, large-scale baroque urbanism acquired associations with imperialism and authoritarian governance, which it carries to this day. But not necessarily, and not always justly. It was the design language adopted by George Washington and his architect Pierre L'Enfant in the late eighteenth century for the new capital of the democratic United States of America. It was employed at a smaller scale in a more rural context by Thomas Jefferson in his campus plan for the University of Virginia. And for some forty years in the late nineteenth and early twentieth centuries, baroque urbanism was adopted again by a modern democracy, promoted throughout the United States by Daniel Burnham and the City Beautiful Movement, ironically to simultaneously *facilitate* robust commerce and *constrain* modern commerce's own imperious tendencies and the resultant physical and environmental chaos. And though orderly and beautiful urban form at the scale of the modern city is probably something only government can oversee, strong metropolitan and city government necessarily precludes neither democracy nor the multiple goods of *subsidiarity*, the Catholic social teaching principle that acknowledges (and mandates recognition of) the multiple realms of legitimate authority in civil society. The gravamen of *After Burnham* is that classical humanist urbanism provides precedents for design at the scale of modernity that also make room for subsidiary institutions – sacred and civic, governmental and non-governmental – and multiple formal expressions of legitimate authority for which today's increasingly authoritarian hyper-modernism has no room.[6]

I will return to the topics of large-scale baroque urbanism, religious pluralism, formal order and legitimate authority. Suffice it to say that here my immediate interest in religion and innovation vis-à-vis Chicago is less in Daniel Burnham's religious beliefs and in the history of baroque urbanism, than in the religious and philosophical assumptions both embedded and evident in the classical humanist tradition of architecture and urbanism that Burnham embraced and promoted for Chicago. Human beings reason – as thinkers, as moral agents, as artisans – in the context of traditions and with reference to ideals, because they are beings so constituted as to both remember, and hope for, the good. This suggests that goodness has both teleological and ontological implications. Insofar as *religion* is a primary way in which human beings acknowledge communally an orientation to the good, religion also provides a context in which to think about teleology, the good and *innovation*.

Classical Humanist Urbanism, Notre Dame and Chicago

Over the last century, the Burnham Plan's forest preserve and lakefront park ambitions have been more successfully realized than its civic and regional ambitions. But the *Plan of Chicago* is also important as perhaps the last great planning proposal before the early-twentieth-century advent of architectural modernism. The latter was the architectural equivalent of the French Revolution, a kind of heretical classicism that itself turned out to be a transitional ideology superseded in the late twentieth century by postmodern architectural hyper-modernism. The Burnham Plan attempted to bring classical humanist aesthetic and moral sensibilities – concerns for beauty, for home – to bear upon the practical problems of a modern metropolitan region, and was arguably the last best effort to do so.

It matters to *After Burnham* that the concerns for both practicality and beauty that characterize the Burnham Plan, and classical humanist architecture and urbanism generally, are both grounded in and characteristic of cultures of *moral and metaphysical realism*, the fundamentals of which may be summarized as (a) reality is real; (b) human beings can know reality truly (albeit only partially); and (c) human beings thrive as both creative artisans and moral agents by progressively conforming themselves to reality truly understood (i.e. we *can* derive 'ought' from 'is').[7] This is significant for at least two reasons: first, because cultures (and sub-cultures) of moral and metaphysical realism may be distinguished from post-modern cultures of moral relativism and epistemological scepticism; and second, because in the West, moral and metaphysical realism have existed within and been carried into the modern world most prominently by biblical religion. Consistent with this, cities that grow within classical humanist cultures of urban design invariably include within themselves prominent places the primary purpose of which – among many secondary purposes – is to acknowledge a sacred order of which every particular city is part of.[8]

Why does an acknowledgement of sacred order in urban form matter *especially* for *After Burnham*? The answer is that it matters both intellectually and existentially. It matters intellectually because this project is undertaken under the auspices and as representative of the University of Notre Dame School of Architecture, for which classical architecture and urbanism is foundational to the curriculum, and which exists as part of the worldwide mission of the Catholic Church.[9] With Catholic Christianity comes Notre Dame's understanding of God, nature, human nature and human flourishing that includes a developed body of social teaching germane to any serious theory and practice of urbanism, understanding such teaching as pertaining to a common good that includes Catholics and non-Catholics alike. With classical humanism comes the approach to architecture and urban design of the School of Architecture, an approach (at least presumably) consonant with Catholicism. Thus it simply seems fitting that we at Notre Dame would and should ask ourselves: What do classical humanist architecture and urbanism, and Catholic Christian theology, anthropology and social teaching, have to do with the challenges of contemporary urbanism? And how do and how ought these subjects – especially the Church's view of human nature – find expression in contemporary urban form?

But an acknowledgement of sacred order also matters existentially, because we who profess and pursue this understanding of architecture and urbanism believe that human flourishing itself is best facilitated by understanding truly and acknowledging the place of human beings in both nature and sacred order. Absent this true understanding and its formal expression, we fear human beings will be more inclined than we already are to get lost in our selfish interests, with adverse consequences penultimate and ultimate.

Understanding man (male and female) as an intermediate being by vocation simultaneously a steward and an artisan, and working within classical humanist traditions of urbanism, *The Notre Dame Plan of Chicago 2109* (hereafter *Chicago 2109*), therefore, envisions how metropolitan Chicago might be re-fashioned so that, about a hundred years out, Chicagoans will occupy metropolitan Chicago's rural and urban landscapes in settlements that locate and express the proper place of human beings within both nature and sacred order; create long-term rather than ephemeral wealth, in places simultaneously durable, convenient and beautiful, and environmentally, economically and culturally sustainable; and promote human flourishing from conception to natural death, over and across generations and into eternity. In these ambitions, *After Burnham* understands *Chicago 2109* as both continuous with Daniel Burnham and an extension of the classical humanist tradition of which he is part, even where we find aspects of Burnham's work deficient and seek to go beyond some of his own specific proposals and concerns. We revisit Burnham not because the *Plan of Chicago* was perfect or its author infallible, but because we observe that metropolitan Chicago today is neither socially nor formally very much like what Burnham envisioned. And Chicago is the worse for it.

Chicago 2015: Problematic Global City

More than a century after the publication of the *Plan of Chicago*, in a time of explosive global urban growth, Chicago presents itself to the world as a global city, one among perhaps a couple dozen critical to a worldwide network of production and exchange.[10] With a Chicagoan in the White House and his former chief of staff as mayor, Chicago's ties to Washington and to international power centres have never been stronger. Downtown Chicago – never more photogenic, never more lively – grew by some 60,000 residents between 2000 and 2010, its symbolic, if not physical, centre the new and wildly popular Millennium Park.

By other markers, however, Chicago is not well. During that same 2000–10 census period, the metropolitan region as a whole – even while growing in net population by about 285,000 (3.5 per cent) – lost more than 7 per cent of its jobs, with a ten-year out-migration of about 550,000 people offset only by the decade's net births. Chicago's apparently most thriving locale, the Loop, lost over 18 per cent of its private sector jobs, and outside the downtown area, the rest of the city lost a quarter million people (85 per cent of them African-American).[11] Both Chicago and Illinois are running record deficits and debts; the gun violence in certain Chicago neighbourhoods far exceeds anything ever witnessed in Tombstone and Deadwood; and the middle-class population in The City That Works has shrunk dramatically, making Chicago an increasingly two-tiered city comprising one class of residents tending towards increasing wealth and another class of (many more) residents tending towards increasing poverty.[12] To the extent current public policy in Chicago is designed for the institutions and executors of the global economy – which in a short-term calculus is low-hanging fruit – downtown Chicago's rising skyline is best understood as a symbol of crony capitalism, that long-standing, cozy, law-blurring public sector/financial sector relationship in Chicago known colloquially as *clout*.

It remains unclear whether Chicago's widening class division is a necessary and systemic feature of global cities and the global economy; whether global cities and the global economy at their current scale are sustainable ventures; and whether global cities can exist with and as part of thriving, diversified and productive local economies. It is clear, however, that Chicago and its suburbs today are neither socially nor formally the kind of metropolitan region envisioned by Daniel Burnham: an urban-agrarian culture of opportunity and broad prosperity, that inculcates character virtue and inspires affection in part by the quality of its built environment and its formal celebration of the institutions of civil society. Moreover, simply on the basis of demographic trends and their pending consequences – retiring Boomers and their health care needs; decades of below-replacement fertility rates worldwide and in America – America's current economic sluggishness may be more than a brief downturn, even if less perilous than the economic fate awaiting Japan, Russia, China, most of Europe and other ageing countries demographically destined to severe population decline by the second half of the twenty-first century. And while Chicago neighbourhoods away from downtown may be thriving or declining, neither current Millennial family structure and child-bearing habits, nor foreseeable economic realities (most especially, infrastructure maintenance), nor the construction quality of their building stock bode well for the future of Chicago's post-1945 automobile suburbs.

It is this historical context for which *Chicago 2109* is envisioned. Taking advantage of Chicago's existing strengths, it imagines metropolitan Chicago in 100 years as a region in its parts and as a whole more intimately related to its immediate natural and agricultural landscape, characterized by a productive economy that may be international, may be national, but will also and at the very least be local, employing more of its residents in economically and environmentally sustainable labour producing tangible goods for local consumption. Before turning to some of the details of *Chicago 2109*, it is important to address some general questions about religion and innovation and about the nature and purposes (the teleology) of architecture and urbanism that the plan itself and the current state of metropolitan Chicago raise.

Religion and Innovation – and Progress

I operate here with a substantive definition of religion as an activity directed towards the sacred, rather than a functionalist definition of religion as a worldview or 'ultimate concern'.[13] Both definitions have their merits. The primary virtue of the functionalist definition is its recognition that even persons who understand themselves to be 'not religious' or as 'postmodern' typically think both in metanarrative and symbolically. Nevertheless, rather than defining religion functionally in terms of metanarrative (e.g. Marxism or Darwinism), or as that which is most important in the life of a person or community (e.g. Annie Savoy's 'Church of Baseball'), I am opting, instead, for a substantive definition: *Religion is a shared acknowledgement of sacred order, oriented communally towards* worship, *and orienting individuals towards* vocation *as their existential relationship to the cosmos*.[14] Although any particular religion will be regarded by outsiders at best as a sub-narrative subject to more or less reductive explanations, for insiders one's own religion typically functions as a *sui generis* metanarrative within which various subsidiary narratives find their place. Religious persons and practices may be more or less good, more or less just, more or less virtuous; and religious truth claims more or less true. But objective goodness, objective justice, objective virtues and objective truth all imply, if not require, an overarching sacred order with reference to which goodness, justice, virtue and truth are defined and measured.

Religion, therefore, is inherently metaphysically realist in character, by which I mean simply that religion generally affirms the realist philosophical assertion that, appearances and cultural narratives to the contrary, being is what it is, and things are what they are[15] (which innovations successful and unsuccessful in their own way will confirm). Furthermore, although related, religion is to be distinguished from the comparatively simpler subject of human spirituality. More precisely, religion engages human spirituality, but in communal ways. Religion is the communal form of human spirituality, in the absence of which acknowledgement of sacred order is not corporately registered in the world, and the public realm yields by default to other corporate human registrations less comprehensive, often less edifying and less benign.

Innovation is almost as complicated, especially when coupled with religion, because (like 'social change' or 'development') an innovation may be good or bad depending upon the *telos* of the contexts, immediate and ultimate, in which the innovation occurs. But presuming a cultural context in which both Western religious narratives and their modern secular counterparts embrace the category of history, by *innovation* I mean *the appearance in the world of something new*, disregarding any qualitative judgement of the novel thing. Nevertheless, in Western culture (*sotto voce*) and in modern culture (*fortissimo*), innovation is generally – if often naively – presumed to be intrinsically good.

Religion may, but need not, be a source of innovation, or, perhaps, it *is* a source of innovation, but not most of the time. Religions typically rely on ritual and authority to reinforce within the religious community – in premodern societies within an entire culture – some shared understanding of what is genuinely true, authoritative and trustworthy. Ritual and authority also 'domesticate' those episodes of spiritual enthusiasm, full of both insight and danger, in which religions both originate and are renewed. Moreover, this caution about enthusiasm is understandable, if only because human communities cannot exist in a perpetual state of ecstasy. (Who would cook and do the dishes?)

So religions, especially to the degree that they function as metanarratives, are inherently conservative, inherently cautious and suspicious about novelty (their adherents perhaps most often the better for it). And yet, because religion is both communal and transformative in the lives of individuals, and even more because religious communities open themselves to a sacred horizon and orient themselves to sacred ideals, neither internal innovations in religious belief and practice nor practical 'secular' innovations inspired by religion and/or undertaken for religious reasons are rationally inconsistent or historically unknown. This is especially true of Judaism and Christianity that take seriously the category of history and understand history teleologically. And in biblical religion there arises the category of *progress* as an especially salutary type of innovation insofar as it is an advancement towards, and both necessarily related and subordinate to, the end (*telos*) that is God.

Progress is especially important in the Christian metanarrative, where history is oriented towards an eschatological fulfilment – classically, a heavenly city – by definition outside history and space–time, though sacramentally present in history and space–time, in relation to which progress in history is possible and real, but not necessary (because it is also possible to regress and fall away). Progress is equally important to architectural modernism, where the eschatological fulfilment is anticipated in history – indeed, is a *necessary* historical event, one with its own urban ideal famously represented in iconic modernist images such as Le Corbusier's

1922 *Plan Voisin* for Paris, published a mere thirteen years after Burnham's *Plan of Chicago*.

Because modernists believed historical progress to be necessary, progress increasingly came to be conflated with change itself and, inevitably, with innovation. Thus today, at a historical moment in which no one believes that the modernist utopia has *not* failed, postmodern persons and hyper-modernist architects, who almost unanimously eschew teleology (and therefore any coherent notion of progress), nevertheless speak blithely of 'progressive' design, the progressiveness of which is evaluated almost entirely in terms of its novelty – an odd historical condition about which one can say without exaggeration that architectural hyper-modernism fetishizes novelty *as* progress. Small wonder that today even well-educated non-architects desiring to understand and characterize 'cutting edge' architecture are so often reduced to verbal vacuities – 'different', 'interesting', 'exciting' – to describe mystifying (and inevitably short-lived) buildings the likes of which, indeed, no one has seen ever before.

But what if we post-moderns have become lazily accustomed to celebrating novelty and innovation rightly in some human endeavours, but wrongly in others? What if genuine progress in architecture and urbanism – a concept making sense only when architecture and urbanism are understood as teleological activities, and their ends correctly understood – refers to innovations generally emerging only slowly in the context of their respective practices, rarely occurring when pursued for their own sake but more often as by-products of pursuing the several true ends of architecture and urbanism? In other words, what if architecture and urbanism are not primarily experimental arts?

The Ends of Architecture and Urbanism[16]

The classical humanist tradition that Notre Dame teaches, in which she participates and which she aspires to improve and extend, is commonly dismissed in both the architectural profession and academy as antiquated, inauthentic and unsuited to contemporary life. How, it is thought, can Notre Dame seriously propose classical humanist architecture and urbanism as normative when these seem so foreign to the way modern people live? Contrary to classical ideals, modern life is more motion than calm, more mobility than place; it emphasizes the disposable over the durable, the temporal over the timeless, novelty over beauty. How in this context can classical humanism architecture and urbanism be 'authentic'? Be authentically modern? Consider other modern practices, randomly chosen, in which innovation is prized: aviation, banking, business, communications media, dentistry, information technology, medicine, the military. No one engaged in, or benefiting from, these practices idealizes old ways of doing them, and each is apparently modern in a way that traditional architecture and urbanism apparently are not. Is this not for classical humanist architects and urbanists a contradiction? Are modern persons who love old buildings and traditional cities living incoherent lives? Guilty of thoughtless nostalgia? Intellectually unserious? Ideologically blinded? This is what critics of traditional architecture and urbanism – some for ideological reasons, some for ostensibly pragmatic reasons – contend.[17] But perhaps they are confusing innovation for progress.

For all their apparent differences, the modern practices cited above have something in common with classical humanist architecture and urbanism: the practitioners of each share a more or less clear and reasonable understanding of the nature and purpose of their respective practice and its ends (*teloi*). This is less true of contemporary architecture and urbanism. Where once there was both theoretical and practical agreement that buildings should be durable, comfortable, beautiful and suitably decorous in their (typically urban) context, today we build everyday buildings for short-term economic gain and monumental buildings as exercises in novelty, self-expression and advertising. The cumulative result is our contemporary built environment of junk and bewilderment – *junkspace*, Dutch hyper-modernist Rem Koolhaas happily terms it.[18] No one responsible for this junky bewildering built environment argues that it represents any shared clear purpose, or accounts it reasonable. We have, rather, the built environment we do *because* we lack any shared architectural and urban ends. Modern junkspace happens when the utilitarian rationality of bureaucracies and developers collides with the architecture-as-experimental-novelty rationale of contemporary architectural culture.

But these ends are not the ends of classical humanism. Notre Dame and a few other architectural communities understand the purpose of classical humanist architecture and urbanism to be good places for human flourishing. It follows from this premise that making buildings and public spaces should be deliberate; that craft and durability are essential to good building; that traditional builders innovate, but only slowly, testing everything and holding fast to what is good; and that all this is true because the ends of architecture and urbanism properly understood are different from, though not unrelated to, the ends of faster-paced characteristically modern activities.

For here is the paradox: even modern human beings fare better in good places. Indeed, persons best able to successfully navigate the changes and uncertainties of the modern world, even life itself, are most often those rooted in stable families in good places. And this suggests the true rationale for classical humanist architecture and urbanism even in the modern world: *a durable and beautiful built environment provides the best physical and spatial context for human life, and thereby supports the different kinds of inventiveness and daring that life – even modern life – demands.* If one grows up in a loving family in a good home in a good town or city, one is likely to carry within oneself a foundational intuition of home throughout one's life, through whatever other uncertainties, dangers and adventures life presents. Making places in which human beings are able to feel at home – even if in this world in which we are destined to die we can never be entirely at home – is a genuine good, a primary purpose of classical humanist architecture and urbanism properly understood, and a primary criterion by which to judge the merits of any town or city at any moment in time, including Chicago.

Chicago 2109 – Solidarity, Subsidiarity, Environmental Stewardship ... and Good Urbanism

Space limitations make it impossible to describe here in detail either the many issues addressed by the scores of drawings in *Chicago 2109* – many of which may be seen and studied on the project website afterburnham.com – or the conjectural 'history of twenty-first-century Chicago' we imagine as the background and precursor to the metropolitan Chicago we envision. We do not presume, however, to work on a blank canvas. Rather, *Chicago 2109* engages the geography, history and culture of Chicago *in media res*, informed throughout by Catholic social teaching principles regarding the dignity of the human person and of human labour, communal solidarity, subsidiarity in civil society, environmental stewardship and public policy attentive to the poor.

So informed, and like the Burnham Plan, *Chicago 2109* entails architecture, urban design and planning at a metropolitan scale encompassing the seven counties of northeastern Illinois, with particular attention to Chicago. Neither predicting nor presuming environmental or economic apocalypse, rather an extended period of twenty-first-century economic and population decline followed by revival, *Chicago 2109* promotes long-term environmental, economic and cultural sustainability in metropolitan Chicago by illustrating good land use, good transportation policy, good building practices and good urban form in a democratic political system characterized by metropolitan and local governments funded by a metropolis-wide *land value tax*,[19] with local governments responsible for their own zoning and development practices in settlements located around existing and improved public transportation lines.

Anticipating (primarily for infrastructure cost and demographic reasons) an inevitable decay and abandonment of post-1945 sprawl suburbs, *Chicago 2109* would reclaim some 70 per cent of metropolitan Chicago's current suburban footprint as mostly pervious open land for villages, hamlets, agriculture, prairie, passive wastewater treatment, forest preserves and commercial forestry (Figure 13.2). By damming and re-reversing the Chicago River and creating new active (city) and passive (town and country) water treatment districts, *Chicago 2109* would supplement and repair Chicago's problematic storm water and wastewater infrastructure, recharge regional aquifers and send as clean water back to the Great Lakes Watershed what is now sent as partially treated wastewater down the Mississippi River valley.

Chicago 2109 retains regional inter-state highways, but would re-urbanize in-city inter-state rights-of-way as parks, real estate and multi-modal transportation corridors. It envisions a re-established metropolitan agrarian-urban culture of rural-to-urban settlements – hamlets, villages, towns, cities – with agricultural and industrial activities, population density and land coverage appropriate to each. It illustrates a metropolitan region of city neighbourhoods and towns along improved and extended city and regional rail lines, and villages and hamlets in the rural landscapes in between.

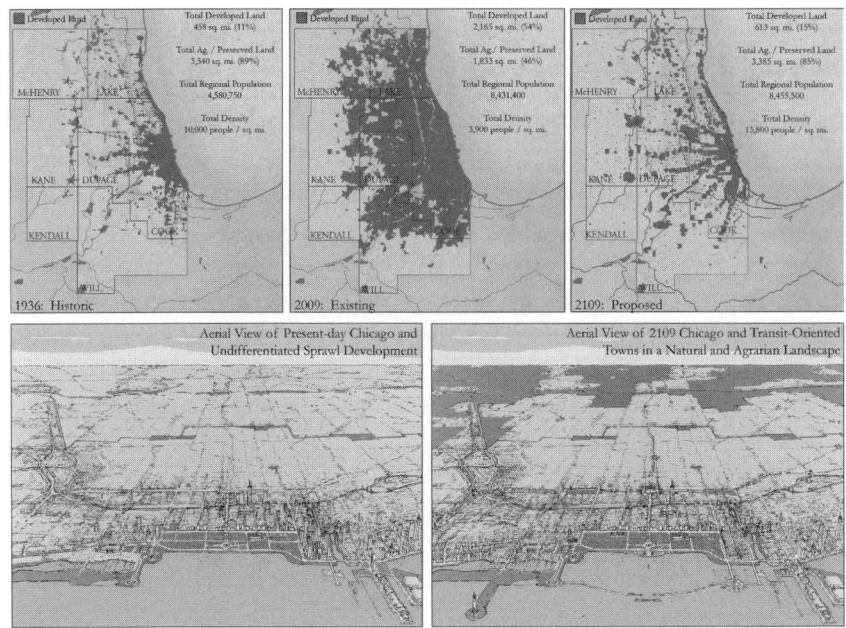

Figure 13.2 *Chicago 2109* – Land Use, existing and proposed. Courtesy Philip Bess.

It would encourage metropolitan Chicago's commercial development with simple form-based zoning codes subservient to local community-based and community-developed master plans. It triples the city's open land, and depicts a public realm of civic and religious buildings, and parks, plazas, squares, avenues, boulevards and streets established as normative and beautiful spaces for all. Finally, though *Chicago 2109* presumes that for economic and environmental reasons, durable and traditional low-embodied-energy materials and methods of construction will be more common in early-twenty-second-century Chicago, and that Chicago's more poorly built late-twentieth- and early-twenty-first-century buildings will not endure for 100 years, it also presumes that even through economic hardship, ways will be found to preserve Chicago's most beloved historic buildings. We imagine too that even when architectural hyper-modernism ceases to be culturally normative (for a combination of cost, durability, aesthetic and environmental reasons), architectural *modernism* will continue in Chicago as a local aesthetic tradition for architects who wish to pursue it and private patrons who are willing to pay for it.

Chicago 2109: Acknowledging Sacred Order

Virtually every walkable human settlement prior to the advent of modernist urbanism acknowledges sacred order in its formal arrangement. Sometimes that acknowledgement is the settlement itself, examples of which in the United States include the historic centres of planned cities like New Haven, Philadelphia, New

Orleans and Savannah. But *ad hoc* acknowledgements of sacred order are likewise evident in virtually every American town and city built prior to 1950, whether it is a church fronting a public square, or multiple churches located along a street.

Daniel Burnham chose not to address the issues of religious pluralism and sacred order in the *Plan of Chicago*, though the Burnham Plan did propose a governmental Civic Centre as a symbolic counterweight to downtown Chicago's commercial centre. Not only was this element of Burnham's Plan never realized, however, but – in a 1960s triumph of utilitarian symbolism over classical humanist ideals – the site proposed in 1909 for Chicago's city hall also became the Chicago Circle Interchange, meeting point of Chicago's several inter-state highways (Figure 13.3).

Chicago 2109 reclaims the freeway interchange site, and re-imagines the *Plan of Chicago*'s Civic Centre originally intended for it. Congress Street is restored as Burnham's east–west 'Grand Axis', now focused on a new 550-foot high-rise City Hall at Congress and Halsted, and a new north–south sacred cross-axis is established one block east of and parallel to Halsted in re-purposed inter-state rights-of-way (Figures 13.4–13.5). In contrast to the civic axis and its focus upon a single building, the sacred axis is a 1.2-mile-long – though symbolically infinite – linear public space – Columbian Exposition Boulevard – devoid of terminating buildings at either end. The new boulevard is fronted and defined along its length by six-storey residential and mixed-use 'background buildings' of mandated limestone or white terra cotta, punctuated by twelve religious buildings located on reserved sites. The sacred buildings depicted include a synagogue; Catholic, Orthodox, Protestant and Mormon

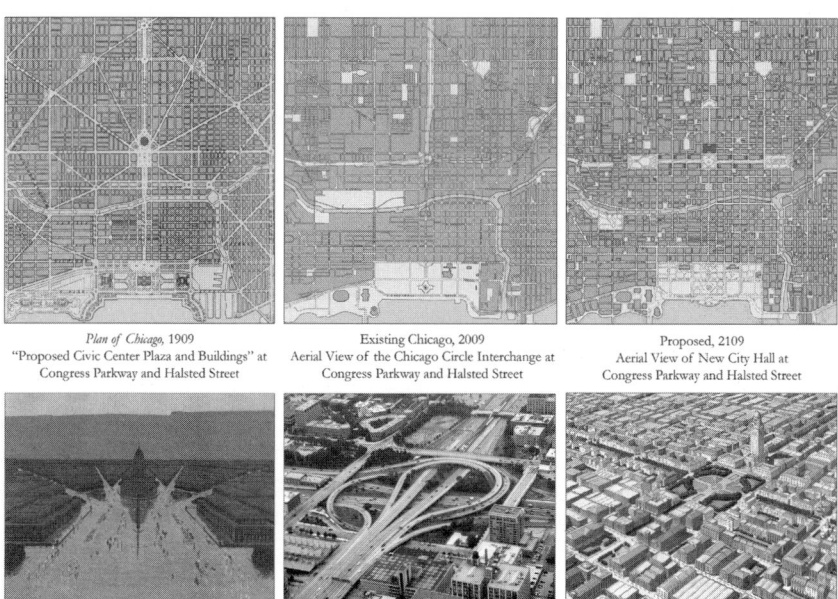

Plan of Chicago, 1909
"Proposed Civic Center Plaza and Buildings" at Congress Parkway and Halsted Street

Existing Chicago, 2009
Aerial View of the Chicago Circle Interchange at Congress Parkway and Halsted Street

Proposed, 2109
Aerial View of New City Hall at Congress Parkway and Halsted Street

Figure 13.3 *Chicago 2109* – The Once and Future Civic Centre. Three images courtesy Philip Bess.

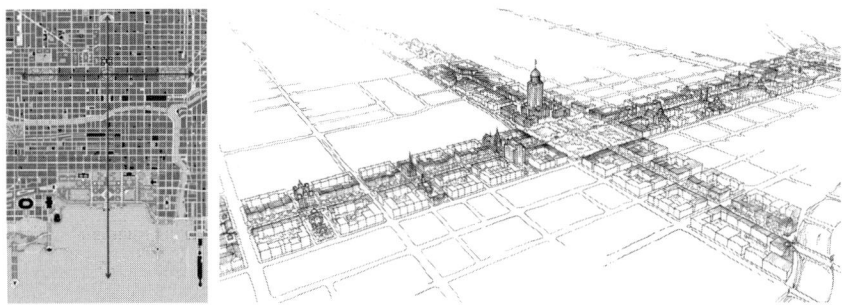

Figure 13.4 *Chicago 2109* – Left: Civic Axis/Sacred Axis Crossing, plan diagram; Right: preliminary perspective study. Courtesy Philip Bess.

Figure 13.5 *Chicago 2109* – Top: Columbian Exposition Boulevard, partial elevation looking west; Bottom Left: Civic Axis/Sacred Axis aerial perspective looking northwest; Bottom Right: Columbian Exposition Boulevard/Sacred Axis, perspective looking north. Courtesy Philip Bess.

churches; a mosque; and Hindu and Buddhist temples, as formal representatives of metropolitan Chicago's religious pluralism.

The proposed new sacred/civic axial crossing – premodern cosmography in a postmodern world – acknowledges formally both the religious dimension of metropolitan Chicago culture and the foundational American principles of religious non-establishment and free exercise. Re-interpreting and extending Burnham's original civic centre, it serves purposes practical and symbolic, mundane and sacred. Practically, it establishes a grand, formal and dense-but-human-scaled mixed-use neighbourhood at the centre of Chicago. Symbolically, it critiques Chicago's crony-capitalist culture and the prevailing hyper-modern urbanism, and better represents the dynamic reciprocity of Chicago's best environmental, commercial, civic and religious sensibilities, ambitions and duties. The result is a baroque-scale classical humanist city centre after Burnham: grounded in principle and informed by historic precedent, simultaneously traditional and new, distinctively American, unique to Chicago, a thing heretofore unseen.

Conclusion

After Burnham is an affectionate alternate reading of Chicago's history and present, and *Chicago 2109* a hopeful vision of Chicago's future. Informed by both a Catholic view of human flourishing and a commitment to the practices and purposes of classical humanist architecture and urbanism, they would identify and correct Chicago's past and present mistakes, and recover, build upon and extend what Chicago and America (and Notre Dame) do best – convinced that what each does best is a genuine contribution to the common good now, and points ultimately to the City of God. We imagine some spiritual descendant of Daniel Burnham, surveying Chicago in a hundred years, writing this:

> If the keynote of early twenty-first-century Chicago was 'clout', entertainment and display, we Chicagoans of today find that our dominant idea is human flourishing. We have ceased to be impressed by graceless and costly architectural ephemera that depend upon and celebrate arrogant privilege, but mystify honest and intelligent working persons. Chicagoans no longer accept an indifference to the middle class and the poor, a utilitarian attitude towards nature and international labour. What we insist upon asking now is this: How do we create opportunities for all Chicagoans to prosper on well-kept farms and in the homes, workshops, stores and offices of the towns and neighbourhoods of metropolitan Chicago? How do we love Chicago into a metropolis of durable, beautiful and ennobling places commensurate with our affection?

What affinities does *After Burnham* have with other explorations of religion and innovation featured in this volume? That remains to be seen. It may be germane to religious communities and economic development in the Global South, especially as manifest in expanding cities, the current livability and sustainability of which remain in question. *After Burnham* may also interest anthropologists, insofar as it includes a cosmographical component proposing to acknowledge in urban form that Chicago is not only a political order within a larger natural context, but also exists within sacred order. Such acknowledgement, we trust the anthropologists will confirm, was typical of premodern human settlements. Only time will tell whether such acknowledgement again becomes common, or whether the postmodern/post-sacred must perforce become the post-*anthropos*.

Intellectually, we hope *Chicago 2109,* in particular, demonstrates how in the modern world it is possible all at once to profess classical humanist architecture and urbanism in local accents, think phenomenologically about religion and religious truth claims, think sociologically about the effects of religion upon individuals and societies – and at the same time work out of an overarching religious and theological metanarrative. For several members of the *Chicago 2109* design team, the Catholic intellectual tradition has informed our work throughout, both substantively and methodologically, and illuminated its various practical and symbolic *teloi*. I do not mean by this that *Chicago 2109* is an argument for Catholic Christianity per se. (If anything, it is more an argument for classical humanist architecture and urbanism.) But it *is* an argument for a holistic view of architecture and urbanism that in its metaphysical realism and sacramental sensibilities, its understanding of nature and human nature, Catholic intellectual culture encourages, and does so in competition with theories and practices by comparison less capacious in their estimations of nature, human nature and the divine. Metanarratives aside, we hope *Chicago 2109*'s environmental, practical and aesthetic merits will appeal immediately to Catholics and non-Catholics, classicists and non-classicists alike, but we want to be clear (if only for ourselves) from whence we come.

In the end, what is new about *Chicago 2109*? A few details at different scales – the town-and-country wastewater treatment; the re-urbanizing of inter-state rights-of-ways; Columbian Exposition Boulevard as sacred axis – but more the effort to look at Chicago carefully and holistically, and in a world of increasingly hyper-modern urbanism to envision a counter-metropolis existing self-consciously for the sake of human flourishing, where beauty matters and parts relate to the whole in a context of sacred order – an effort no other architecture school (or university) appears to be trying to undertake. Whether in the end *Chicago 2109* can be regarded as innovative – or even as progressive, which is our own ambition – is a judgement left to others, and ultimately to God.

14 Technologies of Imagination: Secularism, Transhumanism and the Idiom of Progress

J. BENJAMIN HURLBUT

The project of this volume is to explore the relationship between religion and innovation and specifically to ask: Does religion contribute to innovation? This is an important question, because it runs against the grain of a widely held assumption about the role of religion in the development of post-Enlightenment societies. The grip of this assumption is evident in a wide variety of contexts. In social theory, the notion that advances in knowledge have tended to correspond with corollary displacements of religion has served to ground the thesis that the history of the West is a story of secularization. These transformations are seen as constitutive of modern society and its institutions. A similar, if far less theorized, account is widely present in contemporary cultural vernacular. Religion is seen as a necessarily conservative institution that emphasizes continuity of belief and practice rather than inviting progressive change, whereas (rational, scientific) knowledge aspires to endlessly transgress its own limits and innovate upon existing capacity to know and act upon the world.

Such accounts are simultaneously descriptive and proscriptive: they narrate the history of post-Enlightenment societies, even as they posit a set of natural and necessary relationships between religion and secular institutions. These relationships configure, on the one hand, notions of the forms of meaning and discourse appropriate in the public sphere and to institutions of liberal democracy[1] and, on the other hand, delineations between knowledge and norms and, thus, science and religion.[2] Thus, in running against the grain of widely held views about the separation of religion from secular and scientific institutions, the question invites us to interrogate relationships that have generally been treated as self-evident and fundamental to modernity.

Yet, in querying inter-relations between something called *religion* and something called *innovation*, the question, like the assumptions it perturbs, takes as given categories that are themselves very much situated within those relations. These categories themselves are powerful ordering devices in contemporary public life. Far from being merely descriptive labels, they are constitutive, deployed in the perpetual political work of separating what is shared, secular and even incontestable, from what is private, normative and potentially outside the bounds of shared public meanings. As such, these categories are not mere reflections of social and political forms of life; they also configure them. Indeed, this is what gives the question its import, since these categories reflect our own 'historical situated consciousness'.[3]

The aim of this chapter is to question the question: to interrogate some of the underlying assumptions about innovation and religion that 'make sense' of this question, and that render the presumption that religion inhibits – or at least does very little to enhance – innovation a cultural commonplace. For purposes of my analysis, I will take *innovation* to mean technological innovation. Innovation in contemporary public discourse is generally taken to refer to advances in knowledge, technique or technology. Interpreting innovation as technological unquestionably occludes other important forms of social and intellectual innovation. I take, however, the fact that the term has acquired this *de facto* meaning in our contemporary vernacular to be itself worthy of reflection. Thus, it is important to draw attention precisely to such occlusions and to explore their significance for the way the concept of innovation informs morally and religiously inflected notions of progress, hope, transcendence and the good.

The idea of innovation that circulates in contemporary public discourse is laden with political and normative meanings. The term figures centrally in contemporary ways of talking about human progress, benefit and the good. Yet, the forms of human activity that innovation tends to refer to are relatively narrow in scope. Thus notions of technological innovation become a locus for contending with questions of human purpose that have long been the province of religion. Importantly, my aim is not to suggest that this is to the exclusion of 'the religious', even if it does in some respects marginalize institutional religion. To the contrary, technological projects are often inflected with theological or ethico-religious valences.

I explore these questions through the case of transhumanism, an ideology of radical technological progress that anticipates the transformation of human beings – and transcendence of human limits – through advances in technological capacity. My focus is less on transhumanism as a body of philosophical ideas and more on the *transhumanist imagination*, that is, on the postures towards the future that transhumanism tends to reflect and crystallize. Thus my aim is to place transhumanism in a wider cultural context, attending to the ways the transhumanist imagination trades in more culturally widespread beliefs, values and imaginations of progress.

I approach transhumanism not as a body of philosophical doctrines or a coherent system of beliefs, but rather as a culturally situated project of moral imagination that draws together visions of technological futures, notions of progress (and perfection) and ideas of the human. The imaginations of the (technological) future that are advanced by transhumanists are laden with religious motifs, even as they bear markers of the (radically) secular. They offer narratives of transcendence in technocratic terms. They construct justice, liberty and salvation as technological achievements and, thus, as projects of innovation.[4] And they account for human nature, purpose and meaning in terms of a techno-developmentalist historicism that culminates in an eschaton – the so-called *singularity* (the notion, largely associated with Ray Kurzweil, for the time, soon approaching, when the exponential growth of computing and other technologies reaches the point when artificial intelligence overtakes human thinking with profound and unpredictable consequences).

In this respect, the transhumanist imagination complicates clean distinctions between the religious and the secular. It trades upon the notion of technological innovation as an (inevitable) outgrowth of post-Enlightenment science, and, thus, as of a piece with that most fundamental achievement of secular modernity. Yet, it advances a messianic utopianism replete with the language of salvation and transcendence whose central protagonist is technology. As such, transhumanism is a strange hybrid between the religious and the secular. At the same time, transhumanists draw strong boundaries between religion and secular technoscience. They claim forms of authority that are grounded in a radical denial of (religious) faith and an affirmation of secular modernity. To the question of whether religion inhibits innovation, they answer a resounding 'yes'. As such, transhumanism is a strange entity in a world where ideas and institutions are supposed to map cleanly onto these most basic categories of secular modernity.

The Transhumanist Imagination

Transhumanism refers to the application of science and technology to radically transform the human body. Transhumanists advocate a programme of technological innovation in the name of augmenting human physical and mental capacities. The term variously refers to a body of philosophical ideas, a transnational community of like-minded individuals and an ontological stage of human evolution. The transhuman is conceived as an evolutionary transition between *Homo sapiens* and a technological posthumanism in which the constraints of the human body are transcended through elimination of disease and pain, radical extension of lifespan and mechanical augmentation of human cognitive and physical capacities. Transhumanism is, therefore, a hybrid of a body of predictions about trajectories of technological innovation, a set of philosophical ideas about the role of technology in human life that celebrates these predictions and invites technological transformations of human beings, and a group of people who advocate, support and spearhead projects of innovation that serve these transformative ends. In short, it marries innovation science with an evangelical activism and a technologically grounded philosophical anthropology.

The transhumanist imagination is suffused with religious motifs and eschatological valences. My aim, however, is not to unmask transhumanism as (pseudo)religion, since it is neither religion nor not-religion. Nor is it merely to offer a problem-case in the taxonomy of the religious and the secular. I aim, rather, to show how the overtly eschatological dimensions of transhumanism draw upon a discourse and repertoire of imagination that is more widespread in contemporary society, one that privileges innovation – that is, technological futures – as a locus of moral imagination. These dimensions are hard to see in contemporary innovation discourse. By presenting them in their extreme form in transhumanist imaginations, I aim to draw attention to their more attenuated versions in a less radical and more culturally ubiquitous vision of innovation. My analysis is consonant with a broad literature on the history of science that rejects the narrative of intrinsic and inevitable conflict between religion and science (or for present purposes, technoscience). At the same time, my aim is not merely to trace interconnections and dependences between something called religion and something called science. I aim, rather, to interrogate the work that goes on in drawing a demarcation between them, including the boundary work that transhumanism does in constructing itself as consonant with, and grounded in, secular, enlightened science. I draw attention to the place of technology in what are generally considered to be secular imaginations of progress, and technological futures as a locus of moral-cum-theological imagination.

The technological futures that transhumanists imagine have become increasingly common objects of engagement, anxiety, celebration and critique. Transhumanists like Ray Kurzweil have become public figures. Transhumanist organizations (now generally 'H+') are increasingly common on college campuses, and discussion of the ethics of human enhancement and governance of emerging technologies increasingly engage with transhumanist ideas (sometimes also under the heading of *technological posthumanism*). Transhumanism has become an object of scholarly interest.[5] Bioethicists, including Julian Savelescu, John Harris and others, have introduced transhumanist ideas into mainstream bioethical and policy discussions.[6] On the other side, critics of such approaches have likewise elevated the visibility of transhumanist ideas. A 2004 special issue of *Foreign Policy*, in which leading public intellectuals identified 'the world's most dangerous ideas', included an essay by Francis Fukuyama on 'Transhumanism'.[7] The technological futures that transhumanists imagine have become increasingly common objects of engagement, anxiety, celebration and critique in both American and European contexts.[8] Transhumanism's futurism also reflects wider cultural currents that are partly responsible for its increasing visibility. As such, it offers an entry point for diagnosing cultural phenomena that bear upon the question of the relationship between religion and innovation.

It is easy to see the transhumanist imagination as an extreme ideology, a departure from the more modest (and realistic) visions of technological progress that inform mainstream approaches to innovation. Indeed, transhumanism has generally been analysed as a techno-utopian project, an ideology and a heretical cult. Scholars have examined consonances between transhumanism and other, older heretical and occult religious movements, including Gnosticism, hermeticism, Pelagianism and Arianism.[9] There is much in transhumanist talk to justify this sort of characterization. From outlandish predictions of an imminent technological eschaton, to theologically inflected descriptions of innovation as the path to perfection, there is ample warrant to see transhumanism as culturally 'other' and as appropriating and transforming more measured notions of technological innovation and progress. Philosopher of technology Langdon Winner observes that in transhumanism 'one finds a level of self-indulgence and megalomania that are [sic] off the charts. The greatest puzzle about this fin de siècle fad is how tawdry notions could have attracted such a large audience at all'.[10]

This construction of transhumanism as an extreme ideology distracts, however, from those features of the transhumanist imagination that are commonplace in contemporary cultural postures towards technological visions. Transhumanist imaginations of the technological future may indulge in grandiose production, but they draw upon thinking that is commonly used to anticipate emerging technological change. As transhumanists are quick to point out, many of their ideas simply extend the logic of technological innovation. As Transhumanist Nick Bostrom wrote in response to Fukuyama's article, 'The [transhumanist] agenda is a natural extension of the traditional aims of medicine and technology and offers a great humanitarian opportunity to genuinely improve the human condition'.[11] Perhaps the defining feature of transhumanism is the notion that human quintessence lies in the ability to transcend limitations through technological means. According to Ray Kurzweil, 'the essence of being human is not our limitations – although we do have many – it's our ability to reach beyond our limitations'.[12] In this sense, technology is elevated to an expression of the essentially human and realizes the potential for reweaving the very fabric of the human body. For Kurtzweil, transhumanism is grounded first in scientific observations about the dynamics of technological innovation. He has modelled and quantified rates of technological change to demonstrate that technology is subject to the 'law of accelerating returns'. Technology 'bootstraps' itself, growing ever more powerful, and ever more rapidly transcending prior limitations. It is, according to Kurtzweil, a regular process that can be modelled and predicted, yet one that we tend not to notice. He asserts that most people have an 'intuitive linear' view of history, as opposed to a more enlightened 'historical exponential' view. For him, this is a key distinction between an outmoded humanism and transhumanism. Transhumanists understand the dynamics of technological change and recognize that technological transcendence of human biological constraint is a historical inevitability. Thus, on this account, technology determines and drives history and is the dominant source of transformation of human lives and societies.

The transhumanist imagination is grounded in a commonplace historicism that narrates socio-technical change in terms of technology's developmental trajectory. For instance, Kurtzweil's models are consonant with a body of research that seeks to understand (and predict and control) innovation. By adopting a narrow, temporally circumscribed focus, innovation research tends to suppress questions of the good that arise in relation to transhumanism. This is more a function of the scale of analysis than the analytic framework through which socio-technical change is narrated.

One example of the consonance between transhumanist ideas and the mainstream discourse of innovation is the notion of converging technologies. Articulated in a report on 'Converging Technologies for Improving Human Performance' that was spearheaded by National Science Foundation division director and transhumanist Mikhail Roco, the concept was offered to map strategic opportunities for US federal investment in domains of science and technology that would engender innovation, economic activity and human benefit. The report advocated strategic investment to encourage convergence in the name of beneficial near-term technological and economic benefits. At the same time, it elevated technology to the status of prime mover in reshaping the landscapes of human life. 'Technology will increasingly dominate the world, as population, resource exploitation and potential social conflict grow. Therefore, the success of this convergent technologies priority area is essential to the future of humanity'.[13]

These forms of technocratic prediction easily harmonize with transhumanist narratives of transcendence. One transhumanist advocate writes:

> Our purpose is to transcend our limiting biology and the resulting limitations in our consciousness, thus enabling the rise of new kinds of sentient beings, freed from our genetic limitations in the pursuit of the highest transcendental aspirations and the promotion of cosmic evolution. ... This, I believe, is our calling. To say this may seem to be a leap of faith to some; but when examined carefully ... it simply follows a long-existing evolutionary trend.[14]

The author of the above passage is Ted Chu, former chief economist of the largest sovereign wealth fund in the Middle East. His analysis shifts seamlessly between mundane discussions of innovation trends and technological solutions to an eschatological idiom of cosmic evolution. Similarly, the argument of Kurtzweil's *Age of Spiritual Machines,* which imagines a (utopian) future in which the human being is transcended by new forms of disembodied intelligence, is essentially a playing forward of Moore's law of the rate of increase of computing power.[15] In these accounts, transcendence is a function of inevitable technological trends, and transhumanity is a natural and inevitable waypoint in a process of technological-cum-spiritual transformation. The singularity is at once an eschatological fulfilment of historical destiny and an inevitable outcome of mundane processes of technological change.

These imaginations of human nature, progress and eschaton are rooted in (self-styled) expert accounts of the mechanics of technological innovation. This has two important consequences. First, it frames a radical ontological re-imagining of the human subject as an inevitable consequence of technological progress in secular time. Transhumanism in this vein is not so much a choice (let alone a faith) as a recognition and acknowledgement of historical trends. It takes technology as the frame through which to read historical progress and discovers in it a truer picture of human quintessence and destiny. Second, it constructs the future in terms of inevitable trends that are only known to those experts who understand the dynamics of innovation. Ethical postures that invite transformations of human life are recast as simply accepting and embracing the lives to come. As Gregory Stock puts it: 'The human species is moving out of its childhood. It is time for us to acknowledge our growing powers and begin to take responsibility for them. We have little choice in this, for we have begun to play god in so many of life's intimate realms that we probably could not turn back if we tried.'[16]

In this narrative of inevitability, technology is the locus of agency and the driver of history. It allows transhumanists, as students of the dynamics of innovation, to claim a privileged position in seeing the future and thereby diagnosing those ideas and institutions that are obsolete, or, worse, inhibiting the unfolding of technological progress. Thus, on the one hand, Kurtzweil's predictions are ostensibly value-neutral and objective. On the other, they become the basis for an eschatological vision. This apparent transgression of a secular/religious boundary actually reflects a secular reconstruction of time that first having abandoned historical teleology recovers directionality via the concept of technology.

Technology occupies a powerful position in contemporary understandings of history and social change. Charles Taylor observes that one of the central transitions marked by secular modernity was a profaning of time, rendering it a homogenous container of contingent events.[17] The market is rooted in profane time. It is pure, temporally situated activity, but without direction or purpose beyond the particular, contingent activities of the individuals that make it up. When Francis Fukuyama famously declared the end of history, he was observing that the triumph of capitalism over communism had completed the profaning of time and foreclosed imaginations of historical progress. The last powerful teleological vision of history had given way to 'the end point of mankind's ideological evolution and the universalization of Western liberal democracy as the final form of human government'.[18] In Fukyuma's account, innovation is treated as a function of markets, and technology tends to reinforce market structures. Technological change, therefore, is consistent with historical stasis.

Yet, only a few short years later, Fukuyama declared the 'recommencement of history' under the guise of 'our posthuman future'.[19] In remarkable contrast to *The End of History and the Last Man*, technology becomes an agent of historical change. Fukuyama's declaration that transhumanism is a dangerous idea is built on the same vision of innovation as driver of historical change as Kurtzweil's singularity. Put differently, in both cases, 'technology' is constructed as a locus of agency. Technology brings about re-orderings of life. Questions about the good life then become questions of what sorts of technological futures are desirable. Visions of progress are articulated in terms of imagined technological futures.

This frame privileges technology as a measure of historical change and as a space of imagined futures. It also configures imperatives of action and allocations of power and authority in the present. First, in this frame, social (or socio-technical) change is driven by a small number of elite, creative agents. Innovators innovate, and innovations diffuse out into, and impact upon, the wider world. Second, notions of effects, impacts and consequences are corollary to this asymmetry between elite innovators and wider society. Innovation is characterized as the agent of change whose effects are felt in a passive social world. Third, innovation (and technological change, more broadly) is invoked to distinguish past from future and to narrate progress. In this respect, innovation is a normatively laden concept. It becomes a resource for explaining social change, but at the same time for articulating possible futures and delineating the deficiencies of the present in terms of the forms of innovation that can rectify them. Put differently, imaginations of innovation – of technological emergence and novelty – tend to simultaneously be imaginations of governance – of the right allocations of responsibility for transcending the problems of the present and achieving a better world. Insofar as technological innovation offers the means to (future) material comfort, (future) economic growth and (future) rectification of the infirmities and vulnerabilities of human life, innovation becomes a social imperative. It also becomes the framework through which such problems are diagnosed.

This tendency to imagine the good in terms of technological futures is a defining feature of 'knowledge societies'. It has become central to practices of governance in contemporary democracies.[20] It has also configured a particularly consequential point of contact between religion and innovation as theological engagement with ideas of the human person have since the 1960s been increasingly undertaken in response to, and in terms of, the possibilities of human genetic engineering.[21] This has also been a critical domain for mapping the boundaries between religious and secular reasoning, and their respective roles in public deliberation and democratic governance, both within public controversies around biotechnology, and in the configuration of policy-relevant moral expertise, for instance, in professional bioethics.[22]

These cultural preoccupations reflect a world that is suffused with the products of science and technology, but they also reflect cultural habits of mind. Science and technology are not only material, epistemic and institutional presences in the world, but also objects of collective imagination. Indeed, technological futures become sites of moral imagination in ways that are configured not merely by specific technological possibilities, but by the idea of technology as such.

Making Sense of Technology

The term *technology* is ubiquitous in contemporary public discourse. National development strategies identify 'technological innovation [as] a significant driver of economic growth'.[23] Industries rise and fall on perceptions of the promise of technology sectors.[24] And critics worry about the impact of technology upon social life. 'Is there too much technology in our modern lives?' asks one observer. 'So much of modern life involves us standing absolutely still, like lobotomised privates on parade, while *technology* goes to work'.[25]

Yet, *technology* is a slippery concept. The term seems to refer to something solid, self-contained and independent of the social arrangements from whence it emerges and within which it is embedded. It assumes a kind of agency in common discourse. Technology 'impacts' upon society. Technology moves too fast for society to keep up with it. Technology exacts costs and produces unintended consequences. Yet, despite this discourse of 'autonomous technology',[26] it is difficult to offer a definition of technology as such that does not thoroughly bleed over into the social world from which it is ostensibly independent. Nor can technology be easily decomposed into specific technolog*ies*. The meanings and forms of agency that are attributed to technology dissipate as the unitary figure of technology is broken down into a heterogeneous field of tools and techniques. As much is evident in the fact that the term *technology* is difficult to define.

The *Oxford English Dictionary* offers the following definition: 'The branch of knowledge dealing with the mechanical arts and applied sciences; the study of this. ... The product of such application; technological knowledge or know-how; a technological process, method, or technique. Also: machinery, equipment, etc., developed from the practical application of scientific and technical knowledge.' While this covers some of the relevant territory, none of these terms, whether taken individually or collectively, could substitute for technology in the phrases above without losing important aspects of their meaning.

The historian of technology Thomas Hughes offers another definition: 'Craftsmen, mechanics, inventors, engineers, designers and scientists using tools, machines, and knowledge to create and control a human built world consisting of artifacts and systems associated mostly with the traditional fields of civil, mechanical, electrical, mining, materials and chemical engineering.'[27] This definition has the merit of drawing attention to the situatedness of material technologies within the forms of human knowledge, practice and aspiration that are deployed to manipulate the material world. Yet, in highlighting this embeddedness, Hughes's definition excludes the meanings – and forms of autonomy and agency – that tend to get attributed to *technology* in common speech. Put differently, while Hughes's definition invites us to dissolve technology into the heterogeneous social, material, institutional and epistemic parts that make it up, it distracts from the discursive figure of *technology* as a repository of meaning and an object of collective imagination.

Hughes's contextualist approach is characteristic of the social-scientific analysis of technology. Historians and sociologists of technology have long observed that technologies, whether transformative or mundane, are deeply situated in, emergent from and refractory of the social, political, economic and intellectual worlds that they inhabit, and must be analysed accordingly. The uses technologies are put to, the meanings they acquire and even the functional forms that they take are deeply interwoven with the social realities that surround them.[28] Indeed, analysis of technologies can function as a powerful entry point into interrogating social, political and moral orders, particularly in their material instantiations. Though technological objects are 'taken to be fundamentally neutral as regards their moral standing', they are 'not merely aids to human activity, but also powerful forces acting to reshape that activity and its meaning'. Rejecting the notion of technological determinism – where technology acts upon and shapes society – political theorist Langdon Winner argues that the material effects of technological arrangements are felt only in relation to the genuine choices to construct them and incorporate them into social life in particular ways.[29]

Indeed, scholars in science and technology studies (STS) have extensively criticized the notion of technological determinism (and its cousin in evolutionary economics, path dependency), interrogating the social contingency and historical specificity of technological innovation and its inevitable entanglement with a putatively distinct social sphere. STS scholar Bruno Latour observes: 'Every day in our newspapers we read about more entanglements of all those things that were once imagined to be separable – science, morality, religion, law, technology, finance, and politics. But these things are tangled up together everywhere: in the Intergovernmental Panel on Climate Change, in the space shuttle, and in the Fukushima nuclear power plant.'[30]

Latour argues that a conception of society that overlooks the material and technological arrangements that pervade it is grounded in a false demarcation between nature and culture. Technology dissolves into the myriad forms of capacity, agency and socio-material arrangement that are abroad in the world. For Latour, this contextualism becomes a kind of metaphysics: material artefacts, including technologies, are elevated to agents alongside human actors. 'We are never faced with objects or social relations, we are faced with chains [of humans and nonhumans]'.[31] Technologies are moral actors insofar as machines discipline human agency and responsibility. 'No human is as relentlessly moral as a machine … we have been able to delegate to nonhumans not only force as we have known it for centuries, but also values, duties and ethics'.[32]

Yet, while Latour may offer a means for seeing past the alleged value-neutrality of technological artefacts, he offers scant resources for making sense of technology as an object of collective moral imagination. Observing the disciplining function of the ubiquitous beeping technologies that inhabit our world tells us little about what aspirations to progress inform projects of technological innovation, or why imaginations of right order are articulated in the idiom of technological futures. At best, Latour problematizes the concept of technology as a singular category and its assumed separation from an equally mythical *society*.

The contextualist project of differentiating technology into technologies makes *technology* as an analytic concept problematic. Technologies are always multiple, and always already embedded in socio-technical contexts. The resilience of the concept of technology, however, suggests that, given its powerful presence in public discourse, it does far more work than as a descriptive category of a class of objects.

The term *technology* emerged in the late nineteenth century, displacing 'the mechanical arts'.[33] Cultural historian Leo Marx has noted that technology's 'relative abstractness compared with the "mechanical arts," had a kind of refining, idealizing, or purifying effect upon our increasingly elaborate contrivances for manipulating the object world, thereby protecting them from western culture's ancient fear of contamination by physicality and work'. Thus, as an idealized concept, technology also acquired a particular moral valence. It allowed for a dissociation of technical capacities from the specificities of social life, locating them in a distinct sphere and attributing to them an internal, self-contained logic and momentum of progress. Imagined as a force of social ordering in itself, technology assumes a kind of autonomy in collective imagination. By this token, the notion of the role of technological innovation in social progress shifts from *using* technical capacity to achieve socially defined ends, to social progress itself becoming an expression of technological progress as improvements in human well-being, social order and governance are increasingly understood as technical problems in need of innovative technological solutions.

This attribution of agency and autonomy to technology has several consequences, including 'the illusion that technology drives history'.[34] Importantly for my purposes, it also renders the concept of technology a historicizing frame that is deployed to narrate progress: tracing the history of civilization means drawing a developmental trajectory of progressive technological advance. Hence the commonplace that technology is accelerating, and society is struggling to keep up. This construal ignores the social forces that shape technologies, but it affects the ways in which relationships between technological and social orders are understood and configured, including the ways technologically inflected visions of the future engender tensions between secular and theological discourses of progress. As technology is imagined to be a unified category and an agent of historical progress, it also acquires a moral and messianic role. Technological utopianism is nothing new. Centuries ago, Francis Bacon's *New Atlantis* exemplified the utopia as a tool in political philosophy for articulating political and moral virtues by imagining a materially perfected world. Importantly, for Bacon, utopian imagination was simultaneously technological, political and theological, as human ingenuity became the means to recovering (or reconstructing) a prelapsarian state.

As technology has come to figure in an American vernacular of progress, it has maintained its political and theological valences, but has shed the radical unattainability of utopia (as, literally, 'no place'), and has become central to shared aesthetic and political imaginations of progress. The roots of this run deep, and trace in part to the politics of American religion. Historian David Nye has described the emergence of the 'technological sublime' as a peculiarly American relationship with feats of technological innovation. In the context of American religious pluralism, technological achievements have served as objects of religious-like veneration in American civic life, and thus as loci for constructing unifying visions of progress and collective identity. Far from displacing religious feelings, visions of technological progress have come to be objects of them.[35]

It is easy enough to discern the centrality of projects of technological innovation in constructions of shared political and moral identity. Indeed, political theorist Yaron Ezrahi has argued that science and technology were critical resources to the high modern state in performing its legitimacy.[36] Thus, for instance, John F. Kennedy declared the space programme central to 'the battle that is now going on around the world between freedom and tyranny', that will turn on 'the impact of this adventure on the minds of men everywhere, who are attempting to make a determination of which road they should take'.[37]

Some scholars have argued that the association of technology and secularization is historically false. Sociologist Bronislaw Szerszynski observes that technology 'far from being an instrument of desacralization that strips meaning from nature … serves ceremonial functions in maintaining a particular sacral ordering of nature'.[38] Historian of technology David Noble has demonstrated that technologies most celebrated as achievements of secular modernity are themselves 'rooted in religious myths and ancient imaginings'.[39] These revisionist accounts blur the boundary between religion and (secular) technoscience, but like the contextualist approaches discussed above, they do not yet account for the significance of the categories themselves. Put differently, though particular technologies can be located in a complex socio-historical context, the categories of science and technology, secular society and religion – and the presumed relations between them – remain fundamental concepts in the vocabulary of modernity. And these concepts have a life of their own. The distinction between technology and society, like the distinction between secularism and religion, has important consequences for the ways we govern innovation and confront the perturbations to social and normative order that technological change brings about. When technology is imagined to be autonomous from, even if impacting upon, the social world, we tend neither to ask questions about the normative commitments that are present in our very projects of innovation, nor to see clearly overt transgressions of these distinctions.

Technology, Religion and Secularism

The transhumanist imagination offers a particularly potent example of a vision that transgresses these boundaries while deriving authority from them. It is not easily classified as either an instrumental technological project or a messianic vision. It 'secularizes age old human pursuits of perfection, characteristic of all religions'.[40] Transhumanists use technoscience to locate the project in the tradition of secular enlightenment, while at the same time invoking the authority of science to challenge religion as a repository of ignorance and, furthermore, to diagnose it as a retrograde force with inhibitory effects on the (enlightened) project of innovation-driven redemption. As sociologist and transhumanist W. S. Bainbridge puts it:

> Until this point in history, humanity was ignorant and beset by insoluble problems. Religion assuaged fears, motivated sacrifice and strengthened social solidarity. … However, now it has become an impediment to the full flowering of science and technology and the transformation of humanity. … Humanity is crossing an abyss on a tightrope. Behind us is the old world of religious faith that compensated wretched but fertile people for the misery in their lives. On the other side, if we can only reach it is a new land where we no longer need to live by illusions, where wisdom and procreation are compatible, where truth and life are one.[41]

This remarkable passage transgresses the very line it invokes between premodern religion and post-Enlightenment secularism. As religious studies scholar Linell Cady observes, 'the cultural work of the religion/secular binary lends transhumanism the mantle of the modern, the rational, and the progressive, positioning religion as its antiquated, superstitious and regressive opponent'. She observes that 'the secularization narrative that envisions the differentiation of the various spheres of the market, science, and politics, and the privatization if not demise of religion'[42] is engaged by transhumanism to position itself squarely within secular modernity.

She rightly suggests that cultural formations like transhumanism pose challenges for the secularization thesis and invite attention to the ways in which religion has been reconfigured in novel forms and domains.

Transhumanism may, indeed, reveal the limitations of the secularization thesis, but it also reveals how the categorical distinctions between religious and secular that the thesis invokes have themselves become a cultural resource in the production of authority. And it exposes the ways in which science and technology function as loci of moral (and, indeed, soteriological) imagination within the dominant mappings of secularism. Indeed, Bainbridge's vision of 'the other side' where 'truth and life are one' is but a short distance from his account of convergent technologies that offer 'a new renaissance, embodying a holistic view of technology based on transformative tools, the mathematics of complex systems and unified cause-and-effect understandings of the physical world from the nanoscale to the planetary scale'.[43] This latter formulation, however, was offered in Bainbridge's capacity as a policymaker. It is drawn from a strategic report on US investment in nanotechnology. The secular story of technological redemption that it offers is a familiar one: public investment in converging technologies will 'achieve a tremendous improvement in human abilities, societal outcomes, the nation's productivity, and the quality of life'.[44]

Thus, the task is not to diagnose transhumanism in relation to these separate spheres – for example, to ask: Is it religious or secular? Is it science or ideology? – but to diagnose the ways in which authority is configured by a notion of the secular itself and its relationship to technology, on the one hand, and religion, on the other.

Recently, there has been renewed attention to the idea of the secular in social theory, in part by questioning the idea of secularism as a space of imagination and world ordering in modernity. As sociologists Craig Calhoun, Mark Juergensmeyer and Jonathan VanAntwerpen put it, 'secularism should be seen as presence. It is *something,* and is therefore in need of elaboration and understanding'. They continue, 'the demarcation between religion and the secular is made, not simply found'.[45] This analysis invites questions: How has the concept of secularism as a way of *knowing* society informed the very configuration of that society, and how have the practices, imaginations and norms that sustain that configuration privileged particular ways of knowing and understanding social order under the rubric of secularism? It draws attention to the fact that institutions of knowledge-making are part of the cultural landscape that shape and are shaped by wider configurations.

Like secularism, technology is a presence that is made, not found. It is a collectively imagined figure or an 'imaginary' (a collectively held vision that serves as the basis both for shared understandings and for the practices and commitments that sustain these understandings). These understandings come to be embodied in the material technologies we construct, and are made durable by the ways we organize our habits, sensibilities and norms around our technologies. The ways we tend to confront visions like those of transhumanism reflect an asymmetry between visions of progress articulated in terms of technological futures and visions that draw upon other resources of moral imagination, including theological ones. As Pope

Francis has observed, technology demands critical scrutiny as a common currency of moral imagination:

> In contemporary culture, we often tend to consider the only real truth to be that of technology: truth is what we succeed in building and measuring by our scientific know-how, truth is what works and what makes life easier and more comfortable. Nowadays this appears as the only truth that is certain, the only truth that can be shared, the only truth that can serve as a basis for discussion or for common undertakings.[46]

Technological futures are devices of political ordering in the subtle role of prophesying futures and promising a redeemed world. Consequently, there is a need – and an urgency – to rethink received dogma about the relationship of the religious not merely with the secular, but also the inter-relations that shape notions of science (and technology), secularism and religion in contemporary society.

Yet, the moral imperatives of redeeming suffering, imagining progress and aspiring to the good remain ever present. In our society, they are increasingly understood as imperatives of innovation, and thus are wrapped into the project of imagining – and enacting – technological futures: technological innovation is a domain of moral imagination. Yet, it is a politically asymmetric space in which an elite few claim the authority to see – and make – the future. The autonomy of science as a supposed space of pure knowledge and as a generator of instrumental goods for society is grounded in the notion that it sits apart from public space. Its autonomy is seen as a normative prerequisite for its integrity as an institution of modernity, a configuration that is itself underwritten by a collectively held imagination of science as a creative source of innovation and a driver of history.[48]

This imagination of science places society in a position of perpetual reactivity, awaiting the production of the future by technoscience. It constructs moral postures towards technology as either resistant or accommodating to technoscientific creativity, but not contributory to it. Thus, transhumanists label critics of human biotechnology 'bioconservatives' over against pro-technology 'bioprogressives'.[49] The choice is between inviting or resisting the forward historical movement along the trajectory of technological progress, but the trajectory itself goes unquestioned.

The habit of imagining technology as a driver of history and a wellspring of progress is consequential. Technological futures become a space of imagination within which particular conceptions of progress, of the human person and of the good are engaged, displacing others. Yet, the configuration of that space is determined by authoritative declarations of what revolutions are realistic, what upheavals of social and moral order are inevitable and, thus, what moral anxieties do or do not warrant engagement. Visions of progress, of justice and of redemption are recast in a technological idiom. And theological reflection on the nature of the human person is transmuted into a task of technology assessment.

This reflects a profound attenuation of the repertoire of moral meaning available to engage with the fundamental problems of human nature, dignity and right that are so relevant to contemporary projects of socio-technical transformation. It reflects a cultural self-disciplining and an unwitting delegation to technoscience of authority and responsibility for imagining and enacting the good. It creates a secular priesthood of scientists and innovators. Though there are individuals who happily wear this mantle, I wish to emphatically stress that this position of moral authority is as much imposed upon science by society as it is invited by science. It is an outgrowth of a project of modernity whose imagination of right order unfolds in the ostensibly value-free space of instrumental reason, even as it places constraints on the repertoire of meaning deemed appropriate to processes of public deliberation and democratic governance.

As a technocratic, political and theological project, transhumanism is a particularly visible attempt to claim and occupy this priestly position: to preach a vision of innovation as a gospel of progress and to undertake a mission of world transformation. Yet, the history of the West is littered with messianic cults. Why does this new breed of messianism warrant any more attention than those that have preceded it? There is the simple fact that leading figures in the transhumanist movement occupy positions of privilege in the technoscientific establishment and have control over innovation agendas that are backed by large pools of capital. But in the scheme of things, these represent relatively trivial resources.

Transhumanism warrants attention, rather, because it draws upon – and thus draws attention to – the forms of authority that society has laid at its feet. It is a self-proclaimed priesthood whose proclamations we find hard to dismiss because we have difficulty locating them within the typologies of reason and authority that constitute an idea of secular modernity. In assuming an unprincipled position as followers of technoscience – always lagging behind, yet always anxiously awaiting, whatever future the cornucopia of innovation has in store for us – we find ourselves in the awkward position of being complicit in the imaginations of technology-driven progress, perfection and transcendence that transhumanism trades in.

Conclusion

I return to the question of this volume: does religion contribute to innovation? I have attempted to demonstrate that the question itself should be questioned to elicit the historical consciousness, hermeneutical posture and normative imagination that make it seemingly straightforward. I have argued that the concepts of religion and innovation (and its corollary, technology) evoke an idea of secular modernity that privileges visions of innovation – of possible technological futures – as a site of collective moral imagination and public reasoning. I have argued that imagining futures in a technological idiom imposes constraints for the forms of critique that are admissible in collective sense making. It engenders an asymmetry between competing accounts of what normative questions need to be asked, because those who claim authoritative knowledge of what futures are possible also define terms and agendas for moral deliberation. It reinforces demarcations between knowledge and norms, rationality and religion – demarcations that are in the same moment being systematically transgressed. And in privileging technology as a site of historical agency, it occludes the role of collective imagination in constructing the very constraints that silence counter-imaginations.

Nearly a century ago, the great social theorist of technology Lewis Mumford wrote:

> We sleep under the light of stars that have long since ceased to exist, and we pattern our behavior by ideas which have no reality as soon as we cease to credit them. Whilst it holds together this world of ideas – this idolum – is almost as sound, almost as real, almost as inescapable as the bricks of our houses or the asphalt beneath our feet. ... An idea is a solid fact, a theory is a solid fact, a superstition is a solid fact as long as people continue to regulate their actions in terms of the idea, theory, or superstition; and it is none the less solid because it is conveyed as an image or a breath of sound.[50]

Mumford penned these words in his first book, *The Story of Utopias*. From this survey of imaginations of perfection – worlds fabricated of ideas – he shifted his sights from the idolum to the 'bricks of our houses' and 'the asphalt beneath our feet'. This apparent displacement of attention from the rich idea-world of politics to the instrumentalism of technique, from moral imagination to mundane materiality, in fact reflects a powerful insight about modernity. The *idolum* is inscribed in the technological orders we construct and no less in the technological futures we imagine. Imagined technological futures are rendered 'solid fact' as they are made to regulate the world of moral imagination, delineating the possible and the actual, and constraining the repertoire of meaning that is available in making sense of human progress, purpose and good. And as ideas are ultimately rendered in the brick and mortar of the built technological world, imaginations of progress limned in matter, their newfound solidity may well obscure the contingent configurations that usher them into the world.

Thus, insofar as the question of this volume demands that we analyse a world that we presume to grasp by mapping relations between categories that we presume to understand, the question should be refused. But insofar as it invites us to interrogate concepts and categories that are at once so commonplace that they are exempt from critical examination, yet so consequential in practice that they configure the very shape of human lives, the question is profound and urgent. In the spirit of that invitation, we must therefore also ask: What collectively held visions of right knowledge, reason and progress – solid as brick, yet mere 'breath of sound' – configure and constrain creative innovation in the work of moral imagining? And what repertoires of meaning – religious and otherwise – can engender the humility that this task demands?

Afterword: Innovation and Religion, Today and Tomorrow

ADAM KEIPER

It seems intuitive, doesn't it – the idea that religion is opposed to innovation? After all, many of the most visible aspects of Western religious life seem to incline away from innovation and towards its sometime-opposite: preservation. Religious styles of architecture, modes of dress, rituals and language, and matters of morals and doctrine tend towards the transmission of tradition rather than the embrace of the new. Our eyes can plainly see the evidence of religious conservatism that caught the attention of Émile Durkheim and some of the other early sociologists of religion.[1]

Moreover, nearly everywhere we turn we are told that religion is necessarily opposed to modern science, one of the great wellsprings of innovation. Prominent public issues, ranging from policy disputes (like the teaching of evolution or alternative explanations for human origins in public schools) to moral matters (like some of the implications of the debate about when a human life begins) to more abstract and metaphysical debates (like whether miracles are possible and whether mankind has a special status in the universe), are widely characterized as parts of a broad conflict between science and religion. As the story is usually told, religion stood against the ideas of Galileo and Darwin, two of the foremost figures in the history of science. And now, in bestselling books, on television shows, in articles by public intellectuals and interviews with celebrities, we hear the familiar refrain: religion is the enemy of science; science and religion are at war; science must destroy religion.[2] If religion and modern science are fundamentally at loggerheads, perhaps that antagonism should be understood as religion opposing innovation itself.

And what do we mean by *innovation*? Etymologically, the word refers simply to bringing something new into the world. Its early usage in English often connoted troublesome novelty and pernicious change in the status quo; would-be innovators and their desired innovations merited wariness.[3] But nowadays when we speak of innovation, it is almost always as a term of approbation. Innovation is generally understood to be a good thing. The term is used most often in the context of economics, technology, business and policy: we laud innovators; we celebrate their innovations; our universities and companies hand out an endless variety of innovator awards; we strive to achieve an 'innovation economy'; we launch innovation initiatives and establish innovation hubs; we create blue-ribbon innovation commissions. When innovation is discussed in newspapers and magazines, it is often depicted as elusive, something we crave more of, something at which nations compete to outdo one another. The clichés and mixed metaphors pile high: innovation is a race, or part of an ecosystem, or an engine we need to feed, or a science, or an art or both a science and an art.

Although politicians and the popular press have abused the term *innovation*, we can thank the denizens of America's schools of business and management for making it a buzzword in the first place. Clayton M. Christensen, the Harvard Business School professor arguably most responsible for the ubiquity of innovation talk, laid out the 'principles of disruptive innovation' that businesses could employ to keep up with the changing times – a sort of applied version of Schumpeter's theory of creative destruction.[4] Christensen's wildly popular *The Innovator's Dilemma*, like most of its followers in the unceasing parade of innovation literature, explains innovation as a dichotomy: there is sustaining innovation, which is easy, and there is disruptive innovation, which is difficult but necessary if a business is to survive. Other books describe open versus closed innovation,[5] intersectional versus directional innovation,[6] and so on and on. In each case, the distinction is highly normative: success depends on innovating in the right way. Innovations that are sustaining, incremental, directional and limited are inferior to innovations that are disruptive, non-incremental, non-linear, systemic, radical and 'intersectional' (i.e. that bring together different 'fields, disciplines, or cultures'[7]), since the latter variety will reshape markets and have a noticeable impact on social practices.[8]

The widespread influence on public rhetoric of the innovation literature emanating from US business schools is especially remarkable in the light of the vacuity of that literature's sweeping pronouncements and pat formulas. Consider what Gary Hamel, a consultant and professor described as 'the world's leading expert on business strategy' and 'the world's reigning strategy guru',[9] has had to say about innovation in the 'age of revolution' in which we now live:

> Change has changed. No longer is it additive. No longer does it move in a straight line. ... We have not so much reached the end of history, as Francis Fukuyama would have it, as we have developed the capacity to interrupt history – to escape the linear extrapolation of what was. ... In the age of revolution, the future will be different from the past and, perhaps, infinitely better. Our heritage is no longer our destiny. ... In the age of revolution we will see competition not only between business models, but between innovation regimes. Big science, boffins in their labs, seemingly intractable problems ... this was the innovation regime of the industrial age. ... The new industrial order is the product of a very different type of innovation – one built on neither the slow accretion of scientific knowledge nor the breathless hype of Madison Avenue, but instead by leaps of human imagination.[10]

The quotability of the bromides almost conceals their emptiness. 'Change has changed' in such a way that it no longer moves 'in a straight line'? But no student of history would claim that change – in business or in any other field of human affairs – was ever simply 'additive' and moved in a straight line. (Indeed, if 'linear extrapolation' from the past were possible, then our forebears would have been able to predict the future with perfect accuracy.) 'The future will be different from the past and, perhaps, infinitely better'? The silliness of the first half of that sentence (of course, the future will be different from the past) is only exceeded by the meaninglessness of the second half (what does it mean for the future to be 'infinitely' better?). How strange to imply that the accumulation of scientific knowledge and the advent of the modern advertising industry somehow did not result from 'leaps of human imagination', or indeed, that human imagination has not been responsible for innovation until our own era. And this from the individual ranked as the world's most influential business thinker.[11]

The modish obsession with such a desiccated understanding of innovation, both in the realm of commerce and more generally in public life, bespeaks the 'upsetting and edgy uncertainty', as historian Jill Lepore has put it.[12] The ideology of innovation does not promise us success; the only hope it holds out is the possibility of survival, if we are canny enough to change. And insofar as religion is believed to stand athwart innovation – insofar as it is a source of continuity instead of disruptive change – one gets the sense that the innovationists would have us reject religion. We should embrace the new; religion tends to oppose the new; religion must either keep up or give up.

How much richer is the discussion of religion and innovation in this book! In these pages the presumption that religion is simply opposed to innovation is nowhere to be found. Absent, too, is the assumption that innovation is nearly always a good and desirable thing. The scholars contributing to this anthology tackle a range of complex subjects, from the formative role of religion in pre-Columbian societies to the complicated tales of modern secularism; from the rise of science to the spread of capitalism; from powerful beliefs and abstractions, such as guilt to the most concrete (literally) manifestations of religion, such as architecture. These essays, cliché-smashers all, should help us begin to think more clearly about the ways in which religious beliefs and practices have contributed to changes in human affairs and have, in turn, been shaped by those changes.

Major Trends

It is fitting to conclude this volume with some speculation about what the future, and even the distant future, might hold for religion and innovation. Our conjectures about the future ought to be informed by history – by the lessons of the distant past, and by the broad trends of the last several centuries, some of which have been addressed or at least mentioned already in this book. Modernity has witnessed a series of institutions, beliefs and phenomena that have transformed religious ideas, practices, traditions and functions. Some of those institutions and beliefs have sought to explain the world and to restructure the entirety of human experience, from birth to death and beyond. Some have supplanted aspects of the temporal power of religion, sometimes quite by accident, sometimes with the explicit intention of usurping the power or prestige of religion. Although in our speculation about the decades and even centuries ahead we can only be certain about one thing – that religions will continue to change both from within and from without – the exercise may help illuminate some of the trends taking shape around us.

Let us begin with nationalism, understood here in the most general sense – not as an extreme patriotism that favours one nation over another, but as the very concept of nation state sovereignty. The map of Europe, smeared red in a long century of religious bloodletting, was redrawn with fresh ink in 1648. The new borders channelled common local and regional interests into national ones; religious passions and enmities by no means evaporated, but they were increasingly pooled with other concerns of state and thereby somewhat moderated and made more stable. Although several stateless ethnic and religious groups slipped through the cracks – the Kurds, the Roma and Sinti, the Hmong, the Jews until 1948, and others – the Westphalian system of sovereign states has spread around the globe, ordering and organizing international affairs.[13] When warfare arises that is primarily motivated by religious and ethnic concerns, it has by default usually been understood and treated as a domestic matter or a conflict between separate states.

But various forces and institutions have been chipping away at the nation state paradigm. The nineteenth-century growth of international movements and ideologies, the creation in the twentieth century of intergovernmental organizations like the United Nations and its sprawling bureaucratic apparatus, the expansion of international law for the purposes of peace and commerce and the post-Second World War project of Europeanization have all challenged the Westphalian system.[14] So too has globalism – the spread around the world of people, goods, information and ideas. And sub-state and transnational actors, such as multinational corporations and terrorist networks, have an ability to defy nation states and to influence world events.

While the nation state system will remain resilient as long as the vast preponderance of economic and military 'hard power' is in the control of national governments, these challenges to its dominance raise some provocative questions relating to religion and innovation. For instance, the Peace of Westphalia represented a significant curtailment of the authority of the Church to wield power across borders; therefore, national sovereigns assumed the ultimate authority over matters within their jurisdictions, including the legitimacy and permissibility of different religions. How might religions fare in an era in which the nation state system is weakened? While it is unlikely that the pope, or indeed any transnational religious leadership, will assert direct political power on the world stage anytime soon, the new tools of transportation and communication technology amplify the ability of religions – via commentary and texts, missionaries or messages direct from leaders – to reach believers and find new followers. These practices could strengthen religious institutions and weaken states. And even when the explicit aims of transnational religious movements are extremely unlikely to be realized, the effects of those movements can still be quite profound. For example, the pan-Islamic movements that seek to unite the *ummah* in a new global political order are very unlikely to achieve their aim given the power of the states (Muslim and otherwise) that oppose it, but those movements' propaganda, money and arms have destabilized governments and changed the course of world history.

Thanks to the transportation and information technologies that enable the spread of people and ideas, all the world's religions are jangling up against one another. The inhabitants of cities and countries where commerce thrives have always brushed up against unfamiliar religions. But today, especially due to the global near-ubiquity of television and the internet, even physically remote places can be sites of intimate encounters with foreign beliefs and believers (including, of course, atheistic and anti-religious beliefs and believers). Will these interactions give rise to new antagonisms, new spasms of violence and new pushes for orthodoxy and purity? Or will religious beliefs and practices ebb away when exposed to different beliefs and to unbelief? Will the vast diversity of religious doctrines and practices someday merge into just a few great, global religions, like tiny creeks and rivers all flowing into the oceans? Or will today's religions – not to mention the unfathomable complexity of cultural byways affecting and affected by religions, from food to language to art – result in strange and unpredictable blends?

Some recent examples of syncretism have sought to combine disparate world views and beliefs, have faced the critical scrutiny of both non-believers and orthodox believers and have arguably been stepping stones towards non-belief. Consider the combination of Western and Eastern religious traditions in the United States over the last sixty years. Scholarly interest in Asian philosophy and religion around the turn of the twentieth century led by the 1960s to conceptual efforts to combine Buddhism with the wisdom of the moral teachings of Christianity; this has resulted in a lively and modern American version of Buddhism (sometimes called 'import Buddhism' to distinguish it from 'immigrant Buddhism').[15] But the New Age movement went further, adding cherry-picked elements of Hinduism, Taoism and the mystical traditions of Judaism (Kabbalah) and Islam (Sufism).[16] Cutting-edge and highly exploratory areas of science, like quantum mechanics and consciousness studies, were synthesized, too.[17] This messy concatenation of beliefs never gelled into any widely accepted doctrines or practices, although it lingers on in the eminently quotable clichés about spiritualism that trip off the tongues of pop-culture figures and that weigh down shelves heavy with self-help books.

This brings us to another of the major trends related to religion and innovation: the rise of psychology. The twentieth century saw the spread of this new approach – or really, set of approaches – to understanding and medically treating human beings. In the developed world, psychology and psychiatry came to be recognized as authorities on matters that religion alone could formerly address. And conversely, religions sometimes came to be characterized as therapeutic. Jung captured this notion, writing that 'religions are psychotherapeutic systems in the truest sense of the word, and on the grandest scale. They express the whole range of the psychic problem in mighty images; they are the avowal and recognition of the soul, and at the same time the revelation of the soul's nature'.[18]

The spiritual and metaphysical certainties available to religious believers in previous eras may be harder to come by today, but psychology offers not inconsiderable this-worldly comforts. In the first half of the twentieth century, the pioneers of psychology knowingly explored territory that had been the province of religion. By the second half, some critics were arguing that psychology, in some cases and settings, amounts to a religion – complete with spiritual advisers, rituals of confession and absolution and even sects and prophets.[19] Looking forward, however, the quasi-religious aspects of psychology may recede if the study and healing of the mind give way to the study and treatment of the brain. When psychology was aborning in Europe and the United States, theologians argued vigorously about its importance and cultural meaning.[20] Today, however, it is difficult to find evidence of interest among theologians in grappling with neuroscience. In the Western world, the transition from thinking of the soul as immaterial and immortal to thinking of it as an emergent property of the material and mortal brain may well depend on how successful the medical treatments that neuroscience makes possible are.

Like psychology, many philosophical, political and economic ideas have been described as tantamount to religions, from capitalism to Marxism to democracy to utilitarianism to positivism.[21] In the latter case, the similarity was intentional: Henri de Saint-Simon sketched out plans for temples dedicated to Isaac Newton, and Auguste Comte set himself forward as the *Grand-Prêtre de l'Humanité*, the high priest for all humanity.[22] Others eschew the comparison to religion. Many adherents of secular humanism, for example, feel that describing their views as an alternative to religion is to cede conceptual ground to theism, so they prefer to describe secular humanism as a 'life stance'.[23] In recent years, comparisons to religion have encompassed the environmental movement (which has its own 'saints, sins, prophets, predictions, heretics, demons, sacraments, and rituals'[24]), celebrity culture (wherein we use such theological terms as 'worship, icon, divinity, fall, redemption, and salvation'[25]), the field of sociology (which is 'a profoundly *sacred* project at heart ... animated by *sacred* impulses, driven by *sacred* commitments, and serv[ing] a *sacred* project'[26]) and even consumer technology (where, for example, terms like 'cult', 'acolytes', 'worship' and 'saint' have described affection for the Apple Corporation, its founder and its branded products[27]).[28] Although such comparisons to religion are often superficial or intended as smears, they sometimes highlight intellectual analogies or social similarities that reveal at least indebtedness to religious thought and tradition.

Are there some political conditions that will in the future be more open than others to religion, innovation and religious innovation? Here a set of conflicting tensions comes into play. Liberal democracy permits the free exercise of religion and is conducive to various forms of innovation. But liberal democracy is, by definition, tolerant of a range of beliefs, including unbelief. Social science data suggest that professed unbelief and religious unaffiliation are nearly as common in liberal democracies as under regimes where religion is or was suppressed.[29] If there is some truth to the much-talked-about notion that liberal democracy represents the 'end of history', does the related Hegelian understanding of religion – the understanding that Christianity, although a necessary precondition for liberal democracy, is 'the last great slave ideology' and its 'secularization' and self-abolishment is crucial for 'the completion of the historical process' – suggest that Christian belief and practice will inevitably wane as liberal democracy strengthens and spreads?[30] How can that thesis be reconciled with the brute facts of demography, which show that populations of religious believers are in general more likely to expand while more secularized populations are likely to stabilize or even contract?[31] And what of other religions not so entangled in the Hegelian dialectic process of history, like India's bewildering diversity of religions? The subcontinent is quickly modernizing without undergoing every one of the philosophical and political debates that characterized rising secularization in the West. The richness of religious innovation over the last four generations of rapid modernization in India suggests that liberal democracy and religious belief and practice – including porous religious belief that sees divinity active in the mundane, everyday world – may not be incompatible as the Hegelians suggest.[32]

The Future of Religion and Innovation

The pluralism of liberal democracy has an analogue in the academy. To speak of 'religion' and 'religions' with scholarly detachment is to step outside of one's own beliefs and commitments. This is, on the one hand, an enlarging of the sphere of one's concerns to better and more fully understand human nature; as Max Müller, a founder of the field of comparative religion, famously put it: 'He who knows one [religion], knows none.'[33] On the other hand, this stepping outside can also represent a diminishment. To disinterestedly put contrasting religious beliefs and conflicting truth claims on an equal analytical footing can invite a kind of relativism and can shrink what the experience of religion most truly and fully is.[34] The diminishment is greatest when the scholarly analysis is scientific and reductionist. As early as the 1860s, Edward B. Tylor began to develop an evolutionary interpretation of religion, linking the origins of religion to survival in primitive times and the changes in religion to the shifting needs of human civilization.[35] One of the bestselling books of the late nineteenth century, William Winwood Reade's *The Martyrdom of Man*, made this argument most vividly, depicting religion as an evolved phenomenon that once served an important function, but that humanity has largely outgrown and must now be rid of.[36] Today, it is the biological sciences that carry on in this practice, regularly reporting new evidence or arguments for the proposition that religious, or at least spiritual, tendencies are etched into our genes and our brains.[37] The effort to explain (or explain away) religion is thus interestingly paradoxical: it suggests that we evolved into religious belief and that we can (or must) move beyond it, but it also reminds us that we are stuck with religion since a longing for spirituality and grand metaphysical explanations is permanently baked into our very nature.

But what if human nature is not fixed? Recent technological advances give us new abilities to remake ourselves. 'We, as human beings, have tamed the fire of life', writes the molecular biologist Lee Silver. 'And in so doing, we have gained the power to control the destiny of our species'.[38] Other technologies that do not yet exist but are being hotly pursued by teams of researchers around the world – especially in the so-called 'converging' fields of nanotechnology, biotechnology, information technology and cognitive science and technology – promise even greater power to redesign who and what we are. An age of 'superintelligent' and 'spiritual' machines beckons; minds and machines will merge; we will enjoy bodily immortality; and we will eventually shed our material existence to become beings of almost limitless power and intelligence, with all the cosmos as our playground.[39] This is the promise of transhumanism – the belief that we will leave behind more and more of the constraints of our merely human nature until we become something new, something 'posthuman', something ever more omnipotent and omniscient.[40]

In transhumanism, we see innovation and religion merge: technology and theology become one, and our deep desires for understanding and perfection unite with our hunger for the new. Whether the transhumanist vision is plausible remains to be seen. It may melt away to nothing, as so many other futurist fads have done before it. But the mere prospect that some part of the transhumanist vision might be possible raises three questions with which it is fitting to close this book. First, by what standard can we judge when innovation is in progress, especially as it is seeks after ultimate things? Second, what is the future of religion when mankind's ambition seems directed towards increasingly god-like power and knowledge? And finally, to what extent are we defined not by what we can do and know but by what we cannot, by the incompleteness of it all, by the limits to our understanding of our purpose, origins and ends – and our struggle or graceful acceptance in the face of eternal mystery?

Notes

Introduction

1. Several authors in this volume speak to this widely held assumption. See chapters by Peter Harrison and J. Benjamin Hurlbut, and Adam Keiper's Afterword.

2. The scholarly literature combatting the view that science and religion have been implacable foes is substantial. For accessible introductions to this scholarship, see Ronald L. Numbers (ed.), *Galileo Goes to Jail and Other Myths about Science and Religion* (Cambridge, MA: Harvard University Press, 2009); and Donald A. Yerxa (ed.), *Recent Themes in the History of Science and Religion* (Columbia: University of South Carolina Press, 2009).

3. Colin Renfrew, 'Introduction: Becoming Human: Changing Perspectives on the Emergence of Human Values', in *Becoming Human: Innovation in Prehistoric Material and Spiritual Culture*, ed. Colin Renfrew and Iain Morley (Cambridge: Cambridge University Press, 2009), 3–4.

4. Ian Hodder, 'Conclusions and Evaluation', in *Religion in the Emergence of Civilization: Çatalhöyük as a Case Study*, ed. Ian Hodder (Cambridge: Cambridge University Press, 2010), 340; and Jacques Cauvin, *The Birth of the Gods and the Origins of Agriculture*, trans. Trevor Watkins (Cambridge: Cambridge University Press, 2000).

5. Shah's chapter complements the recent work of intellectual historian Larry Siedentop, who makes the case in *Inventing the Individual: The Origins of Western Liberalism* (London: Allen Lane, 2014) that 'liberal thought is the offspring of Christianity' (332). Unlike Shah who examines the Patristic period, Siedentop focuses on the fourteenth and early fifteenth centuries.

6. Victoria S. Harrison, 'The Pragmatics of Defining Religion in a Multi-Cultural World', *International Journal for Philosophy of Religion* 59 (2006): 140–1.

7. Hodder, 'Conclusions and Evaluation', 332–8. See also Ian Hodder, *Entangled: An Archaeology of the Relationships between Humans and Things* (Malden, MA: Wiley-Blackwell, 2012); and Timothy Insoll, 'Are Archaeologists Afraid of Gods? Some Thoughts on Archaeology and Religion', in *Belief in the Past: The Proceedings of the 2002 Manchester Conference on Archaeology and Religion*, ed. Timothy Insoll (Oxford: Archaeopress, 2004), 1–6.

8. William T. Cavanaugh, *The Myth of Religious Violence: Secular Ideology and the Roots of Modern Conflict* (New York: Oxford University Press), 7–8.

9. See Peter Harrison, *The Territories of Science and Religion* (Chicago: University of Chicago Press, 2015), 1–11, and ch. 4; Peter Harrison, *'Religion' and the Religions in the English Enlightenment* (Cambridge: Cambridge University Press, 1990); Brent Nongbri, *Before Religion: A History of a Modern Concept* (New Haven, CT: Yale University Press, 2013); and Cavanaugh, *Myth of Religious Violence*, 7–8, and ch. 2. For a spirited challenge to those who stress the recent social 'constructedness' of the concept of religion, see Martin Riesebrodt, *The Promise of Salvation: A Theory of Religion*, trans. Steven Rendall (Chicago: University of Chicago Press, 2009), esp. 1–20.

10. Harvey Whitehouse, 'Theorizing Religions Past', in *Theorizing Religions Past: Archaeology, History, and Cognition*, ed. Harvey Whitehouse and Luther H. Martin (Walnut Creek, CA: AltaMira Press, 2004), 230.

11. As philosopher Victoria Harrison has argued, just because a term lacks clear meaning, it does not mean it is analytically unimportant. Harrison, 'Pragmatics of Defining Religion', 144–6.

12. See Scott Berkun, *The Myths of Innovation* (North Sebastopol, CA: O'Reilly Media, 2010), xvi.

13. Michael J. O'Brien and Stephen J. Shennan, 'Issues in Anthropological Studies of Innovation', in *Innovation in Cultural Systems: Contributions from Evolutionary Anthropology*, ed. Michael J. O'Brien and Stephen J. Shennan (Cambridge, MA: MIT Press, 2010), 3–4.

14. H. G. Barnett, *Innovation: The Basis of Cultural Change* (New York: McGraw-Hill, 1953), 7.

15. It should be noted that the possibility of genuine novelty is also conceptually problematic. Innovation does not occur in a vacuum. As one scholar put it, 'Innovation with no tradition at all would produce unintelligibility.' See G. E. R. Lloyd quoted in Armand D'Angour, *The Greeks and the New: Novelty in Ancient Greek Imagination and Experience* (Cambridge: Cambridge University Press, 2011), 24.

16. Innovation remains, as Michael North has recently said about its conceptual twin *novelty*, 'a crucial and yet vague term in the sciences, social sciences, and the arts'. Michael North, *Novelty: A History of the New* (Chicago: University of Chicago Press, 2013), 5–7.

17. Clearly, before anything approaching a general theory can be advanced, more work needs to be done. It would be helpful to have an outline history of religion and innovation to provide the contours of a provisional narrative that would be revised and refined in the light of new research. Such a history might revisit some controversial notions advanced in the twentieth century, including Karl Jaspers' Axial Age thesis (updated by Robert Bellah), Lynn White's work on medieval religion and technological inventiveness, Robert Merton's perspective on the role of Puritan values in helping to motivate scientific activity in the seventeenth century, and even Élie Halévy's views on Methodism as a politically conservative force in the age of the French Revolution.

18. Here I borrow from Michael North's conceptual understanding of novelty as a function of recurrence, recombination or some combination of the two. See North, *Novelty*.

19. Alister McGrath, 'Understanding Cultural and Theological Resistance to Special Divine Action' (lecture, St Anne's College, Oxford, July 2015), http://www.ianramseycentre.info/videos/beyond-modularisation-282.html (accessed 15 February 2015).

Chapter 1

1. Lars Fogelin, 'The Archaeology of Religious Ritual', *Annual Review of Anthropology* 36 (2007): 55–71.

2. David L. Webster, 'On Theocracies', *American Anthropologist* 78, no. 4 (December 1976): 812–28.

3. Émile Durkheim, *The Elementary Forms of the Religious Life: A Study in Religious Sociology*, trans. Joseph Swain (London: Allen & Unwin, 1915).

4. John W. Rick, 'The Evolution of Authority and Power at Chavín de Huántar, Peru', *Archaeological Papers of the American Anthropological Association* 14 (2004): 71–89.

5. Ibid.; and Silvia R. Kemble and John W. Rick, 'Building Authority at Chavín de Huántar: Models of Social Organization and Development in the Initial Period and Early Horizon', in *Andean Archaeology*, ed. Helaine Silverman (Malden, MA: Blackwell), 51–76.

6. Richard L. Burger, *Chavín and the Origins of Andean Civilization* (London: Thames and Hudson, 1992).

7. See John Ware, *A Pueblo Social History: Kinship, Sodality, and Community in the Northern Southwest* (Santa Fe, NM: School for Advanced Research Press, 2014); and Camilla H. Wedgwood, 'The Nature and Function of Secret Societies', *Oceania* 1, no. 2 (July 1930): 129–45.

8. See Michael J. O'Brien and Stephen J. Shennan (eds), *Innovation in Cultural Systems: Contributions from Evolutionary Anthropology* (Cambridge, MA: MIT Press, 2010).

9. Michael B. Schiffer, 'Can Archaeologists Study Processes of Invention?' in Ibid., 235–50.

10. See Ian Hodder, *Entangled: An Archaeology of the Relationships between Humans and Things* (Malden, MA: Wiley-Blackwell, 2012).

11. See examples in Sander E. van der Leeuw and Robin Torrance (eds), *What's New? A Closer Look at the Process of Innovation* (London: Unwin Hyman, 1989).

12. Rick, 'Evolution of Authority and Power at Chavín'. For an example, see Armand D'Angour, *The Greeks and the New: Novelty in Ancient Greek Imagination and Experience* (Cambridge: Cambridge University Press, 2011), esp. 36–63.

13. Peter Kaulicke, 'Espacio y Tiempo en el Periodo Formativo: Una Introducción', *Boletín de Arqueología PUCP* 12 (2008): 9–23.

14. See Ruth Shady Solis and Carlos Leyva (eds), *Los orígenes de la civilización andina y la formación del Estado prístino en el antiguo Perú* (Lima: Instituto Nacional de Cultura, 2003).

15. Shelia Pozorski and Thomas Pozorski, *Early Settlement and Subsistence in the Casma Valley, Peru* (Iowa City: University of Iowa Press, 2006).

16. John W. Rick et al., 'La cronología de Chavín de Huántar y sus implicancias para el Período Formativo', *Boletín de Arqueología PUCP* 13 (2009): 87–132.

17. See the several articles dealing with the Formative period in the *Boletín de Arqueología PUCP* 12 and 13 (2008 and 2009).

18. Rick, 'Evolution of Authority and Power at Chavín'; and Richard L. Burger, 'Unity and Heterogeneity within the Chavín Horizon', in *Peruvian Prehistory: An Overview of*

Pre-Inca and Inca Society, ed. Richard W. Keatinge (Cambridge: Cambridge University Press, 1988), 99–144.

19. John W. Rick, 'Religion and Authority at Chavín de Huántar', in *Chavin: Peru's Enigmatic Temple in the Andes*, ed. Peter Fux (Zürich: Scheidegger & Spiess, 2013), 167–76; Burger, *Chavín and the Origins of Andean Civilization*; Luis G. Lumbreras, *Chavín: Excavaciones Arqueológicas*, 2 vols (Lima: Universidad Alas Peruanas, 2007); and Julio C. Tello, *Chavín: Cultura Matriz de la Civilización Andina*, *Primera parte* (Lima: Universidad Nacional de San Marcos, 1960).

20. John H. Rowe, *Chavín Art: An Inquiry into Its Form and Meaning* (New York: The Museum of Primitive Art, 1962).

21. John W. Rick, 'Un Analisis de los Centros Ceremoniales del Periodo Formativo a Partir de los Estudios en Chavín de Huántar', *Boletín de Arqueología PUCP* 10 (2006): 201–14.

22. Tello, *Chavín: Cultura Matriz*.

23. Lumbreras, *Chavín: Excavaciones Arqueológicas*.

24. Burger, *Chavín and the Origins of Andean Civilization*.

25. Richard L. Burger, 'The Radiocarbon Evidence for the Temporal Priority of Chavín de Huántar', *American Antiquity* 46, no. 3 (1981): 592–602; and Richard L. Burger and Lucy C. Salazar, 'The Manchay Culture and the Coastal Inspiration for Highland Chavín Civilization', in *Chavín: Art, Architecture, and Culture*, ed. William J. Conklin and Jeffrey Quilter (Los Angeles: Cotsen Institute of Archaeology, UCLA, 2008), 85–105.

26. Rick et al., 'La cronología de Chavín'.

27. John W. Rick, 'Context, Construction, and Ritual in the Development of Authority at Chavín de Huántar', in *Chavin: Art, Architecture, and Culture*, ed. Conklin and Quilter, 3–34.

28. Rick et al., 'La cronología de Chavín'.

29. Silvia Rodriguez Kembel, 'The Architecture at the Monumental Center of Chavín de Huántar: Sequence, Transformations, and Chronology', in *Chavin: Art, Architecture, and Culture*, ed. Conklin and Quilter, 35–81; and Silvia Rodriguez Kembel and Herbert Haas, 'Radiocarbon Dates from the Monumental Architecture at Chavín de Huántar, Peru', *Journal of Archaeological Method and Theory* (September 2013): 1–83.

30. Daniel A. Contreras, '(Re)constructing the Sacred: Landscape Geoarchaeology at Chavín de Huántar, Peru', *Archaeological and Anthropological Sciences* (August 2014).

31. John W. Rick, 'Cambio y Continuidad, Diversidad y Coherencia: Perspectivas Sobre Variabilidad en Chavín de Huántar y el Período Formative', *Senri Ethnological Studies* 89 (2014): 261–89; and Seiichi Izumi and Toshihiko Sono, *Andes 2, Excavations at Kotosh, Peru* (Tokyo: Kadokawa Publishing Co., 1963).

32. Burger, *Chavín and the Origins of Andean Civilization*.

33. Luis G. Lumbreras, 'Excavaciones en el Templo Antiguo de Chavín (sector R). Informe de la Sexta Campaña', *Ñawpa Pacha* 15 (1977): 1–38.

34. John W. Rick, 'Architecture and Ritual Space at Chavín de Huántar', in *Chavin: Peru's Enigmatic Temple*, ed. Fux, 151–66.

35. Rick. 'Context, Construction, and Ritual'.

36. Miriam A. Kolar et al., 'Ancient pututus contextualized: Integrative archaeoacoustics at Chavín de Huántar, Peru', in *Flower World: Music Archaeology of the Americas*, ed. Matthias Stöckli and Arnd Adje Both (Berlin: Ekho Verlag, 2012), 23–53.

37. Aldona Jonaitis (ed.), *Chiefly Feasts: The Enduring Kwakiutl Potlatch* (Seattle: University of Washington Press 1991).

38. Contreras, '(Re)constructing the Sacred'.

39. Richard Burger, 'What Kind of Hallucinogenic Snuff Was Used at Chavín de Huántar? An Iconographic Identification', *Ñawpa Pacha* 31, no. 2 (2011): 123–40; and Constantino Manuel Torres, 'Chavín's Psychoactive Pharmacopoeia: The Iconographic Evidence', in *Chavin: Art, Architecture, and Culture*, ed. Conklin and Quilter, 239–59.

40. Kent V. Flannery, 'The Cultural Evolution of Civilizations', *Annual Review of Ecology and Systematics* 3 (1972): 399–426.

41. Rick, 'Evolution of Authority and Power at Chavín'.

42. Flannery, 'Cultural Evolution of Civilizations'.

Chapter 2

1. This chapter was a result of research carried out through a Religion and Innovation in Human Affairs (RIHA) grant from The Historical Society (funded by the John Templeton Foundation). We would especially like to thank the RIHA programme leader and editor of this volume, Donald Yerxa, who offered advice, encouragement and good humour throughout the project. We would also like to thank the people of the lower Río Verde Valley for their friendship and assistance through the years as well as the Consejo de Arqueología and Centro INAH Oaxaca of the Mexican Instituto Nacional de Antropología e Historia. Additional funding for our archaeological research discussed in this chapter has been provided by grants from the following organizations: National Science Foundation (grants BNS-8716332, BCS-0096012, BCS-0202624, BCS-1123388, BCS-1123377), Foundation for the Advancement of Mesoamerican Studies (#99012 with Stacie King), National Geographic Society (grant 3767-88), Wenner-Gren Foundation (GR. 4988), University of Colorado at Boulder (CARTSS, CRCW, Norton Anthropology Fund, and Dean's Fund for Excellence), University of Central Florida Office of Research and Commercialization's In-House grant and start-up fund, Vanderbilt University Research Council and Mellon Fund, Fulbright Foundation, H. John Heinz III Charitable Trust, Explorers Club, Sigma Xi, Association for Women in Science, Women's Forum Foundation of Colorado, Colorado Archaeological Society and Rutgers University.

2. Periodization in Mesoamerican archaeology was originally based on theories of a cultural evolutionary sequence with Formative cultures developing into fluorescent civilizations in the Classic period and then declining in the Post-Classic. This sequence has not held up, however, since in some regions polities reached their greatest scale and complexity in the Formative period and in others not until the Post-Classic. Today these periods are used simply as arbitrary conventions.

3. Robert Carneiro, 'A Theory of the Origin of the State', *Science* 169 (1970): 733–8.

4. Lisa J. Lucero, *Water and Ritual: The Rise and Fall of Classic Maya Rulers* (Austin: University of Texas Press, 2006).

5. John E. Clark and Michael Blake, 'The Power of Prestige: Competitive Generosity and the Emergence of Rank Societies in Lowland Mesoamerica', in *Factional Competition and Political Development in the New World*, ed. Elizabeth M. Brumfiel and John W. Fox (Cambridge: Cambridge University Press, 1994), 17–30.

6. Anthony Giddens, *The Constitution of Society: Outline of the Theory of Structuration* (Berkeley: University of California Press, 1984); Ian Hodder, *Entangled: An Archaeology of the Relationship between Humans and Things* (Malden, MA: Wiley-Blackwell, 2012); and Timothy R. Pauketat, *An Archaeology of the Cosmos: Rethinking Agency and Religion in Ancient America* (London: Routledge, 2012).

7. Sarah B. Barber and Arthur A. Joyce, 'Polity Produced and Community Consumed: Negotiating Political Centralization in the Lower Río Verde Valley, Oaxaca', in *Mesoamerican Ritual Economy*, ed. E. Christian Wells and Karla L. Davis-Salazar (Boulder: University Press of Colorado, 2007), 221–44; and Arthur A. Joyce, 'The Founding of Monte Albán: Sacred Propositions and Social Practices', in *Agency in Archaeology*, ed. Macia-Anne Dobres and John Robb (London: Routledge, 2000), 71–91.

8. David A. Freidel, Linda Schele and Joy Parker, *Maya Cosmos: Three Thousand Years on the Shaman's Path* (New York: William Morrow, 1993); and Fray Bernardino Sahagún, *Florentine Codex: General History of the Things of New Spain*, trans. Charles H. Dibble and Arthur J. O. Anderson. 12 vols (Santa Fe, NM: School of American Research and the University of Utah, 1950–82).

9. John Monaghan, 'Sacrifice, Death, and the Origins of Agriculture in the Codex Vienna', *American Antiquity* 55 (1990): 559–69.

10. Antonia E. Foias, 'Ritual, Politics, and Pottery Economics in the Classic Maya Southern Lowlands', in *Commoner Ritual and Ideology in Ancient Mesoamerica*, ed. Nancy Gonlin and Jon C. Lohse (Boulder: University Press of Colorado, 2007), 167–94.

11. Patricia Plunket (ed.), *Domestic Ritual in Ancient Mesoamerica* (Los Angeles: Cotsen Institute of Archaeology Press, 2002).

12. Scott R. Hutson and Travis W. Stanton, 'Cultural Logic and Practical Reason: The Structure of Discard in Ancient Maya Houselots', *Cambridge Archaeological Journal* 17, no. 2 (2007): 123–44.

13. Joyce, 'Founding of Monte Albán'.

14. Julia A. Hendon, 'Having and Holding: Storage, Memory, Knowledge, and Social Relations', *American Anthropologist* 102, no. 1 (2000): 42–53.

15. Eduardo Viveiros de Castro, 'Exchanging Perspectives: The Transformation of Objects into Subjects in Amerindian Ontologies', *Common Knowledge* 10 (2004): 463–85; and María Nieves Zedeño, 'Animating by Association: Index Objects and Relational Taxonomies', *Cambridge Archaeological Journal* 19, no. 3 (2009): 407–17.

16. See Hodder, *Entangled*.

17. Ibid., especially chs 2–4 and pp. 95–6.

18. Sarah B. Barber, 'Defining Community and Status at Outlying Sites During the Terminal Formative Period', in *Polity and Ecology in Formative Period Coastal Oaxaca*, ed.

Arthur A. Joyce (Boulder: University Press of Colorado, 2013), 165–92; and Arthur A. Joyce, Marcus Winter and Raymond G. Mueller, *Arqueología de la Costa de Oaxaca: Asentamientos del Periodo Formativo en el Valle del Río Verde Inferior* (Oaxaca: Estudios de Antropología e Historia No. 40, Centro INAH Oaxaca, 1998).

19. See *Polity and Ecology in Formative Period Coastal Oaxaca*.

20. Barber and Joyce, 'Polity Produced'.

21. Sarah B. Barber et al., 'Formative Period Burial Practices and Cemeteries', in *Polity and Ecology in Formative Period Coastal Oaxaca*, 97–134; and Arthur A. Joyce et al., 'Negotiating Political Authority and Community in Terminal Formative Coastal Oaxaca', in *Political Strategies in Pre-Columbian Mesoamerica*, ed. Sarah Kurnick and Joanne Baron (Boulder: University Press of Colorado, in press).

22. Brian Stross, 'Seven Ingredients in Mesoamerican Ensoulment', in *The Sowing and the Dawning: Termination, Dedication, and Transformation in the Archaeological and Ethnographic Record of Mesoamerica*, ed. Shirley B. Mock (Albuquerque: University of New Mexico Press, 1998), 31–9.

23. Joyce, 'Founding of Monte Albán'.

24. Monaghan, 'Sacrifice, Death'.

25. John Monaghan, *The Covenants with Earth and Rain* (Norman: University of Oklahoma, 1995).

26. Sarah B. Barber, Andrew Workinger and Arthur Joyce, 'Situational Inalienability and Social Change in Formative Period Coastal Oaxaca', in *Inalienable Possessions in the Archaeology of Mesoamerica*, ed. Brigitte Kovacevich and Michael G. Callaghan (Washington, D.C.: American Anthropological Association, 2014), 38–53; and Joyce et al., 'Negotiating Political Authority'.

27. Sarah B. Barber and Mireya Olvera Sánchez, 'A Divine Wind: The Arts of Death and Music in Terminal Formative Oaxaca', *Ancient Mesoamerica* 23, no. 1 (2012): 9–24.

28. Barber, Workinger and Joyce, 'Situational Inalienability'.

29. Arthur A. Joyce, Marc N. Levine and Sarah B. Barber, 'Place-Making and Power in the Terminal Formative: Excavations on Río Viejo's Acropolis', in *Polity and Ecology in Formative Period Coastal Oaxaca*, 135–64.

30. Joyce et al., 'Negotiating Political Authority'.

31. Monaghan, *Covenants*, 167–89.

32. Arthur A. Joyce, *Mixtecs, Zapotecs, and Chatinos: Ancient Peoples of Southern Mexico* (Malden, MA: Wiley-Blackwell, 2010); and Joyce Marcus and Kent Flannery, *Zapotec Civilization* (London: Thames and Hudson, 1996).

33. Joyce, *Mixtecs*; and Marcus and Flannery, *Zapotec Civilization*.

34. Joyce, 'Founding of Monte Albán'.

35. Marcus and Flannery, *Zapotec Civilization*, 129.

36. Ibid., 131–3.

37. Robert Cahn and Marcus Winter, 'The San José Mogote Danzante', *Indiana* 13 (1993): 39–64.

38. Kent Flannery and Joyce Marcus, 'The Origins of War: New [14]C Dates from Ancient Mexico', *Proceedings of the National Academy of Sciences* 100, no. 20 (2003): 11801–5.

39. Kent Flannery and Joyce Marcus, 'The Rosario Phase and the Origins of Monte Albán', in *The Cloud People: Divergent Evolution of the Zapotec and Mixtec Civilizations*, ed. Kent Flannery and Joyce Marcus (New York: Academic Press, 1983), 74–7.

40. Richard E. Blanton, *Monte Albán: Settlement Patterns at the Ancient Zapotec Capital* (New York: Academic Press, 1978), 44.

41. Joyce, 'Founding of Monte Albán'.

42. Cira Martínez López, 'La residencia de la tumba 7 y su templo: Elementos arquitectónico-religiosos en Monte Albán', in *La Religión de los Binnigula'sa'*, ed. Victor de la Cruz and Marcus Winter (Oaxaca: IEEPO-IOC, 2002), 219–72, 250–5.

43. Joyce, 'Founding of Monte Albán'.

44. Javier Urcid, 'Las oráculos y la guerra: el papel de las narrativas pictóricos en el desarrollo temprano de Monte Albán (500 a.C.–200 d.C.)', in *Monte Albán en la encrucijada regional y disciplinaria: memoria de la quinta Mesa Redonda de Monte Albán*, ed. Nelly M. Robles García and Ángel Rivera Guzmán (Mexico City: Instituto Nacional de Antropología e Historia, 2011), 163–240.

45. Javier Urcid and Arthur Joyce, 'Early Transformations of Monte Albán's Main Plaza and Their Political Implications, 500 BC–AD 200', in *Mesoamerican Plazas*, ed. Kenichiro Tsukamoto and Takeshi Inomata (Tucson: University of Arizona Press, 2014), 149–67.

46. Joyce, *Mixtecs*, 131–41; and Urcid and Joyce, 'Early Transformations'.

47. John E. Clark, 'Ciudades tempranas olmecas', in *Reconstruyendo la ciudad Maya: El urbanismo en las sociedades antiguas*, ed. Andrés Ciudad Ruiz, María Josefa Iglesia Ponce de Léon and María del Carmen Martínez Martínez (Madrid: Sociedad Española de Estudios Mayas, 2001), 183–210; and Marcus Winter, 'La fundación de Monte Albán y los orígenes del urbanismo temprano en los altos de Oaxaca', in *Nuevas ciudades, nuevas patrias. Fundación y relocalización de ciudades en mesoamérica y el mediterráneo antiguo*, ed. María Josefa Ponce de León, Rogelio Valencia Rivera and Andrés Ciudad Ruiz (Madrid: Sociedad Española de Estudios Mayas, 2006), 209–39, 229–31.

48. Elsa M. Redmond and Charles S. Spencer, 'From Raiding to Conquest: Warfare Strategies and Early State Development in Oaxaca, Mexico', in *The Archaeology of Warfare: Prehistories of Raiding and Conquest*, ed. Elizabeth N. Arkush and Mark W. Allen (Gainesville: University Press of Florida, 2006), 336–93.

49. Joyce, *Mixtecs*, 155–9.

50. Redmond and Spencer, 'From Raiding to Conquest'.

51. Robert Markens and Cira Martínez López, 'El Sistema de Producción Cerámica en Monte Albán durante el Preclásico Tardío y el clásico Tardío', in *Bases de la complejidad social en Oaxaca: Memoria de la cuarta Mesa Redonda de Monte Albán*, ed. Nelly Robles García (Mexico City: Instituto Nacional de Antropología e Historia, 2009), 123–52; and Cira Martínez López and Robert Markens, 'Análisis de la función político-económico del conjunto Plataforma Norte lado poniente de la Plaza Principal de Monte Albán', in *Estructuras políticas en el Oaxaca antiguo*, ed. Nelly M. Robles García (Mexico City: Instituto Nacional de Antropología e Historia, 2004), 75–99.

52. Joyce, *Mixtecs*, 159.

Chapter 3

1. For example, see Timothy Insoll (ed.), *The Oxford Handbook of the Archaeology of Ritual and Religion* (Oxford: Oxford University Press, 2011).

2. See James C. Scott, *Domination and the Arts of Resistance: Hidden Transcripts* (New Haven, CT: Yale University Press, 1990).

3. Benjamin Alberti et al., '"Worlds Otherwise": Archaeology, Anthropology, and Ontological Difference', *Current Anthropology* 52, no. 6 (2011): 896–912; Nurit Bird-David, '"Animism" Revisited: Personhood, Environment, and Relational Epistemology', *Current Anthropology* 40, supplement (1999): 67–91; and Graham Harvey, *Animism: Respecting the Living World* (New York: Columbia University Press, 2006).

4. See, for example, Joyce Marcus and Jeremy Sabloff (eds), *The Ancient City: New Perspectives on Urbanism in the Old and New World* (Santa Fe, NM: School for Advanced Research Press, 2008); and Monica L. Smith (ed.), *The Social Construction of Ancient Cities* (Washington, DC: Smithsonian Institution Press, 2003).

5. Henry Marie Brackenridge, *Views of Louisiana Together with a Journal of a Voyage up the Missouri River, in 1811* (Chicago: Quadrangle Books, [1814] 1962).

6. Susan M. Alt, 'A Tale of Two Temples' (paper, Annual Meeting of the Midwestern Archaeological Conference, Columbus, Ohio, 24–6 October, 2013); and Timothy R, Pauketat et al., 'The Emerald Effect: Agency and the Convergence of Earth, Sky, Bodies, and Things' (paper, 70th Annual Southeastern Archaeological Conference, Tampa, FL, 7–10 November 2013).

7. Timothy R. Pauketat and Susan M. Alt (eds), *The Medieval Mississippians: The Cahokian World* (Sante Fe, NW: School for Advanced Research Press, 2014); and Timothy R. Pauketat, Susan M. Alt and Jeffery D. Kruchten, 'City of Earth and Wood: Cahokia and Its Material-Historical Implications', in *A World of Cities*, ed. N. Yoffee (Cambridge: Cambridge University Press, in press 2015).

8. See Marcia-Anne Dobres, *Technology and Social Agency* (Oxford: Blackwell, 2000); Lynn M. Meskell, *Object Worlds in Ancient Egypt: Material Biographies Past and Present* (London: Berg, 2004); and Christopher L. Witmore, 'Symmetrical Archaeology: Excerpts of a Manifesto', *World Archaeology* 39, no. 4 (2007): 546–62.

9. See, for example, Philip Abrams, 'Notes on the Difficulty of Studying the State', *Journal of Historical Sociology* 1 (1988): 58–89; Chris Fowler, *The Archaeology of Personhood: An Anthropological Approach* (London: Routledge, 2004); Rosemary A. Joyce, 'Unintended Consequences? Monumentality as a Novel Experience in Formative Mesoamerica', *Journal of Archaeological Method and Theory* 11 (2004): 5–29; Rosemary A. Joyce and Julia A. Hendon, 'Heterarchy, History, and Material Reality', in *The Archaeology of Communities: A New World Perspective,* ed. M. A. Canuto and J. Yaeger (London: Routledge, 2000), 143–60; Timothy R. Pauketat, 'The Economy of the Moment: Cultural Practices and Mississippian Chiefdoms', in *Archaeological Perspectives on Political Economies*, ed. G. M. Feinman and L. M. Nicholas (Salt Lake City: University of Utah Press, 2004), 25–39; and Timothy R. Pauketat, *Chiefdoms and Other Archaeological Delusions* (Walnut Creek, CA: AltaMira, 2007).

10. Benjamin Alberti et al., 'Worlds Otherwise', 896–912; Benjamin Alberti and Yvonne Marshall, 'Animating Archaeology: Local Theories and Conceptually Open-ended Methodologies', *Cambridge Archaeological Journal* 19, no. 3 (2009): 344–56.

11. See Bird-David, '"Animism" Revisited', 67–91; Harvey, *Animism*; Lee Irwin, *The Dream Seekers: Native American Visionary Traditions of the Great Plains* (Norman: University of Oklahoma, 1994); and Ray A. Williamson, *Living the Sky: The Cosmos of the American Indian* (Norman: University of Oklahoma Press, 1984).

12. See Marilyn Strathern, *The Gender of the Gift: Problems with Women and Problems with Society in Melanesia* (Berkeley: University of Califorina Press, 1988); and Roy Wagner, 'The Fractal Person', in *Big Men and Great Men: Personifications of Power in Melanesia*, ed. M. Godelier and M. Strathern (Cambridge: Cambridge University Press, 1991), 159–73.

13. Vine Deloria, Jr, *God is Red: A Native View of Religion* (Golden, CO: Fulcrum Publishing, 2003); A. I. Hallowell, 'Ojibwa Ontology, Behavior, and World View', in *Culture in History: Essays in Honor of Paul Radin*, ed. S. Diamond (New York: Columbia University Press, 1960), 19–52; and Lee Irwin, *The Dream Seekers: Native American Visionary Traditions of the Great Plains* (Norman: University of Oklahoma Press, 1994).

14. See Åke Hultkrantz, *Belief and Worship in Native North America* (Syracuse, NY: Syracuse University Press, 1981).

15. Severin M. Fowles, *An Archaeology of Doings: Secularism and the Study of Pueblo Religion* (Sante Fe, NM: School for Advanced Research Press, 2013); and David Morgan, *The Sacred Gaze: Religious Visual Culture in Theory and Practice* (Berkeley: University of California Press, 2005).

16. Timothy R. Pauketat, *An Archaeology of the Cosmos: Rethinking Agency and Religion in Ancient America* (London: Routledge, 2013).

17. Joseph Epes Brown, *The Spiritual Legacy of the American Indian* (New York: Crossroad Publishing, 1977), 93 [emphasis added].

18. Pauketat, *Archaeology of the Cosmos*, especially ch. 4.

19. See, for example, Arthur Joyce, 'Sacred Space and Social Relations in the Valley of Oaxaca', in *Mesoamerican Archaeology: Theory and Practice*, ed. J. Hendon and R. A. Joyce (Oxford: Blackwell, 2004), 192–216.

20. David G. Anderson and Robert C. Mainfort (eds), *The Woodland Southeast* (University of Alabama Press, 2002); Kenneth E. Sassaman, *The Eastern Archaic: Historicized* (Lanham, MD: AltaMira Press, 2010); Susan M. Alt, 'Making Mississippian at Cahokia', in *The Oxford Handbook of North American Archaeology*, ed. T. R. Pauketat (Oxford: Oxford University Press, 2012), 497–508; Timothy R. Pauketat, *Ancient Cahokia and the Mississippians* (Cambridge: Cambridge University Press, 2004); and Pauketat et al., 'City of Earth and Wood'.

21. Neal H. Lopinot, 'Cahokian Food Production Reconsidered', in *Cahokia: Domination and Ideology in the Mississippian World*, ed. T. R. Pauketat and T. E. Emerson (Lincoln: University of Nebraska Press, 1997), 52–68; James A. Brown, 'Where's the power in mound building? An Eastern Woodlands Perspective', in *Leadership and Polity in Mississippian Society* [Center for Archaeological Investigations, Occasional Paper

No. 33], ed. B. M. Butler and P. D. Welch (Carbondale: Southern Illinois University, 2006), 197–213; and George R. Milner, *The Cahokia Chiefdom: The Archaeology of a Mississippian Society* (Washington, DC: Smithsonian Institution Press, 1998).

22. Timothy R. Pauketat, 'A Fourth-Generation Synthesis of Cahokia and Mississippianization', *Midcontinental Journal of Archaeology* 27 (2002): 149–70.

23. Pauketat et al., 'City of Earth and Wood'.

24. See, for example, Susan M. Alt, 'Cahokian Change and the Authority of Tradition', in *The Archaeology of Traditions: Agency and History Before and After Columbus*, ed. T. R. Pauketat (Gainesville: University Press of Florida, 2001), 141–56; 'Identities, Traditions, and Diversity in Cahokia's Uplands', *Midcontinental Journal of Archaeology* 27 (2002): 217–36; and 'Unwilling Immigrants: Culture, Change, and the "Other" in Mississippian Societies', in *Invisible Citizens: Slavery in Ancient Pre-State Societies*, ed. C. M. Cameron (Salt Lake City: University of Utah Press, 2008), 205–22.

25. Philip A. Slater, Kristin M. Hedman and Thomas E. Emerson, 'Immigrants at the Mississippian Polity of Cahokia: Strontium Isotope Evidence for Population Movement', *Journal of Archaeological Science* 44 (2014): 117–27.

26. Timothy R. Pauketat et al., 'The Residues of Feasting and Public Ritual at Early Cahokia', *American Antiquity* 67 (2002): 257–79.

27. See Alt, 'Unwilling Immigrants', 205–22; Melvin L. Fowler et al., *The Mound 72 Area: Dedicated and Sacred Space in Early Cahokia* (Springfield: Illinois State Museum, Reports of Investigations, no. 54, 1999); Timothy R. Pauketat, '"Founders" Cults and the Archaeology of *Wa-kan-da*', in *Memory Work: Archaeologies of Material Practices*, ed. B. Mills and W. H. Walker (Sante Fe, NM: School for Advanced Research Press, 2008), 61–79; Timothy R. Pauketat, 'The Missing Persons in Mississippian Mortuaries', in *Mississippian Mortuary Practices: Beyond Hierarchy and the Representationist Perspective*, ed. L. P. Sullivan and R. C. Mainfort (Gainesville: University Press of Florida, 2010), 14–29; and Paula J. Porubcan, 'Human and Nonhuman Surplus Display at Mound 72, Cahokia', in *Mounds, Modoc, and Mesoamerica: Papers in Honor of Melvin L. Fowler*, ed. S. R. Ahler (Springfield: Illinois State Museum, Scientific Papers vol. 28, 2000), 207–25.

28. See Thomas E. Emerson, 'Water, Serpents, and the Underworld: An Exploration into Cahokia Symbolism', in *The Southeastern Ceremonial Complex: Artifacts and Analysis*, ed. P. Galloway (Lincoln: University of Nebraska Press, 1989), 45–92; *Cahokia and the Archaeology of Power* (Tuscaloosa: University of Alabama Press, 1997); 'Cahokian Elite Ideology and the Mississippian Cosmos', in *Cahokia: Domination and Ideology in the Mississippian World*, ed. T. R. Pauketat and T. E. Emerson (Lincoln: University of Nebraska Press, 1997), 190–228; Timothy R. Pauketat, 'The Tragedy of the Commoners', in *Agency in Archaeology*, ed. Marcia-Anne Dobres and John Robb (London: Routlege, 2000), 113–29; Timothy R. Pauketat and Thomas E. Emerson, 'The Representation of Hegemony as Community at Cahokia', in *Material Symbols: Culture and Economy in Prehistory* [Center for Archaeological Investigations, Occasional Paper No. 26], ed. John Robb (Carbondale: Southern Illinois University, 1999), 302–17; Patricia L. Crown et al., 'Ritual Black Drink Consumption at Cahokia', *Proceedings of the National Academy of Sciences* 109, no. 35 (2012): 13, 944–9; Thomas E. Emerson, Susan M. Alt and

Timothy R. Pauketat, 'Locating American Indian Religion at Cahokia and Beyond', in *Religion, Archaeology, and the Material World* [Center for Archaeological Investigations, Occasional Paper No. 36], ed. L. Fogelin (Carbondale: Southern Illinois University, 2008), 216–36; Thomas E. Emerson and Timothy R. Pauketat, 'Historical-Processual Archaeology and Culture Making: Unpacking the Southern Cult and Mississippian Religion', in *Belief in the Past: Theoretical Approaches to the Archaeology of Religion*, ed. D. S. Whitley and K. Hays-Gilpin (Walnut Creek, CA: Left Coast Press, 2008), 167–88; Pauketat, *Archaeology of the Cosmos*; and William F. Romain, 'Moonwatchers of Cahokia', in *Medieval Mississippians: The Cahokian World*, ed. T. R. Pauketat and S. M. Alt (Sante Fe, NM: School for Advanced Research Press, 2014), 33–44.

29. See J. McKim Malville, *A Guide to Prehistoric Astronomy in the Southwest,* rev. edn. (Boulder, CO: Johnson Books, 2008); and Anna Sofaer, *Chaco Astronomy: An Ancient American Cosmology* (Sante Fe, NM: Ocean Tree Books, 2008).

30. Pauketat, *Archaeology of the Cosmos*, 154, 174.

31. Ray Hively and Robert Horn, 'A Statistical Study of Lunar Alignments at the Newark Earthworks', *Midcontinental Journal of Archaeology* 31, no. 2 (2006): 281–322; and 'Hopewell Cosmography at Newark and Chillecothe, Ohio', in *Hopewell Settlement Patterns, Subsistence, and Symbolic Landscapes*, ed. A. M. Byers and D. Wymer (Gainesville: University Press of Florida, 2010), 128–64.

32. William F. Romain, *Shamans of the Lost World: A Cognitive Approach to the Prehistoric Religion of the Ohio Hopewell* (Lanham, MD: AltaMira Press, 2009); 'Moonwatchers of Cahokia', 33–44.

33. See Pauketat, *Archaeology of the Cosmos*.

34. John Francis Snyder, 'Certain Indian Mounds Technically Considered', in *John Francis Snyder: Selected Writings*, ed. C. C. Walton (Springfield: Illinois Historical Society, 1962), 230–73.

35. Pauketat, *Chiefdoms and Other Archaeological Delusions*, especially p. 85.

36. Michael F. Kolb, *Emerald Mound Geo. Report*, submitted to the Illinois State Archaeological Survey, University of Illinois, 2011.

37. B. Jacob Skousen, 'Memory, Monuments, and the Moorehead Phase Occupation at the Emerald Site' (paper, Annual Meeting of the Midwest Archaeological Conference, Columbus, Ohio, 24–7 October 2013).

38. Jeffrey D. Kruchten, 'Early Cahokian Fluidity on the Fringe: Pfeffer Mounds and the Richland Complex' (paper, 57th Annual Southeastern Archaeological Conference, Macon, GA, 9 November 2000); Sarah E. Otten, Melissa Baltus and Timothy R. Pauketat, 'Prayers on Cahokia's Periphery: New Evidence of Temple Ritual and Earthen Symbolism at the Pfeffer Site' (paper, 64th Southeastern Archaeological Conference, Knoxville, TN, 1 November 2007).

39. Alt, 'Tale of Two Temples'.

40. Emerson and Pauketat, 'Historical-Processual Archaeology and Culture Making'.

41. See Emerson, 'Cahokian Elite Ideology and the Mississippian Cosmos'; Emerson, Alt and Pauketat, 'Locating American Indian Religion at Cahokia and Beyond'; Pauketat, *Archaeology of the Cosmos*; and Romain, 'Moonwatchers of Cahokia'.

42. See Thomas E. Emerson, Dale L. McElrath and Andrew C. Fortier (eds), *Late Woodland Societies: Tradition and Transformation across the Midcontinent* (Lincoln: University of Nebraska Press, 2000).

43. Sarah E. Baires et al., 'Fields of Movement in the Ancient Woodlands of North America', in *Archaeology after Interpretation: Returning Materials to Archaeological Theory*, ed. Benjamin Alberti, Andrew M. Jones and Joshua Pollard (Walnut Creek, CA: Left Coast Press, 2013), ch. 10; Melissa R. Baltus and Sarah E. Baires, 'Elements of Power in the Cahokian World', *Journal of Social Archaeology* 12 (2012): 167–92; and Pauketat, '"Founders" Cults'.

44. Pauketat, *Archaeology of the Cosmos*, especially ch. 4.

45. Gordon V. Childe, 'The Urban Revolution', *Town Planning Review* 21 (1950): 3–17.

Chapter 4

1. In the preparation of this essay, I gratefully acknowledge the generous advice and specific recommendations of Robert Louis Wilken. I also thank Matthew Quallen, who provided extraordinary research assistance as well as an extremely perspicuous editorial eye. Most of all, I thank Donald Yerxa and Wilfred McClay. Their intellectual vision and creativity enabled the Religion and Innovation in Human Affairs (RIHA) programme to spawn the scholarly initiatives represented in this volume.

2. See John Rawls, *Political Liberalism* (New York: Columbia University Press, 1993).

3. Perez Zagorin, *How the Idea of Religious Toleration Came to the West* (Princeton, NJ: Princeton University Press, 2003), 16.

4. Ross Koppel, 'Public Policy in Pursuit of Private Happiness', *Contemporary Sociology* 41, no. 1 (January 2012): 49–52.

5. Luke Timothy Johnson, 'Religious Rights and Christian Texts', in *Religious Human Rights in Global Perspective: Religious Perspectives*, ed. John Witte, Jr and Johan D. van der Vyver (The Hague: M. Nijhoff Publishers, 1996), 66.

6. For contending contemporary perspectives in this debate, see Candida Moss, *The Myth of Persecution: How Early Christians Invented a story of Martyrdom* (San Francisco, CA: HarperOne, 2013). Meanwhile, a number of primary sources attest to the widespread persecution of Christians. See, for example, Tacitus, *Annals* 15.44.

7. See Justin Martyr, '*The First Apology of Justin, the Martyr*', ed. and trans. Edward Rochie Hardy, in *Early Christian Fathers*, ed. Cyril C. Richardson [*The Library of Christian Classics*, ed. John Baillie, John T. McNeill and Henry P. van Dusen, vol. 1] (Philadelphia: Westminster Press, 1953); Justin Martyr, '*The Second Apology*', in *The Writings of the Fathers down to A.D. 325,* ed. the Rev. Alexander Roberts and James Donaldson (Edinburgh: T & T Clark, 1867), vol. 1; Athenagoras of Athens, '*A Plea for Christians by Athenagoras the Athenian: Philosopher and Christian*', in *Athenagoras: Legatio and De Resurrectione,* ed. and trans. William R. Schoedel [*Oxford Early Christian Texts*, ed. Henry Chadwick] (Oxford: Oxford University Press, 1972); and Tertullain, '*The Apology*', trans. Rev. S. Thelwall, in *The Writings of the Fathers down to A.D. 325,* ed. Alexander Roberts and James Donaldson (Edinburgh: T & T Clark, 1867), vol. 3.

8. Justin Martyr, '*The First Apology*', ch. 1.

9. Ibid., ch. 3.

10. Ibid.

11. Justin Martyr, '*The Second Apology*', ch. 8.

12. Justin Martyr, '*The First Apology*', ch. 8.

13. '*Plea for Christians by Athenagoras*'.

14. Timothy D. Barnes, 'The Embassy of Athenagoras', *The Journal of Theological Studies* 26 (1975): 111–14.

15. Ibid.

16. '*Plea for Christians by Athenagoras*', ch. 1.

17. Ibid.

18. Edward Gibbon, *The History of the Decline and Fall of the Roman Empire*, ed. J. B. Bury (New York: Fred de Fau and Co., 1906), vol. 1, ch. 2.

19. '*Plea for Christians by Athenagoras*', ch. 3.

20. Tertullian, *Apology* 24.6–10.

21. Tertullian, *Ad Scapulam*, ch. 2, 1–2. The translation of the same text in the *Ante-Nicene Fathers of the Church*, volume 3, is more adventurous, but still properly reflects its unmistakable radicalism: 'However, it is *a fundamental human right, a privilege of nature*, that every man should worship according to his own convictions: one man's religion neither harms nor helps another man.' (emphasis added)

22. Gibbon, *Decline and Fall*, vol. 1, ch. 15.

23. Tertullian, *Apology*, ch. 21.

24. Ibid., ch. 40.

25. Lactantius, *Divine Institutes*, book 5, chs 19–20.

26. Tertullian, *Ad Scapulam*, ch. 5, 5–6, *The Ante-Nicene Fathers of the Church*, vol. 3.

27. Brian Tierney, *The Crisis of Church and State, 1050–1300* (Toronto: University of Toronto Press, 1988), 1.

28. Quoted in Amartya Sen, *Development as Freedom* (New York: Knopf, 1999), 236.

29. Robert Louis Wilken, 'In Defense of Constantine', *First Things* 112 (2001): 36–40; and Peter Leithart, *Defending Constantine: The Twilight of an Empire and the Dawn of Christendom* (Downers Grove, IL: InterVarsity Press, 2010), 112. See especially Elizabeth DePalma Digeser, *The Making of a Christian Empire: Lactantius and Rome* (Ithaca, NY: Cornell University Press, 2000).

30. J. M. Roberts, *The Penguin History of Europe* (London: Penguin Books, 1996), 94. See also Joseph Lecler, *The Two Sovereignties: A Study of the Relationship between Church and State* (New York: Philosophical Library, 1952).

31. Quoting from the text of the Edict in *The Crisis of Empire, AD 193–337*, vol. 12 of *The Cambridge Ancient History*, ed. Alan Bowman, Peter Garnsey and Averil Cameron (Cambridge: Cambridge University Press, 2005), 62.

32. George Weigel, 'Catholicism and Democracy', in *Freedom and Its Discontents*, ed. Weigel (Washington, DC: Ethics and Public Policy Center, 1991), 38.

33. Thomas Jefferson, *Notes on the State of Virginia*, ed. William Pedel (Chapel Hill, NC: University of North Carolina Press, 1954), Query XVII, 159.

34. For this reconstruction of the timing and manner of Jefferson's acquisition of Tertullian's writings, I am indebted to Robert Louis Wilken.

Chapter 5

1. Peter L. Berger (ed.), *The Desecularization of the World: Resurgent Religion and World Politics* (Grand Rapids, MI: Eerdmans, 1999), 2, 9.
2. Monica Duffy Toft, Daniel Philpott and Timothy Samuel Shah, *God's Century: Resurgent Religion and Global Politics* (New York: Norton, 2011).
3. Charles Taylor, *A Secular Age* (Cambridge, MA: Belknap Press of Harvard University Press, 2007).
4. For an alternative typology of secularization accounts to the one set out here, see Ian Hunter, 'Charles Taylor's *A Secular Age* and Secularization in Early Modern Germany', *Modern Intellectual History* 8, no. 3 (2011): 621–46.
5. Bryan Wilson, 'Secularization: The Inherited Model', in *The Sacred in a Secular Age*, ed. Phillip E. Hammond (Berkeley: University of California Press, 1985), 2.
6. J. C. D. Clark, 'Secularization and Modernization: The Failure of a "Grand Narrative"', *The Historical Journal* 55, no. 1 (2012): 190.
7. See Christian Smith, 'Secularizing American Higher Education: The Case of Early American Sociology', in *The Secular Revolution: Power, Interests, and Conflict in the Secularization of American Public Life*, ed. Christian Smith (Berkeley: University of California Press, 2003).
8. Henri de Saint-Simon, *New Christianity*, trans. J. E. Smith (London: B.D. Cousins and P. Wilson, 1834).
9. Auguste Comte, *The Positive Philosophy of Auguste Comte*, trans. Harriet Martineau, 2 vols (London: John Chapman, 1853), vol. 2, 166–7.
10. Émile Durkheim, *The Elementary Forms of Religious Life* [1912], trans. Joseph Swain (London: Allen and Unwin, 1915), 47.
11. Ibid., 427.
12. 'For faith is before all else an impetus to action, while science, no matter how far it may be pushed, always remains at a distance from this. Science is fragmentary and incomplete; it advances but slowly and is never finished; but life cannot wait. The theories that are destined to make men live and act are therefore obliged to pass science and complete it prematurely'. Ibid., 431.
13. Comte, *Positive Philosophy*, 326.
14. Ibid., 167–8.
15. Jean Jacques Rousseau, *The Social Contract and Discourses*, trans. G. D. H. Cole (London: Dent, 1968), 161.
16. On sociology and conjectural history, see Frank Palmeri, 'Conjectural History and the Origins of Sociology', *Studies in Eighteenth-Century Culture* 37 (2008): 1–21.
17. Richard Baxter, *A Christian Directory* in *The Practical Works of Richard Baxter*, 4 vols (London: George Virtue, 1838), vol. 1, 376.

18. Max Weber, *The Protestant Ethic and the Spirit of Capitalism* [1904–5], trans. Talcott Parsons (London: Routledge, 2001), 125.

19. Stephan Richter, 'Martin Luther and the Eurozone: Theology as an Economic Destiny?' *The Globalist*, 14 May 2012, http://www.theglobalist.com/martin-luther-and-the-eurozone-theology-as-an-economic-destiny/ (accessed 6 October 2014). Cf. Chris Bowlby, 'The Eurozone's Religious Faultline', *BBC News Magazine*, 19 July 2012, http://www.bbc.com/news/magazine-18789154 (accessed 6 October 2014).

20. Peter Berger, 'Max Weber is Alive and Well and Living in Guatemala: The Protestant Ethic Today', *The Review of Faith and International Affairs* 8 (2010): 3–9. Cf. 'Faith on the Move: Pentecostalism and its Potential Contribution to Development', Centre for Development and Enterprise, August 2008, http://www.cde.org.za/images/pdf/Faith_on_the_move.pdf (accessed 30 June 2014).

21. Weber, *Protestant Ethic*, 102–25; *Economy and Society: An Outline of Interpretive Sociology*, ed. Guenther Roth and Clause Wittich, 2 vols (Berkeley: University of California Press, 1978), vol. 1, 541–55.

22. For a critical reassessment of the idea of an early modern disenchantment, see Alexandra Walsham, 'The Reformation and the "Disenchantment of the World" Reassessed', *The Historical Journal* 51 (2008): 497–528.

23. Robert K. Merton, *Science, Technology and Society in Seventeenth-Century England* [1938] (New York: Howard Fertig, 2002).

24. Robert K. Merton, *Social Theory and Social Structure*, enlarged edn (New York: Free Press, 1969), 574f.

25. For a discussion of the merits of the Merton Thesis, see I. Bernard Cohen (ed.), *Puritanism and the Rise of Modern Science: The Merton Thesis* (New Brunswick, NJ: Rutgers University Press, 1990); and Charles Webster (ed.), *The Intellectual Revolution of the Seventeenth Century* (London: Routledge & Kegan Paul, 1974). On common misunderstandings, see G. A. Abraham, 'Misunderstanding the Merton Thesis: A Boundary Dispute between History and Sociology', *Isis* 74 (1983): 368–87; Steven Shapin, 'Understanding the Merton Thesis', *Isis* 4 (1988): 594–605; and Peter Harrison, 'Religion and the Early Royal Society', *Science and Christian Belief* 22 (2010): 3–22.

26. See, for example, Charles Webster, *The Great Instauration: Science, Medicine and Reform, 1626–1660* (London: Duckworth, 1975); Peter Harrison, *The Bible, Protestantism and the Rise of Natural Science* (Cambridge: Cambridge University Press, 1998); and *The Fall of Man and the Foundations of Science* (Cambridge: Cambridge University Press, 2007).

27. Steven J. Harris, for example, suggests that to an extent the Jesuit order manifests similar values. See Harris, 'Transposing the Merton Thesis: Apostolic Spirituality and the Establishment of the Jesuit Scientific Tradition', *Science in Context* 3 (1989): 29–65.

28. Weber, *Protestant Ethic*, 124.

29. Ibid.

30. The other obvious group to have addressed the negative consequences of the transition to modernity is the Frankfurt School. See T. W. Adorno with Max Horkheimer, *Dialectic of Enlightenment*, trans. Edmund Jephcott (Stanford: Stanford University Press, 2002);

Jürgen Habermas, *The Philosophical Discourse of Modernity* (Cambridge, MA: MIT Press, 1987); and Martin Jay, *The Dialectical Imagination: A History of the Frankfurt School and the Institute for Social Research 1923–1950* (Berkeley: University of California Press, 1996).

31. Alasdair MacIntyre, *After Virtue: A Study in Moral Theory* (Notre Dame, IN: University of Notre Dame Press, 1981).

32. On this theme, see Peter Harrison, *The Territories of Science and Religion* (Chicago: University of Chicago Press, 2015), ch. 6.

33. Francis Bacon, *Valerius Terminus*, *The Works of Francis Bacon*, ed. James Spedding, Robert Ellis and Douglas Heath, 14 vols (London: Longman and Co., 1860), vol. 3, pp. 221f.; and Joseph Glanvill, 'Modern Improvements of Useful Knowledge', in *Essays on Several Important Subjects in Philosophy and Religion* (London, 1676), 35.

34. R. H. Tawney, *Religion and the Rise of Capitalism* (Harmondsworth: Penguin, 1938), 272.

35. Taylor, *Secular Age*, 4.

36. Ibid., 22, 26–9, 553f.

37. Charles Taylor, 'Western Secularity', in *Rethinking Secularism*, ed. Craig Calhoun, Mark Juergensmeyer and Jonathan VanAntwerpen (Oxford: Oxford University Press, 2011), 39.

38. Ibid., 39–41.

39. Brad Gregory, *The Unintended Reformation: How a Religious Revolution Secularized Society* (Cambridge, MA: Harvard University Press, 2012), ch. 6.

40. Alasdair MacIntyre, *Whose Justice, Which Rationality?* (Notre Dame, IN: University of Notre Dame Press, 1988).

41. Brad Gregory, 'The Intentions of the Unintended Reformation', *Historically Speaking* 13, no. 3 (2012): 2–5.

42. We are here leaving aside the broader question of whether 'religion' itself is a legitimate analytical category. For a discussion of this issue, see Harrison, *Territories of Science and Religion*, ch. 5.

Chapter 6

1. Nicolas de Condorcet, *Condorcet: Political Writings*, ed. Steven Lukes and Nadia Urbinati (Cambridge: Cambridge University Press, 2012), 51, 129.

2. John Draper, *History of the Conflict between Religion and Science* (New York: Appleton, 1874), vii.

3. George Sarton, *The History of Science and the New Humanism* (Bloomington: Indiana University Press, 1962), 10, 43–5. Cf. Sarton, *The Study of the History of Science* [1st ed. 1936] (Harvard: Harvard University Press, 1957), 5.

4. For examples of this historical literature, see David C. Lindberg and Ronald L. Numbers (eds), *God and Nature: Historical Essays on the Encounter between Christianity and Science* (Berkeley: University of California Press, 1986); *When Science and Christianity Meet* (Chicago: University of Chicago Press, 2003); John Hedley Brooke, *Science and Religion: Some Historical Perspectives* (Cambridge: Cambridge University Press,

1991); and Peter Harrison (ed.), *The Cambridge Companion to Science and Religion* (Cambridge: Cambridge University Press, 2010), chs 1–5.

5. 'Science and religion aren't friends', *USA Today*, 11 October 2010, http://usatoday30. usatoday.com/news/opinion/forum/2010-10-11-column11_ST_N.htm (accessed 8 October 2014).

6. The definition is that of Australian philosopher Philip Pettit, cited in Steven Clark, 'Naturalism, Science and the Supernatural', *Sophia* 48 (2009): 127–42.

7. Thomas Henry Huxley, 'Prologue', *Collected Essays* [1892], vol. 5 (Cambridge: Cambridge University Press, 2011), 7.

8. Maarten Boudry, Stefaan Blancke and Johan Braeckman, 'How Not to Attack Intelligent Design Creationism: Philosophical Misconceptions about Methodological Naturalism', *Foundations of Science* 15 (2010): 227–44. Cf. Mario De Caro and David Macarthur, 'The Nature of Naturalism', in *Naturalism in Question*, ed. De Caro and Macarthur (Cambridge, MA: Harvard University Press, 2008), 5–6; and Michael Ruse, *Darwinism and Its Discontents* (New York: Cambridge University Press, 2008), 48.

9. Significant elements of the argument of this section are set out in Chapter 2 of Peter Harrison, *The Territories of Science and Religion* (Chicago: University of Chicago Press, 2015).

10. Kiempe Algra 'The Beginnings of Cosmology', in *The Cambridge Companion to Early Greek Philosophy,* ed. A. A. Long (Cambridge: Cambridge University Press, 1999), 45–65 (quotation is from 48).

11. Andrew Ede and Lesley Cormack, *A History of Science in Society*, 2nd edn (Toronto: University of Toronto Press, 2012), 10.

12. David Deming, *Science and Technology in World History*, vol. 1 (Jefferson, NC: McFarland, 2010), 19; Bryan Bunch and Alexander Hellemans, *The History of Science and Technology*. (Boston: Houghton Mifflin, 2004), 1, 51f., 81, 93, 142; Robert Wilson, *Astronomy through the Ages* (Princeton, NJ: Princeton University Press, 1997), 24; and Paul Davies, *The Goldilocks Enigma: Why is the Universe Just Right for Life?* (London: Penguin, 2007), 14. See also Daniel W. Graham, *The Texts of Early Greek Philosophy* (Cambridge: Cambridge University Press, 2010), 45–6; and S. Sambursky, *The Physical World of the Greeks* (London: Routledge and Kegan Paul, 1956), 3f.

13. Deming, *Science and Technology*, 220; Wilson, *Astronomy through the Ages*, 45; Charles Freeman, *The Closing of the Western Mind* (Oxford: Oxford University Press, 2004), xviii–xix; and Karl Popper, 'The Myth of the Framework', in *The Myth of the Framework: In Defence of Science and Rationality*, ed. M. A. Notturno (London: Routledge, 1996), 42. For nineteenth-century versions of this thesis, see T. H. Huxley, 'The Progress of Science' [1887], *Collected Essays*, vol. 5, 44; John Tyndall, 'Belfast Address', *The Chemical News* 30, no. 769 (1874): 81–93; Draper, *History of the Conflict*; and Andrew Dickson White, *History of the Warfare of Science with Theology in Christendom*, 2 vols (New York: Appleton, 1897).

14. David Sedley, *Creationism and Its Critics in Antiquity* (Berkeley: University of California Press, 2007), 6; and Aëtius. *Doxography* (*Plac.* i. 3: *Dox.* 277).

15. Hermann Diels and Walther Kranz, *Die Fragmente der Vorsokratiker* (Zürich: Weidmann, 1985), [hereafter, DK] 59B12, B13, B14; and J. H. Lesher, 'Mind's Knowledge and Powers of Control in Anaxagoras "DK" B12', *Phronesis*, 40 (1995): 125–42.

16. Werner Jaeger, *The Theology of the Early Greek* Philosophers (Oxford: Blackwell, 1947), v.

17. Sedley, *Creationism and Its* Critics, 2. For a recent account of debates about the supernaturalistic commitments of the preSocratics, see Andrew Gregory, *The Presocratics and the Supernatural* (London: Bloomsbury, 2013).

18. See, for example, Daryn Lehoux, 'Creation Myths and Epistemic Boundaries', *Spontaneous Generations* 3 (2009): 28–34; Luc Brisson, *How Philosophers Saved Myths* (Chicago: University of Chicago Press, 2004); Richard Buxton (ed.), *From Myth to Reason? Studies in the Development of Greek Thought* (Oxford: Oxford University Press, 1999); and Paul Veyne, *Did the Greeks Believe in Their Myths? An Essay on the Constitutive Imagination*, trans. Paula Wissing (Chicago: University of Chicago Press, 1988). See also the classic study of F. M. Cornford, *From Philosophy to Religion* [1912] (Princeton, NJ: Princeton University Press, 1991), 127–30.

19. DK B23, B25.

20. In the case of Heraclitus, the intelligence [*gnômê*] steers all things (DK B41); for Anaxagoras, the *nous* orders and arranges things (DK B12–14); for Aristotle, the divine *nous* draws all things towards their own perfection (*Metaphysics* 1071b3–1072a18).

21. See, for example, David C. Lindberg, 'Science and the Early Church', in *God & Nature*, ed. Lindberg and Numbers, 19–48; Peter Harrison and David Lindberg, 'Early Christianity', in *Science and Religion around the World: Historical Perspectives*, ed. John Hedley Brooke and Ronald L. Numbers (Oxford: Oxford University Press, 2011), 67–91.

22. J. J. Walsh, 'On Christian Atheism', *Vigiliae Christianae* 45 (1991): 255–77; R. Jungkuntz, 'Fathers, Heretics and Epicureans', *Journal of Ecclesiastical History* 17 (1966): 3–10; and A. D. Simpson, 'Epicureans, Christians, Atheists in the Second Century', *Transactions and Proceedings of the American Philological Association* 72 (1941): 372–81.

23. Origen, *Contra Celsum* 5.7; Philoponus *contra Aristotelem ap.* Simplicium *in Cael.* 88, 28–34, in *The Philosophy of the Commentators 200–600 AD*, ed. Richard Sorabji, vol. 2, Physics (London: Duckworth, 2003), 374.

24. With respect to the question of medieval science, see especially David C. Lindberg, *The Beginnings of Western Science*, 2nd edn (Chicago: University of Chicago Press, 2007); Edward Grant, *The Foundations of Science in the Middle Ages: Their Religious, Institutional and Intellectual Contexts* (Cambridge: Cambridge University Press, 1996); and, for a more popular treatment, James Hannam, *God's Philosophers* (London: Icon Books, 2009).

25. Aristotle, *Metaphysics*, 1064a10–1064b13.

26. The other key element concerned criteria for canonization and how miracles might be forensically distinguished from natural occurrences. See Laura Smoller, 'Defining the Boundaries of the Natural in Fifteenth-Century Brittany', *Viator* 28 (1997): 333–59; Peter

Harrison, 'Miracles, Early Modern Science, and Rational Religion', *Church History* 75 (2006): 493–511; and Lorraine Daston, 'Miraculous Facts and Miraculous Evidence in Early Modern Europe', *Critical Inquiry* 18 (1991): 93–124.

27. *Sentences* Bk. II, dist. 18, ch. 6, in *Opera Omnia S. Bonaventurae*, Ad Claras Aquas, 1885, vol. 2, 429–31.

28. Henri de Lubac, *Surnaturel: etudes historiques* (Paris: Aubier, 1946); and Robert Bartlett, *The Natural and the Supernatural in the Middle Ages* (Cambridge: Cambridge University Press, 2008), 1–33.

29. Peter Lombard, *Sentences* Bk. II, dist. 18, ch. 6, in *Opera Omnia S. Bonaventurae*, Ad Claras Aquas, 1885, vol. 2, 429–31.

30. '*dico quod nihil ad me de Dei miraculis, cum ego de naturalibus disseram*'. Albertus Magnus, *De generatione et corruptione* 1.1.22 (Borgnet edition 4, 363); quoted in Edward P. Mahoney, *Two Aristotelians of the Italian Renaissance: Nicoletto Vernia and Agostino Nifo* (Aldershot: Ashgate [Variorum Collected Studies Series], 2000), 359.

31. '*Sed nihil ad nos nunc de Dei miraculis, cum de naturalibus naturaliter disseramus*'. From his *De anima intellectiva*, III, quoted in Ludger Honnefelder et al. (eds), *Albertus Magnus und die Anfänge der Aristoteles-Rezeption im lateinischen Mittelalter* (Münster: Aschendorff, 2005), 264. Also see Ian Maclean, 'The "Sceptical Crisis" Reconsidered: Galen, Rational Medicine and the *Libertas Philosophandi*', *Early Science and Medicine* 11 (2006): 247–74, esp. pp. 260–4.

32. The Condemnation of 1277, which sought to censure some 219 propositions in philosophy and theology at the University of Paris is said to have had the positive effect of promoting hypothetical and counterfactual speculations that were conducive to scientific theorizing. See Pierre Duhem, *Le système du monde, histoire des doctrines cosmologiques de Platon à Copernic*, 10 vols (Paris: Hermann), vol. 7; Grant, *Foundations of Modern Science*, 70–85. But cf. John Murdoch, '1277 and Late Medieval Natural Philosophy', in *Was ist Philosophie im Mittelalter?* ed. Jan Aertsen, Andreas Speer (Berlin, New York: De Gruyter, 1998), 111–21.

33. David Papineau, *Philosophical Naturalism* (Oxford: Blackwell, 1993), 16.

34. From a large literature on the idea of laws of nature, see John Henry, 'Metaphysics and the Origins of Modern Science: Descartes and the Importance of Laws of Nature', *Early Science and Medicine,* 9 (2004): 73–114; Friedrich Steinle, 'The Amalgamation of a Concept: Laws of Nature in the New Sciences', in *Laws of Nature: Essays on the Philosophical, Scientific and Historical Dimensions* ed. Friedel Weinert (Berlin: Walter de Gruyter, 1995), 316–68; and Peter Harrison, 'Laws of Nature in Seventeenth-Century England: From Cambridge Platonism to Newtonianism', in *God, Man, and the Order of Nature: Historical Perspectives* ed. Eric Watkins (Oxford: Oxford University Press, 2013), 127–48.

35. Descartes, *The World*, in *The Philosophical Writings of Descartes*, 2 vols, ed. John Cottingham, Robert Stoothoff and Dugald Murdoch (Cambridge: Cambridge University Press, 1985), [hereafter CSM] vol. 1, 92–3.

36. Descartes, *Discourse on the Method*, CSM 1, 132. Cf. Descartes, *The World*, CSM 2, 96; Descartes, *Principles of Philosophy*, CSM 1, 240.

37. Robert Boyle, *The Excellency of theology compar'd with natural philosophy* (London, 1674), 4; *A Free enquiry into the vulgarly receiv'd notion of nature* (London, 1686), 39–40.

38. *Isaac Newton: The Principia*, trans. I. Bernard Cohen and Anne Whitman (Berkeley: University of California Press, 1999), 397. (Preface to the 2nd edn by Roger Cotes).

39. Richard Bentley, *The Works of Richard Bentley, D.D.*, ed. Alexander Dyce, vol. 3, *Theological Writings* (London: Macpherson, 1838), 74–5.

40. I. B Cohen (ed.), *Isaac Newton's Papers & Letters on Natural Philosophy*, 2nd edn (Cambridge, MA: Harvard University Press, 1978), 279–312 (quotation on 298); and Gregory's Memoranda, 21 December 1705, *David Gregory, Isaac Newton and Their Circle: Extracts from David Gregory's Memoranda 1677–1708*, ed. Walter George Hiscock (Oxford: Oxford University Press, 1937), 30.

41. William Whiston, *A New Theory of the Earth* (London, 1696), 211.

42. Samuel Clarke, *The Works of Samuel Clarke, D.D.*, 2 vols (London: Pr. for John and Paul, 1738), vol. 2, 697, 698. Cf. Joseph Butler, *The Analogy of Religion* (Oxford: Clarendon, 1897), 39, 43f., 50.

43. John Herschel, *A Preliminary Discourse on the Study of Natural Philosophy* (London: Longman, Rees, Orme, Brown and Green, and J. Taylor, 1830), 137.

44. William Whewell, *Astronomy and General Physics considered with Reference to Natural Theology*, 2nd edn (London: William Pickering, 1833), 361–2. This volume was the third of the Bridgewater Treatises.

45. Tyndall, 'Belfast Address', 81.

46. Tyndall derives much of his history from Draper's *History of the Conflict* and Friedrich Lange's *Geschichte des Materialismus und Kritik seiner Bedeutung in der Gegenwart* (Erstdruck: Iserlohn, 1865).

47. Tyndall, 'Belfast Address', 81.

48. Huxley, 'Progress of Science', 38.

49. Ibid., 5.

50. White, *History of Warfare of Science with Theology*, vol.1, ix, 166f.; vol. 2, 26f., 90.

51. Gertrude Lenzer (ed.), *Auguste Comte and Positivism: The Essential Writings* (New York: Harper and Row, 1975), 71–86.

52. Draper, *History of the Conflict*, 246f.

Chapter 7

1. Samuel Johnson, *A Dictionary of the English Language* (1755), I, n.p.; Peter Lake, *Anglicans and Puritans? Presbyterian and English Conformist Thought from Whitgift to Hooker* (London: Unwin Hyman, 1988), 145–238. Cf. Michael Brydon, *The Evolving Reputation of Richard Hooker: An Examination of Responses, 1600–1714* (Oxford: Oxford University Press, 2006).

2. William J. Bulman, *Anglican Enlightenment: Orientalism, Religion and Politics in England and its Empire, 1648–1715* (Cambridge: Cambridge University Press, 2015); and J. G. A. Pocock, *Barbarism and Religion*, 5 vols (Cambridge: Cambridge University Press,

1999–2010). On the historiography of the Enlightenment, see, for example, William J. Bulman, 'Enlightenment and Religious Politics in Restoration England', *History Compass* 10, no. 10 (2012): 752–64; Annelien de Dijn, 'The Politics of Enlightenment: From Peter Gay to Jonathan Israel', *Historical Journal* 55, no. 3 (2012): 785–805; John Robertson, *The Case for the Enlightenment: Scotland and Naples, 1680–1760* (Cambridge: Cambridge University Press, 2005), 1–51; and Jonathan Sheehan, 'Enlightenment, Religion and the Enigma of Secularization: A Review Essay', *American Historical Review* 108, no. 4 (October 2003): 1–36.

3. Brad Gregory, *The Unintended Reformation: How a Religious Revolution Secularized Society* (Cambridge, MA: Harvard University Press, 2012); and Susan Schreiner, *Are You Alone Wise? The Search for Certainty in the Early Modern Era* (Oxford: Oxford University Press, 2010).

4. See Michael J. Braddick, *God's Fury, England's Fire: A New History of the English Civil Wars* (New York: Penguin, 2008).

5. John Henry, 'The Reception of Cartesianism', in *The Oxford Handbook of British Philosophy in the Seventeenth Century*, ed. Peter R. Antsey (Oxford: Oxford University Press, 2013), 116–43.

6. Justin Champion, *The Pillars of Priestcraft Shaken: The Church of England and its Enemies, 1660–1730* (Cambridge: Cambridge University Press, 1992); Pocock, *Barbarism and Religion*; and Bulman, *Anglican Enlightenment*.

7. For this understanding of secularity, see Bulman, *Anglican Enlightenment*; 'Enlightenment for the Culture Wars', in *God in the Enlightenment*, ed. William J. Bulman and Robert G. Ingram (New York: Oxford University Press, 2015).

8. Anthony Grafton, 'A Sketch Map of a Lost Continent: The Republic of Letters', *Republics of Letters* 1, no. 1 (2009): 1–18; and Anne Goldgar, *Impolite Learning: Conduct and Community in the Republic of Letters, 1680–1750* (New Haven, CT: Yale University Press, 1995).

9. Bulman, *Anglican Enlightenment* treats these two innovations more fully. Cf. John Spurr, *The Restoration Church of England, 1646–1689* (New Haven, CT: Yale University Press, 1991).

10. Champion, *Pillars of Priestcraft Shaken*.

11. On the Restoration settlement in general, see Tim Harris, *Restoration: Charles II and His Kingdoms, 1660–1685* (New York: Penguin, 2006).

12. Mordechai Feingold, 'The Humanities', 'Mathematical Sciences and New Philosophies', and 'Oriental Studies', in *The Oxford History of the University of Oxford. Volume 4: Seventeenth-Century Oxford: Oxford University Press,* ed. Nicholas Tyacke (Oxford: Oxford University Press, 1997), 211–358, 359–448, 449–504.

13. Jean-Louis Quantin, *The Church of England and Christian Antiquity: The Construction of a Confessional Identity in the 17th Century* (Oxford: Oxford University Press, 2009); D. C. Douglas, *English Scholars, 1660–1730*, rev. edn (London: Eyre and Spottiswoode, 1951).

14. Richard H. Popkin, *The History of Scepticism: From Savonarola to Bayle* (Oxford: Oxford University Press, 2003).

15. Paul Hazard, *The European Mind, 1680–1715*, trans. J. Lewis May (New York: New York Review of Books, 2013).

16. See especially Joan-Pau Rubiés. 'From Antiquarianism to Philosophical History: India, China, and the World History of Religion in European Thought (1600–1770)', in *Antiquarianism and Intellectual Life in Europe and China, 1500–1800*, ed. P. N. Miller and F. Louis (Ann Arbor: University of Michigan Press, 2012), 313–67; and *Travellers and Cosmographers: Studies in the History of Early Modern Travel and Ethnology* (Aldershot: Ashgate, 2007).

17. On the *Traité*, see Silvia Berti, Françoise Charles-Daubert and Silvia Berti (eds), *Heterodoxy, Spinozism, and Free Thought in Early-Eighteenth-Century Europe: Studies on the Traité des Trois Imposteurs* (Dordrecht: Kluwer, 1996). On Hume's *Natural History of Religion*, see below.

18. William J. Bulman, 'From Anti-Popery and Anti-Puritanism to Orientalism', in *Making the British Empire, 1660–1800*, ed. Jason Peacey (Manchester: Manchester University Press, 2015).

19. Hugh Trevor-Roper, 'The Religious Origins of the Enlightenment', in *The European Witch-Craze*, ed. Trevor-Roper (New York: Harper & Row, 1967), 193–236. See also John Robertson, 'Hugh Trevor-Roper, Intellectual History and "The Religious Origins of the Enlightenment"', *English Historical Review* 124, 511 (2009): 1389–421.

20. B. W. Young, 'William Warburton (1698–1779)', *ODNB*, 57: 268–74. This section's argument will be developed more fully in Robert G. Ingram, *A Warfare upon Earth: Religion and Enlightenment from Newton to Hume* (forthcoming).

21. Jacqueline Rose, *Godly Kingship in Restoration England: The Politics of the Royal Supremacy, 1660–1688* (Cambridge: Cambridge University Press, 2011), 229–74; and Steven Pincus, *1688: The First Modern Revolution* (New Haven, CT: Yale University Press, 2009), 91–302.

22. Henry Horwitz, *Revolution Politicks: The Career of Daniel Finch, Second Earl of Nottingham, 1647–1730* (Cambridge: Cambridge University Press, 1968), 87–95.

23. Richard Burgess Barlow, *Citizenship and Conscience* (Philadelphia: University of Pennsylvania Press, 1962), 15–97.

24. Nigel Aston and Matthew Cragoe (eds), *Anticlericalism in Britain, c. 1500–1914* (Stroud: Sutton, 2000), esp. 42–137.

25. John Locke, *Two Treatises of Government and A Letter Concerning Toleration*, ed. Ian Shapiro (New Haven: Yale University Press, 2003), 215, 220, 244, 246. Cf. Michael J. Buckley, *Denying and Disclosing God: The Ambiguous Progress of Modern Atheism* (New Haven, CT: Yale University Press, 2004).

26. Cf. Jon Parkin, 'Toleration', in *Oxford Handbook of British Philosophy in the Seventeenth Century*, ed. Peter Antsey (Oxford: Oxford University Press, 2013), 609–26; and John Dunn, 'The Grounds for Toleration in the Early Enlightenment', *Proceedings of the British Academy* 186 (2013): 201–9.

27. Robert Cornwall, 'Charles Leslie and the Political Implications of Theology', in *Religious Identities in Britain, 1660–1832*, ed. William Gibson and Robert G. Ingram (Aldershot: Ashgate, 2005), 27–42.

28. William Gibson, *Enlightenment Prelate: Benjamin Hoadly, 1676–1761* (Cambridge: James Clarke, 2004); and Andrew Starkie, *The Church of England and the Bangorian Controversy, 1716–1721* (Woodbridge: Boydell, 2007).

29. Cf. Robert G. Ingram, 'Nature, History and the Search for Order: The Boyle Lectures, 1730–1785', in *God's Bounty? The Churches and the Natural World* (*Studies in Church History*, 46), ed. Tony Claydon and Peter Clarke (Woodbridge: The Boydell Press, 2010), 276–92.

30. Edward Hyde, *The History of the Rebellion and Civil Wars in England* (Oxford, 1826), VII, 507–649; [William Warburton], *The Alliance between Church and State* (1736), v; and George Watson, 'The Augustan Civil War', *The Review of English Studies*, new series 36, no. 143 (1985): 321–37.

31. Stephen Taylor, 'William Warburton and the Alliance of Church and State', *Journal of Ecclesiastical History* 43, no. 2 (1992): 271–86.

32. [Warburton], *Alliance*, 6, 8.

33. Ibid., 8, 10, 13, 24.

34. Ibid., 35, 36, 39, 44.

35. Ibid., 115, 119–21.

36. J. G. A. Pocock, *Barbarism and Religion: Vol. 5. Religion: The First Triumph* (Cambridge: Cambridge University Press, 2011), 230–7; and B. W. Young, *Religion and Enlightenment in Eighteenth-Century England* (Oxford: Oxford University Press, 1998), 167–212.

37. Warburton, *Divine Legation*, I, title page. Cf. see Isabel Rivers, *Reason, Grace and Sentiment: A Study of the Language of Religion and Ethics in England, 1660–1780. Volume 2: Shaftesbury to Hume* (Cambridge: Cambridge University Press, 2000), 7–84.

38. [William Warburton], *Remarks on Mr. David Hume's Essay on the Natural History of Religion* (1757), 8.

39. David Hume, *A Dissertation on the Passions and The Natural History of Religion*, ed. Tom L. Beauchamp (Oxford: Oxford University Press, 2007), 37.

40. R. W. Serjeantson, 'David Hume's *Natural History of Religion* and the End of Modern Eusebianism', in *The Intellectual Consequences of Religious Heterodoxy, c. 1600–1750*, ed. Sarah Mortimer and John Robertson (Leiden: Brill, 2012), 267–95.

41. [Warburton], *Remarks on … the Natural History of Religion*, 26–7, 29–30. Cf. Isabel Rivers, 'Responses to Hume on Religion by Anglicans and Dissenters', *Journal of Ecclesiastical History* 52, no. 4 (2001): 675–95.

42. Scott Mandelbrote, 'Early Modern Natural Theologies', and Matthew Eddy, 'Nineteenth-century Natural Theology', in *The Oxford Handbook of Natural Theology*, ed. Russell Re Manning (Oxford: Oxford University Press, 2013), 57–117; and Brian E. Daley, 'The Church Fathers', and Gerard H. McCarren, 'Development of doctrine', in *The Cambridge Companion to John Henry Newman*, ed. Ian Kerr and Terrence Merrigan (Cambridge: Cambridge University Press, 2009), 29–46, 118–36.

43. Cf. Sarah Coakley, 'Evolution, Cooperation and Divine Providence', in *Evolution, Games and God* (Cambridge, MA: Harvard University Press, 2013), 375–85.

44. For a European-scale presentation of the arguments outlined here, see Bulman and Ingram, *God in the Enlightenment*.

45. Gianna Pomata and Nancy G. Siraisi (eds), *Historia: Empiricism and Erudition in Early Modern Europe* (Cambridge, MA: MIT Press, 2005).

46. Charles Taylor, *Dilemmas and Connections* (Cambridge, MA: Harvard University Press, 2011), 167–380; and *A Secular Age* (Cambridge, MA: The Belknap Press of Harvard University Press, 2007).

47. See, for instance, Peter Dear, *Revolutionizing the Sciences: European Knowledge and Its Ambitions, 1500–1700* (Princeton: Princeton University Press, 2009); and Steven Shapin, *The Scientific Revolution* (Chicago: University of Chicago Press, 1996).

Chapter 8

1. D. E. Kennedy (ed.), *Authorized Pasts: Essays in Official History* (Parkville, VIC: University of Melbourne Press, 1995), 75ff.

2. John R. Gillis (ed.), *Commemorations: The Politics of National Identity* (Princeton, NJ: Princeton University Press, 1994), 3. [emphasis added]

3. Pierre Nora (ed.), *Realms of Memory: Rethinking the French Past*, trans. Arthur Goldhammer (New York: Columbia University Press, 1996), x, 6.

4. Jeffrey K. Olick et al. (eds), *The Collective Memory Reader* (Oxford: Oxford University Press, 2011), 177.

5. I use *historicism* to denote both a heightened historical awareness generally and, more specifically, a post-Enlightenment preoccupation with the scholarly examination of the past. On the term, see Georg Iggers, 'Historicism: The History and Meaning of the Term', *Journal of the History of Ideas* 56 (Spring 1995): 129–52.

6. On the centenary celebrations of 1617, see Hans-Jürgen Schönstädt, *Antichrist, Weltheilsgeschehen und Gottes Werkzeug. Römische Kirche, Reformation und Luther im Spiegel des Reformationsjubiläum 1617* (Wiesbaden: Steiner, 1978).

7. On 1717, see Harm Cordes, *Hilaria evangelica academia: Das Reformationsjubiläum von 1717 an den deutschen lutherischen Universitäten* (Göttingen: Vandenhoeck & Ruprecht, 2006).

8. Klaus Tanner (ed.), *Konstruktion von Geschichte: Jubelrede, Predigt, Protestantische Historiographie* (Leipzing: Evangelische Verlagsanstalt, 2012), 15ff.

9. On the idea of progress in the German Enlightenment, see Sophie Bourgault and Robert Sparkling, *A Companion to Enlightenment Historiography* (Leiden: Brill, 2013), 55–6.

10. John Tonkin, 'Reformation Studies', in *Oxford Encyclopedia of the Reformation,* ed. Hans J. Hillerbrand, vol. 3 (New York: Oxford University Press, 1996), 403–5.

11. Quoted in Ernst Walter Zeeden, *The Legacy of Luther*, trans. Ruth Mary Bethell (London: Hollis & Carter, 1954), 137.

12. Tonkin, 'Reformation Studies', 403.

13. A. J. Dickens and John Tonkin, *The Reformation in Historical Thought* (Cambridge, MA: Harvard University Press, 1985), 116ff. Cf. Pentti Laasonen and Johannes Wallmann (eds), *Der Pietismus in seiner europäischen und außereurpäischen Ausstrahlung* (Helsinki: Suomen Kirkkohistoriallinen Seura, 1992). On the influence of the University of

Halle in general, see Thomas Albert Howard, *Protestant Theology and the Making of the Modern German University* (Oxford: Oxford University Press, 2006), 87–104.

14. Friedrich Meinecke, *Historicism: The Rise of a New Historical Outlook*, trans. J. E. Anderson (New York: Herder and Herder, 1972), liv.

15. See Thomas Nipperdey's very helpful discussion of the 'revolution of historicism', in *Germany from Napoleon to Bismarck, 1800–1866*, trans. Daniel Nolan (Princeton, NJ: Princeton University Press, 1996), 441–71.

16. Quoted in Zeeden, *Legacy of Luther*, 172.

17. Robert Ergang, *Herder and the Foundations of German Nationalism* (New York: Columbia University Press, 1931), 177–212.

18. Stan M. Landry, *Ecumenism, Memory & German Nationalism, 1817–1917* (Syracuse, NY: Syracuse University Press, 2013), 1–6.

19. Nipperdey, *Germany from Napoleon to Bismarck*, 1.

20. Enno Kraehe, *Metternich's German Policy*, vol. 2 (Princeton, NJ: Princeton University Press, 1963), 99–110.

21. Nipperdey, *Germany from Napoleon to Bismarck*, 245.

22. Quote taken from H. W. Koch, *A History of Prussia* (London: Longman, 1978), 209.

23. James J. Sheehan, *German History, 1770–1866* (Oxford: Clarendon Press, 1989), 406–7.

24. On understandings of freedom at this time, see Leonard Krieger, *The German Idea of Freedom* (Boston: Beacon Hill, 1957), 174ff.

25. Thomas Stamm, *König Preussens grosser Zeit: Friedrich Wilhelm III* (Berlin: Sielder, 1992), 150–80.

26. Howard, *Protestant Theology and the Making of the Modern German University*, 235ff.

27. Robert M. Bigler, 'The Rise of Political Protestantism in Nineteenth-Century Germany', *Church History* 34 (1965): 435.

28. Martin Redeker, *Schleiermacher: Life and Thought,* trans. John Wallhausser (Philadelphia: Fortress Press, 1973), 189–91.

29. Walter Elliger (ed.), *Die evangelische Kirche der Union: Ihre Vorgeschichte und Geschichte* (Witten: Luther-Verlag, 1967), 44–5, 195–6.

30. See Klaus Wappler, 'Reformationsjubiläum und Kirchenunion (1817)', in *Die Geschichte der evangelischen Kirche der Union*, ed. J. F. Gerhard and Joachim Rogge, vol. 1 (Leipzig: Evangelische Verlagsanstalt, 1992), 112ff; and Elliger, *Die evangelische Kirche der Union*, 45f.

31. Hugo Schnell, *Martin Luther und die Reformation auf Münzen und Medaillen* (Munich: Klinkhardt & Biermann, 1983), 75, 231 (image #273); and Elliger, *Die evangelsiche Kirche der Union*, 176.

32. John E. Groh, *Nineteenth-Century German Protestantism: The Church as Social Model* (Washington, DC: University of America Press, 1982), 41–3.

33. G. E. Hofmann (ed.), *Ausgewählte Schriften und Predigten des Claus Harms*, vol. 1 (Flensburg: Christian Wolff Verlag, 1955), 204–22.

34. Rainer Fuhrmann (ed.), *Das Reformationsjubiläum 1817: Martin Luther und die Reformation im Urteil der protestantischen Festpredigt des Jahres 1817* (Bonn: Sofortdruck), 35.

35. On the Old Lutheran emigration, see Wilhelm Iwan, *Die altlutherische Auswanderung um die Mitte des 19. Jahrhundert*, 2 vols (Ludwigsburg: Kallenberg, 1943).

36. Kurt Nowak, *Schleiermacher: Leben, Werk und Wirkung* (Göttingen: Vendenhoeck & Ruprecht, 2001), 364–5. See also B. A. Gerrish, 'Schleiermacher and the Reformation: The Question of Doctrinal Development', in *The Old Protestantism and the New: Essays on the Reformation Heritage*, ed. Gerrish (Chicago: University of Chicago Press, 1982), 179–95. On the Protestant view that Catholicism was contaminated by the retention of many 'Jewish' elements, see David Nirenberg, *Anti-Judaism: The Western Tradition* (New York: W. W. Norton, 2013), 246ff.

37. Hans-Joachim Birkner et al. (eds), *Kritische Gesamtausgabe von Friedrich Schleiermacher*, I. 10 (Berlin: Walter de Gruyter, 1990), 11.

38. August Ludwig Hanstein, *Das Jubeljahr der evangelischen Kirche. Vier vorbereitende Predigten* (Berlin: Sander, 1817), 31.

39. Fuhrmann, *Das Reformationsjubiläum 1817,* 54ff; and Lutz Winckler, *Martin Luther als Bürger und Patriot: Das Reformationsjubiläum von 1817 und der politische Protestantismus des Wartburgfestes* (Lübeck: Matthiesen Verlag, 1969), 23ff.

40. Karl Heinrich L. Pölitz, 'Die Änlichkeit des Kampfes um bürgerliche und politische Freiheit in unserm Zeitalter mit dem Kampfe um die religiöse und kirchliche Freiheit im Zeitalter der Reformation', in *Reformations Alamanach für Luthers Verhrer auf das evangelische Jubeljahr 1817*, ed. Friedrich Keyser (Erfurt: G. A. Keysers Buchhandlung, 1819), 123.

41. W. M. L. de Wette, 'Ueber den sittlichen Geist der Reformation in Beziehung auf unsere Zeit' (1817), in Keyser, *Reformations Almanach*, 286–7.

42. Gottfried Erdmann Petri, 'Versuch einer Skitze über die Folgen der Reformation', in Keyser, *Reformations Alamanach*, 170.

43. C. G. F. Goes, *Luthers Kirchenreformation nach ihrer Veranlassung, Eigenthümlichkeit Beschaffenheit und wohlthätigen Wirksamkeit in einigen Kanzelvorträgen am dritten Säkularfeste nebst kurzem Berichte über die hiesige Festfeyerlichkeit* (Erlangen: Palm 1817), 65ff.

44. See Joachim Kruse*, Luthers Leben in Illustrationen des 18. und 19. Jahrhunderts. Kataloge der Kunstsammlungen des Veste Coburg* (Coburg: Die Sammlungen, 1980), 78ff. On earlier images, see See Ruth Kastner, *Geistlicher Rauffhandel: Form und Funktion der illustrierten Flugblätter zum Reformationsjubiiläum in ihrem historischen und publizistischen Kontext* (Frankfurt am Main: Peter Lang, 1982); and John Roger Paas, *The German Political Broadsheet: 1600–1700*, vols 1 and 2 (Wiesbaden: O. Harrassowitz, 1985/6).

45. Hartmut Lehmann, *Luthergedächtnis 1817 bis 2017* (Göttingen: Vandenhoeck & Ruprecht, 2012), 17–34.

46. Fuhrmann, *Das Reformationsjubiläum 1817,* 72.

47. On the awakening movement and its influence in the early nineteenth century, see Robert M. Bigler, *The Politics of German Protestantism: The Rise of the Church Elite in Prussia, 1815–1848* (Berkeley: University of California Press, 1972), 128.

48. An overview of nineteenth-century commemorations is found in Dorothea Wendebourg, 'Die Reformationsjubiläen des 19. Jahrhunderts', *Zeitschrift für Theologie und Kirche* 108 (2011): 270–335.

49. Landry, *Ecumenism, Memory, and German Nationalism*, 90–1.

50. Thomas A. Brady, *The Protestant Reformation in German History*, Occasional Paper no. 22 of the German Historical Institute (Washington, DC: German Historical Institute, 1998), 15. On the large literature from this jubilee, see Hans Dufel, 'Das Luther-Jubiläum 1883', *Zeitschrift für Kirchengeschichte* 95 (1984): 1–94.

51. Lehmann, *Luthergedächtnis*, 59.

52. Ibid., 77ff.

53. Hartmut Lehmann, 'Martin Luther as a National Hero', in *Romantic Nationalism in Europe*, ed. J. C. Eade (Canberra: Australian National University, 1983), 197.

54. All quotations in this paragraph are from Heinrich von Treitschke, *Historische und politische Aufsätze*, vol. 4 (Leipzig: Verlag von S. Hirzel, 1897), 378–84.

55. Ibid., 388.

56. Ibid., 390–2.

57. Ibid., 391.

58. Adolf von Harnack, *Martin Luther in seiner Bedeutung für die Geschichte der Wissenschaft und Bildung* (Giessen: Alfred Töpelmann, 1911). See Jaroslav Pelikan, 'Adolf von Harnack on Luther', in *Interpretations of the Reformer: Essay in Honor of Wilhelm Paulk*, ed. Jaroslav Pelikan (Philadelphia: Fortress Press, 1968), 253–73.

Chapter 9

1. As examples, see Laurence R. Iannacone, 'The Consequences of Religious Market Structure: Adam Smith and the Economics of Religion', *Rationality and Society*, 3 (1991): 156–77; Peter Berger, Grace Davie and Effie Fokas, *Religious America, Secular Europe?* (Aldershot: Ashgate, 2008); and Steve Bruce, *Secularization: In Defence of an Unfashionable Theory* (Oxford: Oxford University Press, 2011).

2. Bret E. Carroll, 'Worlds in Space: American Religious Pluralism in Geographic Perspective', *Journal of the Academy of Religion* 80, no. 2 (June 2012): 304–64. See also Mark Silk, 'Defining Religious Pluralism in America: A Regional Analysis', *Annals of the American Academy of Political and Social Science* 612 (July 2007): 63–81.

3. The literature on the relationship of the separation of church and state to the distinctive development of American religion defies easy summary. Many interpretations have taken their cues from Robert Baird's *Religion in America* (New York: Harper, 1844), which argued that the United States, liberated from the established church structures of Europe, embraced a 'voluntaristic' approach to the social organization of religion that, as a result, inculcated a more vibrant national spiritual life. Voluntary societies even within established church arrangements were common on both sides of the Atlantic, however,

and had deep roots within the Christian tradition. See William H. Brackney, *Christian Voluntarism in Britain and North America: A Bibliography and Critical Assessment* (Westport, CT: Greenwood Press, 1995). Nevertheless, 'voluntarism' as an organizational principle would be applied to congregations and denominations in the United States more thoroughly than in their European counterparts.

4. William Hutchison, *Between the Times: The Travail of the Protestant Establishment, 1900–1960* (Cambridge: Cambridge University Press, 1991), 3–18. See also Tracy Fessenden, *Culture and Redemption: Religion, the Secular, and American Literature* (Princeton, NJ: Princeton University Press, 2007).

5. See David Hempton, *Methodism: Empire of the Spirit* (New Haven, CT: Yale University Press, 2005), 178–201.

6. Eric Baldwin, 'Religious Markets, Capital Markets, and Church Finances in Industrializing America', Presentation at the Conference on Comparative Secularization and Innovation in Europe and the United States, Harvard Divinity School, Cambridge, MA, 1–3 May 2014 (henceforth cited as HDS Secularization & Innovation Conference).

7. John Charles Bennett, 'The English Anglican Practice of Pew-Renting, 1800–1960' (PhD diss., University of Birmingham, 2011).

8. For more on the innovative fundraising techniques of nineteenth-century Protestant churches, see the collected essays in Mark A. Noll (ed.), *God and Mammon: Protestants, Money, and the Market, 1790–1860* (Oxford: Oxford University Press, 2001); and Larry Eskridge and Mark A. Noll (eds), *More Money, More Ministry: Money and Evangelicals in Recent North American History* (Grand Rapids, MI: Eerdmans, 2000).

9. J. C. Ullman, *The Tragic Week: A Study of Anticlericalism in Spain* (Cambridge, MA: Harvard University Press, 1968).

10. S. J. D. Green, 'Church and City Revisited: New Evidence from the North of England, c. 1815–1914', *Northern History* 43 (2006): 352–3.

11. Roger Ottewill, '"Basingstoke Grand Reformation Times" Bazaar 1903: Aspiring Congregationalism', *Congregational History Society Magazine* 5, no. 4 (2009): 305–17.

12. Stewart J. Brown, 'The Established Churches and Secularization in Imperial Britain', c. 1830–1930, HDS Secularization & Innovation Conference. See also Stewart J. Brown, *The National Churches of England, Ireland and Scotland, 1801–1846* (Oxford: Oxford University Press, 2001).

13. Nicholas Hope, *German and Scandinavian Protestantism, 1700–1918* (Oxford: Clarendon Press, 1995), 486.

14. See Rodney Stark and Laurence Iannacone, 'A Supply-Side Reinterpretation of the "Secularization" of Europe', *Journal for the Scientific Study of Religion* 33, no. 3 (1994): 230–52.

15. See Daniel K. Williams, *God's Own Party: The Making of the Christian Right* (New York: Oxford University Press, 2010).

16. Gérard Cholvy and Yves-Marie Hilaire, *Histoire religieuse de la France contemporaine, 1880–1930* (Toulouse: Privat, 1986), 119–20.

17. Michael Snape, 'GI Religion and Post-War Revival in the United States', HDS Secularization & Innovation Conference.

18. See Hempton, *Methodism*.

19. David W. Bebbington, 'Evangelicalism and Secularization in Britain and America from the Eighteenth Century to the Present', HDS Secularization & Innovation Conference.

20. Heather Curtis, 'Media and the Expansion of American Evangelicalism', HDS Secularization & Innovation Conference.

21. Michael J. Crawford, *Seasons of Grace: Colonial New England's Revival Tradition in Its British Context* (New York: Oxford University Press, 1991).

22. See Leigh Schmidt, *Holy Fairs: Scottish Communions and American Revivals in the Early Modern Period* (Princeton, NJ: Princeton University Press, 1989); Russell E. Richey, *Early American Methodism* (Bloomington: Indiana University Press, 1991), ch. 2; and Ann Taves, *Fits, Trances, and Visions: Experiencing Religion and Explaining Experience from Wesley to James* (Princeton, NJ: Princeton University Press, 1999), 76–117.

23. See Julia S. Werner, *The Primitive Methodist Connexion: Its Background and Early History* (Madison: University of Wisconsin Press, 1984).

24. The best overall survey of the long development of American revivalism remains William McLoughlin's *Modern Revivalism: Charles Grandison Finney to Billy Graham* (New York: Ronald Press Co., 1959). But a more recent crop of biographies has done much to supplement our knowledge of this movement. A number of studies explore the direct and indirect influence of American revivalism on Great Britain. For example, see Richard Carwardine, *Transatlantic Revivalism: Popular Evangelicalism in Britain and America, 1790–1865* (Westport, CT: Greenwood Press, 1978).

25. Uta Balbier, 'Billy Graham's Cold War Crusades: Mass Evangelism in the 1950s in Europe and the United States', HDS Secularization & Innovation Conference.

26. Kenneth Wolfe, *The Churches and the British Broadcasting Corporation, 1922–1956* (London: SCM, 1984).

27. Tona J. Hangen, *Redeeming the Dial: Radio, Religion, and Popular Culture in America* (Chapel Hill: University of North Carolina Press, 2002), 21–36.

28. See Norman Grubb, *C. T. Studd: Cricketer and Pioneer* (Atlantic City, NJ: World-wide Revival Prayer Movement, 1937).

29. Larry Eskridge, *God's Forever Family: The Jesus People Movement in America* (New York: Oxford University Press, 2013).

30. For a resonant evocation of this Nonconformist culture, see Clyde Binfield, *So Down to Prayers: Studies in English Nonconformity, 1780–1920* (London: Dent, 1977).

31. Gérard Cholvy and Yves-Marie Hilaire, *Histoire religieuse de la France contemporaine, 1800/1880* (Toulouse: Privat, 1985), 50–7.

32. Jay P. Dolan, *Catholic Revivalism: The American Experience, 1830–1900* (Notre Dame, IN: University of Notre Dame Press, 1978).

33. Tine Van Osselaer, 'Gendering Religion in Modern Europe', HDS Secularization & Innovation Conference, See also, Tine Van Osselaer, *The Pious Sex: Constructions of Masculinity and Femininity in Belgium, c. 1800–1940* (Leuven: Leuven University Press, 2013).

34. David Holland, 'The Enemy of my Enemy is Sometimes Somewhat Useful: The Complicated Relationships of Religious Movements and Secularization', HDS Secularization & Innovation Conference.

35. Pamela J. Walker, *Pulling the Devil's Kingdom Down: The Salvation Army in Victorian Britain* (Berkeley CA: University of California Press, 2001).

36. Thomas Nipperdey, *Religion im Umbruch: Deutschland, 1870–1918* (Munich: C. H. Beck, 1988), 143–53.

37. See Catherine Albanese, *A Republic of Mind and Spirit: A Cultural History of American Metaphysical Religion* (New Haven, CT: Yale University Press, 2007).

38. Evelyn A. Kirkley, *Rational Mothers and Infidel Gentlemen: Gender and American Atheism, 1865–1915* (Syracuse, NY: Syracuse University Press, 2000).

39. Randall Stephens, 'Pentecostalism and Popular Culture in Britain and America in the 1960s and 1970s', HDS Secularization & Innovation Conference.

40. See Grant Wacker, *Early Pentecostals and American Culture* (Cambridge, MA: Harvard University Press, 2001); and Randall Stephens, *The Fire Spreads: Holiness and Pentecostalism in the American South* (Cambridge, MA: Harvard University Press, 2008).

41. Donald G. Charlton, *Secular Religions in France, 1815–1870* (Oxford: University Press, 1963); and T. R. Wright, *The Religion of Humanity* (Cambridge: University Press, 1986).

42. See, for example, Stephen Yeo, 'A New Life: The Religion of Socialism, 1883–1896', *History Workshop Journal* 4, no. 1 (1977): 5–56; and Todd Weir, *Secularism and Religion in Nineteenth-Century Germany: The Fourth Confession* (New York: Cambridge University Press, 2014).

43. Claude Langlois, *Le catholicisme au féminin* (Paris: Cerf, 1984).

44. Christopher Clark, 'The New Catholicism and the European Culture Wars', in *Secular-Catholic Conflict in Nineteenth-Century Europe*, ed. Christopher Clark and Wolfram Kaiser (Cambridge: University Press, 2003), 11–46.

45. Ruth Harris, *Lourdes: Body and Spirit in the Secular Age* (New York: Viking, 1999).

46. Catherine Brekus, *Strangers and Pilgrims: Female Preaching in America, 1740–1845* (Chapel Hill: University of North Carolina Press, 1998).

47. Kathryn Kish Sklar, '"Women Who Speak for an Entire Nation": American and British Women Compared at the World Anti-Slavery Convention, London, 1840', *Pacific Historical Review* 59, no. 4 (November 1990): 453–99.

48. Ann Braude, 'Women's History and Religious Innovation', HDS Secularization & Innovation Conference.

49. John Hall, 'Reform Colleges', HDS Secularization & Innovation Conference.

50. Clyde Binfield, *George Williams and the YMCA* (London: Heinemann, 1973).

51. Tine Van Osselaer, '"Such a Renewal": Christian All-Male Movements in Modern Europe', HDS Secularization & Innovation Conference. Closely related to the question of the masculinity of churchgoers was the question of the church's view of sport. 'Muscular Christianity' was the name popularly given to a movement that began in England in the 1850s and rapidly spread to the USA. See Dominic Erdozain, *The Problem of Pleasure: Sport, Recreation, and the Crisis of Victorian Religion* (Woodbridge: Boydell, 2010), 85–112; Clifford Putney, *Muscular Christianity: Manhood and Sports in Protestant America, 1880–1920* (Cambridge MA: Harvard University Press, 2001), 11–44; and Hugh

McLeod, 'Sport and Christianity in England, c.1790–1914', in *Sports and Christianity: Historical and Contemporary Perspectives*, ed. Nick J. Watson and Andrew Parker (New York: Routledge, 2013), 112–30.

52. R. Laurence Moore, *Selling God: American Religion in the Marketplace of Culture* (Oxford: Oxford University Press, 1994). See also Jerry Z. Park and Joseph Baker, 'What Would Jesus Buy? American Consumption of Religious and Spiritual Material Goods', *Journal for the Scientific Study of Religion* 46, no. 4 (December 2007): 501–17.

53. Bethany Moreton, *To Serve God and Wal-Mart: the Making of American Free Enterprise* (Cambridge, MA: Harvard University Press, 2009).

54. See Catherine Albanese, 'The Culture of Religious Combining: Reflections for the New Millennium', *Cross Currents 50* (Spring/Summer 2000): 16–22; Leigh Eric Schmidt, '"A Church-going People are a Dress-loving People": Clothes, Communication and Religious Culture in Early America', *Church History* 58, no. 1 (March 1989): 36–51; Leigh Eric Schmidt, 'The Easter Parade: Piety, Fashion, and Display', in *Religion and American Culture: A Journal of Interpretation* 4, no. 2 (Summer 1994): 135–64; and Jean M. Bartunek and Boram Do, 'The Sacralization of Christmas Commerce', *Organization* 18, no. 6 (2011): 795–806.

55. Colleen McDannell, 'Mormons, Materialism, and the Struggle Against the Ideology of Separation', HDS Secularization & Innovation Conference.

56. Grace Davie, 'Religion, Territory, and Choice: Contrasting Configurations', HDS Secularization & Innovation Conference.

57. *Christianity Today*, 5 November 1971.

58. Kip Richardson, 'Is Bigger Better? The American Megachurch as Innovation', HDS Secularization & Innovation Conference.

59. H. Paul Douglass, *The Church in the Changing City: Case Studies Illustrating Adaptation* (New York: George H. Doran Co., 1927).

60. Lex Heerma van Voss et al. (eds), *Between Cross and Class: Christian Labor in Europe 1840–2000* (Bern: Peter Lang, 2005).

61. Matthew Pehl, 'The Remaking of the Catholic Working Class, 1919–1945', *Religion and American Culture* 19 (Winter 2009): 37–67.

62. The Manhattan Religious Census of 1902 showed that approximately 50 per cent of the borough's Catholics, but only 25 per cent of Protestants, attended church on the day of the census. Hugh McLeod, *Piety and Poverty: Working Class Religion in Berlin, London and New York, 1870–1914* (New York: Holmes & Meier, 1996), 55. A 2008 Gallup Poll found that nine of the ten states with the highest self-reported church attendance were in the South, the exception being Utah, http://en.wikipedia.org/wiki/Most_Religious_US_states (accessed 25 November 2014).

Chapter 10

1. Robert Woodberry, 'The Missionary Roots of Liberal Democracy', *American Political Science Review* 106, no. 2 (May 2012): 244. Woodberry worked for fifteen years on

this paper before it was published with all its statistical data in the leading political science journal. The correlation between democracy and 'conversionary Protestantism' remained consistent through analysis of fifty variables, in regions around the world.

2. Walter Russell Mead, *Special Providence: American Foreign Policy and How It Changed the World* (New York: Knopf, 2001), 146.

3. David Yui [Yu Rhizang], 'The Present Situation in China', in International Missionary Council, *Addresses and Other Records: Report of the Jerusalem Meeting of the International Missionary Council, March 24th–April 8th, 1928* (London; Oxford University, 1928), 63.

4. See Abigail Green and Vincent Viaene (eds), *Religious Internationals in the Modern World: Globalization and Faith Communities Since 1750* (Basingstoke: Palgrave Macmillan, 2012); John L. Esposito, Darrell J Fasching and Todd Lewis, *Religion and Globalization: World Religions in Historical Perspective* (Oxford: Oxford University Press, 2008); and Dana L. Robert, 'The First Globalization: The Internationalization of the Protestant Missionary Movement between the World Wars', *International Bulletin of Missionary Research* 26, no. 2 (2002): 50–67.

5. See, for example, John Nurser, *For all Peoples and All Nations: The Ecumenical Church and Human Rights* (Washington, DC: Georgetown University Press, 2005); and Martin Erdmann, *Building the Kingdom of God on Earth: The Churches' Contribution to Marshal Public Support for World Order and Peace, 1919–1945* (Eugene, OR: Wipf and Stock, 2005).

6. Now Hokkaido University; University of Massachusetts, Amherst.

7. John F. Howes, *Japan's Modern Prophet: Uchimura Kanzo, 1861–1930* (Vancouver: UBC Press, 2005), 35.

8. Furuya Jun, 'Graduate Student and Quaker', in *Nitobé Inazô: Japan's Bridge Across the Pacific*, ed. John F. Howes (Boulder, CO: Westview Press, 1995), 55–76.

9. Quoted in Yasaka Takagi's introduction to *The Works of Inazô Nitobé* (Tokyo: Kyobunkan Publishing House, 1969–70), vol. I, xiii.

10. Quoted in John F. Howes and George Oshiro, 'Who was Nitobé?' in *Nitobé Inazô*, 10.

11. Nitobé, 'How Geneva Erred', in *Nitobé Inazô: From Bushido to the League of Nations*, ed. Teruhiko Nagao (Sapporo, Japan: Hokkaido University Press, 2006), 100.

12. Inazô Nitobé, *The Japanese Nation; Its Land, Its People, and Its Life, with Special Consideration to Its Relations with the United States* (New York: G. P. Putnam's Sons, 1912).

13. Sandra Wilson, 'The Manchurian Crisis and Moderate Japanese Intellectuals: The Japan Council of the Institute of Pacific Relations', *Modern Asian Studies* 26, no. 3 (1992): 519–20; Tomoko Akami, *Internationalizing the Pacific: The United States, Japan and the Institute of Pacific Relations, 1919–1945* (London: Routledge, 2002); and John N. Thomas, *The Institute of Pacific Relations: Asian Scholars and American Politics* (Seattle: University of Washington Press, 1974).

14. Nitobé quoted in Teruhiko Nagao (ed.), *Nitobé Inazô. From Bushido to the League of Nations* (Sapporo, Japan: Graduate School of Letters, Hokkaido University, 2006), 117.

15. Nitobé, 'Development of International Cooperation', in *Works of Inazô Nitobé*, vol. IV, 310.

16. Ibid., 320–1.

17. Griffis, Introduction to 'Bushido', in *The Works of Inazô Nitobé*, 19.

18. Ibid., 8.

19. Ibid., 133.

20. Ibid., 141.

21. Cyril H. Powles, 'Bushido: Its Admirers and Critics', in Howes, *Nitobé Inazô,* 107.

22. For a discussion of these issues, see Ibid., 107–15; and A. Hamish Ion, 'Japan Watchers, 1903–1931', *Nitobé Inazô,* 79–105.

23. For example, see Powles, 'Bushido', 109.

24. 'Molema, Seetsele Modiri', in *New Dictionary of South African Biography*, ed. E. J. Verwey and Nelly Sonderling (Pretoria: HSRC, 1995), vol. 1, 175–8.

25. Silas M. Molema, *The Bantu Past and Present: an Ethnographical and Historical Study of the Native Races of South Africa* (Edinburgh: W. Green & Son, 1920).

26. Ibid., 203.

27. Ibid., 151.

28. Ibid.

29. Ibid., 152.

30. Ibid., 352.

31. Ibid., 354.

32. *Christ and Human Need 1921* (London: SCM, 1921).

33. (Silas M. Molema) Typescript, 'Race Relations in South Africa. Address to the Synod Missionary Committee [Wesleyan Methodist Church] on the segregation laws in South Africa', Silas T MOLEMA and Solomon T PLAATJE Papers, 1874–1932. Collection: A979.Item Number: H4. University of the Witswatersrand, 4, http://www.historicalpapers.wits.ac.za/?inventory_enhanced/U/Collections&c=157313/R/A979-H4 (accessed 12 December 2013). Although editors of the papers are not entirely certain this speech was by Molema, it is consistent with his phraseology and biography. The Glasgow conference was 4–7 January 1921.

34. Molema, 'Race Relations in South Africa', 4.

35. Ibid., 1.

36. Joseph L. Grabill, *Protestant Diplomacy and the Near East: Missionary Influence on American Policy, 1810–1927* (Minneapolis: University of Minnesota Press, 1971); and Eleanor H. Tejirian and Reeva Spector Simon, *Conflict, Conquest, and Conversion: Two Thousand Years of Christian Missions in the Middle East* (New York: Columbia University Press, 2012).

37. George Antonius, *The Arab Awakening: The Story of the Arab National Movement* (Safety Harbor, FL: Simon Publications, [1939] 2001), 43–55.

38. When the British mandate expired in 1948, Jewish immigrants established the State of Israel by force.

39. John R. Starkey, 'A Talk with Philip Hitti', *Saudi Aramco World* (July/August 1971), http://www.saudiaramcoworld.com/issue/197104/a.talk.with.philip.hitti.htm (accessed 11 January 2014).

40. Philip K. Hitti, 'Characteristics of Syrian Students', *Report of the Conference of the WSCF, Constantinople* (New York: World Student Christian Federation, 1911), 229–30.

41. Philip K. Hitti, *History of the Arabs* (London: Macmillan and Co., 1937).

42. Betty Anderson, *History of American University of Beirut: Arab Nationalism and Liberal Education* (Austin: University of Texas Press, 2011), 48.

43. Quoted in Starkey, 'Talk with Philip Hitti'.

44. For his argument that the Zionist cause was anachronistic and unrealistic, see Philip K. Hitti, 'The Possibility of Union among the Arab States', in *The Quest for Political Unity in World History*, ed. Stanley Pargellis (Washington, DC: Annual Report of the American Historical Association, 1942), vol. 3, 152.

45. Eric J. Hooglund (ed.), *Crossing the Waters. Arabic-Speaking Immigrants to the United States Before 1940* (Washington, DC: Smithsonian Institution Press, 1987), 7.

46. The myth of Phoenician origins adopted by Christian Syrians in the late 1800s gave them pride in a set of ancestors and a cultural lineage separate from Islamic domination. See Asher Kaufman, *Reviving Phoenicia: Reviving Phoenicia The Search for Identity in Lebanon* (London: I. B. Tauris, 2004).

47. Philip K. Hitti, *The Syrians in America* (New York: George H. Doran, 1924), 21. By the time Hitti's *History of the Arabs* came out in 1937, he had shifted his understanding of nationalism to a pan-Arab position, in which Saudi Arabia was the 'cradle' of Semitic peoples, including the Phoenicians, Babylonians and Hebrews. By 1940, he defined Arabs based on linguistics, as those people who speak Arabic, while Arabians are those from the Arabian Peninsula. See Hitti, 'Possibility of Union among the Arab States', 147.

48. Hitti, *Syrians in America*, 23.

49. Ibid., 31, 90.

50. Ibid., 120.

51. Ibid., 121.

52. Critics of Hitti accuse him of being an Orientalist in the negative sense. See, for example, Wail S. Hassan, *Immigrant Narratives: Orientalism and Cultural Translation in Arab American and Arab British Literature* (New York: Oxford University Press, 2011), 13.

Chapter 11

1. The discussion that follows is drawn from the second essay in Friedrich Nietzsche, *On the Genealogy of Morality*, ed. Keith Ansell-Pearson, trans. Carol Diethe, 2nd edn (1887; repr., Cambridge: Cambridge University Press, 2006), 35–67. I here take note of the fact that any discussion of guilt *per se* runs the risk of conflating different meanings of the word: guilt as a forensic or objective term, guilt as culpability, is not the same thing as guilt as a subjective or emotional term. It is the difference between *being* guilty and *feeling* guilty, a difference that is analytically clear, but often difficult to sustain in discussions of particular instances.

2. Ibid., 61–2.

3. Sigmund Freud, *Civilization and Its Discontents*, trans. James Strachey (New York: W. W. Norton, 2005), 137–40.

4. W. H. Auden, 'In Memory of Sigmund Freud', from *Collected Poems* (New York: Vintage, 1991), 273–6.

5. R. T. Kendall, *Total Forgiveness* (Lake Mary, FL: Charisma House, 2007); Sidney B. and Suzanne Simon, *Forgiveness: How to Make Peace With Your Past and Get On With Your Life* (New York: Grand Central Publishing, 1991); Nancy Leigh DeMoss, *Choosing Forgiveness: Your Journey to Freedom* (Chicago: Moody Publishers, 2006); and Neale Donald Walsch and Gerald G. Jampolsky, *Forgiveness: The Greatest Healer of All* (Hillsboro, OR: Beyond Words, 1999).

6. Luskin's book was published by HarperOne in 2003; his Website is at http://learningtoforgive.com/ (accessed 13 October 2014).

7. Gregg Easterbrook 'Forgiveness Is Good For Your Health', *beliefnet* http://www.beliefnet.com/Health/2002/03/Forgiveness-Is-Good-For-Your-Health.aspx (accessed 13 October 2014).

8. Frederic Luskin, 'Forgive for Good' http://learningtoforgive.com/9-steps/ (accessed 24 February 2015).

9. Portia's speech can be found in Act 4, scene 1, 184–205.

10. Luke 23:34.

11. I borrow here from the work of Thomas Haskell, whose brilliant analysis of the changing horizons of moral responsibility has greatly influenced my own view of these matters. See especially his 'Capitalism and the Origins of the Humanitarian Sensibility', in *The Antislavery Debate: Capitalism and Abolitionism as a Problem in Historical Interpretation*, ed. Thomas Bender (Berkeley: University of California Press, 1992), 107–60.

12. For an example of an Olympic-class guilt-producing effort, see 'The Story of Stuff', a widely used, and astonishingly tendentious and manipulative online resource, designed for school children, found at http://storyofstuff.org/ (accessed 14 October 2014).

13. Pascal Bruckner, *The Tyranny of Guilt: An Essay on Western Masochism*, trans. Steven Redall (Princeton, NJ: Princeton University Press, 2010), 1–4.

14. 'Gerontion', in *Complete Poems and Plays* (New York: Harcourt, Brace, 1971), 21.

15. Daniel Mendelsohn, ' Stolen Suffering', *New York Times* (9 March 2008).

16. The book was entitled *Misha: A Memoire of the Holocaust Years* and the author published it under the name Misha Defonseca. According to the Belgian newspaper *Le Soir*, Ms De Wael was the daughter of parents who had collaborated with the Nazis. See Lizzie Dearden', Misha Defonseca: Author Who Made Up Holocaust Memoir Ordered to Repay £13.3m', *The Independent* (12 May 2014). David Mehegan, 'Misha and the Wolves', *Boston.com* (3 March 2008), http://www.boston.com/ae/books/blog/2008/03/misha_and_the_w.html (accessed 13 October 2014).

17. Binjamin Wilkomirski, *Fragments: Memories of a Wartime Childhood* (New York: Schocken, 1997); and Margaret B. Jones, *Love and Consequences: A Memoir of Hope and Survival* (New York: Riverhead, 2008).

18. In a final twist of the case, in May of 2014, the Massachusetts Court of Appeals ruled that De Wael had to forfeit the $22.5 million in royalties that the book had earned her. See http://www.independent.co.uk/arts-entertainment/books/news/author-who-made-up-bestselling-holocaust-memoir-ordered-to-repay-133m-9353897.html; and http://www.courthousenews.com/2014/05/08/67710.htm (both accessed 13 October 2014).

19. Thomas U. Berger, *War, Guilt, and World Politics after World War II* (New York: Cambridge University Press, 2012), 8.

20. See Berger's subtle and thoughtful account of these matters, ibid., 44–5, 144–5, 239.

21. Elazar Barkan, *The Guilt of Nations: Restitution and Negotiating Historical Injustices* (Baltimore, MD: Johns Hopkins University Press, 2000), xxxiii.

22. Herbert Butterfield, *The Whig Interpretation of History* (New York: Norton, 1965), 45–7.

23. David W. Blight, *Race and Reunion: The Civil War in American Memory* (Cambridge, MA: Harvard University Press, 2001).

24. Berger, *War, Guilt, and World Politics*, 39–44.

25. Ibid., 246.

26. Karl Menninger, *Whatever Became of Sin?* (New York: Hawthorn Books, 1973).

27. Andrew Delbanco, *The Death of Satan: How Americans Have Lost the Sense of Evil* (New York: Farrar, Straus and Giroux, 1995), 9.

28. See: Abigail Frymann, 'Church of England Considers Changes to Baptism Service', *Episcopal News Service* (9 January 2014); and Jonathan Petre, 'Welby Casts Out "Sin" from Christenings: Centuries-old Rite Rewritten in "Language of EastEnders" for Modern Congregation', *Daily Mail* (4 January 2014).

29. 'Church of England Accused of Dumbing Down Baptism Service', *The Guardian* (4 January 2014), http://www.theguardian.com/world/2014/jan/05/church-of-england-accused-of-dumbing-down-baptism-service (accessed 14 October 2014).

30. Paula Fredriksen, *Sin: The Early History of an Idea* (Princeton, NJ: Princeton University Press, 2012), 149.

31. Ibid.

32. Ibid., 150.

Chapter 12

1. My education of the impact of Christian faith on economic development began in 1976, when I became introduced to life in the Lingarajapuram slum where my father planted an Anglican church and my mother established the first English-medium school for outcaste children. Even as I observed the devastating impact of poverty and deprivation, I also witnessed the transformation in the economic, social and spiritual lives of numerous Dalit families in our community. I am profoundly grateful to the many Dalit women in Lingarajapuram who shared intimate details of their lives with me over the last ten years. Special thanks go to Donald Yerxa and Wilfred McClay who encouraged me to apply for funding, which greatly expanded the scope of my research. I owe much to Robert Woodberry whose advice on methodology has not only improved the quality of the research but also provided important reassurance. The chapter's shortcomings, however, are mine.

2. Max Weber, *The Protestant Ethic and the Spirit of Capitalism* (London: Routledge, [1930] 2001).

3. Alasdair C. MacIntyre, *After Virtue: A Study in Moral Theory* (Notre Dame, IN: University of Notre Dame Press, 1981).

4. See, Steve Bruce, *God Is Dead: Secularization in the West* (Malden, MA: Blackwell, 2002); Peter L. Berger, *The Sacred Canopy: Elements of a Sociological Theory of Religion* (Garden City, NY: Doubleday, 1967); and Bryan R. Wilson, *Religion in Sociological Perspective* (Oxford: Oxford University Press, 1982).

5. Gerard Debreu, 'The Mathematization of Economic Theory', *The American Economic Review* 81, no.1 (March 1991): 1–7.

6. Paul A. Marshall, *A Kind of Life Imposed on Man: Vocation and Social Order from Tyndale to Locke* (Toronto: University of Toronto Press, 1996).

7. R. H. Tawney, *Religion and the Rise of Capitalism: A Historical Study* (New York: Harcourt, Brace and Co, 1926).

8. Weber, *The Protestant Ethic*, 176.

9. Weber quoted in Stephen P. Turner and Regis A. Factor, *Max Weber as Social Thinker* (Oxford: Routledge, 1994), 61.

10. Weber, *The Protestant Ethic*, 181.

11. Building on a historical review of Bishop Jarrell Wascom Pickett's study of mass conversion movements among outcastes in India in the 1930s, between 2009 and 2011, I conducted a small survey of outcaste female micro-entrepreneurs in Bangalore, India. This study was supported by Peter Berger and the Institute of Culture, Religion and World Affairs at Boston University. In 2011, the John Templeton Foundation funded a pilot study to examine the association between religiously motivated giving and economic outcomes of 300 female micro-entrepreneurs in an urban slum in Bangalore, India. An additional grant from the Religion and Innovation in Human Affairs Project of The Historical Society expanded the study in India and added research sites in Peru and South Sudan. In total, I conducted some 900 face-to-face interviews in Bangalore, India.

12. Navsarjan Trust, 'Understanding Untouchability: A Comprehensive Study of Practices and Conditions' (Washington, DC: Robert Kennedy Center for Justice and Human Rights, 2010).

13. Satish Deshpande, 'Dalits in Muslim and Christian Communities: A Status Report on Current Social Scientific Knowledge', *National Commission for Minorities Government of India* (December 2008), http://ncm.nic.in/pdf/report%20dalit%20%20reservation.pdf (accessed 30 January 2014).

14. Jarrell Waskom Pickett, *Christian Mass Movements in India: A Study with Recommendations* (New York: Abingdon Press, 1933), 36.

15. R. H. Strotz, 'Myopia and Inconsistency in Dynamic Utility Maximization', *Review of Economic Studies* 23, no. 3 (1955–6): 165–80.

16. Sendhil Mullainathan and Eldar Shafir, *Scarcity: Why Having Too Little Means so Much* (New York: Times Books, 2013).

17. B. Douglas Bernheim, Debraj Ray and Sevin Yeltekin, *Poverty and Self-Control* (Cambridge, MA: National Bureau of Economic Research, 2013).

18. Abhijit V. Banerjee and Esther Duflo. *The Economic Lives of the Poor* (London: Centre for Economic Policy Research, 2006), 32.

19. Esther Duflo, 'Human Values and the Design of the Fight against Poverty' (Tanner Lectures, Harvard University, May 2012), http://economics.mit.edu/faculty/eduflo/papers (accessed 28 January 2015).

20. See, *World Values Survey WVS*. (Stockholm, Sweden), 1998, http://www.worldvaluessurvey.org/ (accessed 28 January 2015).

21. A majority of the converts in our study were part of what Shah and Shah call 'storefront' Pentecostal or Charismatic churches. These are independent, indigenous churches that operate in some of the poorest areas in Bangalore. All of the independent churches in our sample area were entirely self-supporting, sustained by the voluntary financial contributions of their members, not by external missions' agencies. See Rebecca Samuel Shah and Timothy Samuel Shah, 'Pentecost amid Pujas: Charismatic Christianity and Dalit Women in Twenty-First Century India', in Robert W. Hefner (ed.), *Global Pentecostalism in the 21st Century* (Bloomington: Indiana University Press, 2013), 194–227.

22. Amartya Sen, *Development As Freedom* (New York: Knopf, 1999).

23. Pope Paul VI, '*Gaudium et Spes*', 7 December 1965, http://www.vatican.va/archive/hist_councils/ii_vatican_council/documents/vat-ii_const_19651207_gaudium-et-spes_en.html (accessed 28 January 2015).

24. *Populorum Progessio*, 26 March 1967, http://www.vatican.va/holy_father/paul_vi/encyclicals/documents/hf_p-vi_enc_26031967_populorum_en.html (accessed 28 January 2015).

25. Amartya Sen, 'Well-being, Agency and Freedom: The Dewey Lectures 1984', *Journal of Philosophy* 82, no. 4 (April 1985): 200.

26. Martha C. Nussbaum, *Women and Human Development: The Capabilities Approach* (Cambridge: Cambridge University Press, 2000), 56.

27. Hernando de Soto, *The Mystery of Capital: Why Capitalism Triumphs in the West and Fails Everywhere Else* (New York: Basic Books, 2000), 6–16 and *passim*.

28. Max Weber, *Economy and Society: An Outline of Interpretive Sociology* (Berkeley: University of California Press, [1956] 1978), 542–4.

29. George A. Akerlof, 'The Missing Motivation in Macroeconomics', *The American Economic Review* 97, no. 1 (March 2007): 5–36.

30. Hanming Fang and Glenn C. Loury, 'Toward an Economic Theory of Dysfunctional Identity', in *The Social Economics of Poverty: On Identities, Communities, Groups, and Networks*, ed. Christopher B. Barrett (London: Routledge, 2005), 12–53.

31. See David Martin, *Tongues of Fire: The Explosion of Protestantism in Latin America* (Oxford: Blackwell, 1990); and Elizabeth E. Brusco, *The Reformation of Machismo: Evangelical Conversion and Gender in Colombia* (Austin: University of Texas Press, 1995).

32. Robert D. Woodberry and Timothy S. Shah, 'Christianity and Democracy: The Pioneering Protestants', *Journal of Democracy* 15, no. 2 (2004): 47–61.

33. For more on this issue, see Jeffry Jacobs and Thomas Osang, 'Religious Values, Beliefs and Economic Development', (paper presented at the Association for the Study of Religion, Economics and Culture, Washington, DC, 2010), http://faculty.smu.edu/tosang/pdf/jo_vbad_32.pdf (accessed 29 January 29 2015); Robert D Woodberry, 'The Shadow of Empire: Christian Missions, Colonial Policy and Democracy in Post-Colonial Societies', (PhD diss., University of North Carolina, Chapel Hill, 2004); Robert W. Hefner

(ed.), *Conversion to Christianity: Historical and Anthropological Perspectives on a Great Transformation* (Berkeley: University of California Press, 1993); and Tim Heaton, James Spencer and Oheneba-Sakyi Yaw, 'Religion and Socioeconomic Attainment in Ghana', *Review of Religious Research* 51, no. 1 (2009): 71–86.

34. Timur Kuran, *The Long Divergence: How Islamic Law Held Back the Middle East* (Princeton, NJ: Princeton University Press, 2011).

35. Denis Goulet, 'Development Experts: The One-Eyed Giants', *World Development* 8, no. 7 (1980): 481–9.

36. Glenn C. Loury, 'On Group Identity and Individual Behavior: Thoughts on The Anatomy of Racial Inequality', *Faith and Economics* 41 (Spring 2003): 8–16.

37. Bruce Wydick, Paul Glewwe and Laine Rutledge, 'Does International Child Sponsorship Work? A Six-Country Study of Impacts on Adult Life Outcomes', *Journal of Political Economy* 121, no. 2 (April 2013): 393–436.

38. Rebecca Samuel Shah and Timothy Samuel Shah, 'How Evangelicalism – Including Pentecostalism – Helps the Poor', in *The Hidden Form of Capital: Spiritual Influences in Societal Progress*, ed. Peter L. Berger and Gordon Redding (London: Anthem Press, 2010), 61–90.

39. Jessica Schicks and Richard Rosenberg, 'Too Much Microcredit? A Survey of the Evidence on Over-Indebtedness', *CGAP Occasional Papers,* no. 19 (September 2011).

Chapter 13

1. Daniel Burnham and Edward Bennett, *Plan of Chicago* (New York: Princeton Architectural Press, 1993 [re-published from 1909]), 32.

2. William Cronon, *Nature's Metropolis: Chicago and the Great West* (New York: Norton, 1991).

3. Ibid., 5–22, 371–86.

4. See Kristen Schafer, 'Fabric of City Life: The Social Agenda in Burnham's Draft of The *Plan of Chicago*' (published as the Introduction to) Burnham and Bennett, *Plan of Chicago* (1993), v–xvi; and 'The Swedenborgian Underpinnings of Burnham's City Planning', unpublished paper delivered at the Seventh Biennial Symposium on the Historic Development of Metropolitan Washington, DC, March 2007. The former is of interest for Burnham's neighbourhood concerns, omitted from the final text of the *Plan of Chicago*; the latter for its detailed account of an 1893 'sermon' by Burnham that makes direct associations between elements of The White City of the World's Columbian Exposition of 1893 and elements of The Heavenly Jerusalem as described in the Book of Revelation. See also Judith McBrien (director), 'Make No Little Plans: Daniel Burnham and the American City [a documentary]', Chicago: The Archimedia Workshop, 2010.

5. Burnham and Bennett, *Plan of Chicago,* 35–6.

6. *Hyper-modernism* here refers to what, outside the discipline of architecture, is called *postmodernism*: essentially subjectivism, relativism and individualism in and at the scale of buildings and cities, a Nietzschean phenomenon lending itself well to both the

avant-garde ambitions of architects and the different ambitions of politicians, financiers and crony-capitalists foreign and domestic. For more on hyper-modernism, see Philip Bess, 'Building on Truth', *First Things* (January 2015), 51–3.

7. Bess, 'Building on Truth', 48.

8. The representation of sacred order in forms of human settlement is not unique to Western culture, but *is* a mark of moral and metaphysical realism, and present virtually everywhere prior to the advent of modernism.

9. To be clear, *Chicago 2109* should not be taken to represent *in its details* a consensus of opinion that, in fact, does not exist at either the University of Notre Dame or her School of Architecture. Rather, it intends to represent a consensus (however tenuous) that *does* exist at Notre Dame: Catholicism as foundational to the University's understanding of the world and her intellectual and moral vocation; and classicism as foundational to the School of Architecture's study and profession of urbanism and architecture.

10. The term *global city* is used here after the work of Saskia Sassen, *The Global City* (Princeton, NJ: Princeton University Press, 1991) and her various interpreters.

11. Aaron Renn, 'The Second Rate City?' *City Journal* (Spring 2012), http://www.city-journal.org/2012/22_2_chicago.html (accessed 18 January 2015).

12. Daniel Kay Hertz, 'Watch Chicago's Middle Class Vanish Before Your Very Eyes', *City Notes* (31 March 2014), http://danielkayhertz.com/2014/03/31/middle-class/ (accessed 18 January 2015).

13. Paul Tillich, *Dynamics of Faith* (New York: Harper & Row, 1957).

14. For a more extended consideration of what I mean by 'the sacred', see Philip Bess, *Till We Have Built Jerusalem* (Wilmington, DE: ISI Books, 2006), ch. 5.

15. Consider, for example, the Zen Buddhist poem/sermon of Ching-yuan, quoted in John G. Rudy, *Wordsworth and the Zen Mind* (Albany: State University of New York Press, 1996), 101: 'Before I had studied Zen for thirty years, I saw mountains as mountains, and waters as waters. When I arrived at a more intimate knowledge, I came to the point where I saw that mountains are not mountains, and waters are not waters. But now that I have got its very substance I am at rest. For it's just that I see mountains once again as mountains, and waters once again as waters.'

16. I have made versions of the argument in this section elsewhere: in *Public Discourse* (8 June 2010), http://www.thepublicdiscourse.com/2010/06/1358/ (accessed 18 January 2015); and in 'Metaphysical Realism, Modernity, and Traditional Cultures of Building', *Why Place Matters*, ed. Wilfred M. McClay and Ted V. McAllister (New York: Encounter, 2014), 131–3.

17. This is most evident in widespread twenty-year criticisms of the alleged conservative agenda of the Congress for the New Urbanism – for a concise and representative summary of such criticisms, see Aaron Passell, *Building the New Urbanism* (New York: Routledge, 2013), ch. 5 – but *mutatis mutandis* applies also to Notre Dame, exacerbated by her Catholic connection. Ironically, Notre Dame's classical humanist architectural curriculum is regarded by some New Urbanists as nostalgic, incoherent and intellectually unserious – mistakenly, we think.

18. Rem Koolhaas, 'Junkspace', *October* 100 (Spring, 2002): 175–90.

19. The Land Value Tax – which replaces other taxes, and taxes only *unimproved* land on the basis of its proximity to socially created value – is an idea most prominently associated with the late-nineteenth-century American Henry George. For a brief summation of the idea, see James Howard Kunstler, *Home From Nowhere* (New York: Touchstone, 1996), ch. 7. It has been adopted in places, usually at the scale of a single town or city, but its beneficial effects seem better suited for the scale of a metropolitan region.

Chapter 14

1. John Rawls, *Political Liberalism*, 2nd edn (Columbia University Press, 2005); and Jürgen Habermas, *The Theory of Communicative Action,* 2 vols (Cambridge: Polity Press, 1986).

2. John H. Evans, *Contested Reproduction: Genetic Technologies, Religion, and Public Debate* (Chicago: University of Chicago Press, 2010); and Thomas F. Gieryn, 'Boundary-Work and the Demarcation of Science from Non-Science: Strains and Interests in Professional Ideologies of Scientists', *American Sociological Review* 48, no. 6 (December 1983): 781–95.

3. Hans-Georg Gadamer, *Truth and Method*, 2nd rev. edn (London: Bloomsbury Academic, 2004).

4. Margarita Boenig-Liptsin and J. Benjamin Hurlbut, 'Technologies of Transcendence and the Singularity University', in *Perfecting Human Futures: Innovation, Secularization and Eschatology*, ed. J. Benjamin Hurlbut and Hava Tirosh-Samuelson (Dordrecht, The Netherlands: Springer, 2015).

5. Maxwell J. Mehlman, *Transhumanist Dreams and Dystopian Nightmares: The Promise and Peril of Genetic Engineering* (Baltimore, MD: Johns Hopkins University Press, 2012).

6. John Harris, *Enhancing Evolution: The Ethical Case for Making Better People* (Princeton, NJ: Princeton University Press, 2010); Ingmar Persson and Julian Savulescu, *Unfit for the Future: The Need for Moral Enhancement* (Oxford: Oxford University Press, 2012); Ronald M. Green, *Babies by Design: The Ethics of Genetic Choice* (New Haven, CT: Yale University Press, 2008); and Allen Buchanan, *Better than Human: The Promise and Perils of Enhancing Ourselves* (New York: Oxford University Press, 2011).

7. Francis Fukuyama, *Our Posthuman Future: Consequences of the Biotechnology Revolution* (New York: Farrar, Straus & Giroux, 2000); Francis Fukuyama, 'Transhumanism', *Foreign Policy* 144 (1 September 2004), http://www.foreignpolicy.com/articles/2004/09/01/transhumanism#sthash.1Fl11MK9.dpbs; and Ted Peters, 'H–: Transhumanism and the Posthuman Future: Will Technological Progress Get Us There?', http://www.metanexus.net/essay/h-transhumanism-and-posthuman-future-will-technological-progress-get-us-there (both accessed 10 April 2014).

8. See, for example, Nick Bostrom and Milan M. Cirkovic, *Global Catastrophic Risks* (Oxford: Oxford University Press, 2008); Pew Research Center, *Living to 120 and Beyond: American's Views on Aging, Medical Advances and Radical Life Extension* (6 August 2013), http://www.pewforum.org/2013/08/06/living-to-120-and-beyond-americans-views-on-aging-medical-advances-and-radical-life-extension/ (accessed

23 January 2015); and Alfred Nordmann, *Converging Technologies – Shaping the Future of European Societies* (Report of the European Commission, 2004), https://ec.europa.eu/research/social-sciences/pdf/ntw-report-alfred-nordmann_en.pdf (accessed 23 January 2015).

9. Steve Fuller and Veronika Lipińska 'Transhumanism for the Encyclopedia of Ethics, Science, Technology and Engineering', *H+ Magazine*, http://hplusmagazine.com/2014/03/30/transhumanism-for-the-encyclopedia-of-ethics-science-technology-and-engineering/ (accessed 8 May 2014); and M. Zimmerman, in Hurlbut and Tirosh-Samuelson, *Perfecting Human Futures*.

10. Langdon Winner, 'Resistance Is Futile: The Posthuman Condition and Its Advocates', in *Is Human Nature Obsolete? Genetics, Bioengineering, and the Future of the Human Condition*, ed. Harold W. Baillie and Timothy Casey (Cambridge, MA: MIT Press, 2005), 410.

11. Mark Solomon and Nick Bostrom, 'The Transhumanist Dream', *Foreign Policy* 146 (1 January 2005): 4.

12. Ray Kurzweil, *The Singularity Is Near: When Humans Transcend Biology* (New York: Penguin Books, 2006), 311.

13. Mihail C. Roco and William Sims Bainbridge (eds), *Converging Technologies for Improving Human Performance: Nanotechnology, Biotechnology, Information Technology and Cognitive Science* (Dordrecht, The Netherlands: Kluwer Academic Publishers, 2003).

14. Ted Chu, *Human Purpose and Transhuman Potential: A Cosmic Vision for Our Future Evolution* (San Rafael, CA: Origin Press, 2014), xx.

15. Ray Kurzweil, *The Age of Spiritual Machines: When Computers Exceed Human Intelligence* (New York: Penguin Books, 2000).

16. Gregory Stock, *Metaman: The Merging of Humans and Machines into a Global Superorganism* (New York: Simon & Schuster, 1993).

17. Charles Taylor, *Modern Social Imaginaries* (Durham, NC: Duke University Press, 2003).

18. Francis Fukuyama, 'The End of History?', in *The National Interest* (Summer 1989): 3–18.

19. Fukuyama, *Our Posthuman Future*.

20. J. Benjamin Hurlbut, 'Remembering the Future: Science, Law, and the Legacy of Asilomar', in *Dreamscapes of Modernity: Sociotechnical Imaginaries and the Fabrication of Power*, ed. Sheila Jasanoff and Sang-Hyun Kim (Chicago: University of Chicago Press, 2015).

21. See, for instance, Jean Bethke Elshtain's excellent study of notions of secular and religious authority in the history of the modern West, which culminates in a discussion of technologies of human genetic enhancement. In these technological aspirations, she sees the ongoing working out of the basic preoccupations of modernity in the ordering of societies and selves. Elshtain, *Sovereignty: God, State, and Self* (New York: Basic Books, 2008).

22. J. Benjamin Hurlbut, 'Experiments in Democracy: The Science, Politics and Ethics of Human Embryo Research in the United States, 1978–2007', PhD diss, Harvard University, 2010; and John H. Evans, *Playing God? Human Genetic Engineering and the Rationalization of Public Bioethical Debate* (Chicago: University of Chicago Press, 2002).

23. US Office of Science and Technology Policy, 'National Bioeconomy Blueprint', http://www.whitehouse.gov/administration/eop/ostp/library/bioeconomy (accessed 8 May 2014).

24. Kaushik Sunder Rajan, *Biocapital: The Constitution of Postgenomic Life* (Durham, NC: Duke University Press, 2006).

25. Stuart Jeffries, 'Is There Too Much Technology in Our Modern Lives?', *The Guardian* (10 April 2014), http://www.theguardian.com/lifeandstyle/2014/apr/10/modern-life-electricity-technology (accessed 15 November 2014).

26. Langdon Winner, *Autonomous Technology: Technics-out-of-Control as a Theme in Political Thought* (Cambridge, MA: MIT Press, 1978).

27. Thomas P. Hughes, *Human-Built World: How to Think about Technology and Culture* (Chicago: University of Chicago Press, 2005), 4.

28. Wiebe E. Bijker et al., *The Social Construction of Technological Systems: New Directions in the Sociology and History of Technology* (Cambridge, MA: MIT Press, 2012).

29. Langdon Winner, *The Whale and the Reactor: A Search for Limits in an Age of High Technology* (Chicago: University of Chicago Press, 1986), 6.

30. Bruno Latour, 'Love Your Monsters: Why We Must Care for Our Technologies As We Do Our Children', *The Breakthrough Journal* (Winter 2012) http://thebreakthrough.org/index.php/journal/past-issues/issue-2/love-your-monsters (accessed 15 November 2014).

31. Bruno Latour, 'Technology is Society Made Durable', in *Sociology of Monsters: Essays on Power, Technology, and Domination*, ed. John Law (London: Routledge, 1991), 110.

32. Bruno Latour, 'Where Are the Missing Masses?', in *Shaping Technology/Building Society: Studies in Sociotechnical Change*, ed. Wiebe E. Bijker and John Law (Cambridge, MA: MIT Press, 1992), 225–58.

33. Leo Marx, 'The Idea of 'Technology' and Postmodern Pessimism', in *Does Technology Drive History? The Dilemma of Technological Determinism*, ed. Merritt Roe Smith and Leo Marx (Cambridge, MA: MIT Press, 1994), 248.

34. Ibid., 249.

35. David E. Nye, *American Technological Sublime* (Cambridge, MA: MIT Press, 1996), xiv.

36. Yaron Ezrahi, *The Descent of Icarus: Science and the Transformation of Contemporary Democracy* (Cambridge, MA: Harvard University Press, 1990).

37. John F. Kennedy, 'Special Message to the Congress on Urgent National Needs', (United States Congress, 25 May 1961), http://www.nasa.gov/vision/space/features/jfk_speech_text.html (accessed 16 November 2014).

38. Bronislaw Szerszynski, *Nature, Technology and the Sacred* (Malden, MA: Wiley-Blackwell, 2005), 172.

39. David F. Noble, *The Religion of Technology: The Divinity of Man and the Spirit of Invention* (New York: Penguin Books, 1999), 3.

40. Hava Tirosh-Samuelson and Kenneth L. Mossman, 'New Perspectives on Transhumanism', in *Building Better Humans? Refocusing the Debate on Transhumanism*, ed. Hava Tirosh-Samuelson and Kenneth L. Mossman (Frankfurt am Main: Peter Lang International Academic Publishers, 2012), 36.

41. William S. Bainbridge, *Across the Secular Abyss: From Faith to Wisdom* (Lexington Books, 2007), 247.

42. Linell E. Cady, 'Religion and the Technowonderland of Transhumanism', in Tirosh-Samuelson and Mossman, *Building Better Humans*, 84, 89.

43. Roco and Bainbridge, *Converging Technologies*, x.

44. Ibid., ix.

45. Craig Calhoun, Mark Juergensmeyer and Jonathan VanAntwerpen, 'Introduction', in *Rethinking Secularism*, ed. Calhoun, Juergensmeyer and VanAntwerpen (Oxford, New York: Oxford University Press, 2011), 5, 20.

46. Pope Francis, 'Encyclical Letter *Lumen Fidei* of the Supreme Pontiff Francis to the Bishops Priests and Deacons Consecrated Persons and the Lay Faithful On Faith', http://w2.vatican.va/content/francesco/en/encyclicals/documents/papa-francesco_20130629_enciclica-lumen-fidei.html (accessed 7 May 2014).

47. Michael Polanyi, 'The Republic of Science', *Minerva* 1 (1962): 54–73.

48. Hurlbut, 'Remembering the Future'.

49. James Hughes, *Citizen Cyborg: Why Democratic Societies Must Respond to the Redesigned Human of the Future* (Boulder, CO: Westview Press, 2004).

50. Lewis Mumford, *The Story of Utopias* (1922; repr., Breinigsville, PA: Girvin Press, 2010), 9.

Afterword

1. Émile Durkheim, *The Elementary Forms of the Religious Life: A Study in Religious Sociology* (London: George Allen & Unwin, 1915), 223.

2. See, for example, Sam Harris, 'Science Must Destroy Religion', in *What Is Your Dangerous Idea*, ed. John Brockman (New York: Harper Perennial, 2007), 148–51; Mano Singham, 'The New War Between Science and Religion', *The Chronicle of Higher Education* (9 May 2010), chronicle.com/article/The-New-War-Between-Science/65400/ (accessed 3 December 2014); 'Real Time with Bill Maher', HBO (13 September 2013); Christopher Hitchens, *God Is Not Great* (New York: Twelve/Hachette, 2007), 46–7, 244; and Richard Dawkins, *The God Delusion* (New York: Houghton Mifflin, 2006), 282–6 and *passim*.

3. Entries for 'innovate, *v.*', 'innovation, *n.*', 'innovative, *adj.*' and 'innovator, *n.*', *OED Online* (Oxford: Oxford University Press, June 2014). Shakespeare has King Henry lament 'hurlyburly innovation' (*Henry IV, Part 1* 5:1); has Sicinius describe Coriolanus as not just a 'traitor' but a 'traitorous innovator, a foe to the public weal' (*Coriolanus* 3:1); and has both Cassio and Rosencrantz use the term 'innovation' negatively (*Othello* 2:3 and *Hamlet* 2:2).

4. Clayton M. Christensen, *The Innovator's Dilemma* (Cambridge, MA: Harvard Business School Press, 1997), xiii. See also Jill Lepore, 'The Disruption Machine', *The New Yorker* (23 June 2014): 30–6; and Patrick Thibodeau, 'Innovation is the most abused word in tech' (online column), *Computerworld* (29 August 2012), http://blogs.computerworld.com/tablets/20914/innovation-most-abused-word-tech (accessed 3 December 2014).

5. Henry W. Chesbrough, *Open Innovation: The New Imperative for Creating and Profiting from Technology* (Cambridge, MA: Harvard Business Review Press, 2003).

6. Frans Johansson, *The Medici Effect: What Elephants and Epidemics Can Teach Us About Innovation* (Cambridge, MA: Harvard Business Review Press, 2004).

7. Ibid., 2.

8. Chesbrough, *Open Innovation*, xx–xii.

9. Chris Lauer, 'Leading the Revolution' (review), *Bloomberg BusinessWeek* (10 June 2008) http://www.businessweek.com/stories/2008-06-10/leading-the-revolutionbusinessweek-business-news-stock-market-and-financial-advice (accessed 3 December 2014).

10. Gary Hamel, *Leading the Revolution: How to Thrive in Turbulent Times by Making Innovation a Way of Life*, rev. edn (Cambridge, MA: Harvard Business School Press, 2002), 4, 10–11, 26–7. The original edition of this book, published in 2000, praised the company Enron at considerable length, hailing its 'uniquely entrepreneurial culture'. After the firm's illegal accounting practices were revealed in 2001 and it went bankrupt, Hamel released an edited version that excised all mention of Enron. Erin White, 'Quest for Innovation, Motivation Inspires the Gurus', *Wall Street Journal* (5 May 2008), B6.

11. Erin White, 'New Breed of Business Gurus Rises', *Wall Street Journal* (5 May 2008): B1.

12. Lepore, 'Disruption Machine', 36.

13. This conventional account of the Westphalian Peace has, of course, been contested but will suffice for present purposes. See, for example, Benno Teschke, 'Theorizing the Westphalian System of States: International Relations from Absolutism to Capitalism', *European Journal of International Relations* 8, no. 1 (March 2002): 5–48.

14. Stephen D. Krasner, 'Westphalia and All That', in *Ideas and Foreign Policy: Beliefs, Institutions, and Political* Change, ed. Judith Goldstein and Robert Keohane (Ithaca, NY: Cornell University Press, 1993), 235–64.

15. Martin J. Verhoeven, 'Science through Buddhist Eyes', *The New Atlantis* 39 (Summer 2013): 107–11. Roughly one million Americans *not* of Asian descent describe themselves as Buddhists. See Pew Forum on Religion and Public Life, 'Asian Americans: A Mosaic of Faiths', (19 July 2012): 14, 36.

16. James R. Lewis, *Perspectives on the New Age*, (Albany: State University of New York Press, 1992), *passim*.

17. Verhoeven, 'Science through Buddhist Eyes', 110–11.

18. Carl Jung, 'The State of Psychotherapy Today', in *Collected Works of C.J. Jung, Volume 10: Civilization in Transition*, ed. and trans. Gerhard Adler and R. F. C. Hull, 2nd edn (Princeton, NJ: Princeton University Press, 1970), 172.

19. Paul C. Vitz, *Psychology as Religion: The Cult of Self-Worship*, 2nd edn (Grand Rapids, MI: Eerdmans, 1994).

20. Terry D. Cooper, *Paul Tillich and Psychology* (Macon, GA: Mercer University Press, 2005), *passim*.

21. Robert H. Nelson, 'The Secular Religions of Progress', *The New Atlantis* 39 (Summer 2013): 38–50.

22. Ibid., 42.

23. See, for example, the many instances of the term on the website of the American Humanist Association (americanhumanist.org).

24. Joel Garreau, 'Environmentalism as Religion', *The New Atlantis* 28 (Summer 2010): 67.

25. Pete Ward, *Gods Behaving Badly* (Waco, TX: Baylor University Press, 2011), 6.

26. Christian Smith, *The Sacred Project of American Sociology* (New York: Oxford University Press, 2014), x.

27. See, for example, Michael E. Brooks, 'Death of Secular Saint Steve Jobs in a Theologically Devoid Culture', *Christian Post* (28 October 2011), christianpost.com/news/death-of-secular-saint-steve-jobs-in-a-theologically-devoid-culture-59595/ (accessed 3 December 2014). See also Brett T. Robinson, 'The Marriage of Religion and Technology: Reading Apple's Allegorical Advertising', *Second Nature* (27 January 2014), secondnaturejournal.com/the-marriage-of-religion-and-technology-reading-apples-allegorical-advertising/ (accessed 3 December 2014). One Jesuit university reportedly found a clever way to invert the technology-as-religion trope: by adopting the slogan: 'Our CEO mastered social networking 2,000 years before Mark Zuckerberg was born.' Jaron Lanier, *Who Owns the Future* (New York: Simon and Schuster, 2013), 190.

28. These neo-quasi-religions sometimes collide, as celebrities and tech gurus become involved in environmental activism. 'I needed something outside of myself to believe in', the Hollywood actor Harrison Ford recently said in a celebrity-studded documentary series, 'and I found in nature a kind of a god'. *Days of Living Dangerously*, James Cameron *et al.* producers, Showtime (2014).

29. Pew Forum on Religion and Public Life, 'The Global Religious Landscape' (December 2012), 24–7.

30. Francis Fukuyama, *The End of History and the Last Man* (New York: Free Press, 1992), 198, 216–17.

31. Phillip Longman, *The Empty Cradle: How Falling Birthrates Threaten World Prosperity and What to Do About It* (New York: Basic, 2004), 33–4; and Jonathan V. Last, *What to Expect When No One's Expecting: America's Coming Demographic Disaster* (New York: Encounter, 2013), 84–7, 169–70.

32. See, for example, William Dalrymple, *Nine Lives: In Search of the Sacred in Modern India* (New York: Alfred A. Knopf, 2010).

33. F. Max Müller, *Introduction to the Science of Religion*, 2nd edn (London: Longmans, Green, and Co., 1882), 13. [original in italics]

34. This diminishment is a fundamental trait of much modern scholarship about religion, and one that has been challenged in recent years, most trenchantly in Timothy Fitzgerald, *The Ideology of Religious Studies* (New York: Oxford University Press, 2000).

35. Edward B. Tylor, *Researches into the Early History of Mankind and the Development of Civilization* (London: John Murray, 1865).

36. William Winwood Reade, *The Martyrydom of Man*, 18th edn (London: Kegan Paul, Trench, Trübner, & Co., 1910), 505, 516ff.

37. For a taste, see Andrew Newberg, Eugene D'Aquili and Vince Rause, *Why God Won't Go Away: Brain Science and the Biology of Belief* (New York: Ballantine, 2001); Dean

Hamer, *The God Gene: How Faith Is Hardwired into Our Genes* (New York: Doubleday, 2004); and Barbara Bradley Hagerty, *Fingerprints of God: The Search for the Science of Spirituality* (New York: Riverhead, 2009).

38. Lee Silver, *Remaking Eden: How Genetic Engineering and Cloning Will Transform the American Family* (New York: Avon, 1998), 17.

39. Nick Bostrom, *Superintelligence: Paths, Dangers, Strategies* (Oxford: Oxford University Press, 2014); and Ray Kurzweil, *The Age of Spiritual Machines: When Computers Exceed Human Intelligence* (New York: Viking, 1999).

40. Charles T. Rubin, *Eclipse of Man: Human Extinction and the Meaning of Progress* (New York: Encounter, 2014), *passim*. See also Robert M. Geraci, *Apocalyptic AI: Visions of Heaven in Robotics, Artificial Intelligence, and Virtual Reality* (New York: Oxford University Press, 2010); Christina Bieber Lake, *Prophets of the Posthuman: American Fiction, Biotechnology, and the Ethics of Personhood* (Notre Dame, IN: Notre Dame Press, 2013); and Hans Moravec, *Mind Children: The Future of Robot and Human Intelligence* (Cambridge, MA: Harvard University Press, 1988).

Selected Bibliography

This bibliography is limited to the major works cited by the contributors. Full references can be viewed in the citations provided at the end of each chapter.

Books

Alberti, Benjamin, Andrew M. Jones and Joshua Pollard (eds). *Archaeology after Interpretation: Returning Materials to Archaeological Theory*. Walnut Creek, CA: Left Coast Press, 2013.

Bainbridge, William S. *Across the Secular Abyss: From Faith to Wisdom*. Lexington Books, 2007.

Banerjee, Abhijit V. and Esther Duflo. *The Economic Lives of the Poor*. London: Centre for Economic Policy Research, 2006.

Barkan, Elazar. *The Guilt of Nations: Restitution and Negotiating Historical Injustices*. Baltimore, MD: Johns Hopkins University Press, 2000.

Barnett, H. G. *Innovation: The Basis of Cultural Change*. New York: McGraw-Hill, 1953.

Bellah, Robert. *Religion in Human Evolution: From the Paleolithic to the Axial Age*. Cambridge, MA: Belknap Press of Harvard University Press, 2011.

Bellah, Robert and Hans Joas (eds). *The Axial Age and Its Consequences*. Cambridge, MA: Belknap Press of Harvard University Press, 2012.

Berger, Peter L. *The Sacred Canopy: Elements of a Sociological Theory of Religion*. Garden City, NY: Doubleday, 1967.

Berger, Peter L. (ed.). *The Desecularization of the World: Resurgent Religion and World Politics*. Grand Rapids, MI: Eerdmans, 1999.

Berger, Peter, Grace Davie and Effie Fokas. *Religious America, Secular Europe?* Aldershot: Ashgate, 2008.

Berger, Thomas U. *War, Guilt, and World Politics after World War II*. New York: Cambridge University Press, 2012.

Berkun, Scott. *The Myths of Innovation*. North Sebastopol, CA: O'Reilly Media, 2010.

Bess, Philip. *Till We Have Built Jerusalem: Architecture, Urbanism, and the Sacred*. Wilmington, DE: ISI Books, 2006.

Bijker, Wiebe E., Thomas P. Hughes and Trevor Pinch (eds). *The Social Construction of Technological Systems: New Directions in the Sociology and History of Technology*. Cambridge, MA: MIT Press, 2012.

Brekus, Catherine. *Strangers and Pilgrims: Female Preaching in America, 1740–1845*. Chapel Hill: University of North Carolina Press, 1998.

Bruce, Steve. *Secularization: In Defence of an Unfashionable Theory*. Oxford: Oxford University Press, 2011.

Bruckner, Pascal. *The Tyranny of Guilt: An Essay on Western Masochism*. Translated by Steven Redall. Princeton, NJ: Princeton University Press, 2010.

Buchanan, Allen. *Better than Human: The Promise and Perils of Enhancing Ourselves*. New York: Oxford University Press, 2011.

Bulman, William J. *Anglican Enlightenment: Orientalism, Religion and Politics in England and its Empire, 1648–1715*. Cambridge: Cambridge University Press, 2015.

Bulman, William J. and Robert G. Ingram (eds). *God in the Enlightenment*. New York: Oxford University Press, 2015.

Burger, Richard L. *Chavín and the Origins of Andean Civilization*. London: Thames and Hudson, 1992.

Burnham, Daniel and Edward Bennett, *Plan of Chicago*. 1909. Reprint, New York: Princeton Architectural Press, 1993.

Calhoun, Craig, Mark Juergensmeyer and Jonathan VanAntwerpen (eds). *Rethinking Secularism*. Oxford: Oxford University Press, 2011.

Carwardine, Richard. *Transatlantic Revivalism: Popular Evangelicalism in Britain and America, 1790–1865*. Westport, CT: Greenwood Press, 1978.

Cauvin, Jacques. *The Birth of the Gods and the Origins of Agriculture*. Translated by Trevor Watkins. Cambridge: Cambridge University Press, 2000.

Cavanaugh, William T. *The Myth of Religious Violence: Secular Ideology and the Roots of Modern Conflict*. New York: Oxford University Press, 2009.

Chesbrough, Henry W. *Open Innovation: The New Imperative for Creating and Profiting from Technology*. Cambridge, MA: Harvard Business Review Press, 2003.

Christensen, Clayton M. *The Innovator's Dilemma*. Cambridge, MA: Harvard Business School Press, 1997.

Cronon, William. *Nature's Metropolis: Chicago and the Great West*. New York: Norton, 1991.

D'Angour, Armand. *The Greeks and the New: Novelty in Ancient Greek Imagination and Experience*. Cambridge: Cambridge University Press, 2011.

Dear, Peter. *Revolutionizing the Sciences: European Knowledge and Its Ambitions, 1500–1700*. Princeton, NJ: Princeton University Press, 2009.

Delbanco, Andrew. *The Death of Satan: How Americans Have Lost the Sense of Evil*. New York: Farrar, Straus and Giroux, 1995.

Digeser, Elizabeth DePalma. *The Making of a Christian Empire: Lactantius and Rome*. Ithaca, NY: Cornell University Press, 2000.

Dodgson, Mark and David Gann. *Innovation: A Very Short Introduction*. Oxford: Oxford University Press, 2010.

Draper, John. *History of the Conflict between Religion and Science*. New York: Appleton, 1874.

Durkheim, Émile. *The Elementary Forms of the Religious Life: A Study in Religious Sociology*. Translated by Joseph Swain. London: Allen & Unwin, 1915.

Eskridge, Larry. *God's Forever Family: The Jesus People Movement in America*. New York: Oxford University Press, 2013.

Eskridge, Larry and Mark A. Noll (eds). *More Money, More Ministry: Money and Evangelicals in Recent North American History*. Grand Rapids, MI: Eerdmans, 2000.

Esposito, John L., Darrell J. Fasching, and Todd Lewis. *Religion and Globalization: World Religions in Historical Perspective*. Oxford: Oxford University Press, 2008.

Evans, John H. *Contested Reproduction: Genetic Technologies, Religion, and Public Debate*. Chicago: University of Chicago Press, 2010.

Evans, John H. *Playing God? Human Genetic Engineering and the Rationalization of Public Bioethical Debate*. Chicago: University of Chicago Press, 2002.

Fagerberg, Jan, David C. Mowery, and Richard R. Nelson (eds). *The Oxford Handbook on Innovation*. Oxford: Oxford University Press, 2006.

Fowler, Chris. *The Archaeology of Personhood: An Anthropological Approach*. London: Routledge, 2004.

Fredriksen, Paula. *Sin: The Early History of an Idea*. Princeton, NJ: Princeton University Press, 2012.

Freud, Sigmund. *Civilization and Its Discontents*. 1930. Translated by James Strachey. Reprint, New York: W. W. Norton, 2005.

Fukuyama, Francis. *Our Posthuman Future: Consequences of the Biotechnology Revolution*. New York: Farrar, Straus & Giroux, 2000.

Green, Abigail and Vincent Viaene (eds). *Religious Internationals in the Modern World: Globalization and Faith Communities Since 1750*. Basingstoke: Palgrave Macmillan, 2012.

Green, Ronald M. *Babies by Design: The Ethics of Genetic Choice*. New Haven, CT: Yale University Press, 2008.

Gregory, Brad. *The Unintended Reformation: How a Religious Revolution Secularized Society*. Cambridge, MA: Harvard University Press, 2012.

Hamel, Gary. *Leading the Revolution: How to Thrive in Turbulent Times by Making Innovation a Way of Life*. Rev. edn. Cambridge, MA: Harvard Business School Press, 2002.

Hangen, Tona J. *Redeeming the Dial: Radio, Religion, and Popular Culture in America*. Chapel Hill: University of North Carolina Press, 2002.

Harris, John. *Enhancing Evolution: The Ethical Case for Making Better People*. Princeton, NJ: Princeton University Press, 2010.

Harrison, Peter. *The Bible, Protestantism and the Rise of Natural Science*. Cambridge: Cambridge University Press, 1998.

Harrison, Peter. *The Fall of Man and the Foundations of Science*. Cambridge: Cambridge University Press, 2007.

Harrison, Peter. *'Religion' and the Religions in the English Enlightenment*. Cambridge: Cambridge University Press, 1990.

Harrison, Peter. *The Territories of Science and Religion*. Chicago: University of Chicago Press, 2015.

Harrison, Peter (ed.). *The Cambridge Companion to Science and Religion*. Cambridge: Cambridge University Press, 2010.

Hassan, Wail S. *Immigrant Narratives: Orientalism and Cultural Translation in Arab American and Arab British Literature*. New York: Oxford University Press, 2011.

Hazard, Paul. *The European Mind, 1680–1715*. Translated by J. Lewis May. New York: New York Review of Books, 2013.

Hefner, Robert W. (ed.). *Conversion to Christianity: Historical and Anthropological Perspectives on a Great Transformation*. Berkeley: University of California Press, 1993.

Hellemans, Alexander. *The History of Science and Technology*. Boston: Houghton Mifflin, 2004.

Hempton, David. *Methodism: Empire of the Spirit*. New Haven, CT: Yale University Press, 2005.

Hitti, Philip K. *History of the Arabs*. London: Macmillan and Co., 1937.

Hitti, Philip K. *The Syrians in America*. New York: George H. Doran, 1924.

Hodder, Ian. *Entangled: An Archaeology of the Relationship between Humans and Things*. Malden, MA: Wiley-Blackwell, 2012.

Hodder, Ian (ed.). *Religion in the Emergence of Civilization: Çatalhöyük as a Case Study*. Cambridge: Cambridge University Press, 2010.

Howard, Thomas Albert. *Protestant Theology and the Making of the Modern German University*. Oxford: Oxford University Press, 2006.

Hughes, James. *Citizen Cyborg: Why Democratic Societies Must Respond to the Redesigned Human of the Future*. Boulder, CO: Westview Press, 2004.

Hughes, Thomas P. *Human-Built World: How to Think about Technology and Culture*. Chicago: University of Chicago Press, 2005.

Hurlbut, J. Benjamin and Hava Tirosh-Samuelson (eds). *Perfecting Human Futures: Innovation, Secularization and Eschatology*. Dordrecht, The Netherlands: Springer, 2015.

Insoll, Timothy. *Archaeology, Ritual, Religion*. London: Routledge, 2004.

Insoll, Timothy (ed.). *The Oxford Handbook of the Archaeology of Ritual and Religion*. Oxford: Oxford University Press, 2011.

Jaspers, Karl. *The Origin and Goal of History*. London: Routledge & Kegan Paul, 1953.

Johnson, Steven. *Where Good Ideas Come From: The Natural History of Innovation*. New York: Riverhead Books, 2010.

Joyce, Arthur A. *Mixtecs, Zapotecs, and Chatinos: Ancient Peoples of Southern Mexico*. Malden, MA: Wiley-Blackwell, 2010.

Kurzweil, Ray. *The Age of Spiritual Machines: When Computers Exceed Human Intelligence*. New York: Penguin Books, 2000.

Kurzweil, Ray. *The Singularity Is Near: When Humans Transcend Biology*. New York: Penguin Books, 2006.

Leithart, Peter. *Defending Constantine: The Twilight of an Empire and the Dawn of Christendom*. Downers Grove, IL: InterVarsity Press, 2010.

Lindberg, David C. and Ronald L. Numbers (eds) *God and Nature: Historical Essays on the Encounter between Christianity and Science*. Berkeley: University of California Press, 1986.

Lindberg, David C. and Ronald L. Numbers (eds). *When Science and Christianity Meet*. Chicago: University of Chicago Press, 2003.

McClay, Wilfred M. and Ted V. McAllister (eds). *Why Place Matters*. New York: Encounter Books, 2014.

McCraw, Thomas K. *Prophet of Innovation: Joseph Schumpeter and Creative Destruction*. Cambridge, MA: Belknap Press of Harvard University Press, 2007.

MacIntyre, Alasdair. *After Virtue: A Study in Moral Theory*. Notre Dame, IN: Notre Dame University Press, 1981.

McLeod, Hugh. *Piety and Poverty: Working Class Religion in Berlin, London and New York, 1870–1914*. New York: Holmes & Meier, 1996.

Marcus, Joyce and Jeremy Sabloff (eds). *The Ancient City: New Perspectives on Urbanism in the Old and New World*. Santa Fe, NM: School for Advanced Research Press, 2008.

Marshall, Paul A. *A Kind of Life Imposed on Man: Vocation and Social Order from Tyndale to Locke*. Toronto: University of Toronto Press, 1996.

Martin, David. *Religion and Power: No Logos without Mythos*. Farnham, Surrey: Ashgate, 2014.

Mehlman, Maxwell J. *Transhumanist Dreams and Dystopian Nightmares: The Promise and Peril of Genetic Engineering*. Baltimore, MD: Johns Hopkins University Press, 2012.

Menninger, Karl. *Whatever Became of Sin?* New York: Hawthorn Books, 1973.

Molema, Silas M. *The Bantu Past and Present: an Ethnographical and Historical Study of the Native Races of South Africa*. Edinburgh: W. Green & Son, 1920.

Morgan, David. *The Sacred Gaze: Religious Visual Culture in Theory and Practice*. Berkeley: University of California Press, 2005.

Nitobé, Inazô. *From Bushido to the League of Nations*. Edited by Teruhiko Nagao. Sapporo, Japan: Hokkaido University Press, 2006.

Nitobé, Inazô. *Japan's Bridge Across the Pacific*. Edited by John F. Howes. Boulder, CO: Westview Press, 1995.

Nietzsche, Friedrich. *On the Genealogy of Morality*. 1887. Edited by Keith Ansell-Pearson. Translated by Carol Diethe. Cambridge: Cambridge University Press, 2006.

Noble, David F. *The Religion of Technology: The Divinity of Man and the Spirit of Invention*. New York: Penguin Books, 1999.

Noll, Mark A. (ed.). *God and Mammon: Protestants, Money, and the Market, 1790–1860*. Oxford: Oxford University Press, 2001.

Nongbri, Brent. *Before Religion: A History of a Modern Concept*. New Haven, CT: Yale University Press, 2013.

North, Michael. *Novelty: A History of the New*. Chicago: University of Chicago Press, 2013.

Numbers, Ronald L. (ed.). *Galileo Goes to Jail and Other Myths about Science and Religion*. Cambridge, MA: Harvard University Press, 2009.

Nurser, John. *For all Peoples and All Nations: The Ecumenical Church and Human Rights*. Washington, DC: Georgetown University Press, 2005.

Nye, David E. *American Technological Sublime*. Cambridge, MA: MIT Press, 1996.

O'Brien Michael J. and Stephen J. Shennan (eds). *Innovation in Cultural Systems: Contributions from Evolutionary Anthropology*. Cambridge, MA: MIT Press, 2010.

Passell, Aaron. *Building the New Urbanism*. New York: Routledge, 2013.

Pauketat, Timothy R. *Ancient Cahokia and the Mississippians*. Cambridge: Cambridge University Press, 2004.

Pauketat, Timothy R. *An Archaeology of the Cosmos: Rethinking Agency and Religion in Ancient America*. London: Routledge, 2013.

Pauketat, Timothy R. *Chiefdoms and Other Archaeological Delusions*. Walnut Creek, CA: AltaMira, 2007.

Pauketat, Timothy R. and Susan M. Alt (eds). *The Medieval Mississippians: The Cahokian World*. Sante Fe, NW: School for Advanced Research Press, 2014.

Persson, Ingmar and Julian Savulescu. *Unfit for the Future: The Need for Moral Enhancement*. Oxford: Oxford University Press, 2012.

Pickett, Jarrell Waskom. *Christian Mass Movements in India: A Study with Recommendations*. New York: Abingdon Press, 1933.

Pocock, J. G. A. *Barbarism and Religion*. 5 vols. Cambridge: Cambridge University Press, 1999–2010.

Putney, Clifford. *Muscular Christianity: Manhood and Sports in Protestant America, 1880–1920*. Cambridge, MA: Harvard University Press, 2001.

Renfrew, Colin and Iain Morley (eds). *Becoming Human: Innovation in Prehistoric Material and Spiritual Culture*. New York: Cambridge University Press, 2009.

Riesebrodt, Martin. *The Promise of Salvation: A Theory of Religion*. Translated by Steven Rendall. Chicago: University of Chicago Press, 2009.

Roco, Mihail C. and William S. Bainbridge (eds). *Converging Technologies for Improving Human Performance: Nanotechnology, Biotechnology, Information Technology and Cognitive Science*. Dordrecht, The Netherlands: Kluwer Academic Publishers, 2003.

Rogers, Everett M. *Diffusion of Innovations*. 5th edn. New York: Free Press, 2003.

Sarton, George. *The History of Science and the New Humanism* (Bloomington: Indiana University Press, 1962.

Sen, Amartya. *Development As Freedom*. New York: Knopf, 1999.

Shapin, Steven. *The Scientific Revolution*. Chicago: University of Chicago Press, 1996.

Siedentop, Larry. *Inventing the Individual: The Origins of Western Liberalism*. London: Allen Lane, 2014.

Smith, Christian (ed.). *The Secular Revolution: Power, Interests, and Conflict in the Secularization of American Public Life*. Berkeley: University of California Press, 2003.

Smith, Merritt Roe and Leo Marx (eds). *Does Technology Drive History? The Dilemma of Technological Determinism*. Cambridge, MA: The MIT Press, 1994.

Stark, Rodney. *For the Glory of God: How Monotheism Led to Reformations, Science, Witch-hunts, and the End of Slavery*. Princeton, NJ: Princeton University Press, 2003.

Stark, Rodney. *One True God: Historical Consequences of Monotheism*. Princeton, NJ: Princeton University Press, 2001.

Stark, Rodney. *The Victory of Reason: How Christianity Led to Freedom, Capitalism, and Western Success*. New York: Random House, 2005.

Szerszynski, Bronislaw. *Nature, Technology, and the Sacred*. Malden, MA: Wiley-Blackwell, 2005.

Tawney, R. H. *Religion and the Rise of Capitalism: A Historical Study*. New York: Harcourt, Brace and Co, 1926.

Taylor, Charles. *Dilemmas and Connections*. Cambridge, MA: Harvard University Press, 2011.

Taylor, Charles. *Modern Social Imaginaries*. Durham, NC: Duke University Press, 2003.

Taylor, Charles. *A Secular Age*. Cambridge, MA: Belknap Press of Harvard University Press, 2007.

Tejirian, Eleanor H. and Reeva Spector Simon. *Conflict, Conquest, and Conversion: Two Thousand Years of Christian Missions in the Middle East*. New York: Columbia University Press, 2012.

Tirosh-Samuelson, Hava and Kenneth L. Mossman (eds). *Building Better Humans? Refocusing the Debate on Transhumanism*. Frankfurt am Main: Peter Lang International Academic Publishers, 2012.

Toft, Monica Duffy, Daniel Philpott, and Timothy Samuel Shah. *God's Century: Resurgent Religion and Global Politics*. New York: Norton, 2011.

Turner, Stephen P. and Regis A. Factor. *Max Weber as Social Thinker*. Oxford: Routledge, 1994.

van der Leeuw, Sander E. and Robin Torrance (eds). *What's New? A Closer Look at the Process of Innovation*. London: Unwin Hyman, 1989.

Weber, Max. *Economy and Society: An Outline of Interpretive Sociology*. 1922. Edited by Guenther Roth and Claus Wittich. Berkeley: University of California Press, 1978.

Weber, Max. *The Protestant Ethic and the Spirit of Capitalism*. 1904–5. Translated by Talcott Parsons. Reprint, London: Routledge, 2001.

White, Andrew Dickson. *History of the Warfare of Science with Theology in Christendom*. 2 vols. New York: Appleton, 1897.

White, Lynn Jr. *Medieval Religion and Technology*. Berkeley: University of California Press, 1978.

White, Lynn Jr. *Medieval Technology and Social Change*. Oxford: Oxford University Press, 1962.

Whitehouse, Harvey and Luther H. Martin (eds). *Theorizing Religions Past: Archaeology, History, and Cognition*. Walnut Creek, CA: AltaMira Press, 2004.

Whitley, David S. and Kelly Hays-Gilpin (eds). *Belief in the Past: Theoretical Approaches to the Archaeology of Religion*. Walnut Creek, CA: Left Coast Press, 2008.

Winner, Langdon. *Autonomous Technology: Technics-out-of-Control as a Theme in Political Thought*. Cambridge, MA: The MIT Press, 1978.

Winner, Langdon. *The Whale and the Reactor: A Search for Limits in an Age of High Technology*. Chicago: University of Chicago Press, 1986.

Yerxa, Donald A. (ed.). *Recent Themes in the History of Science and Religion*. Columbia: University of South Carolina Press, 2009.

Young, B. W. *Religion and Enlightenment in Eighteenth-Century England*. Oxford: Oxford University Press, 1998.

Zagorin, Perez. *How the Idea of Religious Toleration Came to the West*. Princeton, NJ: Princeton University Press, 2003.

Chapters and Articles

Akerlof, George A. 'The Missing Motivation in Macroeconomics'. *American Economic Review* 97, no. 1 (March 2007): 5–36.

Alt, Susan M. 'Cahokian Change and the Authority of Tradition'. In *The Archaeology of Traditions: Agency and History Before and After Columbus*, edited by Timothy R. Pauketat, 141–56. Gainesville: University Press of Florida, 2001.

Alt, Susan M. 'Making Mississippian at Cahokia'. In *The Oxford Handbook of North American Archaeology*, edited by Timothy R. Pauketat, 497–508. Oxford: Oxford University Press, 2012.

Barber, Sarah B. and Mireya Olvera Sánchez, 'A Divine Wind: The Arts of Death and Music in Terminal Formative Oaxaca'. *Ancient Mesoamerica* 23, no. 1 (2012): 9–24.

Bess, Philip, 'Building on Truth'. *First Things* (January 2015): 47–53.

Bulman, William J. 'Enlightenment and Religious Politics in Restoration England'. *History Compass* 10, no. 10 (2012): 752–64.

Carroll, Bret E. 'Worlds in Space: American Religious Pluralism in Geographic Perspective'. *Journal of the Academy of Religion* 80, no. 2 (June 2012): 304–64.

Clark, J. C. D. 'Secularization and Modernization: The Failure of a "Grand Narrative"'. *The Historical Journal* 55, no. 1 (March 2012): 161–94.

Clark, Steven. 'Naturalism, Science and the Supernatural'. *Sophia* 48 (2009): 127–42.

Daston, Lorraine. 'Miraculous Facts and Miraculous Evidence in Early Modern Europe'. *Critical Inquiry* 18 (1991): 93–124.

de Castro, Eduardo Viveiros. 'Exchanging Perspectives: The Transformation of Objects into Subjects in Amerindian Ontologies'. *Common Knowledge* 10 (2004): 463–85.

Dunn, John. 'The Grounds for Toleration in the Early Enlightenment'. *Proceedings of the British Academy* 186 (2013): 201–9.

Fogelin, Lars. 'The Archaeology of Religious Ritual'. *Annual Review of Anthropology* 36 (2007): 55–71.

Green, S. J. D. 'Church and City Revisited: New Evidence from the North of England, c. 1815–1914'. *Northern History* 43 (2006): 345–60.

Gregory, Brad. 'The Intentions of the Unintended Reformation'. *Historically Speaking* 13, no. 3 (2012): 2–5.

Harrison, Peter. 'Miracles, Early Modern Science, and Rational Religion'. *Church History* 75 (2006): 493–511.

Harrison, Peter. 'Religion and the Early Royal Society'. *Science and Christian Belief* 22 (2010): 3–22.

Harrison, Victoria S. 'The Pragmatics of Defining Religion in a Multi-Cultural World'. *International Journal for Philosophy of Religion* 59 (2006): 140–1.

Ingram, Robert G. 'Nature, History and the Search for Order: The Boyle Lectures, 1730–1785'. In *God's Bounty? The Churches and the Natural World*, edited by Tony Claydon and Peter Clarke, 276–92. Woodbridge: The Boydell Press, 2010.

Insoll, Timothy. 'Are Archaeologists Afraid of Gods? Some Thoughts on Archaeology and Religion'. In *Belief in the Past: The Proceedings of the 2002 Manchester Conference on Archaeology and Religion*, edited by Timothy Insoll, 1–6. Oxford: Archaeopress, 2004.

Joyce, Arthur A. 'The Founding of Monte Albán: Sacred Propositions and Social Practices'. In *Agency in Archaeology*, edited by Macia-Anne Dobres and John Robb, 71–91. London: Routledge, 2000.

Kembel, Silvia Rodriguez. 'The Architecture at the Monumental Center of Chavín de Huántar: Sequence, Transformations, and Chronology'. In *Chavin: Art, Architecture, and Culture*, edited by William J. Conklin and Jeffrey Quilter, 35–81. Los Angeles: Cotsen Institute of Archaeology, UCLA, 2008.

Koolhaas, Rem. 'Junkspace'. *October* 100 (Spring, 2002): 175–90.

Lepore, Jill. 'The Disruption Machine'. *The New Yorker* (23 June 2014): 30–6.

McLeod, Hugh. 'Sport and Christianity in England, c.1790–1914'. In *Sports and Christianity: Historical and Contemporary Perspectives*, edited by Nick J. Watson and Andrew Parker, 112–30. New York: Routledge, 2013.

Nelson, Robert H. 'The Secular Religions of Progress'. *The New Atlantis* 39 (Summer 2013): 38–50.

Pauketat, Timothy R. 'Founders' Cults and the Archaeology of Wa-kan-da'. In *Memory Work: Archaeologies of Material Practices*, edited by Barbara J. Mills and William H. Walker, 61–79. Sante Fe, NM: School for Advanced Research Press, 2008.

Rick, John W. 'Context, Construction, and Ritual in the Development of Authority at Chavín de Huántar'. In *Chavin: Art, Architecture, and Culture*, edited by William J. Conklin and Jeffrey Quilter, 3–34. Los Angeles: Cotsen Institute of Archaeology, UCLA, 2008.

Rick, John W. 'The Evolution of Authority and Power at Chavín de Huántar, Peru'. *Archaeological Papers of the American Anthropological Association* 14 (2004): 71–89.

Rick, John W. 'Religion and Authority at Chavín de Huántar'. In *Chavin: Peru's Enigmatic Temple in the Andes*, edited by Peter Fux, 167–76. Zürich: Scheidegger & Spiess, 2013.

Robert, Dana L. 'The First Globalization: The Internationalization of the Protestant Missionary Movement between the World Wars'. *International Bulletin of Missionary Research* 26, no. 2 (2002): 50–67.

Sen, Amartya. 'Wellbeing, Agency and Freedom: The Dewey Lectures 1984'. *Journal of Philosophy* 82, no. 4 (April 1985): 169–221.

Shah, Rebecca Samuel and Timothy Samuel Shah. 'How Evangelicalism — Including Pentecostalism — Helps the Poor'. In *The Hidden Form of Capital Spiritual Influences in Societal Progress*, edited by Peter L. Berger and Gordon Redding, 61–90. London: Anthem Press, 2010.

Shah, Rebecca Samuel and Timothy Samuel Shah. 'Pentecost amid Pujas: Charismatic Christianity and Dalit Women in Twenty-First Century India'. In *Global Pentecostalism in the 21st Century*, edited by Robert W. Hefner, 194–227. Bloomington: Indiana University Press, 2013.

Sheehan, Jonathan. 'Enlightenment, Religion and the Enigma of Secularization: A Review Essay'. *American Historical Review* 108, no. 4 (October 2003): 1–36.

Solomon, Mark and Nick Bostrom, 'The Transhumanist Dream'. *Foreign Policy* 146 (1 January 2005): 4–10.

Stark, Rodney and Laurence Iannacone. 'A Supply-Side Reinterpretation of the "Secularization" of Europe'. *Journal for the Scientific Study of Religion* 33, no. 3 (1994): 230–52.

Walsham, Alexandra. 'The Reformation and the "Disenchantment of the World" Reassessed'. *The Historical Journal* 51 (2008): 497–528.

Wilken, Robert Louis. 'In Defense of Constantine'. *First Things* 112 (2001): 36–40.

Woodberry, Robert D. 'The Missionary Roots of Liberal Democracy'. *American Political Science Review* 106, no. 2 (May 2012): 244–74.

Woodberry, Robert D. and Timothy S. Shah. 'Christianity and Democracy: The Pioneering Protestants'. *Journal of Democracy* 15, no. 2 (2004): 47–61.

Contributors

SUSAN M. ALT is an associate professor of anthropology at Indiana University, Bloomington. Her current research deals with the relationships between the Emerald complex, Cahokia and the Yankeetown culture of Southwestern Indiana. She is the editor of *Ancient Complexities: New Perspectives in Pre-Columbian North America* (Utah, 2010).

SARAH B. BARBER is an associate professor of anthropology at the University of Central Florida. Her research focuses on the origins of early complex societies in ancient Mexico. Her work has been published in a number of academic journals and edited volumes. She is currently completing a book on *Religion and Political Innovation in Formative Period Mesoamerica* and an edited volume on *Religion and Politics in the Ancient Americas*.

PHILIP H. BESS is a professor of architecture at the University of Notre Dame, where he teaches urban design and theory, and from 2004 to 2014 was the School of Architecture's Director of Graduate Studies. He is the author of numerous articles and three books, including *Till We Have Built Jerusalem: Architecture, Urbanism, and the Sacred* (ISI, 2006).

WILLIAM J. BULMAN is an assistant professor of history at Lehigh University, where he is also the Inaugural Digital Scholarship Faculty Fellow. His research centres on the politics, religion and culture of seventeenth- and eighteenth-century Britain and its empire. His major publications include *Anglican Enlightenment: Orientalism, Religion and Politics in England and its Empire, 1648–1715* (Cambridge, 2015) and *God in the Enlightenment* (Oxford, 2015, co-edited with Robert G. Ingram).

PETER HARRISON is an Australian Laureate Fellow and director of the Institute for Advanced Studies in the Humanities at the University of Queensland. He was previously the Idreos Professor of Science and Religion at the University of Oxford. He has published extensively in the area of intellectual history with a focus on the philosophical, scientific and religious thought of the early modern period. His six books include *The Territories of Science and Religion* (Chicago, 2015) – a revised version of his 2012 Gifford Lectures – and *The Fall of Man and the Foundations of Science* (Cambridge, 2007).

DAVID N. HEMPTON is the Alonzo L. McDonald Family Professor of Evangelical Theological Studies, the John Lord O'Brian Professor of Divinity and dean of the faculty at Harvard Divinity School. A fellow of the Royal Historical Society, Dean Hempton is the author of several award-winning books, including *Methodism: Empire of the Spirit* (Yale, 2005) and *The Church in the Long Eighteenth Century* (I. B. Tauris, 2011).

THOMAS ALBERT HOWARD holds the Stephen Phillips Chair of History at Gordon College, where he directs the Center for Faith and Inquiry. He is the author of several books, including the award-winning *Protestant Theology and the Making of the Modern German University* (Oxford, 2006) and *God and the Atlantic: America, Europe, and the Religious Divide* (Oxford, 2011).

J. BENJAMIN HURLBUT is an assistant professor in the School of Life Sciences at Arizona State University. His research lies at the intersection of science and technology studies, bioethics and political theory. He has authored or co-authored articles in a number of journals, including *Nature*, *The Scientist* and the *Journal of Policy Analysis and Management*, and is completing a book on human embryo research and public bioethics in the United States.

ROBERT G. INGRAM is an associate professor of history at Ohio University and the director of the George Washington Forum on American Ideas, Politics, and Institutions. He is the author of *Religion, Reform and Modernity the Eighteenth Century: Thomas Secker and the Church of England* (Boydell, 2007) and co-editor (with William Gibson) of *Religious Identities in Britain, 1660–1832* (Ashgate, 2005) and (with William J. Bulman) of *God in the Enlightenment* (Oxford, 2015).

ARTHUR A. JOYCE is professor of anthropology at the University of Colorado, Boulder. Since 1986, he has conducted interdisciplinary archaeological research in Oaxaca, Mexico. He is author of *Mixtecs, Zapotecs, and Chatinos: Ancient Peoples of Southern Mexico* (Wiley-Blackwell, 2010) and *El Pueblo de la Tierra del Cielo: Arqueología de la Mixteca de la Costa* (Centro INAH Oaxaca, 2014), as well as editor of *Polity and Ecology in Formative Period Coastal Oaxaca* (Colorado, 2013).

ADAM KEIPER is the editor of *The New Atlantis: A Journal of Technology and Society*, as well as of the New Atlantis Books series and the website TheNewAtlantis.com. He is also a fellow at the Ethics and Public Policy Center, where he directs the programme on Science, Technology and Society, and a contributing editor to *National Affairs* and *Current*.

WILFRED M. McCLAY holds the G. T. and Libby Blankenship Chair in the History of Liberty at the University of Oklahoma and is the director of the Center for the History of Liberty. His field of expertise is American intellectual history. Among his books are the award-winning *The Masterless: Self and Society in Modern America* (North Carolina, 1994); *Religion Returns to the Public Square: Faith and Policy in America* (Johns Hopkins, 2003); *Figures in the Carpet: Finding the Human Person in the American Past* (Eerdmans, 2007); and *Why Place Matters: Geography, Identity, and Public Life in Modern America* (Encounter, 2014).

HUGH McLEOD is emeritus professor of Church History at the University of Birmingham. A member of the British Academy, he works on the social history of religion in Western Europe and the USA in the nineteenth and twentieth centuries. His books include *Secularisation in Western Europe, 1848–1914* (Palgrave Macmillan, 2000) and *The Religious Crisis of the 1960s* (Oxford, 2007). He edited the *Cambridge History of Christianity, Volume IX: World Christianities, c.1914–c.2000* (2006).

TIMOTHY R. PAUKETAT is an archaeologist and professor of anthropology and medieval studies at the University of Illinois in Urbana-Champaign. He is the author or editor of a dozen books, including *An Archaeology of the Cosmos* (Routledge 2013). His recent field excavations have taken place in western Wisconsin and at the Emerald Acropolis, both religious shrine complexes connected to the ancient city of Cahokia.

JOHN W. RICK is an associate professor of anthropology at Stanford University. He directs a major research project at the monumental World Heritage site of Chavín de Huántar aimed at exploring the foundations of authority in the central Andes. He has published extensively on Chavín de Huántar in a variety of academic journals and scholarly anthologies.

DANA L. ROBERT is the Truman Collins Professor of World Christianity and History of Mission and director of the Center for Global Christianity and Mission at the Boston University School of Theology. At Boston University, she directs one of the oldest doctoral programmes in Mission Studies and World Christianity in the United States. Among her books are *Converting Colonialism: Visions and Realities in Mission History, 1706–1914* (editor, Eerdmans, 2008) and *Christian Mission: How Christianity Became a World Religion* (Wiley-Blackwell, now in 6th printing).

REBECCA SAMUEL SHAH is a research fellow at the Berkley Center for Religion, Peace, and World Affairs, Georgetown University, and an associate scholar with the Berkley Center's Religious Freedom Project. An economist by training, Shah has been the project leader and principal investigator for two research initiatives on religion, entrepreneurship and economic development in the modern world. Her work has been published in a number of scholarly anthologies.

TIMOTHY SAMUEL SHAH is associate director of the Religious Freedom Project at the Berkley Center for Religion, Peace, and World Affairs and visiting assistant professor in the Government Department at Georgetown University. A political scientist specializing in the relationship between religion and political freedom in theory, history and contemporary practice, Shah is co-author of *God's Century: Resurgent Religion and Global Politics* (Norton, 2011) and is editor of a series on 'Evangelical Christianity and Democracy in the Global South'. His articles on religion and global politics have appeared in *Foreign Affairs*, *Foreign Policy*, the *Journal of Democracy*, the *Review of Politics* and elsewhere.

DONALD A. YERXA is emeritus professor of history at Eastern Nazarene College, editor of *Fides et Historia* and former senior editor of *Historically Speaking*. He is the author, co-author or editor of a dozen books, including, most recently, *British Abolitionism and the Question of Moral Progress in History* (editor, South Carolina, 2012). He directed The Historical Society's 'Religion and Innovation in Human Affairs' grants programme from 2011 until 2014.

Index